A Limey from Lyme

About the Author

Glen Herbert was a boatman at the Cobb in Lyme Regis where he took tourists on boat trips during the summer months and travelled the world out of season mainly to the Americas. He is currently a teacher living in Salisbury, England and intends to get a bigger boat.

Glen Herbert

A Limey from Lyme

Olympia Publishers
London

www.olympiapublishers.com

OLYMPIA PAPERBACK EDITION

Copyright ©Glen Herbert 2016

The right of Glen Herbert to be identified as author of this work has been asserted in accordance with sections 77 and 78 of the
Copyright, Designs and Patents Act 1988.

All Rights Reserved

No reproduction, copy or transmission of this publication may be made without written permission.
No paragraph of this publication may be reproduced, copied or transmitted save with the written permission of the publisher,
or in accordance with the provisions of the Copyright Act 1956 (as amended).

Any person who commits any unauthorised act in relation to this publication may be liable to criminal prosecution and civil claims for damage.

A CIP catalogue record for this title is available from the British Library.

ISBN: 978-1-84897-649-8

(Olympia Publishers is part of Ashwell Publishing Ltd)

First published *in 2016*

Olympia Publishers
60 Cannon Street
London
EC4N 6NP

Printed in Great Britain

Dedication

For Jan and her daughters Ellie and Alice

Acknowledgement

My special thanks to the many friends I have now made on both sides of the Atlantic and to the helpful staff of the UK county record offices for Dorset, Devon, Somerset and Wiltshire, The Public Records Office, British Library Map Room, House of Lords Parliamentary Archives, The Church of England Record Office and in the USA, the Jamestown Visitor Center and the brilliant minds of the National Aeronautics and Space Administration. The graphologist report by Margaret Webb and reference to the lifetime work of past historians such as Richard Hakluyt, George Roberts, Cyril Wanklyn and the eyewitness account of the Boston Tea Party by the American revolutionary George Hewes, helped me on the historical content of this work. Thanks to the modern day local historian, Natalie Manifold, who not only corrected me on some of my most outlandish theories but also introduced me to Cambridge University lecturer, Mike Clark, who painstakingly pieced together my rough notes and travel logs into this more recognizable book.

saepius foris experiri

CHAPTER 1

"Life is either a daring adventure, or nothing. Security does not exist in nature, nor do the children of men as a whole experience it. Avoiding danger is no safer in the long run than exposure."
- Helen Keller

After passing through the automatic doors of the air conditioned environment, I inhaled the sub-tropical humidity and gasped it out.

"Hey Bud, need a cab?"

At that same moment, a nearby car accidentally rammed another parked yellow cab, and during the ensuing chaos of cops and security guards closing in on an irate commuter still trying to rush for the flight he was no longer going to catch, I suddenly realised how much I missed the quiet solitude of the rolling hills of Dorset, and chugging along its tranquil coast in my boat. I was just about to turn back for the next flight home when Mohammed, the driver with intact yellow bodywork, continued with, "I can take you to a safe family motel, not far from here and not expensive."

I hesitated; it did seem a good idea, as it had been a long flight, and after a good night's sleep I could always return home tomorrow. Little did I know at the time, but I had just made the most important decision in my life, and before I knew it we tore off along the Hialleah Freeway towards downtown. As is the case with most cab drivers - and Iranian ones are no exception - I heard his whole life story within the next twenty minute fare. He had escaped the regime of the Ayatollah to start a new life, which impressed me, as it must have been more of a culture shock for him to enter this country than for myself, even if Dorset seems more placid than both.

My first step on American soil had almost been my last, and I will always be indebted to that cab driver who had talked me out of catching that next flight home just moments after I stepped onto the sidewalk of Miami Airport. Had we not met, what a terrible loss it would have been for me, as from that humble beginning, my interest in the Americas kindled and developed into a lifelong passion.

After that tediously long flight across the Atlantic, and what seemed to me like an equally lengthy process of immigration and baggage claim, I walked through arrivals with a small backpack, wondering what all the fuss had been about. The smell of popcorn and hotdogs were my first sensory perception of this new world, followed very quickly by the noise and bustle of mass consumerism. Then, as if witnessing a total eclipse of the sun, a shadow loomed over me as three females walked by. I stared in disbelief, as I had never before seen obesity on this scale. The three of them appeared like escapees from Jurassic Park. The largest one had gulped down the remaining contents of a half-gallon container of soda and slammed it through the swing lid of a nearby trash can, when, turning to her equally grotesque and huge companions, she complained, "Hey you guys, I'm starving... Let's go eat!"

Like a pack of reptilian carnivores, they stalked off looking for prey. I tried to clear my mind of prejudiced thoughts, but it was too late, as doubt suddenly popped into my head that the airport's whole supply of hotdogs would have been enough to satisfy their appetites.

In my motel room that night, I began to rediscover myself, along with the subtle differences between British and American cultures. To start with, the case of beer that I had just purchased from the Winn-Dixie store across the road had pop-tops instead of pull-rings. I could use a TV remote to surf over fifty channels, while back home in those times we still had only four. Surprisingly, even today, neither culture has perfected a remote that is user friendly! On the science fiction channel I came across the new *Star Trek* series with an elderly Captain Jean-Luc Picard at the helm long before it had ever been aired in the UK, where the much older Captain Kirk had been rerunning his five-year mission for almost two decades. Today, with the power of the Internet, this cultural difference is closing fast, but at the time it seemed as if I had not only been transported across the Atlantic, but also a decade into the future.

From this future world, I thought back to my early childhood and my first day at school, as I walked along the tall gothic corridors of Burdett Coutts Primary. I stopped to look up at a poster of probably the most famous photograph ever taken. Seen for the first time from space was the complete globe of the Earth, taken by the Apollo Eight astronauts. I remember shortly afterwards being assembled in the main hall with the rest of the school, in front of an old communal black and white telly, the type that you had to slap on the top to clear the picture, and when it did, a fuzzy upside down image appeared of a white blob, which slowly ascended up the screen and stopped. The whole room of noisy kids went quite with bated breath as we heard those enigmatic words for the first time.

"That's one small step for man, one giant leap for mankind."

At break, I ran out into the school yard oblivious to what was really happening in the world around me, but I remember older kids talking about a place called America and it was people from there who had gone to the Moon. The sixties were a confusing time for a child, as it seemed almost anything was possible. In the same week of the moon landing, the original *Star Trek* series was first aired on British television, and for a while afterwards I thought it had been Captain Kirk who had gone to the Moon, and not some obscure organisation called NASA. The Vietnam War was in full swing, along with the emergence of 'Flower Power' and the hippy peace movement. It took a while, but eventually I grasped the concept that a very clever man called Kennedy had inspired his people in America to put a man on the Moon, and that he wanted to end this war but was sadly murdered for it. So it could be argued that, at the tender age of seven, my interest in this strange foreign place first started.

'Tuesday's child is full of grace'; and on that particular day, Bob Dylan made his first public début. Number one in the British music charts was Shirley Bassey with 'Reach for the Stars' - rather fitting, as it was also the year that the Soviet Cosmonaut Yuri Gagarin became the first man in space. Kennedy retaliated by announcing the American goal of reaching the Moon before the end of that decade. It was also the time of the sealing of the East German border, the 'Bay of Pigs Cuba Crisis' and the start of the Cold War, which was the real inspiration for placing a man on the Moon. This was no place for the likes of Captain Kirk, since both Democrats and Communists alike realised that a Moon base could be used to launch a nuclear holocaust, potentially leaving a world Spock would have described as, 'Life Jim, but not as we know it!'

My earliest childhood memory that I suppose could be associated with adventure is when I was about a year old and my mother took me into the garden, amidst a basket of laundry. It was a hot summer's day and she sat me on the grass and pegged clothes out on the line. As soon as her back was turned, I crawled along the lawn, through a gap in the hedge and into woodland. I stood up in amazement at my discovery of a strange new world. A field of bluebells stretched out as far as I could see and swayed gently like waves on the warm summer breeze, all beneath an equally azure blue sky. Bewildered, I recall crying my little eyes out as I realised I was lost and alone and away from the security of familiar things. I suppose, like the explorer who discovered the vast ocean that doubled the size of the known world, you could say that this baby Balboa had discovered his own Pacific.

Born the eldest of four children to a farm labourer, it was here in Dorset where I was raised, until my father joined the army and we moved to London. Now, as a 'Military Brat', I would sometimes accompany him to work on Saturday mornings to feed sugar cubes to the Queen's horses at Wellington Barracks. On one particular excursion, we stopped off at a secondhand bookshop in Victoria which, to my surprise, on a recent trip down Memory Lane has only recently closed down! It was here that I was first introduced to American imports, such as D.C. and Marvel comics - so much more interesting than the mundane British *Beano* or *Dandy*.

Here I discovered a whole library of American culture, and I couldn't get enough of it. I spent my weekly pocket money buying new issues and exchanging read copies on a two for one basis. My knowledge of this strange foreign place started to grow; its full name I now knew to be the United States of America. I learned that others as well as Captain Kirk had been to the Moon, and they had superheroes such as Batman and Spiderman who beat up the bad guys with colourful *POWs* and *WHAMs*. But they still had time to do the

American thing and help old ladies across the road. They had a friendly ghost called Casper, who wasn't at all scary, and a boy called Richie Rich, who was always bored because he could have anything he desired, since his dad was the largest realtor in the States. The military exploits of Sad Sac were probably my favourite, as they gave me an insight into the day-to-day running of the American Army; it seemed familiar but at times surprisingly different to that of the British Household Cavalry, as I compared the two during those Saturday morning excursions to the royal stables.

I remember once, as a child still young enough not to have any sense of the value of money, being given one of those big old pennies not long before decimalisation, and walking into the local sweetshop on my way to school. Here, two builders who were renovating the premises decided to have some fun and pretended to be the shopkeeper and his assistant. I left the premises struggling to carry one of those big old glass jars packed to the brim with every type of sweet you could possibly imagine, and with change of a halfpenny. Ah the innocence of youth - those were the days!

The first morning in the States, I woke up, showered and dressed and, with a change of heart, decided I was going to stick around for a while and explore this strange new world; after all, it was the home to my fondest childhood memories. I checked out of the motel, and purchased a roadmap at the nearby service station, where I noticed fuel was less than half price compared to the UK. I sat on my backpack beneath the shade of a palm tree in the early morning sun, observing what an organised road system they have. The east-to-west running routes were always numbered evenly, while south-to-north were odd. So without even looking at a map, I knew roughly where I was anywhere in the country. For example, if I was at the road junction of 1 and 10, I know I was in the southeast, while a road junction of, say, 92 and 93, placed me in the northwest. I decided I was going to hitchhike north to Jacksonville, pickup the transcontinental highway and then make it up as I went along, heading west across the vast continent.

Moments later, I staggered off the road, more in shock than in pain, looking down at the bloodied sear mark on my jeans above my right knee. Just as I had started hitchhiking, an extended arm had appeared from a passing car; then the crack of a pistol shot and the sting from the passing bullet.

"My God, someone has just shot me!"

As amazing as it sounds, I had barely been in the country twenty-four hours, and already those crazy Americans were trying to kill me! Bewildered and unsure of what I should do next, I just carried on hitchhiking and tried to justify that it was something else other than a bullet, but still to this day I cannot. It *was* a bullet, and it was a very near miss. Another car passed and another arm was extended. I panicked and dove for cover behind some scrub, before realising with some embarrassment that this time it was just the passenger airing his hand in the midday humidity. Years later, on another journey across the States, I met a road engineer who told me he'd been shot at no less than five times in the course of his career building bridges. He told me that it was a gang initiation, whereby a new member had to kill or at least try to kill someone so that other members could hold it against him or her if he or she should ever try to turn state evidence against them.

"Long time since I seen a hitchhiker here in Little Cuba," said the old hippy as I clambered into the passenger seat of the battered truck, relieved that I had finally got a lift. It would turn out to be the first of many to come.

"Little Cuba," I exclaimed. "What sort of place is it? I'm sure someone just tried to shoot me!"

"Man, you from Australia or summin'? 'Cos you're well on the wrong side of the tracks out here."

"Err no, I'm British," I said, wondering where the tracks were.

"A Limey, eh? Well, welcome to America boy, but you definitely ain't to be out there… This is the hood, the drug capital of the U.S. of A.."

I knew the expression 'Limey' had originated as a nickname for British sailors who, in days of old, used lime juice to prevent scurvy. I was obviously not so streetwise at the time to realise that the term 'hood' was used for more than a car bonnet, but I was starting to learn fast, and my throwback buddy from the sixties was about to provide me with some invaluable help. His explanation went something like this:

When Castro started his Communist regime, he took back property and land from Cubans made rich by unfair American commercial intervention. These Cubans were allowed to immigrate to Miami - thus 'Little Cuba' - and America started its sanction policy on mainland Cuba at the start of the Cold War. Whatever your view on Castro, it's best to find out first what camp a particular Cuban is in before discussing anything further about him, simply because Hispanic emotional opinion either for or against Castro can flare up and tempers can fly! But one thing for certain about this man is that he fills a very interesting chapter in American political history, and oddly enough, for or against, one cannot help but have admiration for him.

All cities have a commercial centre, an area for the masses to live and work and places for the wealthy, such as local industrialists. As industry changes, so the wealthy move away, and where land is limited (as in European cities), the poorer parts are rejuvenated; a good example of this are the docklands of London. But across the pond, our ex-colonial cousins have the space for cities to continually expand even over the railtracks from the commercial centre, without having to rejuvenate the poorer parts - hence the hood. Like all over the world, the ghetto crime rate is high and illegal narcotics become a major problem. Where these areas are rejuvenated, these problems can be overcome, but in the ever-expanding hood it only gets worse, and the highly addictive crack cocaine is slowly decimating the youth of America.

My first destination was the Kennedy Space Centre, and my hippy friend drove me as far north as Titusville. Thick cloud cover and early evening made it appear darker than it really was. It was early October, which in Florida is still the hurricane season, generally running from about July to October, and officially ending on the first day of November. A tropical storm built up and it started to rain as I stood on the side of the road, deciding where to go next. I donned my waterproofs and watched a hurricane cloud give off a spectacular lightning display over the intercoastal waterway. But this was no ordinary lightning storm; this was a tropical one, which can be very unpredictable. The rain lashed down even heavier and I started timing the distance from the storm as I heard a loud crack of thunder. They say only a dead man can hear and see lightning at the same time. I started to worry when, using the old 'Mississippi Missouri one, Mississippi Missouri two', etc., to time it, I could only get to the first M in the time it took me to see the lightning before I could hear the thunder. *This was too close for comfort*, I thought, as I saw a neon Budweiser sign glowing through the deluge of rain and rushed on into the entrance of a nearby bar on the street corner.

    I was inside a crowded sports bar, but instead of some ballgame on the big screens, the shuttle Discovery was touching down on the Californian salt flats at the other end of the continent where it was still daylight. This was the culmination of the first successful mission since the Challenger disaster. I then heard cheers and saw tears and baseball caps flying, since Titusville relies on the space programme for its livelihood. It was as real to these people as an office or a shop is as a workplace back home. The space programme was back on; mortgages and car loans could once again be paid.

    I soon struck up a conversation with the locals seated around one of those circular bars that I had only previously ever seen in *Cheers*. I corrected them that I was British and not Australian, and that I wanted to visit the Space Center. The friendly locals told me the history as I listened to them in awe. Near here on Cape Canaveral is where the space programme had begun. It was a natural choice; even Jules Verne had predicted this part of Florida in his novel *A Trip to the Moon and Around It*, almost a century before it was ever used. The Cape has everything that is needed; a firing range of ten thousand miles over water to the east, it is near the equator and in the correct direction for launching into the earth's spin and located where malfunctioning rockets would not endanger human life. Also, the isolation made it ideal for security purposes.

    Just after the Second World War, President Harry Truman authorised the activation of the Cape testing ground and the infamous German V-2s, the doodlebugs used to bomb London, were converted into Redstone rockets for the US Army by the captured ex-Nazi Werner Von Braun in Huntsville, Alabama and hauled over primitive roads to the tip of the Cape. The first successful launch was Bumper, which travelled only ten miles, launched from a painter's scaffold next to an old tar-paper bathhouse, protected by sandbags that was used as the control centre. As things became more ambitious, a converted oil derrick became the launchpad. Staff lived nearby in small mobile homes known as trailers and rode bicycles home for lunch, but I think the expression 'trailer-trash' hadn't been invented back then. A larger building was eventually erected, but launching the converted V-2 was still a risky business. One Redstone turned over at launch and exploded just outside the new building, to the accompaniment of shouts and panic. Another veered off course into the village of Cape Canaveral, which is known affectionately today by the locals as Cape Carnival due to its high population of crack cocaine addicts. Luckily a safety officer managed to blow it up, but fragments of the rocket sprayed a trailer park and set scrub alight. For a number of days afterwards, guards were still killing an infestation of rattle snakes which had escaped the burning bushes.

Meanwhile, the Soviet Union's Sputnik bleeped its way around the Earth; a nervous Congress passed the Space Act; and the National Aeronautics and Space Administration - or NASA, as we know it today - was born. Things became a little more serious out on the Cape, since it was obvious that nuclear weapons could now be carried by rockets. First, the monkey Ham was launched into space at around the same time the Russians launched the first human into space, Yuri Gargarin. NASA started the one man Mercury program and Alan Shepard became the first American in space. The Soviet Premier Nikita Khrushchev had maliciously joked that his fifteen minute suborbital flight was just a 'flea jump' compared to his own cosmonaut, who had spent hours in earth's orbit. This so annoyed President Kennedy, and so determined was he to end the missile gap of the Cold War, that he made the famous speech that galvanised all Americans:"I believe that this nation should commit itself to achieving the goal, before this decade is out, of landing a man on the Moon and returning him safely to the Earth."

As a direct challenge to the Soviet Union, the Space Race was born. Despite his speech, the Russians were still far ahead in the race; while Cosmonauts orbited the earth many times on each flight, NASA could only manage a monkey for a couple of orbits at the very best. So when John Glenn - who, incidentally, is my namesake - became the first American in orbit, he became a national hero. This was despite the fact that the mission was ended prematurely when an errant warning light signaled a malfunction and his spacecraft *Friendship 7* entered the atmosphere with chunks peeling off and passing his view port. Being the cool character that he is, his pulse rate never once fluctuated on his entry back to Earth. He is certainly of the 'Right Stuff', and had achieved what Kennedy wished -that was all that counted. John Glenn was flown to West Palm Beach after splash down to meet the elated president. With Kennedy were his wife, Jackie, and their young daughter, Caroline. Glenn later recalled in his autobiography *A Memoir* that 'Caroline obviously expected someone else, because when she was introduced to me [she] looked around and asked, "Where's the monkey?"'

Next to me at the bar, a NASA contractor recollected those heady years when the impetus was on to land a man on the Moon. A much larger rocket was needed for a Moon shot than the old Redstone converted V-2s that tossed Mercury astronauts into low Earth orbit. Next came the larger two-man Gemini rockets launched by Titans; although larger than the Redstone, an even larger rocket would be needed, and so the *Saturn V* was born. By now Congress was pouring money into NASA, and at the peak of the Apollo moon program, over four hundred thousand people all across the States were working on it. The complex at the Cape grew immensely, and it is now named Cape Kennedy after the recently assassinated president. Titusville grew, and the contractor told me how he had worked on the construction of the gigantic fifty-storey Vehicle Assembly Building, "which you can't miss, Limey, as it's the first thing you'll see as you head out on the Cape."

VAB1, the largest man-made construction on Earth, was needed before they could assemble the largest vehicle to leave the Earth; the *Saturn V* rocket. He told me how they had to bore down 160 feet to the limestone bedrock below the sand, and use four thousand steel pilings to anchor the huge structure in place. His eyes sparkled as he explained that the water and salt took on an electrical charge, and by the time they capped this awesome structure with a roof, a storm cloud had built up indoors with its own thunder and lightning! The building had to be neutralised because NASA had just built itself the largest wet-cell battery on Earth. Everything about Apollo was monstrous, but it's one thing to be told that the engines give a thrust of 1.6 million pounds at take-off, and another to be told by someone else - who had by now leaned across the bar to join in the conversation - that he was made rich by men going to the Moon because it was his job to replace smashed windows in many of the Titusville homes after each Apollo launch!

The following day, with my head still spinning from the conversations I'd had with the locals in that bar, I crossed to the Cape and entered the Kennedy Space Center to see for myself the huge beast of a machine. As the locals told me, the first thing I saw from a distance was the isolated VAB1 building. As I got closer, I noticed that in the corner of one wall was painted the American flag; one star alone was larger than a human. The rocket garden had a fascinating display of space vehicles, dating right back to Tom Wolfe's 'The Right Stuff' era - the Mercury/Redstone of Alan Shepard, the Mercury/Atlas of John Glenn and then through the Gemini /Titan class to the modern day shuttle. Now lodged in the new Apollo/Saturn V Center was the Goddess herself, dwarfing in size all the other rockets put together.

I took the tourist bus and the driver stopped us inside a track made by the crawler and teased us with the question, "Now, where do you think the crawler is?" The largest wheeled vehicle on Earth was designed to transport the *Saturn V* from the assembly building to the launchpad; now it's used for the shuttle. By the mid-sixties, the Cape was first open to visitors. Two of its earliest were Walt and Roy Disney, who noticed the Cape's obvious ability to attract tourists, and so decided to erect their theme park in nearby Orlando. We passed launch pad 34, never to be used again as it now stands as a ghostly memorial dedicated to Ed White, Roger Chaffee and Commander Gus Grissom, the last of the Right Stuff's super seven, who was the first man to go into space twice and would have been the first person to have flown in all Mercury, Gemini and Apollo programs had the three of them not lost their lives in the tragic fire of Apollo 1.

Towards the end of the sixties, NASA was feeling a sense of urgency, for Kennedy had promised the world that America would have a man on the Moon by the end of the decade. The deadline was approaching fast; with only fifteen months to go, the first manned Apollo was launched – Apollo 8, whose crew, Borman, Lovell and Anders, not only took the famous picture I recall seeing on my first day at school but who, on Christmas Eve, also broadcasted a message of peace to the Earth, in the form of a reading from Genesis, with Borman adding, "And from the crew of Apollo 8, we close with good night; good luck, a Merry Christmas, and God bless all of you - all of you on the good Earth".

As inspiring as it was, the world was waiting for the grand slam – the actual Moon landing! On launch day, the roads around Titusville and Cocoa Beach, further to the south of the Cape, were jammed with the well over a million spectators, who made their way along the beaches and the landward side of the Indian River to watch launch pad 39A across the water. Throughout the night, floodlights illuminated the thirty-six storey *Saturn V* rocket and its supporting umbilical tower. At the Kennedy Space Center, a large grandstand was assembled for the many thousands of dignitaries and reporters from around the world for the greatest firework display of all time. Astronauts Neil Armstrong, Edwin Aldrin, and Michael Collins suited up and, with their helmets on, silence surrounded them.

"I hear only the squish of my awkward yellow rubber galoshes and the hiss of oxygen…"

Collins later recalled in his book *Carrying the Fire* that, on that morning after breakfast, they left in an air-conditioned van for the launch pad eight miles away. Armstrong entered the command module and took position on the left. He was followed five minutes later by Collins squishing along in his space-wellies, who took a final look around: "… On my right the most colossal pile of machinery ever assembled. If I cover my right eye, I see the Florida of Ponce de Leon… If I cover my left eye, I see civilisation and technology… and a frightening array of wires!"

He sat on the right, with Aldrin in the centre. Then came the wait; at 9:29:51am EDT, the mighty first stage engines burst into life, and the astronauts were thrown left and right against their straps in the now shaking command module. T-Zero was exactly 9:30am; hold-down clamps were released and the beast was loose as it roared upward towards the Moon, in probably the most famous and widely publicised space flight of all time. Everyone at one point must have had that frightening thought – would it explode? But the only damage was from the blast of the Apollo engines at take-off, which was so great that windows in Titusville over thirty miles away cracked, and the new friend I had made in the bar became rich overnight with a contract from NASA to replace them.

It took four exciting days to reach the Moon and, while skimming over the crater-pocked surface, Collins found it "stark", "barren and downright scary". Armstrong and Aldrin left Collins alone in the Command module as they descended to the Moon's surface in the lunar module *Eagle*. A spellbound audience on Earth watched as Armstrong later opened the hatch and gingerly stepped down the ladder. As his foot touched the surface and he made that famous speech, I sat at the back of the crowded school hall, cricking my neck at the telly to get a better view, and wondered why the image had been so much clearer just a few days before when Captain Kirk was giving Spock orders aboard the USS Enterprise! Such was my ignorance as a seven-year-old in that crazy period towards the close of the sixties.

As we all know today, the race for the Moon had been fuelled by the Cold War and a clever speech by the brilliant John Kennedy. So how ironic it was that he was no longer alive to see his dream fulfilled and that his political rival Richard Nixon was to give the moonwalkers a congratulatory speech? It had taken almost quarter of a million of the best brains in the world to come together to share ideas of how we were to colonise the Solar System and live permanently on places like the Moon and Mars, so that someday we may even reach for the stars - and Apollo was the answer. The Apollo program turned out as possibly the greatest disappointment of all time, as it never achieved the real goal it was supposed to; a money-conscious Congress axed it just a few years later after only a dozen men had set foot on the Moon, and boldly leapt to a place where none would ever return.

It has now been such a long time since man last stood upon the surface of another world that soon no one will be left alive to recount the personal experience of what it was like, and we are starting to breed a whole generation who doubts that it ever happened. Andrew Smith, in his book *Moondust*, mentions the day he was unable to interview the elderly Buzz Aldrin - and yes, he was the role model for this same generation's Buzz Lightyear, which probably doesn't help matters - because, with his staunchly religious upbringing, he was so unprepared and angry when a reporter thrust a Bible in his face and insisted "swear on this that you went to the moon" that in response he punched him and was subsequently arrested. I further read that, when he was asked by the British comedian interviewer Ali-G, "So what was it like to be just the second man on the moon?", Aldrin proved he was obviously in a better mood that day, as he just smiled.

In my early days of backpacking around Europe, I met the charismatic Jim Irwin in a marquee on the seafront in the French Riviera. Now a reverend, he was lecturing on his religious experiences on the way back from the Moon. Not only was he a good, honest, religious man but I personally had the chance to speak to him and shook the hand of this Apollo 15 veteran who had driven the lunar buggy. So to any would be Moon-landing hoaxer, I would suggest they get out more often! As Eugene Cernan, the last man ever to walk on the Moon, once said, "Truth needs no defence... Nobody can take those footsteps I made on the surface of the Moon away from me."

Incidentally, his widely acclaimed last words before launching off the lunar surface -"Let's get this mother out of here!"- are, I believe, an urban myth.

Leaving the Space Center, I walked out onto the NASA Parkway and tried hitchhiking; not a good move, as I spotted many alligators in amongst the swamps on either side of the road and they had also spotted me! They say in Florida that if you don't like the weather then wait five minutes, which did work to my advantage, being hot as hell after the inclement weather we had just had. The road dried up very quickly as the beady eyes of the gators occasionally bobbed up out of the water looking at their potential next meal – me! But the road surface was too hot for them, and this gave me the time to hitch a ride before the road cooled again during the next shower. From here, I travelled on through the rich green subtropical Everglades to the coast road known as A1A. Then north, spending the night on a remote sandy beach, where I soaked my weary feet in the Atlantic and watched a row of pelicans fly across the crest of a wave looking for the unwary cat fish in the surf; the sun set behind me as I gazed out to sea. I climbed into my sleeping bag as the lightning from more storm clouds lit up the dusky horizon. I fell asleep thinking of those footsteps left behind on the Moon, and wondering when the time will arrive for more to be added.

The Ponce de Leon that Collins mentioned was in fact the Spanish Conquistador Don Juan Ponce de Leon, who had arrived with Columbus on his second voyage to the New World. He first became a governor of Puerto Rico, and it is said that this is where he first heard of the legendary 'Fountain of Youth' from the locals. A few years later, another Conquistador, Amerigo Vespucci, had discovered and claimed the Southern part of the mainland continent of the New World for Spain; the whole continent was named 'America' after him. It was Leon's intention to do the same for the northern part of the continent and so he claimed the island of La Florida, naming it either after the abundance of flowers, or because he arrived during Easter, which is the Spanish festival of flowers. He landed somewhere near today's St. Augustine, where his 'Fountain of Youth' can still be found, and when I arrived there, much to my dismay, I found out that it no longer worked, the little spring having obviously become polluted in the intervening years!

Saint Augustine, along with Pensacola, which Leon also founded, are apparently the two oldest European settlements in the States, but neither may be correct as he encountered at least one Native American in Florida who could speak Spanish, indicating an even older settlement may have existed somewhere else. I was astonished to find an old stone fortress at an inlet on the intercoastal waterway. This is the Castillo de San Marcos and wasn't even the first one built here, but the tenth! The previous ones had been built from wood, and one of them was burnt to the ground by Francis Drake. Those bloodthirsty British attacked again several years after the stone one was complete and torched the town, but that time the fortress remained intact.

While hitchhiking on the outskirts of Jacksonville, a 'cop' car pulled up with lights flashing, and someone I could only describe as Judge Dredd stepped out of it.

"Is there a problem, officer?"

He slowly walked towards me as his utility belt of pistol, cuffs and nightstick glistened in the morning sun. He took off his reflective sunglasses to make eye contact,

"Could I see your I.D., sir?"

I proffered him my passport.

"You ain't from around here, are you boy?" he asked, flicking through the pages.

"No sir, I'm from Britain."

He pulled out a pen and black book and made a note of this.

"A Limey, eh? Where are you from in Britain?"

"Lyme Regis." He smirked and made a note of this, too.

"A Limey from Lyme Regis, eh?"

Finding this mildly amusing, he returned to the car, shaking his head.

He radioed through to check to see if I had any outstanding warrants, but with a clean slate, he returned my passport and issued me with a warning ticket. From that point onwards, I knew I had to become a bit more streetwise for my own survival.

"Okay then, the reason why I stopped you hitchhiking is because you're in a bad area; a lot of drugs and crime here! You're in America now and you'll find things are a lot different over here than back in little ole England. So even though it's against regulations, what I'm going to do is give you a lift to a safe spot."

What a nice man, I thought, as I bundled myself and my backpack into the rear of the bulletproof-screened vehicle and travelled in style through the hood on the next leg of my journey.

The following morning, I found myself sipping from a bottomless cup of coffee at a diner in Baldwin County, somewhere in the suburbs of Jacksonville. I had finally reached I-10, the transcontinental highway, and I was now completely out of dollars. I asked the waitress where I could exchange sterling, and she looked at me as if I were from Mars. Sitting next to me at the counter, a truck driver overheard my accent, and before I knew it I was helping him deliver hotel security safes all over Jacksonville on my first day of gainful employment in the States, for which I earned forty bucks.

Back on I-10 was the most frightening three-day experience of my life, as I hitched along the Florida Panhandle and met every kind of weirdo imaginable - from drug addicts and sexual perverts, to religious fanatics who really thought the world was about to end, and even a driver so drunk he zigzagged back and forth across the freeway while swigging from a bottle of gin! Every lift was like entering the 'Twilight Zone'; it was as though the whole world had gone mad and I just did not know what to expect next. One simple rule about hitchhiking in the States is don't! The cop who gave me the lift a few days earlier was right; things were very different over here. I had already realised how much faster the pace of life was compared to anywhere else I had ever been, and this tended to reflect in the people; everything was taken to the extreme and I had to stop playing the naive tourist and get streetwise the American way, before it killed me.

I thought back to the truck driver who had employed me for the day, and when we shook hands and parted, he gave me a piece of advice which was worth a thousand times more than he paid me. A low budget traveler like me should only ever get a lift with truck drivers; they travel the longest distances and most of them need the company to relieve the boredom. This was the only safe way to travel the States, and as Americans liked the British accent it was easy enough for me to ask for a ride at truck stops. Some drivers couldn't give me a lift for insurance reasons, but most of them would ignore this, and as I discovered in the next few weeks, all of them were of good character - a breed apart, as they would look out and help each other on their long journeys around the continent. They are the modern day cowboys, and it is to them that I owe everything.

We passed a chain-gang of prisoners digging at the roadside as the sixteen-wheeler roared across the Florida/Alabama state line, with the Confederate southern cross flying and the words 'Proud to be a Redneck' on the windscreen. The driver was on the CB radio and it sounded like astronaut comm traffic as he called other truckers in an attempt to get me a connecting lift.

"Anyone going west from Mobile on I-10? I have a Limey here who needs a ride."

Coincidently, in the background, the radio blasted out Skynyrd's, '...Big wheels keep on turning / Carry me home to see my kin / Singing songs about the southland / I miss Alabama once again / And I think its a sin, yes...'

We passed road junctions with romantic names like Spanish Fort, Gulf Shores and Fairhope, and the surrounding lush green of the subtropics suddenly broke into blue as we trundled onto the Mobile Bay bridge and a rich clear sky reflected off the Gulf of Mexico.

'…Sweet home Alabama / Where the skies are so blue / Sweet home Alabama / Lord, I'm coming home to you.'

In the far distance I could see the skyscrapers of the commercial centre, reminding me I was still in America, and across the bay as far as the eye could see were marker buoys for fishing traps and shipping lanes. Even though I'd never been here before, it really did feel like coming home.

I have often heard people complain 'why go to America? It's so over commercialised, so false and it just doesn't have the culture and history as we do back in Europe.' Well, think again, as the first European to clasp his eyes on this part of the States was a Welsh prince called Madoc, who set sail from Rhos-on-Sea and founded a colony somewhere near here. Nothing surprising about this, you may think, until you find out that it was in the twelfth century, three centuries before Columbus. Madoc was one of the many children of King Owain Gwynedd; upon his death, fighting broke out among the possible successors. Madoc was so disheartened, says the story, that he and a brother decided to explore the Western Ocean with a small fleet of ships. They discovered a distant and abundant land where one hundred men disembarked to form a colony, before Madoc and the others returned to Wales to recruit settlers. After gathering ten ships of men and women, the prince sailed west a second time, never to return. Legend has it that Madoc's colonists are supposed to have travelled up the many vast river systems here and settled with friendly Native Americans.

This always remained a legend until the late seventeenth-century, when the Welshman Morgan Jones, an Oxford University-educated reverend, was captured by a tribe of Tuscaroras in an area we now know as South Carolina. They were about to kill him when he muttered a few words in Welsh, and to his surprise the Indians understood and released him. Not only did Morgan Jones assert that this story was true, but he made a formal affidavit to that effect on returning to the British Colonies sixteen years later. Folklore has long claimed that Louisville, Kentucky was also once home to a colony of Welsh-speaking Indians. Even in the late eighteenth-century, John Sevier, who became the first governor of Tennessee, was told by an old Cherokee chief named Oconostota of ancient fortifications built along the Alabama River by white people who had once lived in the area as a protection against his Cherokee ancestors. They were called 'Welsh' and their leader was 'Modok'. As unbelievable as this may sound, even Lewis and Clark were asked to look out for Welsh-speaking Indians when they went on their expedition across this vast continent.

The Elizabethan historian Richard Hakluyt (Hack-loot) records Madoc's story in his own work from an earlier source by the historian George Peckham. Both were Elizabethan propagandists, and therefore it is so easy to discount such stories as British claims in the New World against those of Spain. But let's not be too hasty here; even if the story of Madoc is just that, we know from discoveries by the Norwegian historian Helge Ingstad that the Viking Lief Erikkson had a colony in Newfoundland, which he called Vinland some five centuries before Columbus. So why not others?

The anthropologist Thor Heyerdahl made his famous crossing of the Pacific in the 'Kon Tiki', a balsa wood raft, proving that the South American Olmecs could be ancestors to the Polynesians. He was convinced of this from the similarity of the huge rock statues of carved heads in South America with those on Easter Island. The statues have distinctly negroid features, so why not extend this theory back to Africa? Could the Olmecs themselves have sailed the Atlantic from Africa as long ago again before the Vikings – why not? It's certainly a shorter distance and therefore an easier trip than crossing the Pacific, and West African myths do tell about people going west across the ocean on rafts; even Columbus had recorded seeing West African traders in Central America near present-day Panama.

Once in the tradewinds, it is possible for a small vessel to cross the Atlantic in as little as two to three weeks. It's easy if you know what you are doing, and I should know, as even I would later do it. This is a relatively short period of time for a fishing boat or a merchant vessel to be at sea and consequently was not an impossible task long before Columbus. Breton fisherman trawled the North Atlantic for months at a time long before 1492, and may well have seen the American coastline, if not landed there.

More convincing still is the hard evidence that exists, of which some goes back as far again in time as that of Erikson to Columbus, such as Roman coins found in Venezuela and a clay head of a third-century Roman doll found in a twelfth-century tomb in Mexico. In the ashen ruins of Pompeii in Italy is a wall painting of a pineapple, which at the time only grew in South America. The earliest examples of pottery in the western hemisphere have been found in a village in Ecuador, which is almost identical to pottery made in Japan at that time. Modern day chemical tests on Egyptian mummies have found traces of tobacco and cocaine, which some have proposed was brought to them by Carthaginian merchants. Even Roman shipwrecks have been found just off the coast of Rio de Janeiro, but are now subject to a Brazilian government cover-up, because the first one was discovered by a diver during the Columbus' 500th anniversary celebration – how embarrassing is that?

Most of this evidence is inconclusive on its own, but when you combine the little bits together, there is an overall pattern to support a whole new subject known as 'Pre-Columbian Oceanic Diffusion'; and someday soon, when archaeologists have discovered more evidence, I think we may be in for a few surprises. Just imagine it - the Roman Empire sending fleets of ships across the Atlantic to trade pottery, chickens, cloth and whatever else they could offer the Olmecs for gold, fruit, cocoa and even tobacco, long before Columbus sailed his ocean blue.

The truck driver dropped me off in downtown Mobile before heading north on I-165. It was now getting dark and so, guided by the nearest neon Budweiser sign, I wandered off into another bar. Overhead were rotating fans and an old vintage Wurlitzer jukebox still in mint condition in the corner. It was like stepping back in time, and it was here, seated at the bar next to me, that I was first introduced to that good oldSouthern hospitality from a Southern Belle, as we struck an immediate friendship. Even to this day the expression, "Where ya'll from, honey?", spoken with that Southern drawl, still makes me grow weak at the knees.

I remained in Mobile with her for about two weeks, time enough to acclimatise. Old Civil War stately homes, Mark Twain, 'grits' for breakfast, drive-in-movies, all-you-can-eat diners, the Bible Belt, Martin Luther King, the smell of wood pulp from the paper mills, ice cold Dr Pepper from the bottle, corndogs, chilli-cheesedogs, Willie

Mays (baseball legend), Crimson Tide cheerleaders, burgers all-the-way, a much vaster selection of magazines than anything I've ever seen in the UK, and an almost infinite variety of candy. It was terrific and I experienced all this, strangely enough, in an environment similar to *Back to the Future*, where Doc and Marty are transported back in time to the fifties.

"Limey, you definitely ain't from around here," she laughed, as I posted another letter home in a trashcan.

It took me a while to kick the habit, confusing trashcans with postboxes and dustbins for mailboxes. The following day, after mailing an empty soda can, we drove down to the beach on Gulf Shores in her 1976 Ford Mustang. She wanted to buy a lottery ticket and, since gambling is illegal in Alabama, we drove to a small wooden shack on the beach, a liquor and package store just on the Florida/Alabama state line known as the Florabama, where you can purchase a state lottery ticket on the Florida side. The beach, nicknamed the Redneck Riviera, had white sugar sand that squeaked as you walked along it, and stretched, uninhabited east and west, as far as the eye could see. With a back drop of fresh water lagoons surrounded by subtropical jungle and fir trees, it was the most beautiful and unspoilt stretch of coastline I'd ever seen, and would be a place I would get to know and return to for many years to come, before most of it disappeared.

The population of the States is over four times that of the UK, and with almost forty times the area; it equates to everything back home being about ten times more congested. This is obviously not noticeable in a city in either country, but to get my head around the scale of size and distance, I started to estimate everything in the States on a scale of ten greater than anything back home. Take, for instance, a short distance to travel in the UK is say ten miles, while a typical long journey would be a hundred miles. In the States, it's equivalent to a hundred and a thousand miles respectively. This seemed to make sense. For example, in the UK, the furthest you can go inland from the coast is less than a hundred miles, while in the USA it's about a thousand miles.

"You ever seen a bridge four miles long?" asked the Connecticut driver in his Yankee accent as we rode along the North Causeway

Boulevard towards Lake Pontchartrain, Louisiana. I had to think twice about this question. The Severn Bridge back home is probably the longest bridge I'd ever seen, and that couldn't be more than a mile long.

"No, I haven't," was my reply as we rode crossed the Pontchartrain and I tried to see where the bridge ended but couldn't. I looked into the wing-mirror and slowly watched the land diminish in size until it too disappeared, all around us from horizon to horizon was just water and the bridge causeway.

"This bridge is more than four miles!" I exclaimed.

"Hell son, I didn't say four miles, I said twenty-four miles long!"

I was later to find out that the Lake Pontchartrain Causeway consists of two parallel bridges and is actually the longest in the world by total length. In fact, four of the ten longest bridges in the world are in the state of Louisiana. The lake itself was named after Louis Phélypeaux, Comte de Pontchartrain, a French minister to King Louis XIV, after whom Louisiana is named. It's a place where today most of its inhabitants claim descent from the French. We crossed the bridge and I was dropped off in New Orleans at a junction close to the French Quarter. From here I walked down Bourbon Street admiring the old French colonial buildings and visiting its many jazz bars. This was once the main seaport to the vast colony of New France, which had stretched from here to Canada.

This French colony was established after the exploration of the Saint Lawrence River by the sixteenth-century explorer Jacques Cartier, who happened to give Canada its name. The greedy British, always trying to be the ultimate superpower in colonial expansionism, then arrived to conquer New France, but it wasn't long before they had their comeuppance when America beat the British in the War of Independence, and New France ended up with the Spanish after the Seven Years War before being returned to the French. Napoleon then decided to sell this vast colony to the United States so that he could raise funds for his conquest of Europe, making everyone as bad as those greedy British.

I walked from one bar to another with a plastic takeout glass of beer listening to different jazz musicians and refuelling with dollar draughts. No open container restrictions here, and you might wonder why. This is because Bourbon Street is owned by local police chiefs and that part of the French Quarter is a law unto itself. From a nearby cellar bar I could hear a Louis Armstrong rendition: 'I see trees of green, red roses too / I see them bloom for me and you / And I think to myself what a wonderful world…'

"Bet you five bucks I can guess where you got dem shoes," said a young black boy, looking down at my old worn out deckshoes.

"… I see skies of blue and clouds of white / The bright blessed day, the dark sacred night / And I think to myself what a wonderful world…'

"Deal," and waved him a fiver; it seemed a safe bet. How was he ever to know where I bought the shoes?

'… The colours of the rainbow so pretty in the sky / Are also on the faces of people going by / I see friends shaking hands saying "how do you do?" / They're really saying "I love you"…'

"You got dem shoes on de sidewalk on Bourbon Street,", -and with that he took the note and walked off.

"… I hear babies crying, I watch them grow / They'll learn much more than I'll never know / And I think to myself what a wonderful world / Yes, I think to myself, what a wonderful world.'

Like the Pontchartrain Bridge, the French Quarter miraculously survived the terrible devastation of Hurricane Katrina and today is happily regaining its reputation and charm as one of the most popular tourist destinations in the States. It is a special place with its French and Afro-American cultural influences; I mean, where else in the world can you listen to the music of the great Louis Armstrong while dining on diverse Cajun culinary delights such as frogs' legs, clam chowder, gumbo or alligator, during a 'female mud wrestling' match!?

It is no great surprise to learn that the Native American Indian name for the Mississippi translates to Great River - specifically 'Father of Waters' - and crossing it is entering Indian territory, since today ninety percent of all native Americans live here, having been forced west by the US government due to the white population explosion in the nineteenth-century. President Andrew Jackson signed the Indian Removal Act that authorised the removal, forcible if necessary, of Native Americans in the east to the new designated Indian Territory west of the Mississippi, mainly Oklahoma. The

Cherokee of Georgia were the hardest hit, as a quarter of them died during their forcible removal, known today as the 'Trail of Tears'. Further disruption of Indian culture was caused during the Gold Rush, when whites then also decided to move west.

At Lafayette, which is named after the French hero who helped Washington defeat the British, I got a lift from a truck driver who was hauling goods into Texas. As we crossed the state line at a town named Orange, I noticed the first mile marker read '880', and for the next three laborious days of hitched rides I watched them slowly dwindle down to zero. Everything about Texas is huge; it has an area over five times that of England and is mainly ranch country. The King Ranch in the South West corner of the state was once the largest in the world and the birthplace of American ranching; it covered an area that was twice the size of my home county Dorset, but has now been divided into two.

One evening, somewhere west of San Antonio, I noticed the prairies turn into scrubland and then desert. I was now in the vast wilderness of the Midwest, and was dropped off at a truck stop literally in the middle of nowhere. I slumped my backpack on the sand away from the noise of the interstate, and watched trucks from a distance entering the gas station like worn out oxen from a hard day's work in the field. It was a pleasant warm evening as I lay in my sleeping bag and gazed up at the spectacular starlit sky that one can only ever experience in the desert, away from any light pollution. I had never before seen the Milky Way so bright and clear; it stretched northeast to southwest, and the shooting stars seemed so close that you could almost put out your hand to catch them. As a waning full moon rose, I fell asleep thinking that this was the life, and it really was a daring adventure.

The following morning I rose early, stuffed my sleeping bag into my backpack and walked along a dusty track to a roadside diner as a glorious red sun sprung up and long shadows stretched out across the desert. An old Harley biker pulled up as I rummaged in my pocket for a spare shower pass, which had been given to me the previous day by a trucker for a fuel purchase. My first shower in almost a week, and it was a luxury not to be forgotten in that hot dusty climate; the pass even included a bar of soap, shampoo and a towel – what service! After the shower I walked in for breakfast.

"So, how are you doing today?" asked the trucker sitting next to me, as if he'd known me all my life.

"Er… Fine thanks, how are you?" I replied, a little surprised at the familiarity.

I was to find out that this was just typical American hospitality, so much less reserved than us Europeans are they. Americans, for some reason, are so much more open than Brits that in five minutes, not only will they tell a stranger their life story but that of the wife and kids, how much they earn and the size of their home, while the best you would ever get from a Brit under similar circumstances is polite conversation concerning the weather.

"Hey man, where you from? Australia or summit?" asked the trucker as the biker complained to the waitress about his steak and eggs.

She apologised. "I'm sorry sir, I'll get you another."

Without even inspecting the plate, she emptied the contents straight into the trashcan and ordered it again. The steak was so big it could have lasted me a week.

"Hey man, this is Texas - steaks are cheap. And anyway she only cares about her tip," laughed the trucker who noticed my astonishment as it was thrown away.

I then found out why the service here was so good and how the American tipping system works. It's good etiquette to tip twenty percent of the total price for food and drinks to the service staff. This is counteracted by waitresses and bar staff being paid less than minimum wage, or in most cases almost nothing! This explains why food and drink is generally much cheaper than in Europe, as the overheads are less and the service much better, since staff work for tips. A good server in the States can expect to earn $100 for every $50 of equivalent paid work back in Britain.

As the mile-markers dwindled down to 4, 3, 2 and finally 1, we crossed the state line into New Mexico and the trucker told me of a diner back in Texas just off the old Route 66 where they served a 72 ounce steak. It's a free meal if you can eat it within an hour along with all the trimmings, which include a baked potato, salad, dinner roll and a shrimp cocktail. I would have struggled with the extra sized trimmings, let alone the four and a half pounder top sirloin steak as well. Yet he knew people who could easily do it. I thought of the monstrous females I had met the day I arrived in Miami and wondered about them!

Later research on this place led me to discover that this famous steakhouse is in northern Texas, and only onein five of the 42,000 attempts to date have achieved the colossal steak meal within the time limit. The youngest was an eleven year-old boy and the eldest a sixtynine-year-old grandmother. The wrestler Klondike Bill ate two of the dinners within the one-hour time limit. But be warned, you have to be prepared to pay for your meal if you fail to finish it in the specified time limit. At the time of writing, it cost about a hundred dollars, which did not include the good old American gratuity tip - and to think, some people back home say America has no culture!

Out in the desert, it was just me and a straight, featureless road running from horizon to horizon. As I stood alone on the side of the freeway trying to hitch a ride from the occasional passing truck, a blimp appeared from nowhere advertising Coca Cola, and flew right over me. To my surprise it was followed shortly afterwards by another airship, this time advertising Pepsi. *Only in America*, I thought. *Who in hell except me is ever going to see this all the way out here?* This was a result of the Cola Wars, and at the time they were at their height - literally.

These two massive corporations competing against each other resulted in a whole new range of soft drink variations, including sugar-free, cherry, vanilla, citrus, orange, root beer and ice tea which, in this climate, became my favourite. Coke further teamed up with McDonald's, while Pepsi did the same for Burger King - and yes, would you believe it, the Burger Wars began. At this time, food was cheap if you chose to dine at these places, as one company tried to outdo the other in a price war which, on my budget, was a real bonus. You could find a McDonald's with a billboard or poster advertising Coke in the most unlikely and remotest parts of America, and just across the road, a Burger King advertising Pepsi. Except for the names, they both seem exactly alike to me, and I would often joke to

Americans that I always dined at one then occasionally dined at the other for a change!

'On a dark desert highway, / Cool wind in my hair, / Warm smell of "colitas" / Rising up through the air, / Up ahead in the distance / I saw a shimmering light, / My head grew heavy and my sight grew dim, / I had to stop for the night..."

We passed through an Apache reservation just outside of Alamogordo, and at the trading posts you could purchase objects as diverse as tinned rattle snake to a Totem pole, obviously now for tourists. Just as the Deep South has its own beauty, that of the subtropical jungle, so too the desert has beauty of its own. Here, it becomes difficult to drive west in the evenings and east in the mornings because of the setting or rising sun, which just seems to hover above the horizon, and the shadows of the mountainous desert take on strange colossal shapes with hues of red and orange.

'... Welcome to the Hotel California, / Such a lovely place, (Such a lovely place) / Such a lovely face / Plenty of room at the Hotel California, / Any time of year, (Any time of year) / You can find it here.'

I remember passing signs for Tuscon and Phoenix in Arizona at night, and then hitting the busy early rush hour traffic on an eight lane freeway on the outskirts of Los Angeles. California was originally part of the Spanish Empire, after it was taken from the Native American Indians. The names of major cities still remind you of these colonial times, such as San Diego (Saint James), San Francisco (Saint Francis of Assisi) and the state capital Sacramento (Sacrament). Los Angeles - the city of Angels - is the most misleading name, as I can safely vouch that it's the worse place I've ever visited anywhere in the world. Except for my visit to the Spruce Goose and Queen Mary along the seafront, I hated everything about this City of Angels. The people are rude and greedy and the over sprawling city ugly, with streets that smell of urine. So much for not being able to leave Hotel California, as even the church made me unwelcome by locking me out of the YMCA after I had paid for a much-needed bed for the night. Why the rich and famous should ever choose to live here is beyond me! I left thinking that the place should be twinned with a crater on the surface of the Moon, as both have something in common - no atmosphere!

I travelled south on a bus for several hours before I realised I had read the scale on the city map wrong and had, in fact, covered over a hundred miles just to get to the city limit, this place was so big! Here I got off the bus where, coincidentally, a sign read, 'Welcome to Los Angeles, twinned with the crater Tycho'. On I-5 I got a lift with a nice family in the back of a pick-up truck all the way down to San Diego; it was great, as a breeze cooled me down in the dry heat and I soon forgot all about La La Land.

From here I caught another bus to the border with Mexico; it seemed a wasted opportunity to have travelled so far and have come so close to not visit it, so I decided to make a short excursion across the border. I entered Tijuana, and for a moment it seemed I was back in L.A. At this time, the Border Patrol was a lot more relaxed than in today's post 9/11 'Homeland Security' hysteria. Poor wetbacks openly swam the Rio Grande in broad daylight, and it appeared as if the flood gates to the Third World had been thrown wide open, as thousands of poor Mexican families poured into the States for a better way of life. I was going in the opposite direction, which seemed quite lonely in comparison - just myself and a handful of American tourists.

At the bus station, I was very nearly given an on-the-spot fine for drinking a beer by a couple of dodgy-looking police officers, but managed to bluff my way out as a poor naive tourist, which I suppose I was. The bus to South Nogales was about to leave so I quickly bought a ticket, hid my passport in my backpack in case of pickpockets, and then stashed it in the luggage compartment. I somehow didn't trust anyone here - they all seemed so poor and desperate, just waiting for the opportunity to rob a rich-looking gringo. I watched the driver lock the luggage compartment, and then entered the crowded bus to end up squeezed between two fat people for the duration of the trip.

At dusk the following night, I sat down on the wooden sidewalk in despair after spending my last ten peso note on a packet of cheap cigarettes and a beer. The street ended at the border fence to the United States. I found Mexico dirty and rundown; wherever you looked, the litter-strewn streets were cracked and dotted with potholes, and the buildings ready for demolition. Yet a few feet away on the other side of the tall wire fence, everything is immaculate and the buildings luxurious. How was I supposed to know that I should have bought a luggage label? I had been in a rush to catch the bus and no-one had told me. During the previous night we had stopped en-route to Nogales, and of course my unlabelled backpack had been dropped off in the middle of nowhere - or stolen.

What the hell was I going to do now? No money, no passport and thousands of miles from home without even essentials such as a backpack and a sleeping bag.

It was the low point of my life, and I had never felt this depressed before. The nearest British Embassy was in Mexico City, and how difficult would it be to get there without any money? It had been dangerous enough hitchhiking the States, and I could only imagine Mexico at the time as being much worse. As dusk approached, I noticed lots of little Mexican children running in the streets dressed for Halloween, ready for trick or treat time. Casper the Ghost and a little female devil with pigtails and horns came up to me,

"Hey Gringo... Treek a treat?"

What the hell?, I thought, and gave them the little change I had left. Better treat, as I'd had enough bad luck for one day. Then a thought occurred. Hang on a minute... It's Halloween in the States, not here in Mexico, where it was the Catholic All Saints day! Then my two little intelligent demons, realising my pathetic predicament, asked,"Gringo USA, Gringo USA?" pointing towards a crowd of children gathered around a point at the border.

"That's it!" I exclaimed, realising that the poor Mexican kids were trick or treating on the rich American side by dressing up and climbing through a hole in the fence!

"Com Gringo, Com... USA."

The scene that followed would have had the devil himself doubling up with laughter. I slipped through the gap in the border fence, and it seemed the very gates of hell itself had opened up, as little witches in pointed hats, vampires with huge white blooded fangs, ghouls and demons darted off in every direction on the American side. The American Border Patrol just stood around doing nothing - almost certainly a well-rehearsed nothing, based on previous years' experience - as the harmless kids ran off into the streets and towards the homes of middle town America.

The border patrol did nothing, that is, until they saw my tall silhouette emerge amongst all those smaller demons! Searchlights came on and sirens blared as I ran like hell into the back streets of downtown North Nogales. Behind me, I could hear the screeching tires of military jeeps, as the race was on, and now it really did feel like the gates of Hell had just been opened. I ran around a corner then down a dark alley and - you guessed it - straight into a dead end!

"What the hell now?"

Then, with a bit of quick thinking, I pulled off my blue jumper, slung it into a nearby trashcan, turned around and calmly walked back towards the noise and commotion. Within a few more seconds, a Jeep pulled up and a torch light shone into my face.

"Good evening, Officer, is there a problem?" I asked the blinding light in my best English accent.

"Can I see your I.D.?" asked the light in a stern voice.

I told a bit of a white lie by explaining that I had been robbed here in the States as opposed to Mexico, for fear of being deported back there – and, of course, I was just about to report it to the local police. The officer was no fool; he knew I was the wetback they were after, and he knew I was no Mexican one at that, from my accent and blue eyes (although with bronzed tan and ragged clothes, the rest of me did look like one after having been on the road for over two months).

At the Nogales police station, I was treated as a bit of a celebrity by two pretty female officers.

"We seem to have ourselves a real tourist this time," said one to the other as she smiled at me.

"He's all the way from England, Great Britain."

The place even had its own department for looking after destitute tourists and I was given my own en-suite room in a local motel and even food stamps to buy meals and new clothes from the local mall – incredible! I even managed to borrow money off the local attorney, a father to one of the female officers, until I arranged a money transfer from Britain. It was like being on an all-expenses-paid holiday, and on the day my money transfer arrived, I offered the attorney interest on his loan, but he refused.

"No, I'm not in the money loaning business. I just did that as a favour."

So I bought the pretty female officers flowers as a thank you, which they set up in their office - what great people these Americans were. From the local thrift store I purchased a secondhand backpack with a sleeping bag, and before I knew it I was back on the road again, hitchhiking north across the Arizona desert.

In Monument Valley I passed the unforgettable backdrop of the two Mitten Mountains, used in countless cowboy films, and carried on into the Grand Canyon National Park, arriving to view it during a spectacular red sunset. Words or pictures cannot describe what I saw next because of the vast scale and beauty of it all. The person I had met hitchhiking to the canyon turned out to be a fantastic guide, who led me out onto a rock stack in the Canyon, telling me to cover my eyes. At the correct position he told me to open my eyes for the most spectacular view I have ever seen. The Colorado River was the sheer drop of a mile below, the canyon 18 miles wide and 277 miles long, covering an area over a million acres.

"God's country," said my guide, and one could easily imagine Him using it as the mould for the Himalayas when he created the world.

West again into the desert, I passed the Hoover Dam and avoided the turning for Las Vegas, as it is not my sort of thing. I just cannot do tacky – until, that is, a truck driver told me about Lake Havasu City, the planned community created by the industrialist Robert McCulloch. He was the man who bought London Bridge, disassembled it block by block and had the marked stones shipped across the Atlantic to reassemble it here. I remember this as a child, when McCulloch produced chainsaws in California, and for tax purposes moved his factories and associated community of workers to Arizona, where the state tax was more beneficial to him. To enable him to do this, he had to have something other than a scorching hot desert of nothing to attract the community of workers that he needed. So he bought London Bridge for $2.5 million from the City of London when it was replaced, and paid a further $7 million to reassemble it. Allegedly, when the bridge was finally erected, McCulloch was horrified to discover that he had bought the wrong bridge, as he thought he was buying the more recognisable Tower Bridge. This was genius by accident, because he became famous overnight as the man who bought the wrong London bridge, and many wanted to move to his new community and work for him.

At first, London Bridge appeared like a mirage in the middle of this flat, featureless desert, but as I got closer and touched it, noticing the numbered markings on the block work used to help assemble it in the correct order, it was real enough. I walked along the bridge peering through the balustrades, as I had done as a child all those years ago, but instead of the Thames below, there was an artificial reservoir instead. In the middle of the bridge, a Beefeater guard marched up and down. I never pointed out the obvious mistake that these Beefeaters guarded the crown jewels, not bridges, because in some bizarre way it all fitted in so well. On the other side of the bridge, I came across McCulloch's version of an English village, with timber built shops and a post office, with strange pointed roofs and signs advertising 'Real English Muffins' and 'A Spot of Tea', whatever that is! Well, I had to take my hat off to the guy in admiration, because not only had he got the wrong bridge, but he had got everything else wrong in such a perfect way. It was like being in some weird London of an alternate universe – it was superb.

Further west through the Mojave Desert, I passed a huge junkyard, not of cars but, would you believe, aeroplanes. These disused military and passenger planes remained rust free in the dry desert climate, and the whole collection made a splendid museum. My last lift across this exciting and beautiful continent took me beneath the arch of the Golden Gate Bridge in San Francisco, and to secure the completion of my transcontinental voyage I paddled my feet in the Pacific as I had done at the outset in the Atlantic at Saint Augustine. After I completed this ceremonial task, I took a picture of the bridge with one of those cheap disposable cameras and thought of naming it 'Off the tourist beaten track', which my journey had been. As I turned around, I realised that it would not be a suitable name, as a whole coach load of Japanese tourists stood taking the same picture with their expensive Fuji cameras.

That evening, I made my way to Fisherman's Wharf and watched dolphins playing in the bay. A cold mist with a light rain blew in off the ocean. Now exhausted, I took shelter behind the wheelhouse of a moored fishing boat and fell asleep. The following morning, I awoke to the consternation of many irate Chinese fishermen running around and shouting at me. Surprised as they were to find someone who had the sheer audacity to just go and sleep on someone else's boat, I simply apologised as I stepped the gunwale and back onto the wooden boardwalk.

It was getting colder as fall started to set in the northern hemisphere, and as I was unprepared for the harsh conditions of a North American winter, so I would follow in the footsteps of what the Americans term 'Snow Birds', the elderly and rich retired couples who migrate to the south for the winter in their luxurious mobile homes. But I would do it slightly differently, and within two weeks, I was back in the Deep South and penniless once more. One thing that I had learned on this adventure was how to be streetwise the American way, and so I pawned my watch and purchased equipment for use in the rich colonial and Civil War homes in the leaf strewn streets of downtown Mobile, where I had a business idea.

"Martha, come look here at the yardman; he's a God damn Limey," he exclaimed in a Southern drawl as I made a cold call at one of the many rich downtown homes, towing a secondhand rusty lawn mower with one hand, and grasping a garden rake with the other.

The first job I got was at an attorney's office just off Government Street, a point of interest that I will return to later. It was not long before my new business idea started to boom; everyone seem to like the idea of a Limey yardman and the good old Southern hospitality and community spirit found in Dixie made it a great place to be one. Even there, the inevitable winter set in and the gardening work dwindled to nothing, but I had raised enough cash to head back into Florida.

On Christmas Day I reached Key Largo, and stood before Humphrey Bogart's *African Queen*, where it was actually filmed, and not in the African Tropics as portrayed. I travelled to Key West in search of Hemingway Country, named after the author whose macho interests included fishing, hunting, boxing and running with the bulls in Pamplona. A veteran of the first World War, he had travelled the world and wrote of it in such classics as *Snows of Kilimanjaro*, set in Africa, to *The Old Man and The Sea*, set in nearby Cuba. So you can well imagine my surprise when I finally arrived to find a vast gay community! At first, I found this rather unnerving as a heterosexual but, like the American girls, they did love the English accents, and it wasn't long before I had made some good friends. I continued my newfound career, and while gardening for one gentleman, he told me that as a child he'd once been employed as the author's bellboy and told me how much Hemingway hated cats – obviously not macho enough for him. Yet at Hemingway's home you can see the famous 'Hemingway Cats' and tourists having their photos taken with them - enough, I'm sure, to turn poor old 'Hem' in the grave.

I was then employed by a troubleshooter, whose job it was to look after the properties of the deceased until the will was sorted. One particular property was a beautiful colonial mansion, and it was my job to box away all the books in the library. Of course I was in my element, and was forever being told off for reading the books rather than boxing them. One day, while browsing a pile of 1950s magazines my boss came in and lost his temper.

"Limey, I keep telling you to box them, not read them," he said, thrusting a pile of books under my nose.

Balancing on top of the pile was a first edition Hemingway hardback. I grabbed it, opened the front cover and showed him what it read, exclaiming, "That's why I read them!" The troubleshooter stared in astonishment at the dedication: 'To Major Spottswood, with best wishes, E. Hemingway'. Not bad for a day's work, and that is basically how I managed to pay for my flight home. With a bronzed tan and scruffy attire of faded jeans and T-shirt, I appeared more as a homeless transient rather than a tourist back at Miami Airport. As the wheels lifted off the runway, I left American soil with a heavy heart; this had been one hell of a trip - the adventure of a lifetime - and I had grown from hating to loving this exciting place.

CHAPTER 2

'What is history but a fable agreed upon?'
 - Napoleon Bonaparte

On my way home on the A35 I had a break from hitchhiking and stopped at a McDonald's on the outskirts of Dorchester. It was a cold, brisk February day and I noticed the bemused look on the faces of the two girls behind the counter at my tan and attire. As I left with my heavily overpriced burger thinking, "This just ain't America", I heard one whisper to the other, "I think he must be Australian!"

God forbid, I thought, *I'm a Limey from Lyme.*

My final lift dropped me off at the top of the steep incline to Cobb Road, named after its ancient stone harbour. This was my workplace as a boatman during the summer months, where I took tourists out on fishing trips. It was one of those unusual sunny days in winter with a cloudless blue sky, but still an angry grey sea broke over giant boulders placed at the end of the harbour wall as I walked the last few steps of my long journey. I had always taken these rocks for granted and now wondered what the purpose of them was. The Cobb had never had any use for them in the past. My train of thought was suddenly broken, as it occurred to me that what I had just experienced in the States had its origins in places like this, here in the West Country. I had effectively been to a home away from home.

As I mulled this thought over, I walked past the Crab Shop, where two locals - one an old retired boatman and the other a retired gas fitter - sat outside, patiently waiting to pounce upon an unwary, out-of-season tourist and sell them something fishy they'd never expected.

"Morning Victor, morning Fred."

I waited for some enthusiastic welcome home after my long absence.

"Morning boy," was the reply in unison, as if they had just seen me the day before and not some five months previously.

That's what I love about this place; its old, timeless characters and the fact that nothing ever seems to change. Every day is Groundhog Day in Lyme. I turned the corner on the seaward side of the Cobb Arms towards my parents' burger bar. Mother came out of the kiosk to greet me, obviously glad to see her little boy safely home; okay, so I'm the eldest of four, but mothers will be mothers. Dad, always the cynic, just grinned and rebuked,"Glad you're back and safely in one piece. You had better get changed, it's Mr F's funeral at one o'clock!"

"Albert has passed away?" I exclaimed. Lyme's 'Old Man of the Sea' had gone on his final voyage.

The nickname 'Mr F' had been coined due to his frequent and colourful use of the 'F' word in every sentence. Albert had been a boatman – a man of the Cobb, like my father and, much more recently, me. I was the youngest and least experienced, and we both knew Albert had been the eldest and most experienced. Lyme is full of eccentric characters, drawing a parallel with what I had just experienced in the States, but the common links run much deeper than this.

Both Albert and Victor were the last of the old school of seadogs who worked the Cobb as boatmen, running pleasure trips back before the Second World War. Only then, during those dark years, had they taken time off to serve in the Navy to do their bit for God, King and Country. Albert had served aboard a minesweeper and was the sole survivor after a German U-boat torpedoed it in the English Channel. While in the freezing cold seas he happened upon a mid-Channel marker buoy with a bell, which he clung onto for dear life until an Allied ship just happened to pass by and rescue him! You just don't seem to get that breed of human anymore.

The most senior of the old seadogs in Lyme never spoke to, or ever acknowledged, each other. I was told that they had had a disagreement many years ago and never forgave each other over it. I found this very odd, and it's only because of my interest in travel history that time would reveal the truth behind this disagreement. Just as I had grown to love the States, the inverse would happen for Lyme. In a sense, both Albert and Victor, along with my father, had been my mentors as I trained to become a boatman. They taught me the skill of touting - the verbal promotion of boat trips; the better you are at it, the more passengers you get, and the more you earn.

"Any more for the next boat trip? An hour round the bay mackerel fishing," could be heard echoing from the Cobb on those hot summer days, as boatmen competed with each other to fill their boats with customers. Yet my first season as a fully-fledged boatman would be the last for many of the old school of seadogs. A cold northeasterly wind blew for the whole month of July, known locally as the 'Charmouth Funnel'. 'Wind in the east, fish bite least, wind in the west, fish bite best', as the old saying went. But the old wisdom made no difference, as it was far too rough to take anyone out on boat trips fishing at all, when the schools broke up towards the end of the month and the town flooded with tourists for the summer holidays. On the last day of the month, the wind dropped altogether and I remember Mr F's pale blue eyes peer at me through his sunburned, walnut-faced features as he said,"You've seen it blow a fucking nor'east all fucking month, now watch it blow a fucking sou'wester all fucking August!"

So it did, and consequently there was no long hot summer for the season of '87, and hardly anyone worked the tripping boats. How Albert knew that would happen, when even today the Met Office cannot always get the following day's weather right, had puzzled me at the time. But now I know that it was from his long experience as a boatman at the Cobb. Victor and he had over a century's experience of watching sea conditions between them, and every now and then they had experienced one of those gale force seasons. Dressed in my suit, I sat morosely at the back of the church at Mr F's funeral and listened to the vicar make his speech about this 'Man of the Cobb'. I sat near the Mary Anning window, dedicated to the local palaeontologist, and stared out and thought, *She sells sea shells on the seashore, the shells she sells are sea shells I'm sure*, the childish poem dedicated to her. Albert was going to give me the marks for a fishing ground for my three hour twilight angling trip, but he never did and now I would never know it – just a little thing, but a fragment of our history gone forever!

On the day of my boatman's exam, all the boatmen stood along the railings at the entrance to the Cobb to watch, as I nervously waited for the harbourmaster to arrive – *nothing like working under pressure*, I thought. You could hear a pin drop in the silence – it was the peak of the hot summer of '86, yet no one was touting; everyone had come to a pause to watch me take the exam.

I had managed to memorise the seaway code throughout that season. Early in the morning, before we started work, another boatman would let me take his boat off the mooring and take it out to sea to practice the man overboard drill on my own. He looked at me now and could tell I was nervous.

"Don't you worry, Glen, you can't do anything wrong that hasn't been done wrong by any of us before".

Ron Higgs, the proud Welshman who was the comedian amongst us, proceeded to tell me the tale of when he came back into the Cobb, under full steam with a boatload of passengers, and leisurely knocked the gear lever astern as he approached the harbour wall. The lever snapped off and tumbled between his legs, and along the deck. He mimicked himself desperately fumbling around for it as the tripping boat collided into the Cobb.

"It crumpled up like a crushed matchbox, and full o' passengers too," he said, in his strong accent.

I was splitting my sides with laughter as another senior boatman glared over at him. It had been his boat that Ron was running that particular season, a fact which only brought more tears to my eyes.

Finally my moment had arrived, as *Herbert Paul* came chugging up alongside the quay and the passengers disembarked after their one-hour trip around the bay. As it was peak season, any test would have to be taken in-between trips. I stepped aboard, restarted the engine and waited with bated breath as the harbourmaster arrived in his crisp white shirt and shiny boots, clipboard in hand. I momentarily left the helm to help him aboard, and in the meantime the boat drifted aground. I panicked and opened up the engine to drive her off the sandbar, but too late - she was stuck. In the corner of my eye, I could see Albert leaning over the railings, shake his head and place it in his folded arms.

Another boatman yelled down, "Knock it out of gear and use the tiller to push her free."

I did and, well, would you believe it? It worked!

An hour later, I tied the dinghy up after placing the *Herbert Paul* back on her mooring, and as I climbed the ladder to the outhaul, my father's head peered over the Cobb wall and asked, "Well, did you pass?"

"Yes," I grinned.

"Well, it's a bloody good thing I didn't take you for the test, as you would have failed!"

It took a long time for me to live that one down. I had managed to do something that no other boatman had ever done - gone aground during my exam… and passed! The commercial fisherman, as well as the boatmen at the Cobb, nicknamed me 'Gone-Aground-Glen' for many years to come.

… And those immortal Lyme family names! Curtis, Gear, Gratton, Henley, Higgs, Hodder, Homyer, Humphrey, Legg, Rattenbury, Talbot and Woodroffe, of which some have been associated with the Cobb for almost a century, while others can be traced right back to the reign of Elizabeth the First. I have missed out many other local family names, but one thing is for sure; there's not a true 'Herbert' amongst them until more recent times.

Lyme locals have often joked that you're not a local until your family line stretches back at least four generations. This seems a reasonable criterion to me, as some of those names go back at least four times longer than that! The nickname for a non-local is a 'grockle', a slightly dismissive term for a tourist, which some say may have originated from a cartoon strip in the children's comic book *Dandy*, entitled 'Danny and his Grockle'. The Grockle was a magical, dragon-like creature, and visitors resembled him because of their boorishness and clownish behaviour. Other scholars have suggested that it might originate in a comparison of red-faced tourists in baggy clothing with handkerchiefs on their heads to 'Grock', the famous clown. However, the origin to this word appears very old indeed, since it has been used for centuries in the New Forest area of Hampshire to describe outsiders. In more recent times, it has spread to other parts of the south coast and, indeed, elsewhere in the world - including the former colonies of Rhodesia - as a term for a foreigner. Today, one often hears in Lyme, "Bloody grockles and their caravans, always jamming up the roads!" or "The seagulls are a real problem, they will even nick your ice-cream 'cos the grockles feed 'em chips!"

Dorset born and Dorset bred, strong in the arm and thick in the head I may be, but as it was not in my adopted home of Lyme, I am also a grockle and, as I tell everyone, I'm just a bit keener than the rest! And so it will always be, until my family name fulfils that not so unreasonable criterion - possibly sometime towards the close of the 22nd century!

These days, it seems to be commonly accepted that we live in a world of unprecedented, dazzling change. With globalisation, national frontiers are collapsing around us and technological innovations are reshaping our lives in ways we can hardly comprehend. Within seconds, from almost anywhere on the planet, one can contact almost anyone else and feign authority on any subject by consulting the ultimate library of the Internet. The future is approaching at such an alarming rate that sometime soon our own grandparents will find a world that is completely incomprehensible to them. But in reality, it is just our obsession with novelty, our ignorance of deeper historical patterns and the arrogant insistence of our own self-importance that leads us to these assumptions. I must admit that I was guilty of this myself before I started out on my own voyage of discovery. Yet perhaps, for most of us, our supposedly exciting times are really rather dull, as there's nothing very new about our obsession with the new.

Take, for example, the interesting fact that, a little further west of Lyme along the valley of the River Axe, if you know where to look, can be found the ruins of the lost city of Moridunum. This ancient Roman city wasn't even small compared to today's standards, as it stretched inland from a port at the river estuary as far as the nearby town of Axminster, and along the coast as far as Lyme, where the remains of a Roman villa with mosaic flooring can still be viewed in Uplyme. The city existed throughout the second and third centuries and may well have been moved and rebuilt several times during that period, due to the shrinking and meandering nature of the once much larger river estuary. The Romans named Lyme as Londinium, the same name given to this country's capital city. It's only conjecture, but when the Axe estuary finally silted up, a new location for a harbour was chosen at Lyme; this may very well not be the case, but historians have argued about the possibility of another that may have predated the medieval Cobb. Lyme gets its name from the river Lym, and on pre-Victorian maps this is spelt 'Lima', which could have indicated a river smaller than the once mighty Axe, or may refer to a harbour not so grand where the river once ran.

Records or evidence of a Roman harbour in Lyme are scant, if non-existent, but it is interesting to note that, like at Axmouth, a Roman road ran very near the coast here before most of it was destroyed by eroding cliffs during the middle of last century. A harbour at the river estuary almost certainly predates that of the Cobb, with a road that ran along the riverbanks connecting it to this Roman road.

Over seventeen centuries ago, in the heyday of Moridunum, the Roman Empire was at its apogee, stretching from Asia across the whole known world of Europe and North Africa; it may even have had links as far away as the Americas. It incorporated the religions and customs of all the known nations of the world, and maintained communication links between any two places within the empire, such as its capital Rome, and such remote places as the 'Port of Moridunum', or a possible Port Londinium (Lyme). A branch road ran from here up the Axe Valley, linking it to the Fosse Way, which further connected Exeter to Lincoln. Now, just think about this point for a moment: goods were imported by ship from all over the world to this little known port of today, and then transported to the far north of the country using a communication link, almost two thousand years before Ebay! Today, the Internet consists of ninetypercent local traffic, and most of us use this kind of technology to do remarkably old-fashioned things. Almost all the other types of technology that the Romans never had, and which we take for granted today, such as the electric kettle, television, the car and even man on the Moon, are inventions that are now decades old.

Now, suppose I had been born a century earlier than I really was and lived until I was, say, eighty. This would be a rare old age for those days, but certainly not impossible. I would have been born into a rural landscape of horse-drawn carts, freezing winters and limited horizons, in an age of sailing ships and steam power. A young Victoria would be on the throne, and the British Empire would be expanding at an alarming rate. The human psyche was different from that of today, as everything was achieved for God, Queen and Country. People tended to put their whole hearts and souls into everything they did, with a religiously perfectionist zeal. Just take a look around you now at any old Regency or Victorian building, bridge, canal or even the Cobb, and try to imagine how much effort or cost it would take to replicate something of equal standard today - if it were at all possible! The whole of human history is about empire building, and while we live in the age of the crumbled British Empire, our colonial cousins are living in the heyday of an expanding one. Regardless of all that, I would have seen in a lifetime the advent of cars, motorised shipping, the first manned flight, telecommunication, motion pictures, domestic electricity, mass education, votes for women, the effect of two World Wars and, possibly, the invention of rocket power which would someday place a man on the Moon. Now, ask yourself: who could possibly expect to experience such changes in a lifetime today?

If you take a stroll around Lyme's little stone harbour during a calm summer day, you will see families sunbathing on the beach while children build sandcastles. Further along the harbour, pleasure boats are launched off the slipway or untied from a mooring and head out through the harbour entrance to sail, water ski or embark on an angling trip. Your walk will end at the pier head by the harbour entrance and you can enjoy the breathtaking view of the majestic cliffs across the bay and the town nestled comfortably in the Lym Valley, and only wonder if there is a more tranquil place in the whole world. It is hard to imagine what a turbulent history this little town has had, and what it must have really been like in days gone by.

The town's existence has depended upon the Cobb, this small artificial harbour, for at least eight centuries and, believe it or not, the real turbulence is yet to happen. To completely understand this, we have to start from the very beginning, which is the Cotton Records. These were assembled by Sir Robert Bruce Cotton, then by his son and grandson, and contain some of the greatest treasures of British literature and history, including two of the four surviving copies of the

Magna Carta, an impressive collection of sixteenth- to seventeenth century maps and state papers, the Lindisfarne Gospels and the unique manuscript of *Beowulf*. It is the largest collection of Anglo-Saxon manuscripts in the world, and it includes the earliest written record of Lyme.

It was during the time of Charlemagne that Lyme was founded, and the evidence for this is in an extract from these unique and priceless Saxon chronicles, manuscribed in Latin, and part of a volume containing seventeen documents concerning the bishopric and monastery at Sherborne. This includes five charters from the Abbey of Horton and all of them have been preserved in the impressive Sherborne Cartulary. One of these charters has an equally impressive catalogue number of BL/Add/MS/46487/c/1150/S 263, and is of significant importance for three reasons. At least ninety nine percent of the human race would not understand it. The majority of the remaining few who can, such as my erstwhile and long-suffering girlfriend at the time I was researching this book, will not give a damn, and the last is that this charter is the oldest record of Lyme's existence.

The manuscript very roughly translates (I did this myself with the power of the Internet): "And in the 774th year of the reign of our Lord Jesus Christ and the good government of the Saxon King Cynewulf (Kin-Woolf) of Wessex granted one hide of land (which is about one hundred and twenty acres) to his venerable Bishop of Sherborne with a grant to fit out purification equipment." The land was on the west bank of the river known as the Lim, when this whole valley may well have been a salt marsh. Here, seawater could be drawn from a well and boiled by monks to produce salt for the 'seasoning of food', where seasoning, in this respect, meant as a preservative for fish or meat. This was signed by Cynewulf, king of the 'aforementioned' land, and by his nobles with such illustrious names as Æthelmodus, Scilling, Hemele, Cærdic, Æthelnoþ, Æthelmund, Wigferth - and how can anyone forget good old Bishop Ecgbaldi?

It has been suggested that, long before this estate's subdivision, an earlier single one may have possibly been based on the Roman villa at Holcombe in nearby Uplyme, in the suburbs of Moridunum. The land was then given over to Glastonbury Abbey by King Athelstan, and was subsequently passed on to Lady Huna by King Eadwig. The Norman Conquest changed all this and the Domesday survey, which took twenty years to complete, shows us that most of the land of the Saxon nobility throughout England was granted to William the Conqueror's followers. This survey was very thorough, and it is recorded by one of his counsellors that a second set of surveyors were sent out to check the initial work and report culprits back to the king. It would take a further nine centuries before such a concise survey would ever be conducted again and then only because of the threat of a Nazi invasion.

At this time, Dorset had a handful of boroughs, including Dorchester, Bridport, Wareham, Shafsbury and possibly Wimborne Minster, with Lyme coming under the Dorset western hundred of Whitchurch Canonicorum. The survey described it as divided into three packages.

The Bishop of Salisbury had a house there which paid six pence, this being the old English currency that survived a millennium, only ending as recently as 1971 (the year of decimalisation), a four acre meadow and land for one 'plough', which is a unit of measure representing the area of land that could be ploughed by an eight-ox plough team in a given time. It had never paid tax prior to this time, but fishermen paid fifteen shillings to the monks for landing fish, and this right (would you believe?) lasted for a further nine centuries! Saint Mary's Church of Glastonbury paid tax for three hides, land for four ploughs. A person called Wulfgeat leased land from the Abbot, and had two ploughs, nine villagers, six smallholders, a four acre meadow, a two-by-four furlong pasture, ten acres of woodland, and thirteen salt workers who paid thirteen shillings, resulting in a total tax value for Lyme of sixty shillings.

Still today in Uplyme, the ruins of a mill can be found on the northern extremity of the old borough. This seventeenth-century thatched building, with its wooden paddles, has been the site of a cornmill since Anglo-Saxon times, as part of a manor that belonged to Glastonbury Abbey, while the town mill is of more recent times.

Land was also held by the king's servant, William Bellet, after Aelfeva held it. Before the Norman Conquest, it paid tax for one hide, land for one plough, a villager with half a plough - which is just four oxen - fourteen salt workers, a mill which was almost certainly a watermill for grinding corn, as windmills were not introduced into this country until much later, a three acre meadow, a one-by-four furlong pasture, one square furlong of woodland, all with a total value of sixty shillings. If we assume that the fishermen paid the same rate as the salt workers, then we have sixty workers, including William and Wulfgeat. Now, if we further assume that the average Catholic family of the time numbered six, we have a total community population approaching four hundred, which, surprisingly is just a factor of ten less than today. Exchange salt workers for boatmen at the Cobb, and nothing much else appears to have changed!

The earliest indication of a possible harbour in Lyme is during the reign of King Alfred, the founder of the first Saxon Navy, who used moorings here during a battle with the Danes. Yet, three centuries later, the Doomsday Book does not mention one, although fishermen could land fish here. Later records indicate that one may have existed as early as the thirteenth-century, since the 'Calender of Liberate Rolls,' held in the Dorset History Centre, is an order sending one 'Walter King' on a tour of inspection to Southampton, Poole, Lyme, Exeter, Plymouth and Falmouth. That entry treats Lyme as though it were a port. Salt was the main industry of Lyme until a little after this time, as I have already said, when Axmouth harbour was made unnavigable by a major landslip at Haven Cliff. Lyme may have taken advantage of this opportunity and developed its own harbour for shipping, possibly at the river estuary.

Lyme became a 'Regis' in the thirteenth century when it was granted a royal charter by Edward I, better known as 'Longshanks', the Plantagenet king famous for conquering large parts of Wales, and almost doing the same to the whole of Scotland. After giving Lyme its privileges, both as a borough and a port, he gave the town to his sister Margaret, Queen of Scotland. After this, the place was acquired by the family of Bayeux, famous for the tapestry that recorded the Norman Conquest, before being transferred by marriage to Elias de Rabayne, whose nephew, Peter Baudrat, made a further transfer back to the crown in the early fourteenth-century, when Edward II became lord of one moiety of the borough. It became a prosperous shipbuilding centre during the Hundred Years' War, and for the siege of Calais, it provided

Edward III with four ships and sixty two mariners. At this point, a charter made the town royal property again, having similar powers to the Cinque Ports, indicating its importance. This charter is a beautiful ancient scroll, handwritten in French and etched, no doubt using a feather pen, of which a translation reveals a decree…

"That no Burgess (Freeman) shall engage in trial by combat."

Wow! What a statement, I thought, when I first read the transcript of those enigmatic words in some dusty and dark archive. My mind's eye conjured up a more chivalrous time, of knights charging about on the battlefield in shining white armour, as court minstrels sung about their bravery in seeking the Holy Grail or rescuing damsels in distress from dangerous dragons - or whatever else they did in those times. I later wondered just how chivalrous these knights may have been, when considering the involvement of Sir John Matravers (of Dorset's Lychett Matravers) in the sickening execution of Longshanks' son, the future king Edward II. Although it is unlikely that Edward's execution actually involved having a red hot poker inserted into his rectum as later accounts state, such cruelty wasn't beyond Matravers. Edward was not - a macho warlord like his father, but rather a gentle, homosexual intellectual who was a founder of colleges at both Oxford and Cambridge.

Over the years, the package of Lyme, originally held by Saint Mary's Church, became the tithings (estate) of the local Colway Manor house. According to the Regency historian Roberts, in his *The History of Lyme Regis, Dorset From the Earliest Periods to the Present Day*, this manor gelded the king's service for three hides, and was a parcel of the inheritance of Alured de Nichole, held by knight's service by the Abbot of Glastonbury, then by Robert Fitz-Pain for the same. After this, the manor was passed on by charter to John Bleyon, then Walter de Carmino, then Ralph de Carmino, the Bonviles of Chuton, then onto Margaret wife of Hugh Courtney, then to Joan, wife of Thomas, son of Richard Carew Knight and then his daughters and heirs - and then I got lost somewhere about here!

But I do know that an actual harbour called 'the Cobb' is first mentioned in a written account during the reign of Edward III, when it was described as a work of timber and stone damaged by storms. The stones were actually huge boulders, used in its construction by means of being floated between barrels to the previously storm-damaged part of the harbour, and stacked loose between oak piles. Later, during my travels in Mexico, between Campeche and Champoton on the Yucatan peninsula, I came across a similar construction with much larger boulders, built for the Gulf oil industry, and probably the nearest thing you can find today that looks anything like the original Cobb.

The Cobb was initially detached from the shore at high tide to let shingle pass through by the action of longshore drift, making it self-sluicing, while the earlier harbour built at the estuary was sluiced clean by the river. Lyme is totally exposed to southwesterly gales in the direction of the open Atlantic, so the shape of the Cobb has been naturally curved towards this direction in its construction, producing both a harbour and breakwater. The presence of the Cobb allowed Lyme Regis to become a shipbuilding centre, and an important port for trading products. In the first year of Richard II's reign, it was totally destroyed again in a storm, leading to the destruction of many homes and much shipping; the mention of this indicates the importance of the Cobb as a sea defence for the town, as well as a port.

In the Hundred Years' War, the Cobb's ships and boats were used to transport Henry V's invasion force across the Channel to France for the Battle of Agincourt. An old seafarer had once told me that the longbow archers who had been the cause of the victory at Agincourt had, on the return voyage, introduced the bowline knot to the boatmen that brought them safely back across the Channel; this is commonly used to tie a vessel at the Cobb today. I haven't ever been able to verify this, but it is a nice story, and I cannot tie one without thinking of it. Incidentally, he also told me that the difference between a ship and a boat is that you can carry a boat on a ship, but you cannot carry a ship on a boat!

"Always trust your compass!" barked my sergeant, while on manoeuvres in the Welsh mountains during a cold, bleak winter's night. Needless to say, this was during my short stint in the Territorial Army. But that blunt sentence would turn out to be the best piece of advice in my life. Once I was completely sure I had the correct bearings, I walked off and into the most atrocious weather conditions one could possibly imagine, which is normal for a blustery, cold

February night on the Brecon Beacons. This was my first solo hike across a terrain so barren, so devoid of life, that even the British Army call it 'Moon Country.' But unlike the Moon (and Los Angeles), it had an atmosphere so thick that my visibility was almost down to zero in the driving sleet and pouring rain as I descended a river valley, and then into a thick blanket of ice-cold fog all the way to my next rendezvous point. When I reached that light in the bitter, cold darkness, I was exhilarated. I had just been taught my first lesson in character building – independence. This changed my life; from trusting a compass bearing to reading maps and later on sea charts, my fascination grew into an obsession for travel and the history of exploration.

Not too far from where my sergeant was barking orders – unless, of course, you have to hike it! – is Hereford Cathedral, and one of the most expensive maps in the world, the 'Mappa Mundi,' created by Richard of Haldingham at about the same time as Longshanks' charter for Lyme. It was recently valued at a cool £7 million by Sotheby's, and was very nearly sold to raise funds to maintain the cathedral's library of chained books. Had it not been for a public outcry, and the Getty Foundation stepping in with the ready cash to save it, Britain would no doubt have lost one of its finest treasures.

This medieval map of the world is painted on a single sheet of vellum (dried calfskin), and depicts the known world as interpreted by the Christian theological beliefs of the time. Classified as a 'T-O' map, it shows the known single continent of the world as circular 'O', roughly covering the maximum extent of the Holy Roman Empire and the known lands of Asia, intersected by a 'T'-shaped inland sea which depicts the Mediterranean. The centre to this continent is Jerusalem, influenced not just by the Bible but also the Crusades to the Holy Land that were occurring at this time. The surrounding sea connects this single giant landmass to the edge of the world, where the unwary navigator would sail over its edge into oblivion.

East is at the top, where Heaven is situated, with God seated on his throne overlooking his six-day creation. Between heaven and earth is a small circular island depicting Paradise - the Garden of Eden - protected by a wall of fire with Adam and Eve in the middle, standing by the forbidden Tree of Knowledge. And what a marvellous creation this 'Narnia' or 'Middle Earth' is. Scattered around the shores of the inland sea and along the banks of its river valleys are beautiful cities with fairytale castles. An elongated shape of the British Isles can be seen at about the position of seven on a clock face, distorted either by design, or to show curvature, as it was known as far back as ancient Greek times that the Earth was curved and not flat. Across this strange world, at roughly one on a clock face, at the far end of the continent is a giant red sea in the position of the Ganges.

The remoter parts of the world are populated with fantastic creatures such as Cyclops, griffins and a phoenix, obviously due to Greek mythological influence, as well as dragons, mermaids, and sciapodes (also known as Monopods), which are single-legged humanoids that hop around rather than walk; one can be seen resting in Africa and using his single giant foot as a sunshade! There, too, is the dreaded anthropophagi, a headless humanoid with eyes set in the chest and a hungry mouth set at the abdomen, who goes around devouring babies! The idea was no doubt influenced by cannibalism. Amongst many others is a centaur wrongly labelled as a faun, giant ants that dig up gold and guard it, and the mandrake, a plant with strange aphrodisiac and narcotic powers, which shrieked and caused insanity if one tried to uproot it!

Imagine going through some magic wardrobe into this Narnia, with your rolled-up vellum map, and transported into this world! Being a low-budget traveller, and at a cost of £7 million, I would obviously only take one copy with me! What true-blooded traveller would not want to explore this magical world - except, of course, avoiding meeting any of those nasty anthropophagi? Yet, as amazing as it sounds, people have done so - at least in their imaginations. The self-proclaimed knight, Sir John Mandeville, who was possibly the monk Jehan de Mandeville, published a book of a journey across this strange world. First published in French in the fourteenth-century, he describes meeting all these weird and wonderful creatures.

A century earlier, maps such as these may have even influenced notables like Marco Polo in writing of their own travels throughout a similar world. In his book *Le Livre de Merveilles* (*The Book of Wonders),* Polo travelled throughout the Far East and became an important figure under the great Kublai Khan. He describes an army so vast that if the archers alone fired off a single volley then the arrows would blot out the light of the sun! Had he travelled the real world, and not the imaginary one of the Mappa Mundi, he would have realised an ancient custom that prevailed in the whole of the Far East, but had yet to be introduced into Europe. This was the drinking of tea; never once does he mention the stuff! The good old cuppa - or, rather, the omission of it - is proof enough for modern historians to throw a shadow of doubt rather than countless arrows on the travels of Mr Polo. Nevertheless, it is not of real importance if these accounts are fact, fiction or both. Rather, the important thing is that such stories later influenced Columbus, who had a copy of both of these books when he set off on his famous voyage.

In 1492, Columbus sailed the ocean blue and found... Japan! Actually, 'Cinpangu', the European name for Japan; at least that's where he thought he was when he arrived in the West Indies! Well, it was obvious, wasn't it? Everyone knew the world was round rather than flat by this time, so if you took one of those vellum maps and wrapped it around a globe, then where the two blue edges of the map touched was the western route to the Spice Islands that Columbus had just taken. Even the Spanish Inquisition had interviewed Columbus before he set off on his daring voyage; not because the world was flat instead of round, as the Church doctrine of the time would have you believe, but out of concern that he would reach the Garden of Eden and mess up Paradise a second time.

Columbus had therefore set his route just north of the Garden of Eden Isles, and knew that he had reached an offshore island of Cinpangu. After he erected a cross and proclaimed this new land for Christendom (and his Spanish benefactors), he managed to confirm his exact location from the natives when he presented them with a drawing of a Chinaman with slanted eyes and a pointed hat (honest!). The natives were pretty sure that such people lived on the inner part of the island, pointing Columbus in that direction and repeating its name in their native tongue ('inner island' sounded like 'Cubanna', and just 'island' like 'Cuba'). Cubanna/Cinpangu sounded the same to Columbus; he was convinced he had finally reached Japan and so, to this day, Cuba has remained its name.

Returning to Spain with this conclusive piece of evidence, he reported his findings to the Spanish court of Ferdinand and Isabella, and revealed the discovery of the western route to the silk and spice trade. Columbus even died believing that he had found an offshore island of Japan and not that of a vast new continent, or New World, as it did not exist on the maps of the old. Later on, the explorer and cartographer Amerigo Vespucci realised Columbus had made a mistake, and so had the honour of having this new continent named after himself; thus Amerigus – America, and not Columbus – Columbia. Poor old Christopher! If only he had not relied so much upon those blasted vellum maps.

After his victory at Bosworth Field against Richard III, Henry VII ascended the throne after the War of the Roses and wished to make a marriage treaty with Spain. This was a wise move, as the Spanish were rapidly becoming the world's first super power, with the discovery and impending colonisation of the New World. So a solemn betrothal of Henry's son, Prince Arthur, to Spain's Princess Catherine of Aragon was made at Woodstock, and the marriage took place later in Saint Paul's Cathedral. Unfortunately, Arthur died the following year, and arrangements were then hastily made to betroth Catherine to Henry's second son, the future Henry VIII. The consequences of this marriage would have a dire effect on English involvement in the world superpower game.

Also at this time, the bitterness caused by Longshank's Wars with Scotland had not yet been forgotten, and the Scottish were always ready for conflict with the English - even siding with the French, who were also bitter enemies of the English after the Hundred Years' War. Even though France had finally beaten England, it had left their country in ruins. Henry VII wisely aimed at a lasting peace with Scotland, which would also end the long friendship of Scotland and France. It was decided that Henry's daughter Margaret, the future Mary Queen of Scots, should be married to the Scottish King James IV. From this marriage was descended James VI of Scotland, who later became King James I of England.

Unlike for the Spanish and Portuguese, it was difficult for England to get in early with these new voyages of discovery because of problems related to the recent War of the Roses. When the Genoese navigator Giovanni Cabotto (John Cabot) came to Bristol to seek financial aid from English sea merchants, having been refused by Spain and Portugal, Henry VII showed an interest. Bristol was then the second city in England, and the port most interested in increased trade from new discoveries; and so, Henry financed a voyage of discovery for Cabot and his son, who were the first to reach North America on behalf of the English, and who later on searched for a route to the Indies and the Spice Islands. This was a year before Vasco da Gama, the Portuguese mariner who found an easterly sea route to India around the Cape of Good Hope. The Cabots were not solely in the service of England. Sebastian Cabot, the son, was employed by the King of Spain, and by the Emperor Charles V, and by the Venetians; he made several voyages of discovery for them also. He later became a map-maker for Henry VIII, who sent him to try again to discover the North-West Passage and a route around North America for the Spice Islands.

Although it was Eleanor of Aquitaine, the mother to Richard the Lionheart, who enacted the laws of Oleron, the first codes of maritime law, which founded our navy, it was Henry VIII who was to become known as the 'Father of the English Navy'. By increasing the number of ships and introducing heavy guns into these ships, he did away with archers and hand-to hand-combat, and these improved vessels became the perfect tools for voyages of discovery. Sadly, Henry had no real interest in establishing a New World colony using his new navy, but instead had more of an interest in trying to sire an heir for the throne by one of his many wives. He undid much of the work of his father by divorcing Catherine of Aragon, and in the process he abolished the Catholic religion in England, which did not help matters, as the two greatest empire building nations at the time were Catholic; the Portuguese, seeking an eastern route to the Spice Islands and China around Africa, and the Spanish, seeking a western route to the same place around America.

The Pope then divided the world in half for these two great exploring Catholic nations, according to a meridian drawn at thirty eight degrees west; all new lands discovered east of this demarcation line belonged to the Portuguese, and those west to the Spanish, although in fact it was a semi-meridian, as no one knew at the time exactly where the other half should be placed. The following year, at the Treaty of Tordesillas, the line was moved further west by about nine degrees after it was realised just how advantageous this division had been for the Spanish. That is why today, Brazil is the only Portuguese speaking country in Latin America.

While the Spanish and Portuguese, then the only world superpowers, were seeking trade routes around the Earth, the English were mainly confined to coastal shipping and some trade with Europe. Even this was limited, due to plunder by pirates such as the Barbary Corsairs, who ransacked not only trade ships, but also fishing boats returning from the rich fishing grounds off Newfoundland. The Christian captives from these frequent attacks were sold into the Islamic white slave trade unless a ransom could be raised for their release.

In September 1521, the forty tonne bark *Patience* from Lyme was bound for Malaga, but within the straits of Gibraltar was captured by a Turkish Man-O-War, who, having riffled her and cut her masts, set the ship on fire with all her goods. William Hyett, the Master and part-owner of the vessel, was freed after redeeming himself by paying a large ransom. The remaining crew of eight men and two boys were put into slavery until a ransom of £250 could be raised.

The captives included the local mariners John Thomas, William Milplie, Thomas Gammydge, Elias Ralph, David Seuey, Isaac Thomas, Peter Rogers, John Braddicke, Thomas Coxe and Elias Ralph the Younger. Most of these Lyme men were married and had young children. At the time, this sum of money was such a huge amount that a letter was drafted in Parliament as a patent to raise this sum from the alms and 'charitable benevolence from all its loving and Christian subjects throughout the counties of Dorset, Devon, Wiltshire, Somerset and Gloucester'.

With the Dissolution of the Monasteries by Henry VIII, and the end to the Catholic faith in England, the death knell was struck for England's involvement in any new voyages of discoveries alongside the Catholic superpowers; and so the English nation would have to go-it-alone. It was during Henry's naval building days that he provided an annual grant of twenty pounds for the maintenance of the Cobb in Lyme. This would later be withdrawn by Bloody Mary because the heretic townsfolk remained predominately Protestant when she was trying to restore the Catholic faith, but she did grant a weekly market day and annual fair; making the locals lucky heretics indeed, when the practice was to be burnt at the stake rather than merely having a grant revoked! Queen Mary was the daughter of Catherine of Aragon, and granddaughter to Ferdinand and Isabella of Spain, thus making her the staunch Catholic that she was. Wealthy merchants who lived in Lyme now maintained the harbour at their own expense, but by the time of Lyme's next charter in the reign of Mary's stepsister Elizabeth, most of them were deceased.

Longshanks had granted the 'Burrough of Lyme Regis' with its first charter, and Queen Elizabeth I granted the first act of Parliament for the upkeep of the Cobb - not just through custom duties from imported goods, but also in the purchase of titles for Lyme's wealthier merchants and landowners, showing again the importance of the Cobb as a port.

This act was drafted on the 13th of March 1585, and had the full title of, 'An Act for the maintenance of the Peere and Cobb of Lyme Regis in the county of Dorsett'. It is also known as '27 Elizabeth I', since it was created in the twenty-seventh year of Her Majesty's reign. This important historical document explains why the Cobb was such an important harbour for shipping, 'for it lieth in the great bay that extendeth from the Isle of Portland...'. This island is now called Portland Bill, because a shingle bank thrown up by a hurricane in 1824 joined it to the mainland, '...to the Haven of Dartmouth' forty three miles in distance, covering the same area as modern day metropolitan London.

In the days of sail, it was dangerous to be caught in the bay during a southwesterly gale, for it easily resulted in shipwreck upon its rocky shoreline. It was therefore imperative to maintain a safe haven for ships. Today, Lyme Bay has over a thousand recorded wrecks, and it is estimated that there are double this figure. What is washed up from all these wrecks places the coastline within the top ten richest places for treasure trove in the British Isles. Even today, the modern motorised tripping boats always head into the wind when taking passengers on a one-hour mackerel fishing trip, because when the engines fail (as they sometimes do), they are then blown back into the safe haven of the Cobb rather than onto the rocky coastline.

Money from the ancient Cobb duties was paid to the Mayor and Burgesses (Freemen) of Lyme on goods that had been imported or exported from the Cobb. But this alone was not enough to maintain the pier, which was described as being constructed from many great oak piles filled in with rocks, but which had now fallen into decay due to worms known as 'Artes', and thus needed rebuilding - not just after each storm but now at each tide. The act goes on to argue that it costs a lot to fetch the rocks, which are over two miles further away than before, and so, like everything else, costs are greater now than in the past. If nothing is done with "Speedy Redress", then the harbour will fall into utter ruin - as it did in the time of Edward III, when it was destroyed along with part of the town in a great gale. Many of the local mariners, who relied upon the Cobb for work, became unemployed as well as homeless.

A piece of ordinance in the form of a cannon was also maintained for the town's defence from the Barbary Corsairs, and this also had costs for its operation and ammunition, so the Cobb would have the same privileges as the Cinque Ports (originally five ports, hence the French 'cinque'), whose councils traditionally maintained defence contingents for the realm of England. A prudent move indeed, as the Spanish Armada's arrival in Lyme Bay was only three years away!

So, starting from the next Feast of Pentecost, the fiftieth day after Easter, the import/export duties would be increased, except for a 'Fardel (Bundle) of Woollen and Linen Clothe', which was decreased from 11d to 3d to safeguard the interests of the burgeoning English wool-weaving industry. Every 'Tunn' of sweet wines, 'Oyles' and 'Sacks' increased from 4d to 8d, and other wines or other 'Grape Ware' would be 6d. The 'Killage for each Ship, Vessel or Cockboate' was increased from 4d to 6d and 'Every Tunn of Merchandize weighed at the Queens beame' was increased from 2d to 4d. Any 'Master of ship, Owner, Factour or Dealer' who refused to pay this amount would have goods impounded until the debt was clear.

Even though it was manuscribed in the much easier Middle English, it still took me over a month to transcribe this document - only to discover a much better transcription left behind by the

Edwardian historian Cyril Wanklyn. Such is life! Anyway, the act gave the Mayor the power to 'appoint two sufficient persons of the town' as officers, to keep an account which 'shall be delivered to the Leete on the Feast of Saint Michael the Archangel', the local court, on September 29th. Merchants from the nearby market towns of Chard and Taunton would then check the accounts on this 'Law Day', and a fine of £40 could be imposed on the officers for any errors. No wonder, then, that the accounts in the ensuing years were so meticulously accurate, as this fine was double the annual cost to maintain the whole harbour. We know today, from the accounts by the 'two sufficient persons' of William Elleson and Robert Barons, that shipping was now steadily increasing at the end of the sixteenth-century.

The famous philosopher Francis Bacon was also the parliamentary representative for Melcombe Regis, near Portland, and he reported that the Lords' List of Acts included two private measures which were not in the Commons Register. One of these was the Cobb Act, then due for renewal. Some members of Parliament objected to the continuation of this act, possibly because the reduced import duty on foreign wool was affecting the local wool industry. The diarist at this point reveals his antiquarian interests, explaining that it was called the 'Cobb' because it was built by an ancestor of Lord Cobham of Colway, the Lord of the Manor, and so it passed through Parliament for another ten years.

Roberts, the Regency historian, speaks of a document in the Tower of London 2 Edward III (1328), which contains the earliest mention of the Cobb, and was of earlier construction than this reign. This fits in well with Henry De Cobham, 1st Baron Cobham of Kent. Records are scant, but it appears that his father was a brother to another Henry De Cobbeham, of Roundall, 'the elder', but this Cobham died long before the harbour in Lyme gained its name. During the reign of Edward I, Henry 'the younger' married Maud, the widow of Matthew de Columbers, and was given the manor of Chesbury in Wiltshire as a dowry. He then became a knight and was sent to keep the islands of 'Gerneseye' and 'Gereseye' as a Justice of the Peace.

He was also appointed custodian of all Templar lands in Surrey and Sussex, since the Knights Templar had come under attack by papal bull for heresy in France, where Jacques de Molay, the last Grand Master of the Order, was burned at the stake. During the reign of Edward II, Henry first became Lord Warden of the Cinque Ports and held the title of Sheriff of Kent.

During Edward III's reign, Henry was ordered to cause sixty oak trees to be felled in the wood of Assheburnham for use in the construction at Peveneseye Castle. Could Henry have also been ordered to do the same for the reconstruction of the storm-damaged harbour in Lyme? One can only guess, but what is certain is that future charters and Cobb acts have always empowered Lyme, just as is the case for the Cinque Ports; and as Lord Warden, Sir Henry would have been responsible for a confederation of ports along the south coast, as a defence during the Hundred Years' War. He died at the grand old age - for the time - of seventy-nine in Hacche, Somerset, now known as Hatch Beauchamp, possibly while on a visit to the family of John Beauchamp, whose daughter was the wife to his son, the second Baron Cobham, an Admiral.

He is buried in the former Beauchamp Chapel, at Stoke-sub-Hamdon, once the chapel of Saint Nicholas, the chantry chapel attached to the castle - a fortified manor house - at Stoke. John Leland visited here in 1540, and described the notable ruins of a great manor place and ancient chapel. He also describes the tombs in the chapel, but the inscriptions were so defaced they could not be read except for that of Matthew de Gourney, and by the time of the visit of Thomas Gerard of Trent in 1633, that had also been defaced. Today this exact same spot is in the garden of the Dairy Cottage of Rookery Farm in Castle Street, near Ham Hill, which is not a million miles from Lyme. On a recent pilgrimage to the burial site of this medieval knight, I noticed the cottage deserted with scaffolding against it for renovation, the garden lawn overgrown and nothing but a rotary washing line marked the spot. I couldn't help but wonder, *How did the Cobb get its name?* -a question historians have been asking for centuries. I'd bet anything this is the most plausible answer.

A young Elizabethan dandy, who also had connections with Lyme, first came to the Queen's attention by tactfully placing his expensive cloak over a muddy puddle, thus preventing good old Bessie from getting her feet soggy. Unlike the present members of the Royal household, they didn't wear wellies in those days. This was a tactful move indeed by the discerning Walter Raleigh, who quickly became a royal favourite and an intimate of the Queen; how intimate he became exactly, when she was twenty years his elder, is still debated by historians today. It is said that once, while he was in the Queen's bedchamber, he caught her notice while she was reading by using his diamond ring to scratch upon a pane of glass the words, 'Fain would I climb, yet I fear to fall.' The Queen noticed this and so completed the verse by scratching beneath with an even larger diamond ring, 'If thy heart fails thee, climb not at all.'

So Raleigh chose to climb, and what great heights he reached as a court favourite, with estates in Ireland, the Governorship of Jersey, and special importing and exporting privileges. His country seat was at nearby Sherborne Castle in Dorset, and he often ventured into Lyme, no doubt to exercise his special importing privileges - notably for French wine.

Of the seven most famous and infamous buccaneers of the Elizabethan age, one was a Yorkshireman, and the remaining six, including Raleigh, were locals from here in the West Country. Each of them earned knighthoods and were known as 'privateers' at the time, as the term 'pirate' had yet to be invented; yet pirates as in the modern sense of the word they were. The young Walter Raleigh had been influenced by his elder half-brother Humphrey Gilbert on the idea of a Protestant English colony in the New World, to compete against the Catholic Spanish, and after a failed voyage to North America, they had both turned to piracy by looting the Spanish on the return trip.

Gilbert was an Oxford graduate who also inspired the Yorkshireman Martin Frobisher, who was himself no scholar, but was renowned for his strength and bravery. He became fascinated by the possibility of the mythical Northwest Passage to Cathay (now China) and the silk and spice trade, via a route that supposedly led around the top end of the North American continent, for which the Cabots had been searching years before. Frobisher later started the Cathay Company and, at just twenty years old, he started his piracy career after being captured and imprisoned by the Portuguese in Guiana, before managing to escape. Another associate of Gilbert's was John Hawkins, the prototype Elizabethan pirate, who also became a slave trader. His son, Richard Hawkins, followed in the family profession, and lived on to be the last of this 'old school' of Elizabethan privateers.

The remaining two were Richard Grenville, immortalised by the poet Tennyson for his last battle, but who was an aggressive young man who once killed someone in a street fight; and the most notorious one of them all, a cousin to Hawkins, Francis Drake. Drake is said to have singed the King of Spain's beard, thrashed the Spanish Armada after a game of bowls, and become the first Englishman to sail around the world, looting Spanish shipping and New World colonies along the way! Whatever our opinion of these seafaring rogues from our own perspective in the political correct society of the twenty-first century, one thing is for certain; they shaped a future between them that would bring the English into the world superpower game, and that created our 'Golden Age of Exploration'. All of them can be associated with the little town of Lyme.

The highest cliff face on the south coast of England is 'Golden Cap', and the view from its summit on a clear day will afford three counties. South across the bay from here was my workplace. The coastline stretches in an arc from Portland Bill in the east to Start Point to the west, with Lyme Regis near the northern cusp of the bay. The beach has intrigued geologists for centuries, due to the shingle shore whose pebbles gradually decrease in size west of Portland, with a size-profile so perfect that fishermen who beached at night could tell their position along the coast just by the size of the stones. This coastline now has World Heritage status, mainly due to fossils from the Jurassic period, which can be found towards the western end of the bay at Charmouth. The Jurassic coast will always have a geologist with his hammer lurking somewhere; at sea, one can always spot them in their brightly coloured hard hats and, if close enough to the shore, from the chipping sound of hammers and the splitting of stone. The best time to look for fossils is after stormy or wet weather, when the Blue Lias clay of the cliff erodes away to reveal them. The open Atlantic lies towards the southwest, so one would expect longshore drift to run from west to east along the beach, and therefore the graduation in stone size should be in the opposite direction; this is what so intrigues geologists.

Local boatmen will have their own opinion about this. Most evenings throughout the summer season, I would take anglers out on a three-hour twilight fishing trip, and anchoring on the intended fishing hotspot is not always that easy. To do so, you have to take into account the combined wind and tide directions, so that you can drop your anchor from the bow without getting the rope tangled. A little experience of wrapping the anchor rope around the rudder a few times during a windless, becalmed sea will soon make you realise that an incoming tide runs from the southeast in a northwesterly direction, which accounts for the grading of the pebbles on Chesil Beach. Why this tidal flow is in the opposite direction is most likely due to fluid dynamics, and the pooling of water from that of the deeper English Channel further offshore in the relative shallow bay. An incoming tide up the Channel meets the outgoing tide down the channel just off Portland Bill - known locally as 'The Portland Race' - and the direction of the grading of the pebbles is down to Lyme Bay's distorted tidal curve.

One particular evening, while on such a fishing trip, I anchored the *Herbert Paul* just west of the majestic Golden Cap. According to the log, it was 18:30 GMT on Saturday June 3rd 1989, and us grockles couldn't even catch a cold, let alone a fish. A gentle breeze started to blow - 'the Charmouth Funnel'- and in the anticipated eagerness and silence while waiting for that first catch, all you could hear was the creaking of the wooden floorboards. As the boat started to swing on its anchor rope, you could then hear the rudder gently squeaking on its pintail. *Uh oh*, I thought, *That's not a good sign*. Then it started.

"Huuuugh Weee!"

One, I thought, as a glassy-eyed passenger stared at his vomit now trailing alongside the boat, and then again,"Huuuugh Weee!"

Carrots! But I haven't eaten carrots for ages! Then someone else started.

"Huuuugh Weee!"

Two, I thought, at which point the second green faced passenger commented,"Oh God! What I would give to be back commuting on the Northern line right now!"

Londoners!, I thought, *Don't ya just love 'em?* I don't think any of them had ever seen the sea before, let alone gone out on a boat. In situations like this, one tries to liven things up. A large jellyfish floated by, so I scooped it up with a net and flopped it on the deck. I did this not only to get it away from the trail of vomit, but also to show the passengers that we had finally caught something.

"The locals call this a Dustbin Jellyfish because they grow to the size of a dustbin but its proper name is..."

"Huuuugh Weee!"

Three.

"...Rhizastoma Octopus and unlike the Portuguese Man-O-War this is a real jellyfish." I lifted up one of its tentacles with the net handle. "See, it has eight tentacles just like an octopus."

"Huuuugh Weee!"

Four, then two more in unison,

"Huuuugh Weee!"

"Raaalf," followed by spluttered coughing.

That's six - half my Cockney crew seasick, and not a fish in sight - better do something quick or I will never get repeat custom from this lot!, I thought and continued, "Does anyone know the plural of Octopus?"

"Is it Octopi?" asked a non-seasicker.

"No."

"How about Octopussy... Huuuugh Weee!"

"No... Give up? Well its Octop..."

"Look at all the fish he's catching! Why don't we go over there?" exclaimed the first seasicker, pointing like the fisherman in the *The Boyhood of Raleigh*.

Further inshore, Pinhay Pete was aboard his boat with a farmer friend hauling in a surface net, teeming with sea bass. Pete and his friend only did this as a hobby, yet they were hauling in one of the biggest catches I've ever seen. Mr F had been the one who gave him his nickname, because his real name was Pete and he lived over near Pinhay Bay.

"Reel in, we are moving," I shouted, started the engine and hauled in the anchor. We motored over closer as they continued to haul in the catch. I anchored up again and waved across to them. They waved back and continued hauling in, as if it were the most natural thing in the world that sea bass were so plentiful.

How on Earth does he do it? I thought. The anchor lodged into a rock ledge and the boat swung around, so we started fishing again. At this point, the heavens opened up and it poured with rain - and it's an open boat.

At exactly 21:00 GMT, the *Herbert Paul* chugged back into the Cobb with a full complement of twelve seasick landlubbers and a giant jellyfish as the only catch of the evening. The shivering, wet passengers dragged themselves onto the quay and slouched off around the High Wall, never to be seen again.

The following morning, while strolling to work, I passed the local butchers and noticed un-skinned rabbits hung up in the window. A mischievous idea occurred to me, so I purchased one. Now, old sea lore in the West Country can be very superstitious and held as truth by some, especially the old school of fisherman and boatmen. For example, at Beer, the fishermen will not put to sea if anyone mentions the colour green, for fear of never returning to the green land. Where this superstition came from is anyone's guess, but Lyme does have its own - namely that it is unlucky to mention the word 'rabbit' at sea! At Portland Quarry, it was unlucky to mention this 'bunny' word for fear of seeing a rabbit bolting from its warren, which indicated an imminent avalanche was about to take place, and it has been conjectured that this tradition may have been imported into the Cobb.

Pinhay and his friend not only set nets but lobster pots as well, and after briefing my younger brother Darren and good friend Nick Gear, the three of us sailed off along the coast early that evening towards one of his pots, dead rabbit in hand. The *Herbert Paul* cut in close to Pinhay Bay and we hauled up one of his pots and I stuffed the dead rabbit inside. As I knocked the engine astern it cut, and in the eerie silence, the rabbit's head bobbed up out of the water with wet floppy ears, the black eyes staring up at us. The three of us looked at each other in horror before I leaned over, grabbed the rabbit, and fixed it permanently back in the pot. After that little scare, we chuckled all the way back to the harbour and then went for a beer in my local, the Royal Standard, to wait to see what would happen next.

Later that evening, as regular as clockwork, in strolled Pete with his farmer friend.

"Evening Pete," I said cheerfully, as they bought a beer and walked over towards our table.

"Any good tonight?" asked Nick, hiding a grin as he sipped his beer.

They sat down next to us with faces as pale as ghosts. Pete then craned his neck over towards me, nervously looked around in case anyone was listening and whispered into my ear, "Someone has put the fisherman's death wish on us!"

"Oh really? Whatever makes you think that?"

"Well, you know the animal that you never mention at sea…?"

"What, the albatross?" I interrupted, then quickly took a sip, almost choking on my pint.

"No, not that one!" replied Pete, then the farmer put up two fingers and wiggled them.

"That one." This time I almost choked, but spluttered out the beer and kept up the serious pretence.

"Oh, that one… Well, what about it?"

"Well, someone put one inside one of our pots!"

"You can't be serious, Pete? Who would do a thing like that?"

He shrugged nervously.

"You do shoot your pots in very close; maybe it fell off the cliffs and just got washed in?"

"Well, I thought of that, but then I realised it had been tied in by its ears!"

I never saw Pete at sea again. Being the rural type that he is, I understand he took up beekeeping as a new hobby instead - such a waste for the best fisherman that ever set out from the Cobb.

As a royal favourite, Raleigh used his new-found wealth wisely and received a patent from the Queen to establish an English colony in North America that read:'An Act for the confirmation of the Queen's Majesty's letters patent granted to Walter Raleigh, Esquire, touching the discovery and inhabiting of certain foreign lands and countries.' Raleigh had discovered a land that the natives called 'Wyngandacoia', which he later changed to 'Virginia' in honour of the Virgin Queen. The act further enacted that 'he, his heirs and assigns, may have, hold, and enjoy the said lands forever, according to the full tenor of the said letters patent.' The bill had its first reading in the House of Lords at about the same time that Lyme received its first Cobb Act. One wonders whether it was also Raleigh's intention to use such ports as these in the West Country as springboards to establish English colonies in the New World. This letter patent would remain binding and in legal force for all Virginian colonists until the American year of Independence!

The Queen was not keen on the idea of her new court favourite being away from her too long on any of these dangerous excursions to the New World, and so banned him from going on any further voyages himself. Which is just as well, since his half-brother, Gilbert, tragically went down with his ship on the return voyage only the previous year, while sitting at the helm and reading a book in rough seas off the coast of Canada - remaining the Oxford educated intellect to the very end.

Inspired by Gilbert, as were so many others, the first Virginia voyage Raleigh financed with his new patent from the Queen departed from the West Country in two barks captained by Philip Amadas and Arthur Barlow in 1584. Their mission was to explore the eastern coast of North America and find a suitable location for the first colony. A meeting with the friendly Native American Croatan of the Carolina Algonquians saw the recommendation of Roanoke Island off the coast of present-day North Carolina. Raleigh decided this was to be the spot for his colony and again he wanted to go but the Queen intervened and Sir Richard Grenville led the next expedition in his place.

The following year, a colony of a hundred men, many of them veteran soldiers who had fought to establish English rule in Ireland, was established on Roanoke Island. It was left under the management of Ralph Lane, from Lympstone in Devon and whose mother, Maud, was a cousin of Catherine Parr, the last queen consort to Henry VIII. Lane became an equerry under the Queen, carrying out duties as an officer of the royal household, which included law enforcement and customs duties. The voyage on board the vessel *Tiger*, which had brought them there proved difficult, as Lane found himself at odds with the aggressive leadership of Grenville, who had transported and landed them, then returned to England for supplies.

The colonists were not prepared for such a venture, and not experienced enough for the colonisation of a vast wilderness, which was already occupied by the indigenous Native American Indians. Known as 'planters' at the time, they did very little planting, but instead relied heavily upon the Indians to provide them with food. It was not long before they started to upset the natives through the use of such tactics as kidnapping and holding them hostage in exchange for information. This may have worked during the suppression necessary to establish English rule in Ireland, but was not so successful here in the New World.

Lane led an expedition to explore the Roanoke River and the possibility of finding a Fountain of Youth. Well, why not? Ponce De Leon had long ago discovered one in Florida, so why not have one here in Virginia? At about this time, the natives in the village of Aquascogoc were blamed for stealing a silver cup, and relations with a neighbouring tribe had degraded to such a degree that the Englishmen attacked them and killed the tribal chief Wingina. To make matters worse, Grenville's return was delayed, and the colonists became desperate for supplies.

Fortunately, after destroying the Spanish colony of Saint Augustine in Florida, and the possible poisoning of its Fountain of Youth - which could explain why it never worked when I visited - Francis Drake put in at Roanoke to find out how the new colony was surviving. As things could not have been worse, the entire colony returned with him to England, leaving behind just fifteen of his own men. The relief fleet arrived shortly after the departure of Drake's fleet with the colonists. Finding the colony abandoned, Grenville also decided to return to England, making the establishment of the first English colony in the New World a complete failure. Lane would participate in several more expeditions to Virginia, until he was appointed muster-master general of Ireland, where he suffered severe wounds in an Irish uprising against the crown, from which he never recovered.

Another group of colonists, led by John White, who had been on previous expeditions to Roanoke, was sent by Raleigh. This time, the plan was for a more permanent colony, as both men and women were sent and White's daughter would deliver the first English child born in the Americas - Virginia Dare, who increased the population to one hundred and sixteen. The new colonists were to pick up Drake's men left behind at Roanoke, and then settle farther north in the Chesapeake

Bay area; however, no trace of the fifteen were found, other than the bones of a single man. White reestablished relations with the Croatans on present-day Hatteras Island, who told him that the men had been attacked, and that nine survivors had sailed north along the coast.

When White tried to contact the other tribes that Ralph Lane had attacked, they refused to meet with the new colonists. George Howe was killed by the natives while searching for crabs alone in Albemarle Sound and, fearing for their lives, the colonists convinced White to return to England to explain the colony's situation and get more help.

After leaving behind most of the colonists, including his granddaughter, White returned to England and barely survived the stormy crossing, before arriving to discover that England was about to go to war with the Spanish. It would take a further two years before a resupply attempt could be made for the colonists, as all seaworthy vessels had been requisitioned for the defence of the realm.

White eventually gained passage on a privateering expedition that agreed to stop off at Roanoke on the way back from the Caribbean. He landed on the same day as his granddaughter's third birthday, but found the settlement deserted. He organised a search party, but the men with him could find no trace of the colonists. About a hundred men, women, and children had simply disappeared, leaving behind no sign of a struggle or a battle. The only clues as to what may have happened were the word 'Croatoan' carved into a post of the fort and 'Cro' carved into a nearby tree. Two buried skeletons were found, and all the houses and fortifications had been dismantled. White wondered whether the colonists moved to Croatoan Island, but he was unable to conduct another search as a massive storm was brewing, and his men were afraid to stay any longer. The next day, White stood on the deck of the ship and watched, helplessly, as he left Roanoke Island for the last time.

Even to this day, nothing is known of this 'Lost Colony' - it is all still a mystery. Had they been killed or dispersed and absorbed by either the local Croatan or Hatteras Indians, or even the Algonquian people? No one knows. Maybe, someday in the future, DNA analysis of Native American descendants may help to resolve this puzzle.

At the beginning of May, a thick bank of fog rolled into the bay. These 'May Mists' are not unusual for the time of year, which is also the time when the sea temperature reaches a critical threshold, and plankton sea life starts to bloom at an exponential rate. This is known as 'May-Water', and is not a good time for anglers, since fish have gorged themselves and are not tempted by bait. During such a fishing trip, as the thick fog rolled in, I warned some tourists on a self-drive to return to harbour whilst they could still see it.

The following day, the mist had lifted and this was the start of a brilliant heatwave that granted uninterrupted good weather until the beginning of August. This was to be a ninety seven-day continuous summer and I lost a bet with Nick by just three days that I could have a record one hundred uninterrupted sunny, calm days at sea! The high summer of '89 was to become the hottest since records began; it even beat that of the legendary '76, which had been the driest sixteen month period on record. This summer's heatwave would not be broken again until the high of '95, which has subsequently become the warmest and driest two-month period on record in Lyme Bay. In those interim years, I worked the summers on the boats in Lyme and travelled abroad to even hotter climes during the miserable British winters, mainly to the Deep South of the USA.

During my time in Lyme, my local had been the Royal Standard, whose premises have a history as long as that of the United States. The beer garden runs out onto a sand bar formed by the restriction of longshore drift by the rows of giant boulders propped up against the Cobb. Again, I wondered at the reason for having them, since without them, the pub would stand on the edge of the harbour's inner wall, making it possible to moor up beside the pub at the end of each day. It did in the past, and if you look carefully to the rear of the kiosks, including my parents' burger bar, you can still see the old mooring rings where coal colliers once tied up to exchange their cargo for cement extracted from the surrounding cliffs at the cement factory, where the present day Boat Building Academy now stands.

The roof support of the pub is an old ship's main mast, and if one stands by the fireplace you can still see where the sheaves have been cut to tie sheets to its base. This is the oldest part of the building, and one can only wonder what particular ship was used for its construction. An American Second World War veteran, who had returned to visit the place where he had been billeted, told me that back then this small area was the only part of the pub with spittoons on a sawdust covered floor. Old fishermen have spoken of a broth continuously heated over a coal-fired stove by the landlady, and replenished with any available ingredients as it ran low. Before researching for this book, this is all the history I ever knew about the Cobb and the buildings that stood on it.

My typical day as a boatman started when the tide permitted me to paddle my dinghy across the silted up harbour from the out-haul to the *Herbert Paul*. Switch on the battery, start the engine, pump the bilges and tighten the stern tube greaser before pulling her clear of the moorings and knocking her into gear, chugging over to Victoria pier for my first one-hour trip of the day. Throughout the day, I would negotiate all states of the tide at the Cobb, as previously booked passengers came out on either mackerel fishing or sightseeing trips. My last one-hour trip would be followed by the three-hour twilight fishing trip on busy summer days, and it wasn't unusual for me to end it here in my local.

Those hot summers marched on, and my appearance changed to that of an old weather-beaten seadog, as my arms and face bronzed, my hair bleached blond, while the rest of my body remained Lily-white, since I covered it for protection from skin cancer. At this time, boatmen at the Cobb all wore symbolic blue fisherman's smocks, similar in appearance to an artist's smock, which not only made you look the part of a rustic weather-beaten sea salt, but had its practical purposes as a windproof and protection from the sun.

One particular night after work, seated by the fireplace of my local beneath that old ship mast, I sat drinking with Nick and John, a friend we had not seen for a while. He had recently purchased a beautiful twenty-four foot wooden yacht in London, and had sailed her down the Thames and along the south coast to Lyme. That night, the three of us discussed the possibility of sailing across to France, and as the evening rolled on with the rounds of beers we consumed, so the plan took shape. Except for John's recent trip coasting the English Channel, none of us had ever done anything like this before.

The following morning, with all three of us aboard John's yacht, we set sail off across the bay in a southeasterly direction. We passed the inshore fishing grounds known as the Tenants, six miles offshore. This was the furthest I had been. John studied the chart with meticulous precision.

"The chart is wrong!" John appeared to ignore my comment as he took a bearing.

"The bay has a distorted tidal curve."

He held the compass up and took another bearing of some land feature, then replied,"Well, the chart's accurate enough to get us here."

"He's right you know; just keep away from the shambles", interjected Nick.

We passed the southern tip of Portland Bill, where the incoming tide up the Channel meets the outgoing tide as it still runs out. Through binoculars, we watched the rapids in the distance, which made the sea appear as if it were boiling.

The tide can run anything up to a speed of four knots in the opposite direction to the Admiralty Charts, so a distance-run fix cannot be determined because your true speed is unknown. John used landmarks to fix our position, which worked perfectly well until the land dropped out of view and then night fell. At this point, we had determined our magnetic bearing to Cherbourg and steered by the compass. As we crossed the shipping lane south of the bay, we decided to work shifts at the helm, two on and one off every four hours. John took to his bunk on the first watch, leaving Nick and I at the helm.

As the stars appeared in the night sky, I started to tell Nick all about them. He remained very quiet as I spoke; at the time, one could only assume that he found the subject interesting. When a thick blanket of fog rolled in he let out a sigh of relief.

"Oh, thank God for that!"

"What do you mean?"

"At least the cloud cover will stop you going on about those bloody stars!"

"But don't you see? It's easy to steer by the stars when you know where to look."

"Well, what's the point if you have a compass?"

Good point, indeed. Why have a starlit and infinite universe with all its wonders, if the little boat we are in has a compass?

In the darkness, the visibility dropped to almost zero. We sailed on in complete silence for about an hour then…

"Did you see that?"

"See what?"

"There's it again… A light!"

I squinted but couldn't see anything in the darkness.

"Where?"

Nick pointed in the darkness to a spot that seemed as dark as anywhere else.

"Quick! Get John."

I called below, and within a few seconds I could make out the silhouette of our Captain poke his head out of the hatchway, rubbing his eyes. Still half asleep, he asked the same question and Nick pointed again.

"Can't see anything… What colour is the light?"

"Red," replied Nick, as I'm still squinting in the darkness at what seems nothing.

"Red… Uh… Okay, over on the helm and turn to port," ordered John.

I could now just make out a red pinpoint of light… then suddenly realised the mistake.

"Starboard!" I exclaimed. "Bloody starboard! Turn to starboard!"

"He's right," replied John. "Hard to starboard."

Nick rolled his eyes and pulled the tiller back over onto the opposite tack, and out of the darkness appeared the bridge of a cargo ship!

"Bloody hell! Quick, everyone clip on your harness," ordered our now wide-awake and alert Captain.

The little yacht veered away from the rapidly moving steel wall of the hull, over a giant wave and then bobbed like a cork over the stern wake.

"Phew… That was close!" exclaimed John, as our bow dipped into the sea, spray threw up into the air and water ran along the deck.

"Close!? It's a wonder we never scratched the paintwork!"

If it had not been for the quick change of decision and the swiftness of the helm, then none of us would be alive today to tell the tale. Years later, the three of us can joke about this event and our naivety, but at the time, it was a hard lesson we had learned and a mistake that none of us would ever repeat again.

The following morning, after crossing the Hurd Deeps, we arrived inside the safe confines of the giant, Napoleonic walls of Cherbourg harbour - a sharp contrast to the much smaller Cobb we had left just twenty-four hours previously. We passed a ferry full of screaming British school kids on their return home. Union Jack flags fluttered in the breeze as they waved and cheered at us as we passed. As translator, it was my duty to arrange a mooring berth but... I'd forgotten my French! John took the radio microphone out of my hand and asked for a mooring in perfect English, and we got a reply back in equally good English from the French authorities. We later found ourselves in probably the only English pub in Cherbourg with English girls, and the following morning, we filled the hull up with cheap booze and cigarettes from a very English-looking supermarket. Funny that we can now claim to have sailed all the way to France and back, but never actually saw France! Except, of course, for those giant harbour walls, which ironically had been designed to keep us British out!

At dusk, on our return voyage home, Nick and I took our turn at the helm as John took to his berth, before Nick moaned, "I'm not doing the same watch with Glen if he is going to go on about those bloody stars again!"

John immediately turned around and came back up out of the cockpit; as Captain, it was now his duty to resolve his first potential mutiny.

"Okay... Right, you're to remain at the tiller and Glen, you're to keep watch and check the compass bearing... And no lecturing about the stars."

In the gloomy silence, we sailed across the Channel and on into the night. Nothing was said between us for ages until I stated an obvious observation.

"The Moon's setting."

"Yes, I know."

"I didn't say anything about stars."

"Yes, I know. "He was now annoyed… and the moon did set… and in the light, pollution-free environment, the stars burst out in true splendour with a spectacular backdrop view of the Milky Way.

We both just looked up in awe and Nick just couldn't help himself, "My God, look at all those stars!"

"Yes, I know," was my only response.

By dawn, we slipped back into Lyme Bay to an equally spectacular sunrise over Golden Cap, which turned the sea into the colour of molten copper. This had been my first real sailing trip, and although in years to come the boats would get bigger and the trips further away from home, that first trip would always be… Well, certainly the most interesting!

Tension between the Catholic Spanish and the Protestant English had risen to a new height. Even though the English had yet to establish a permanent colony in the New World, they had become a thorn in the side of the Spanish, with English pirates looting the treasure ships returning to Spain with rich cargo, which itself had been looted from the New World. King Philip II of Spain was compelled to send his army, the most powerful in Europe, across the Channel for an invasion of England. This army had almost crushed the Dutch resistance in the northern provinces of the Spanish-controlled Netherlands, under the formidable command of the Duke of Palma. The plan was to launch an Armada under the command of the equally formidable Medina Sidonia, to transport this army across the Channel to England - not so much to conquer, but to restore the Catholic faith and church property, stolen years before by Henry VIII. Philip had the full consent from the Pope for this invasion.

The Armada set sail from Lisbon with one hundred and sixty ships and about nineteen thousand men, and reached Plymouth on the English South coast in adverse summer sea conditions. As legend has it, this is where the first engagement between the English and Spanish took place, after Drake had finished his game of bowls. In reality, it was very different as the Armada reached Plymouth Sound during the Spring Tides; the lowest low tide was at around midday and the highest high tide about six hours later. At low water, it was impossible for the Spanish to enter Plymouth Hove, although Sidonia had called a Council of War to discuss the option of entering on a making tide and attacking the English fleet still aground on their moorings. He decided against this, as he was under strict instruction from the Spanish King to continue on to his rendezvous point with Palma somewhere on the Flanders coast.

English intelligence had been expecting the Armada for some time, but they were not sure if it was to be an attack on themselves or the Dutch. A freebooter quickly informed Plymouth after he had first spotted the Armada off the Isles of Scilly, and news travelled fast of the impending invasion, as prearranged beacons along the South coast all the way to London were set alight. Sidonia had no way of contacting Palma, and if there had been a pre-arranged rendezvous point, his long voyage to England would have far exceeded any time window of opportunity to transport Palma's army from Flanders to England for the invasion. Dutch ships guarded the Flanders coast, so a rendezvous point could not be held open indefinitely.

This was the biggest mistake of the Spanish, for if they had managed this feat on time, then England would not only have been confronted with the largest fleet of all time, but the largest army in Europe, with battle-hardened Spanish soldiers to contend with for the land-based invasion.

At dusk, the incoming tide floated the English fleet at Plymouth long after Drake's alleged game of bowls, and fifty-five ships under the command of Admiral Lord Howard of Effingham raced out of the Hoe and into the Sound in hot pursuit of the Armada, east into Oceanus Britannicus - now the English Channel. Outnumbered and outmanned by the larger Spanish fleet, this was known as the Western Fleet. Another fleet awaited the Spanish at Tilbury Docks, where Queen Elizabeth, seated on a white horse, would soon be rallying the remainder of her captains and crew together for probably her most famous speech.

"My loving people, we have been persuaded by some that are careful of our safety, to take heed how we commit ourselves to armed multitudes for fear of treachery. Let tyrants fear. I have always so behaved myself that, under God, I have placed my chief strength and safeguard in the loyal hearts and goodwill of my subjects. And therefore I am come amongst you all, as you see at this time, not for my recreation and disport, but being resolved, in the midst and heat of the battle, to live or die amongst you all; to lay down for my God, and for my kingdom, and for my people, my honour and my blood even in the dust. I know I have the body of a week and feeble woman, but I have the heart and stomach of a king, and a king of England too. And think foul scorn that Palma or Spain, or any Prince of Europe, should dare to invade the borders of my realm!"

Powerful words indeed, and in the true style of England's Warrior Queen.

The Western Fleet was comprised of both naval and armed merchant ships. The English ships were much smaller than the Spanish, and therefore much lighter and swifter. As one crewmember noted on the approach, the Spanish galleons were "of a large bigness…and so high they resembled huge castles."

The two fleets had designed ships for very different methods of battle. The Spanish had aimed for grappling and boarding the enemy at close range and overpowering with greater numbers of men, while the English used their dexterity to keep their distance through the use of cannons with greater ranged artillery capabilities. Only three of the English fleet were as large the Spanish ships -*Elizabeth Jonas*, the *Bear* and *The Triumph*, the last of which, captained by Sir Martin Frobisher, was of over a thousand tonnes, making it in fact the largest ship of both fleets, The Admiral was in the *Ark Royal*, of eight hundred tonnes, thirty-two guns and about four hundred men, Sir Francis Drake was appointed Vice-Admiral in the *Revenge,* and Sir John Hawkins was Rear-Admiral in the *Victory*; his son was Captain of the *Swallow*.

The Admiral selected Drake to lead the fleet in his much lighter and faster ship, and further seawards was the *Margaret and John*, sailed by a privateer; at a quarter of the weight of the Ark Royal, it was the fastest ship in the fleet. This ship sped on ahead of the Western fleet, and was the first to encounter the Armada. It was now getting dark as the Spanish manoeuvred into a defensive crescent shape that curved back towards the west. This they did in squalid westerly seas, and the first casualties of war were self-inflicted, as Pedro de Valdes' ship *Nuestra Senora del Rosario* collided with another Andalusian ship and lost her bowsprit. A terrific gunpowder explosion resulted aboard the *San Salvador,* as the collision set the poop ablaze and disintegrated two decks of the stern castle. Both ships were then towed by supply ships, but the cable to the Rosario snapped and Medina Sidonia was advised to quickly proceed with the Armada. As it was getting dark, he reluctantly decided to abandon the *Rosario* - his second mistake. The swift *Margaret and John* soon caught up with the abandoned *Rosario* somewhere off Stert (Start) Point at the western extremity of Lyme Bay, and this is where the fighting began.

In the vanguard of the English fleet, the privateer came across the damaged *Rosario* with a galleass and a pinnace alongside. They immediately fled, leaving the *Rosario* to her fate. The *Margaret and John* set off a volley of musketry at what appeared to be a deserted ship, and was immediately answered with a broadside from several large guns. The privateer returned the broadside, then quickly moved to a safer distance. Howard heard the cannonade; it was about midnight and he sent a pinnace alongside the *Margaret and John,* with the instruction that the English fleet was to remain together and the *Rosario* was to be ignored. Howard was now concerned that the Armada was closing in on Torbay. The English continued on into Lyme Bay, with Howard closely following the stern lantern of Drakes *Revenge*. In the early hours of Monday morning, Howard lost sight of the stern light – the first mistake of the English that nearly had disastrous consequences - but he then noticed it further up along the coast, so ordered more sail to be put out to catch her up.

In the early daylight hours, Howard realised to his horror that the light he had been following was not from Drake; in fact, it wasn't that of any English ship, but rather that of the Spanish flagship. He had the *Bear* and *Mary Rose* with him, and they were well inside the horns of the defensive crescent of the one hundred and thirty war ships of the Armada! To make matters worse, as dawn approached from behind the distant Golden Cap, the squalid westerly changed into an easterly – the wind following the sun, as it invariably does in the bay. Not only was Howard in a very tricky position, but the Spanish had now gained the weather gauge. Howard quickly ordered the three ships about and, before he had noticed, Sidonia had not only lost the opportunity of dispatching three English ships, but the admiral of the fleet as well.

What the bloody hell had happened to Drake? When Howard returned to the English fleet, Drake reported that he had seen shadows of ships, which he assumed were the Armada doubling back to the west; he extinguished his stern lantern so as not to mislead the fleet as he turned around to challenge them. It turned out that these ships were innocent German merchant ships, although no one else in the fleet had seen them. At this point, Drake just happened upon the damaged *Rosario*, captured it, and ordered the *Roebuck* to transport his new prize into Torbay after taking Don Pedro de Veldes as prisoner and handing him over to Howard. How Drake managed to get away with this is still a mystery; he had purposely not kept to his station on the *Revenge*, but instead had looted the spoils of war and placed the flagship and commander of the whole English fleet at risk. Not only did the Spanish lose a forty-six gunner, but fifty five thousand gold ducats were found in the Captain's cabin as well – a lucky prize indeed for the pirate Drake!

The Armada entered a becalmed Lyme Bay, the wind having now completely dropped away. Around noon, the Spanish had yet another casualty, as the damaged *San Salvador* started to take in water. Her pumps were unable to cope with the rapidly flooding bilges and she started sinking. The crew were rescued and dispersed amongst the other ships. When the English arrived, the *San Salvador* had been abandoned. Howard inspected her and found that shot and powder had been left aboard, stowed away in the forehold. Captain Fleming managed to secure a line from his pinnace and tow her into Weymouth harbour. Meanwhile, further east in the bay, the Spanish had rearranged the defensive crescent shape of the Armada into two columns, with the larger, more powerful fighting ships in the stern column in defence against the approaching English, and the remainder in the van.

The following morning was a Tuesday, and a fresh breeze came up from the east, again in the dawn light. Howard observed the Spanish tacking on a northeasterly route towards the land. From ashore, especially from somewhere like Lyme, it must have caused quite a stir in the town to see these "very stately built ships" resembling "huge castles" bearing down upon the Cobb. Any local mariner would have realised that the tide was currently slack (high) early that morning, and if a landing was to be achieved it would be immediate, or else later that very evening. The town would, no doubt, have panicked while assembling some makeshift defence, transporting shot and powder around the Cobb for its single piece of ordinance. However, Sidonia had other plans, and it must have been quite a relief for the townsfolk when he ordered a new course and the Armada suddenly turned on a new tack to the southeast towards the Isle of Portland, and away from Lyme.

Lyme did have a contingency plan, should the Spanish have chosen to land sixty foot of soldiers. One can only wonder what they could have achieved against such a vast army. Lyme also contributed three ships to the English fleet, six times less than London, indicating the Cobb's relative size and importance at this time. These ships were the *Jacob*, of ninety tons and forty men; the smaller *Thomas Bonaventure*, of sixty tons and thirty men; and another *Revenge* (not Drake's ship), also of sixty tons and thirty men. This last little ship would later engage the Spanish in what most maritime history scholars today believe to be the most famous and spectacular sea battle of all time!

The English fleet were further out to sea, but Howard could easily see the Armada as they came abeam of Portland. He worried about Weymouth, just as he had about Torbay the day before. The Spanish were too far inshore to be outflanked by the English, and Howard knew he would be unable to weather the Isle of Portland before them. When Sidonia noticed the English fleet, he led the galleons of the vanguard to intercept for an attack. Howard ordered the fleet to come about on the opposite reach to the south-southwest, and it must have been an awesome sight to behold as the two columns closed in upon each other.

The English fleet of fifty five ships, fluttering the red and white of the George Cross, met the larger Spanish ships, of over twice the number, flying red pennants with a yellow cross, and the flags of the medieval kingdoms of Aragon, Castile, Leon and Navarra high from the masts of these floating castles. Even today, the accounts from both the English and Spanish of this engagement make for interesting reading.

First the two columns approached each other to within culverin range, of musket shot and of half-musket shot. It then became clear that the English, even on this new tack, would be cut off and both sides erupted into cannonades of flame and smoke. The smoke was so thick and the noise so terrific that it could be seen and heard right across the bay - the older and more experienced sea salts had never seen anything like it before. Neither side underestimated the other, as Sedonia later wrote of the English ships: "Being very nimble and of such good steerage, they did with them whatever they desired". Howard would later recall the morning of the first day of battle and how "we durst not adventure to put amongst them, there fleet being so strong."

Both he and Sidonia were in the thick of the fighting and, as the tide turned and started flooding (rising), so followed the wind, as it sometimes does here, and the whole battle drifted north-west back into Lyme Bay. There followed a curious battle with heavy exchanges of fire, but which neither side seem to be winning, as the Spanish were unable to approach and board the swifter English ships, whilst the English fleet were starting to run low on ammunition. Later records of the battle state that it was "confusion enough", while an English master gunner recalls, "What can be said but our sins was the cause that so much powder and shot spent, and so long time in fight, and in comparison thereof so little harm."

If it all seemed confusing enough then, imagine how confusing it was to retrace the events of this 'Battle of Lyme Bay' over four centuries later!

So the wind and tide held from the southeast as another, smaller, battle was raging, with Martin Frobisher at anchor under the lee of Portland. *Triumph* and five London merchantmen were in the heat of battle with four galleasses. The galleasses had both oar and sail power and so did not have to rely so much on the wind as did their counterparts. One questions why Frobisher had chosen to anchor here. Had he been unable to weather Portland and so anchored to wait for the battle to blow back towards him (as it did), or was it because he had a more cunning plan? Just to the east of the southern tip of Portland is a long shallow bank of sand and broken shell known as 'The Shambles', and the tidal race there sets towards it. To reach and do battle with *Triumph*, using the shortest route, one would have to cross this tidal race at a speed of about four knots. To give this death trap a wide berth, a sailing ship would have to lose the weather gauge and negotiate the tidal currents. Either way, Frobisher was in a very good position and he was a brilliant seafarer, so it is unlikely that he didn't know about this local piece of knowledge.

Frobisher was a pirate in the true sense of the word, and had already made three voyages to the North American continent, looking for the fabled Northwest Passage. He returned with what he thought was gold-bearing ore. This turned out to be mistaken, as was the location of the Northwest Passage, but the Queen named the new lands that he found 'Meta Incognita', and the bay he thought was the passage is still known today as Frobisher Bay. Although he never found any gold while searching for the Northwest Passage, Frobisher did find a most valuable treasure. Washed up on the icy shores of northern Canada, he found a white spiral horn sticking up out of the beach which "caught the sun's rays like spun glass". To Frobisher and the rest of Elizabethan society this could only be one thing; the horn of a unicorn. Upon his return, it was presented to Queen Elizabeth. To this day it is known as the Horn of Windsor and is still part of the Crown Jewels. Some stuffy old academics today claim that it is a narwhal's horn, but don't listen to them; I mean, how absurd is that!? Even in those times, royal goblets were lined with such stuff, in the belief that when a unicorn horn came into contact with poison, it would cause the drink to froth - a useful aid for the Queen to have at mealtimes after all the enemies she had acquired from her dispute with Spain, and by placing Mary Queen of Scots under house arrest.

The Spanish soon gave up the fight at this point and continued east along the coast. This was a relief for the English, who had now run out of ammunition and returned to port at Weymouth for more. A few days later, both the Western and Eastern fleets joined up and engaged the Armada at Gravelines, where the main battle took place. The tough Yorkshireman Frobisher was later knighted for his role in the battle by helping to disperse the Armada using fire ships. After the battle, he accused Drake of being a traitor and coward for turning to piracy during the chase... Fresh, for someone who had started such a career so young.

In all, the combined English fleet had over two hundred ships and an unknown number of Dutch ships joined the Protestant cause. Outnumbered, with fewer men, less ammunition, and the weather against them, the Armada battled its way around the British Isles, which lead to nothing short of disaster for the Spanish. Shipwreck followed shipwreck along the west coast of Ireland and by the time Sidonia limped back into Spain on the 23rd of September of 1588, no less than twenty thousand of his crew had been killed and the grand, invincible Armada had been reduced in size by two thirds! King Philip was furious with the Duke, stating, "I sent you out to fight men, not God's wind and waves".

The outcome for the English was one of the most decisive victories in naval history. In Spain, Sidonia surprisingly kept his position, and a newer and more powerful Navy would be built up that would never again suffer such defeat. Sidonia later on lost another squadron to the Dutch off Gibraltar, and it is said his folly made the Duke a satirical target by Miguel Cervantes of Don Quixote fame. This is probably unfair, as Medina Sidonia never once believed it was possible to beat the English in home waters and was against the idea of the invasion from the outset. He was chosen to lead the Armada by King Philip not because of his sea battle experience, but because he was completely loyal to the King and would have followed his instruction to the letter even to the death, unlike other, more experienced, officers.

What became of that little pinnace of Lyme? Three years later, *Revenge* became involved in the most famous sea battle in English maritime history, in which the impossibly arrogant Grenville (with just this one ship), fought single handed an armada of (get this!) fifty-three Spanish ships, in a frenzied twelve-hour sea battle while on a piracy excursion in the waters of Flores in the Azores. This bravery and arrogance beggars belief, and the news of the death of Grenville and the last stand of *Revenge* was later returned to England by way of another Lyme ship, passing into history as a paragon of British maritime heroism, immortalised by the poetical works of Raleigh and later Tennyson: "At Flores, in the Azores, Sir Richard Grenville lay, and a pinnace, like a flutter'd bird, came flying from far away; 'Spanish ships of war at sea! We have sighted fifty-three!' Then sware Lord Thomas Howard: 'Fore God I am no coward…'"

I panicked when I recognised someone amongst my next boat load of passengers. The local novelist John Fowles stepped aboard *Herbert Paul* with a young boy who was his step-grandson… there hadn't been a single fish in the bay for ages! Taking money from grockles for a mackerel fishing trip when you know there aren't any fish around, is one thing, but not from the very person who allegedly put Lyme on the map. I seated them both next to me at the stern, the prime spot to catch fish when trolling, and freshly baited the best hand-lines I had, then proceeded to unwind them and struck up a conversation with Lyme's most famous recluse, as I was pretty sure nothing else was about to happen.

John lived at Belmont, just up the road from the Cobb. This had also been the home of Eleanor Coade, of Coade Stone fame, whose uncle had earlier leased it from the Corporation. Four members of the Coade family were mayors for Lyme throughout the seventeenth- and eighteenth-centuries, and not without controversy. When the wool trade declined, the wealthy wool merchant George Coade moved with his family to London. There he died, leaving the family bankrupt, although his daughter Eleanor had already established a drapery business. In the same year, she bought into one of several unsuccessful 'artificial stone' businesses in King's Arms Stairs, Lambeth, on the opposite bank of the Thames to the Houses of Parliament (in the future the site would be occupied by County Hall). Eleanor sacked the former owner and took the business over completely. She improved the formula by producing a moulded ceramic product more durable than stone itself.

It was probably Jane Austen who first used the Cobb in literature, for the setting where her heroine Louisa Musgrove's fall resulted in a twist of fate for the plot's love-triangle. Later on, the poet Coleridge would come to inspect the Cobb and the plight of Monmouth. He allegedly claimed that he had no interest in the ill-fated Duke, demanding instead, "Take me to the spot where Louisa Musgrove fell!" Even to this day, the exact location of this fictitious place is still debated amongst Austenites.

John Fowles also used it and became one of the world's most prolific authors, with some of his works making it to the big screen, including the locally-filmed *The French Lieutenant's Woman,* starring Jeremy Irons and Meryl Streep. He much appreciated the work of Austen, and his own heroine, Sarah Woodruff, is likened to Louisa Musgrove of *Persuasion*. I remember it well when it was filmed while I was still a student at the local Woodroffe (Woodruff!) School. I even gate crashed a film crew party and was immediately escorted out of it by none other than Miss Streep herself… I never liked any of her films anyway… Except, of course, for *The Deer Hunter*, which is only a bit 'Streepy' at the beginning.

Not only were free illegal narcotics and the loss of virginity introduced to underage girls at the school boarding house by London's yuppie, film star hangers-on, but the whole town was given a complete facelift to revert back to the mid-nineteenth century. Ships' masts were erected at the Cobb for the appearance of a commercial seaport, as it would have been in the olden days of sail. The main street of the town was repainted to give it an even more rustic 'olde worlde' look, with a plastic, imitation cobblestone street laid out, with chickens and sheep running around on the site of the former 'Shambles' marketplace. Even a horse and dray were brought into the town, and many of the locals went about their daily lives in period costume.

The opening scene begins with the lovelorn Sarah, played by Streep. Okay, I admit it, I like this film as well! She walks to the end of the High Wall and stares out to sea, waves surmounting the harbour as she yearns for her long-lost lover, and that windswept look backwards will forever epitomise the Cobb in its defiance against nature. Okay, I admit it further - Meryl Streep isn't such a bad actress after all! Not that I ever hold much of a grudge, but I wish she hadn't thrown me out of her party! The film was a box office hit, and the Cobb has forever been inundated with visitors, who come not only to find the spot where Louisa fell, but now to stand where Sarah stood.

I did everything I possibly could to catch a fish, but nothing; I varied the engine speed to troll at various depths and went to all my favourite fishing grounds but again, nothing! Then, within minutes of the hour being up, the nephew caught a mackerel! I was more elated than anyone, as it was the first fish I had seen in weeks. It was such a relief.

"Thank God for that! My whole reputation depended on that fish!" I exclaimed, and flicked our solitary catch into the bucket, broke its neck and strung it up for young master Fowles to take home for tea.

"Yes, it did!" quipped John seriously, but I'm sure beneath his beard I could glimpse a smirk.

John Fowles loved Lyme; he was curator of the local museum and did much work transcribing old borough documents. Some of the locals described him as cantankerous, snobbish and outspoken, since in his journals he had described them as, "The dullest and most abominably retarded community one can imagine", adding, "the poverty of this town, of provincial England, is a shock, like something from the Gulag Archipelago."

In this he may well have been right, but for reasons for which he was partly to blame. He was an intelligent and talented man, yet mysteriously, he seemed very ignorant of the history of the place that he loved, especially since, being the prolific author of *The French Lieutenant's Woman*, he went on to help with the screenplay.

It may have been a work of fiction, but you would have expected someone like Fowles to get the historical facts right. In the first chapter, he states, "the Cobb has changed very little since the year of which I write". He describes the area as being empty and desolate in 1867: "No house lay visibly then". Here, he was in error, as many workers' cottages had been erected for the cement works, the then big industry employing hundreds of men, women and children. It was extremely noisy and dirty work, with rock imports from the surrounding cliffs being crushed then heated in smoky, coal-fired kilns and the resultant bricks being exported by horse drawn carriage, using a small gauged railway track that ran around the Cobb. Our sweet little lovelorn Sarah may well have had an appearance a little more than windswept had she tried to venture anywhere near the Cobb in those days.

Raleigh's fall was not due to his failure to establish a permanent colony in the New World, but for his association with one of the Queen's ladies in waiting, Elizabeth Throckmorton, yet another person who can be associated with Lyme. Both her father and brother had been former mayors and parliamentary representatives to the town, and may well have influenced the passing of the Cobb Act.

The Queen was furious when she discovered that he had secretly married, and that Raleigh's young bride was expecting a child. Raleigh was immediately imprisoned in the Tower of London. Isn't it ironic that this small fishing village, whose tiny population would soon have such an important role in the establishment of an American colony, produced a resident who nearly brought about its downfall at the outset? Poor Mrs Raleigh miscarried the child later that year. The Queen allowed Raleigh to organise the colony from prison, and eventually forgave and released him. His relation with the Queen would never be the same again, as she subsequently allowed him to go on one of his dangerous voyages, indicating that he was now considered expendable.

It was in the bath, of all places, where I finished reading Melville's *Moby Dick*. I closed the book, placed it on the floor and started to fall asleep, thinking of those passionate words of Captain Ahab as he thrust the handheld harpoon into the great white beast.

"For hate's sake I despise thee, from hell's heart I stab at thee, with my last breath I spit my last curse at thee."

I slowly sank down into the bath and water shot up my nose. Spluttering and coughing, I awoke, and like Ishmael, the sole survivor of the story's sunken whaler, I was still alive, notwithstanding that my adventure had taken me no further than the bathroom. The reason that I mention this is that the next time I fell asleep in the bath, I was woken by a loud rap on the door and shouting before water shot up my nose again, "Glen, get your boat off the mooring, a humpback whale has been sighted in the Bay!"

Just like Moby, this was a one-off phenomenon. A humpback whale sighting in British coastal waters was as rare as Frobisher's unicorn horn. I quickly dried, dressed, ran down to the Cobb, untied the dinghy from the outhaul, paddled across the harbour and took *Herbert Paul* off its moorings in record time - my hair was still wet!

The varnished mahogany on oak hull glistened in the evening sun as I pulled up alongside the pier, and Darren and several other friends clambered aboard before I nosed out of the harbour into a southeasterly swell. A lone herring gull hovered in the air above us and cormorants, perched on rocks ashore with wings outstretched, stared at us curiously as we sailed pass. They hold this heraldic posture to dry themselves after diving for eels.

"About two miles south of Burton Bradstock" was the reply I received over the radio from a local fisherman. That was roughly seven to eight miles southeast, and an estimated journey time of about an hour. After a quick glance at the compass, we headed in that direction and cut the swell diagonally, so the hull could gently roll over the oncoming waves, rather than plough straight through them and soak us. We passed the Blue Lias cliffs to our port, famous for Jurassic period fossils. We passed the majestic Golden Cap, the highest cliff face on the south coast of England. The evening sun reflected off its limestone shale crown, a sharp contrast to the darker coloured clays below.

After an hour, we spotted a small flotilla of boats on the horizon. Through the binoculars, we took turns on look-out from the bow for anything unusual. The wind rattled through the mast staves as we continued to cut through the sea. In the distance, we thought we could make out the occasional burst of white surf. At that distance it was difficult to tell if it was something big swimming amongst the boats or the wind breaking the crest of waves into white horses.

As we approached the other boats, we could see nothing unusual, so I slowed us down and knocked the engine out of gear. We all listened. You could now hear the gentle lapping of the sea against the wooden hull and the creak of floorboards.

The previous summer, a basking shark the size of *Herbert Paul* had nearly rammed the hull as I motored by and surprised it! I did this for the tourists onboard to take photos but should have made a bit more of a noise on the approach – the poor thing was so startled. Schools of bottle-nosed dolphins can be common at times and over the years, I've ran with many along the coast. Probably the most spectacular scenes to date have been those rare moments when countless numbers of giant jelly-fish drift into the bay. These are rhizostoma octopus, which I mentioned earlier; the French call them 'Medusa tête', because they appear similar to a Gorgon's head as they drift by. The most unusual thing I had seen up until this point was probably an angler on a deep sea fishing trip catch a mackerel on an un-baited hook out of water! The hungry little mite had leaped up out of the sea for the glistening hook. Other unusual catches had been a full sized trigger fish and a five-bearded rocklin, but never had I seen anything as unusual as a humpback whale in British coastal waters.

In the silence we continued looking around, but there was nothing. Suddenly, the huge mass of a humpback breached up out of the sea to the stern of *Herbert Paul*. I turned around just in time to see it and received the spray from its blow-hole in my face; then, as quickly as it appeared, it disappeared back into the deep. Everyone was speechless, and Chris, with his video camera, caught a classic shot with a look of astonishment from me in the foreground. I quickly started the engine as my immediate thought was of a collision with this huge thing, as had nearly happened with the basking shark the previous summer.

As the engine shuddered into life and we cut through the sea, the whale followed, thinking we wanted to play. This magnificent beast swam elegantly alongside us, sometimes just inches from the gunwales. The distinct markings of its barnacle-encrusted snout, the unmistakable huge body and white fins made it a humpback for sure. I knocked the engine out of gear when I realised it was playing with us, and it swam beneath the boat. The black mass remained motionless. Had it emerged just a few inches, we would have been high and dry upon its back - and to think this was just a calf.

I stepped across to the bow as my whole body raced with adrenaline and dished out lifejackets from the locker. I wasn't taking any chances as I checked that Darren's - my kid brother, - was firmly tied. The excitement aboard was ecstatic. I had seen whales before in the bay, but only pilots. During a trip to the States, I had seen a whole school of Californian greys offshore from San Diego, but nothing like this.

"It's a calf searching for its mother, probably lost," suggested someone. Chris had by now wedged his foot beneath a seat and the bulkhead to steady himself, as he leaned right out filming this awesome beast. By now, everyone with a camera was taking photos, and other boats of the flotilla came alongside. Chris' younger brother Jason had donned his diving gear and flipped over backwards from the gunwale. *Getting the best view of all*, I thought enviously. We watched as the huge white fins broke the surface and it swam to other boats, looking for the next playmate.

I started up the engine; this time the wind blew from astern, making a smoother ride, and the whale leapt up out of the water again and followed us. It must have liked the sound of my engine. It swam so close that Darren was fortunate enough to stroke it. We must have been making a speed of eight knots on the crest of a wave with the breaching whale alongside. It was just like something out of the *Moby*

Dick novel, especially when someone couldn't resist shouting, "There she blows!"

A little while later, someone reminded me of Jason. *Oh God!*, I thought, *I'd completely forgotten about him*. I steered a sharp course away from 'Moby' and went back looking for our diver. It was lucky he had his wetsuit on, as we hauled him back inside the boat shivering; the poor bugger had missed everything!

I then realised that we had now lost Moby to the other boats of the flotilla, and by the time we caught up, it was following them into the sunset. Eventually, the other boats returned home and again we had Moby to ourselves. It followed us as far as Golden Cap where it disappeared. It was dark by the time we returned to the Cobb.

By the following day, the BBC had heard about Chris' video and sent a despatch rider down from London to retrieve a copy. On the television that evening, millions watched the footage of Darren stroking a humpback whale as it swam alongside *Herbert Paul*. A few weeks later, I heard a conversation on the ship-to-shore that Moby had been spotted far out in the English Channel. A group of humpbacks do migrate between the Azores and the Arctic and, even though the chances are slim, it is possible for one to bear a little bit too much to the East and lose itself somewhere up along the Channel. There have only ever been two recorded sightings of humpback whales off the Dorset coast during the twentieth century, and Wednesday 17th June, 1992 - Moby - had been the last one.

A century after Columbus discovered his offshore island of Japan, almost to the day, Raleigh had embarked on a piracy expedition to another nearby offshore island in a region that had now become known as the West Indies (once it was realised it was nowhere near the East!). He heard the fable of El Dorado, the legendary city of gold, and foolishly believed every word of it. Raleigh became obsessed with El Dorado, just as Frobisher had been in seeking a northwest passage. In fact, the passage does exist but it wasn't confirmed until much later, when Roald Amundsen became the first to traverse the passage - and then only by canoe! It was originally thought that El Dorado was in the mountains of Colombia, near present day Bogota. But no such kingdom of gold was ever found by the Spanish. The search moved east until it found its current location in a place known today as Guiana.

The quest to conquer the New World was highly influenced by the search for the city of El Dorado. The legend of El Dorado first appeared around the 1530s, when the story about an Indian chief covered in gold dust was told. Martinez claimed that he was rescued by the native Indians after he had been charged for negligence after a stock of powder exploded, and he was sent drifting up the Orinoco River in a canoe. After being captured by the natives, they took him to a city with bandages over his eyes. After the bandages were removed, he opened his eyes and as far as the eyes could see, stretching all around him, "were houses of shining gold and dazzling precious stones".

Martinez said that he and his guides had arrived at the King's palace in Manoa, after walking through the city for a full day and that "the emperor was known as El Dorado; for his bath every morning, showers of gold dust were blown through myriads of tubes."

De Berrio wrote in a letter to the Council of the Indies, "If God aids me to settle Guiana, Trinidad will be the richest trade centre of the Indies, for if Guiana was one twentieth of what it was supposed to be, it would be richer than Peru."

The whole of Europe was ablaze with these stories and the hunt for El Dorado started when Raleigh was in the West Indies. After returning to England, he sent out an expedition to Guiana under Captain Whiddon to make enquires about El Dorado, but it came up with nothing definite about the place. Raleigh himself then went to Guiana, after burning down St. Joseph, the capital of Trinidad, which was a Spanish colony. He and his men started up the Orinoco River searching for this fabled land of gold, and for many days they suffered hardship after hardship, being exposed to the torturing tropical sun and heavy pouring rain. With no success, Raleigh returned to England where he published a book called *The Discoverie of Guiana* and wrote, "Whatever prince shall possess it, that prince shall be lord of more gold, and of more cities and people than either the King of Spain or the great Turk."

Raleigh was charged for treason by James I for attacking the Spanish colony, and was imprisoned in the Tower of London again.

While he was in prison, he sent Lawrence Keymis back to Guiana, who explored the area and then returned to England, reporting back to Raleigh. He claimed that El Dorado was situated on the Rupununi in Essequibo, the largest county of Guyana. When Raleigh was released from prison, he was given permission by James I to obtain these treasures for the royal coffers. His friends helped him financially and he set sail with fourteen vessels, in search of El Dorado.

After Raleigh became sick and weak from the attacks by the Spanish in the Americas, he disappointingly returned to England, where he was imprisoned again and sentenced to death on trumped up charges of plotting with the Spanish. Raleigh met his death on the scaffold at Old Palace Yard, Westminster. On the scaffold, he showed remarkable courage and placidity; after inspecting the headsman's axe, he remarked: "This is sharp medicine, but it is a physician for all diseases."

He declined a blindfold, but according to legend was permitted to smoke his pipe; supposedly the first time the now traditional indulgence of a condemned man had been extended. He made a moving and dignified speech to the crowd and, before placing his head on the block, proceeded to each corner of the scaffold, kneeling and asking the onlookers to pray for him. When finally Raleigh placed his head on the block, somebody noticed that he was facing the wrong direction and suggested that he should face "the East of our Lord's arising."

Raleigh replied, "So thy heart be right, it is no great matter which way thy head lieth."

But, to oblige the crowd, he stood up and rearranged himself. When he made the signal that he was ready, the axe man hesitated, so Raleigh's last words were: "Strike man, strike!"

When the executioner had severed his head he held it up to the crowd and exclaimed, "Never a better head in all of England could be cut off!"

The Lord of the Manor of Lyme, Henry Brooke 11th Lord Cobham, together with his brother, George Brooke, and others, were arrested for their involvement in the alleged 'Raleigh Conspiracy' against King James I. Following his trial, Cobham was attainted and condemned to death; he was not, however, executed but rather committed to the

Tower of London, where he remained for the rest of his life. Following his attainder, Cobham Hall and his other estates were granted by King James I to his own wife.

This conspiracy was allegedly started by English Catholics to remove King James I from the throne and replace him with his cousin Arabella Stuart, who was a staunch Catholic. Raleigh had been imprisoned in the Tower of London for thirteen years before he was released for his failed attempt to discover the fabled El Dorado. The main plot was allegedly led by Lord Cobham who, with his brother Sir George Brooke and Baron Thomas Grey, had planned to raise an army to march on London to take over the Government. Cobham was accused of negotiating with the Count of Aremberg to arrange a huge sum of money from Spain. He was to travel to Spain, collect the money, and return via Jersey, where Raleigh was once the governor. Both of them were then to divide up the money and decide how best to spend it to raise an army.

Raleigh's involvement is unlikely, and almost certainly an excuse by the jealous king to have him executed after his failure to revitalise the royal coffers from his venture in the New World. All of his property was confiscated after his execution, including nearby Sherborne Castle, which was passed on to the Digby family. Cobham's execution was scheduled for the year after Raleigh's and a private act of James I had decreed the "Vesting in the Crown the estates of Lord Cobham and George Brooke, attained of high treason, with a confirmation of grants made by the King."

The Colway estate then came into the possession of the Henley family, whose main manor house was nearby Leigh House, in Chard. The combined estates of this wealthy family now stretched across three counties - Somerset, Devon and Dorset. During the English Civil War, Henry Henley was a colonel in the Parliamentary Army, and became the elected MP for Dorset in the First Protectorate Parliament after the war, and later MP for Lyme.

When Charles I raised the Royal Standard in Nottingham, the country split and civil war was declared. Like most wars of the seventeenth-century, it was not a long, drawn-out affair. Roads were no more than tracks, and wet weather could easily make them unusable. Armies therefore lacked mobility, which resulted in long periods of time when no fighting took place. The English Civil War can actually be summarised in three major battles – Edge Hill, Marston Moor and Naseby. At Edge Hill, both sides claimed a win, with many smaller battles resulting equally indecisively. Oliver Cromwell then formed his New Model Army – the Roundheads, or Ironsides, who would achieve a decisive outcome in the next major battle at Marston Moor, leading to the Royalists losing control of the North of England. At Coventry, a prison was built for captured Royalists, and this is how the expression 'to be sent to Coventry' came about, meaning 'to be ostracised'. Naseby was the final battleground that brought victory to the Roundheads and Parliament, but a small skirmish back in the West Country also resulted in a decisive victory and that is what concerns us next.

Bloody Mary had once labelled Lyme "that heretic town" because of the populace's refusal to return to the Catholic faith, and the town has often had a reputation for radical thinking and being a pain in the side of Royals. It had become strongly Puritan, and this is thought to be the main reasons for taking the side of Cromwell during the Civil War. Prince Maurice, a nephew to the king, decided to lay siege to Lyme, considering it as just "breakfast work". Three months later, the forces of the flamboyant and haughty prince withdrew after sustaining heavy losses and being utterly defeated by this "vile little fishing town defended by a small dry ditch". Lyme had on its side colonel Henry Henley, and his mansion at Lyme was taken by Maurice, who used it as the Royalist headquarters for the siege along with nearby Haye House. Colway was so badly battered during the war that the ruins were occupied as a farmhouse for a very long time afterwards.

Parliamentarian Lyme also had the very gifted military strategist Robert Blake who, after the war, became the Admiral famous for defeating the Barbary Corsairs that still plagued the south coast of England. The Royalist forces far outnumbered the locals, and it is said that even the town's women dressed up as men to create the allusion of swelled ranks. They certainly carried supplies and ammunition to the troops, in some cases firing weapons for them. Years after the siege a poem named 'Joanereidos' was dedicated to the women of Lyme, where this Amazonian army was compared to Joan of Arc!

The Royalist forces were unrelenting in their attack on Lyme, using wildfire to burn the houses and bombarding the town with cannon fire and musket shot, which even today can still be found while digging in the garden, or searching around the Cobb at low water. Even a witch was used to cast spells upon the locals, but all was to no avail, with the Royalists forces ending up in second place.

Royalist strongholds around the country gradually started to fall, as the war progressed into the mid -1600s. It wasn't only poetical works that were inspired by events in the English Civil War, but also children's nursery rhymes. For example, at Colchester, the Royalist forces had a huge cannon known as Humpty Dumpty mounted on the city wall, which prevented Cromwell's forces from getting anywhere near them.

"Humpty Dumpty sat on a great wall…"Until, that is, some ingenious Roundhead realised that destroying the wall beneath would render the cannon obsolete…"Humpty Dumpty had a great fall, and all the king's horses and all the king's men couldn't put Humpty together again."

Back in Dorset, the main Royalist stronghold had been at Corfe Castle, which would have been an ideal seat for Humpty Dumpty, as it had much thicker walls that were far more impenetrable to cannon fire. During the second siege of this great fortress, a member of the Royalist garrison named Pittman betrayed them, and opened up the gates for the Roundheads who stormed the castle. After its capture, the castle was completely destroyed with explosives and undermined, to make sure that it would never stand as the impenetrable Royalist stronghold that it had once been.

The Battle of Naseby had been the one that had inflicted the fatal blow, with a combined army from a Scottish and Parliamentary alliance. Charles I was captured but briefly escaped to start the short-lived Second Civil War. He was defeated at Preston and at a trial in Westminster Hall, the captured king was found guilty for he had "Traitorously and maliciously levied war against the present Parliament and the people therein represented". He thus became the last British monarch to be executed!

Almost all of the buildings in Lyme had been destroyed during the war, but the Cobb survived and had been the main bulwark for the town's defences by facilitating the resupply of the Parliamentary forces. So it is ironic that, for reasons I will explain later, unknown by its populace at the time, Lyme had fought against a monarch who, a decade before his execution, had done something for the town that would help preserve it and its harbour five centuries later, and explain the reason for that rock ballast on the end of the Cobb.

Even the young Prince of Wales, who would become the future King Charles II, barely escaped with his life; after the Battle of Worcester he fled to Boscobel where he famously hid in an oak tree before heading south across the Cotswolds and over the Mendips towards the south coast. He was being pursued by Parliamentarians and so hid again - this time for almost three weeks at Trent Manor near Yeovil, owned by Colonel Wyndham. From here, he left on horseback with Juliana Coningsby disguised as mistress and servant, and after the Restoration, Juliana was rewarded with a pension of £200 a year for her bravery. At Charmouth they stayed the night at the Queen's Arms, accompanied by Colonel Wyndham, Lord Wilmot and a servant.

Stephen Limbry of Lyme was a Captain to a thirty tonne ship, who had prearranged to take them to France for £60. Mrs Limbry became aware of her husband's secret rendezvous, and locked him in his room and hid his trousers, so that he missed his appointment. Meanwhile, back in Charmouth, Hammett the blacksmith had become suspicious of a shoe he was replacing on Wilmot's horse; it had come from Worcester. He and the stable boy reported this to the local Puritan Minister, Bartholomew Wesley, the great-grandfather to the founder of the Wesleyan Methodists. This resulted in a chase to Bridport, where Charles had preceded them. Charles was intending to dine at the George, but departed rather hurriedly when he realised he had Parliamentarians hot on his tail again. He galloped east out of Bridport, then turned off at Lee Lane and put up for the night at another George in Broadwindsor. The place was then overrun with Parliamentarians searching for the prince, who again managed to avoid them and returned to Trent. From here they travelled further east over the South Downs to Shoreham, from where they successfully sailed to France, where Charles remained until the Restoration.

After the Restoration, the Henley loyalty to the Parliamentary cause would be their downfall, as Robert Henley was one of those implicated in the Rye House Plot, in which a group of conservative members of Parliament (who later styled themselves as Whigs) planned to capture and murder Charles II and his brother James, for fear of them both becoming Catholic sympathisers. James had actually converted to the Catholic faith, and it was argued that he should cease to be an heir to the throne. Henley, who protested his innocence in a long and convincing speech, was found guilty of treason by the corrupt court, and was subsequently hanged, drawn and quartered. Shortly afterwards, it was proven that he was indeed innocent.

Meanwhile, a real conspirator, James Scott Duke of Monmouth, the eldest illegitimate son of Charles II and his mistress Lucy Walters, fled abroad with plans for another ambitious scheme. When Charles II died, he left no direct heir by marriage, and so his brother ascended the throne as James II, also VII of Scotland and II of Ireland, just to confuse matters. James was unpopular because of his conversion to the Catholic faith, with many people still opposed to the idea of a 'popish king'.

On Midsummer's Day 1685, a ship bearing the Royal Standard was sighted just west of the Cobb. Aboard was the Duke of Monmouth, the illegitimate son of Charles II, who had been in self-imposed exile in Holland, planning an invasion to overthrow this 'popish king' and to place himself upon the throne. According to the accounts of the historian Roberts, "Great numbers assembled to welcome the Duke's arrival and enlist under his standard."

At this time, the Cobb did not join the mainland and the Duke would have soaked his feet had he tried stepping from the boat that paddled him ashore.

"A Lieutenant Bagster of the Navy, who happened to be close to the beach in a boat, jumped into the water, and presented his knee for the duke to step on, which he did, and then reached the shore without inconvenience. He then turned to Lieutenant Bagster, and familiarly striking him on the shoulder, said, 'Brave young man, you will join me?' His intrepid answer is worth recording, - 'No, sir! I have sworn to be true to my king, and no consideration shall move me from my fidelity.'"

Although the Duke was tall, dark and handsome, he was an utter moron, and the planned invasion was to be his downfall. Despite this, he was popular with the locals and Roberts further recalls in his own time that,"... an old woman named Curtis, lately deceased, said her grandfather was obliged to fly for having broken open the town-hall door, in order to give the duke possession, and never more returned."

Many locals and those from the surrounding area joined Monmouth, including such notables as the novelist Daniel Defoe of *Robinson Crusoe* fame. It is worth noting what this great writer said of the Cobb at this time:"They have a good harbour; but 'tis such a one as is not in all Britain besides, if there is such a one in any part of the world."

The Duke's untrained land force of some three thousand followers initiated the 'Pitchfork Rebellion'. This Army was defeated at the Battle of Sedgemoor near Taunton, within a couple of weeks of the Duke's landing. The Government sent Judge Jeffereys to make a sharp retribution, and in the Bloody Assizes that followed, hundreds were either executed or transported to the American colonies. In Lyme, ninety-nine men were arrested and twelve of them executed on the beach where the Duke had landed, still known today as 'Monmouth's Beach.'

Monmouth fled from the battlefield, but was later captured hiding in a ditch. After making a grovelling plea to the King, begging for mercy, and claiming a conversion to Catholicism, he was beheaded on Tower Hill within a month of his landing. The execution was a messy affair, taking several blows of the axe, and then the executioner using a knife to sever the spinal cord. The King then realised that no portrait of the Duke existed and, as it was so unbecoming to execute such a person without a portrait when he was still alive, he ordered the chief surgeon to sew the head back on, the scar being hidden with a scarf. The painting is the only known official rendition of the Duke, and now hangs in the National Gallery.

Today, as you walk into the Royal Lion Hotel in Lyme, you will see a small portrait upon the wooden panelling on the right hand side of the foyer. This little portrait has been much neglected over the years. Some of the paintwork has even been damaged with blue tack from overlaying posters. I have always said that if it were a portrait of who

I think it is, then it would be worth more than the whole hotel. Lyme is steeped in history, and it saddens me that we neglect so much of it. The United States has less European history than this little town, yet the little that they have they seem to take much better care of than we do of ours! I believe that this painting is the only portrait of the Duke when he was still alive, and must be protected from further damage for future generations. I just hate this sort of neglect!

On a bleak moor three miles outside of Chesterfield, Derbyshire, the Earl of Devonshire, from nearby Chatsworth Manor, met with the Earl of Danby and John D'Arcy. They secretly met in an alehouse to plan the Glorious Revolution to overthrow James II and restore a Protestant King. Three years after the Duke of Monmouth's ill-fated attempt for the crown, William of Orange completed a successful invasion using a similar plan, except that he landed with a much larger army at nearby Brixham. This time, James II fled to France and William's invasion lead to a free parliament, with himself and his wife becoming King William III and Queen Mary, in whose honour Williamsburg and Maryland in the Americas were named. During the time from Raleigh's execution until now, a permanent colonial America had been established that would remain British for at least another century and the little town of Lyme had again played its part - but how?, you may well wonder.

CHAPTER 3

"Never wait for trouble."
  - Chuck Yeager

It was a cold February day when I stood on the snowcapped banks of the Chesapeake and looked up at the statue of a person with such a common name as John Smith. He gazed out across the Atlantic towards his home in Gravesend, England, some four thousand miles away. Standing humbly at the base of its plinth had been the culmination of two years on the road travelling the North American continent, spread over three consecutive trips; this particular one had taken almost a year. The epitaph at the base of the monument simply read: 'Captain John Smith, Governor of Virginia, 1608' - a modest description for this larger-than-life character, whose exploits would someday be compared to those of the Arabian Nights, with achievements enough for the lifetimes of many merchant venturers, let alone a single person.

Had it not been for this man, I thought, *how different the world around us would be today*. Back in his time, the Spanish empire was the only real superpower ready to grab the whole of the New World for itself. Because of Smith, England had finally made a foothold in the Americas, and would now become a serious competitor in this world superpower game, starting a chain of events that would lead to the formation of the modern United States.

Inside the nearby Jamestown Visitor Center, I was very curious and asked lots of questions. When the friendly staff realised where I was from, and the interest I evidently had in the history of this particular part of Virginia, they could not have treated me better, and I was invited into an anteroom and allowed to paw through copies of the original accounts of the founding of the Jamestown colony. It had been a fortunate time to make these trips back and forth across the Atlantic, as back home in Lyme, we had three consecutive bad seasons on the boats; what better way to escape from it all than to use the knowledge I had gained from my first trip here, how to make a low budget road trip of the States?

So what else was happening in the world at the same time as the start of the first permanent English settlement in the Americas? It had long been realised that Cuba was not some offshore island to Japan, and so Havana had been officially named as its capital. The Bank of Genoa became bankrupt, proving even then that the banking system doesn't work. This was also the start of the Renaissance period and the first fully developed opera, *Orfeo*, would be performed at Mantua's Court Theatre, with music by Claudio Monteverdi, who employed a new treatment of discords to provide emotional and dramatic values. While this was being performed, a large bright comet appeared high above. It was Halley's Comet, as yet to be named by him, passing as it returned to the inner solar system on its seventy-six year orbit about the Sun. Kepler, the great astronomer of the time, thought that the returning comet was moving along in a straight line and was just passing through the solar system. It would take one more revolution of the sun - a 'Halley Comet Year' if you like - before Edmund Halley realised it was indeed in orbit and, just like the planets, was here to stay and so had the honour of having it named after him.

The comet inspired Shakespeare, and in *Julius Caesar* he wrote: "When beggars die, there are no comets seen; The heavens themselves blaze forth the death of princes."

But this Halley year did not appear to signify the death of any prince, but rather that of the new Jamestown colony; had it not been for the intervention of John Smith, then it would almost certainly have died. The events that were about to follow would further inspire Shakespeare's *The Tempest*.

Born in Willoughby, England, John Smith was a natural adventurer, having left home at just sixteen after his father died. He began his adventures by joining volunteers in France, who were fighting for Dutch independence from Spain. During the sea voyage to mainland

Europe, he was regarded as a bad omen, and was allegedly cast overboard in a stormy sea. He survived and two years later, he set off into the Mediterranean, working on a merchant ship. At the turn of the century, he joined the Austrian forces to fight the Turks in the Long War. He proved to be a valiant soldier and was promoted to captain while fighting in Hungary. Here, he was wounded in battle in Transylvania, where he was captured and sold into slavery to a Turk. This Turk then sent Smith as a gift to his sweetheart in Istanbul. According to Smith, the girl fell in love with him and sent him to her brother for training in the Turkish imperial service. Smith reputedly escaped by murdering the brother, and returned to Transylvania, fleeing through Russia and Poland. After being released from service and receiving a large reward, he travelled all over Europe and North Africa, finally returning to England.

Here, Smith became involved with the Virginia Company and its plans to colonise Virginia. By this time, another charter had been granted by King James I, after whom the new colony was named. Smith was part of the famous expedition that finally reached Virginia, after enduring a lengthy voyage of over four months at sea in three tiny ships. During this time, a sealed box that listed the names of the seven Council members who were to govern the colony was opened. Smith's name was amongst those on the list, and by the month of May, one year previous to that of the comet, the settlers landed at Jamestown to begin the task of surviving in a new environment.

The harsh winter, lack of fresh water, and the spread of disease made life in Jamestown difficult for the settlers. Attacks by the native Algonquian Indians made things intolerable. The natives hoped that the settlers would give up and leave, and so continuously raided their camps, stealing pistols, gunpowder, and other necessary supplies. John Smith did his best to fight off the Indians, and his leadership skills helped the colonists.

By the end of that first year, Smith and some companions were ambushed by Indian deer hunters. After killing the other Englishmen, the Indians carried Smith back to their powerful chief, Powhatan, to decide his fate. Powhatan was apparently greatly impressed by Smith's self-confidence, as well as such mystical instruments as an ivory and glass pocket compass that he had in his possession. Smith was questioned about his colony and then made to take part in some sort of ritual or trial, after which, in keeping with an Indian custom, he was made a subordinate Chief of the tribe. Powhatan's eleven-year-old daughter, Pocahontas, took part in the ceremony in some way. Smith was constantly unsure of what was going to happen to him, and he was convinced afterwards that Pocahontas had saved his life. Smith was released in friendship after about four weeks and returned to Jamestown. Whatever happened during his captivity, Smith had singlehandedly made peace with the Native Americans, something that was imperative for the survival of the English colony.

Meanwhile, dissent within the colony fermented due to lack of supplies, laziness, and periodic attempts at desertion by many of the colonists, as well as personal conflicts among Smith and various leaders, and disagreements over new policies being formulated in London. As a result, Smith left Jamestown to explore and map the Chesapeake Bay region and search for badly-needed food supplies. Although sometimes vain and boastful, he was a brilliant leader and even after an argument with the colonists - who had nearly hanged him - he eventually won their respect. Due to bad government and near chaos, Smith was eventually elected president of the local Council.

He instituted a policy of rigid discipline, strengthened defences, and encouraged farming with this admonishment: "He who does not work, will not eat". He added that, "a plaine soldier that can use a pick-axe and a spade is better than five knights". It is only because of his strong leadership skills and success in making peace with the Native Americans, who taught the colonists how to obtain food and survive the harsh winter conditions, that the settlement survived and grew during the following year. Unfortunately, he was accidentally injured by a gunpowder explosion and had to return to England for treatment, never again to return to Virginia.

In recent decades, an urban myth has grown up around a love affair between Smith and Pocahontas. This was never the case, for two reasons. Firstly, because of the age difference between them; when Smith met Pocahontas, she was just a child, and Smith was actually old enough to be her father. Secondly, both had always treated each other as brother and sister, and through this friendship Pocahontas was introduced to John Rolfe, whom she later married when he became a widower. This would initiate the first introduction of a Red Indian woman into Shakespearean London society; the Virginia Colony's sponsors found it difficult to lure new colonists and investors to Jamestown, and so they used Pocahontas as a symbol to convince people that the New World's natives were now friendly, and the settlement a safe place to live in.

It must have been a strange affair for Pocahontas not only to visit Jacobean London society, accompanied by a group of about eleven other Powhatan natives dressed in traditional native American attire, which no doubt the crowds would have gawked at in disbelief, but then to be presented at court to King James I and Queen Anne at a masque performed by Ben Johnson, where it is recorded that she was suitably seated to suit her status. In a sense, she was our first American Ambassador, and by all accounts was a very popular one. Even the Bishop of London was so impressed by her that someone stated that he, "entertained her with festival state and pomp beyond what I have seen in his greate hospitalitie afforded to other ladies."

There was, however, some confusion when Pocahontas was introduced to the royal household, as she wasn't completely sure which person amongst them was supposed to be the King! According to Smith, this matter was clarified by the end of the evening. This can easily be imagined, considering that James I had no interest in an American colony - even the name 'Jamestown' was most likely coined by the Virginia Company as a propagandist attempt to make him interested. He had Raleigh executed merely on a jealous whim, and preferred the company of young boys to women. His appearance was never very regal, being such a dirty little urchin that another ambassador from Europe even recorded that you could always tell what the King of England had eaten weeks previously by the food stains left on his tunic!

Pocahontas was entertained at various other society gatherings, but unfortunately never met Shakespeare, as sadly the great Bard had passed away just a few weeks before her arrival. Despite this, Pocahontas did have the opportunity to see a performance of his last - and many say his most favourite - play *The Tempest*. This is ironic, as the events that had followed in the time after John Smith's departure from Jamestown had, like the comet, inspired Shakespeare to write this play.

After almost a year in England, Rolfe and his popular wife, who had taken London by such storm, had boarded a ship down the Thames to return to Virginia. However, the ship had only gone as far as Gravesend before Pocahontas became gravely ill; there she was taken ashore, but died shortly afterward. At the time, the cause of her death was unknown, but it is suspected today to have been smallpox. According to Rolfe, she died in his arms, uttering the last words, "all must die, but 'tis enough that our child liveth". Her funeral took place in the parish church of Saint George's, Gravesend. The site of her grave is unknown, but her memory is honoured with a lifesize bronze statue in the grounds of the little church there. When I visited that statue and humbly stood beneath it, I noticed that, ironically, it stares in the opposite direction to Smith's statue, and instead gazes out across the Atlantic in the direction of her home some four thousand miles away.

It is interesting to note that Pocahontas and Rolfe's child, Thomas, was born before his parents left the New World for England. Through this son, Pocahontas has many living descendants, and today several families in Virginia can trace their roots to her and Chief Powhatan, including such notable individuals as the astronomer Percival Lowell and the former First Lady Nancy Reagan.

My year-long trip travelling the North American continent had started on the last day of September, at the end of the 1992 season when I sat on the back seat of the X31 and took my last glimpse of the Cobb as a fierce equinox gale crashed over the rock armament at the southern end of the High Wall - again, I wondered at its purpose. The Axminster bus pulled out of Lyme, and I lost my line of thought, as next came train, plane and New York City, and the beginning of a new adventure.

After Pocahontas had passed away, Smith continued to actively promote the colonisation of the Americas in London, but due to his independent and maverick behaviour, he had become unpopular with the Virginia Company, which denied him further opportunities to return to Jamestown. This notwithstanding, with the approval of the Prince of Wales - later King Charles I - he returned to the New World in a successful voyage to the Maine and Massachusetts bay areas, which he named New England. After this, he spent the rest of his life writing books about the New World until passing away at the age of fifty-one.

With John Smith away from the Jamestown colony, his strict disciplinary rule of 'no work, no food' were ignored and the colony was set to fail again. Had it not been for the intervention of someone with the same diplomatic and leadership attributes as John Smith, then the demise of England's first colony in the New World would have been inevitable, and this is where Lyme's parliamentary representative and Admiral helped to change the course of history.

Born in Lyme, Sir George Somers was the son of John Somers and both had been associates of Raleigh and Drake. His career as a merchant trader and privateer made him a wealthy man and he was able to buy Berne Manor in nearby Whitchurch Canonicorum. Just like Smith, Somers also had a colourful life, since, as a privateer, he took part in the sacking of Caracas in Venezuela and commanded HMS *Vanguard*, which captured a Spanish treasure ship. He also captained HMS *Swiftsure* during the attack of the Spanish fleet off Kinsale, and helped repel the Spanish invasion of Ireland. For these acts he was knighted by James I, and became a Member of Parliament for Lyme Regis.

In 1609, Somers was made admiral of the Virginia Company's third supply and relief fleet for Jamestown, aged just one year short of that at which Smith had died. In April of that year he was in Lyme, as witnessed by a dated signature in the Lyme Borough Court Book. From here, he must have gone straight to Plymouth, as on the 2nd of June, he sailed aboard *Sea Venture*, the flagship of the seven-ship fleet, towing two additional pinnaces and carrying about six hundred colonists, destined for the new colony in Virginia.

I flew into New York City at night and looked down at the Manhattan skyline and its chequered array of street lights and skyscrapers that appear to stretch out into infinity; the view was like something out of *Star Wars*. That evening I went to a bar and met the friendly Irish in Hell's Kitchen, the Irish quarter of New York, and the following morning I walked off my hangover around the equally friendly Afro-American neighbourhood of the Bronx! It was only later

I found out what a bloody foolish thing I had just done. You don't go walking around any 'hood', let alone one of New York's, on your own if you are white, and it was only because I was British that I had got away with it. I fled across the George Washington Bridge to New Jersey, just as its namesake had done in retreat from the British some two centuries previously. Here, many of the houses still exist from that time, making them the oldest European homes in the States.

I arrived unannounced at a retirement home in North Haven, Connecticut, as this was my first planned destination on this particular trip to the States. The security guard looked at me suspiciously as I explained who I was, then went off to check my story; after a while a frail little old lady arrived, peered at me through the glass screen of the security doors, then smiled as she recognised who I was, despite the ocean and the three generations that separated us. She nodded to the security guard and the doors slid open. This was my grandmother's sister on my mother's side, who had married an American serviceman shortly after the Second World War, making my great-aunt Doris a 'G.I. bride'. My great-uncle had now passed away, but from them I can proudly claim to have many second cousins among our ex-colonial cousins.

What a bizarre time I had on that visit, and what an incredible lady Doris Gainsford was, a lovely person who wanted to know all about the 'Old Country' and what everyone in my family was currently doing. She then got out the family album, and I was astonished to discover what a beautiful English rose she had been in her youth, when she married her handsome, chisel-jawed soldier who had survived the war to rid the world of Fascism. She turned the pages in the album of old black and white photographs of herself and her husband, taken on the return voyage to the States aboard a Cunard steamship. Each picture captured a little of something that we have lost in our current, artificial, mundane society. The innocence of the young married couple standing on the wooden boardwalk deck alongside brass polished handrails, tightly holding hands and so obviously in love, with a plume of smoke billowing out of the ship's funnel in the background. Another photo shows the ballroom with its hanging chandeliers and rotary fans, with other passengers correctly dressed for dinner and the newlyweds sat next to the wizened, middle-aged sea Captain at his table. It was like a scene from the movie *Titanic*, the difference being that this was to be a successful crossing and a happy ending. Their children and grandchildren, my second cousins, were spread all over New England, and I had an opportunity to speak too many of them on the phone. I now have proof of being an American, as I had traced my family relatives there!

I spent the night in the guestroom, and the following morning I had tea with lots of little old ladies from their best chinaware. Most of them were also former British G.I. brides, and each of them had their own stories to tell me of similar *Titanic*-esque crossings with albums and memorabilia to prove it. Mentioning *Titanic*, I had once been similarly impressed back in Lyme when I was fortunate enough to meet another little old lady, this time aboard my own boat on a trip around the bay. When I let her steer the helm, she bowled me over by telling me she was the last living person to survive the sinking of *Titanic*, but as its youngest passenger (at just a few weeks old), she could obviously not recall anything about it. I did quip that she need not worry, as we were a long way off from any icebergs.

An elderly gentleman named Bill, a friend of Aunt Doris, drove me to the Amtrak station later that day, stopping off to show me the statue of the Unity of the States. He was a nice old boy who told me all about his thirty-eight year career on the railroads, and how much New England had changed just in his own lifetime. On Amtrak, I continued my journey to nearby Old Lyme, and at the Florence Griswold Museum, I discovered to my surprise that eighty square miles of land were granted to Mathew Griswold in the mid-seventeenth century. The General Court ordered that, "Ye plantations on ye east side river over against say-brooke for ye future to be named Lyme."

The Griswolds had become a prosperous family of merchants by trading with the new colonies, and had achieved enough wealth to buy into part of it, naming it after their home town in the 'Old World', Lyme Regis. Another interesting parallel to be discovered here in New England is 'Lyme's Disease', an infection carried by deer ticks which, if goes unchecked, manifests the same symptoms as arthritis. Ironic that the disease has now been discovered in deer ticks in the nature reserve known as the 'Undercliff' to the west of Lyme Regis.

Next, I visited Mystic, which is surprisingly very similar in appearance to a Cornish fishing village, while further along at Stonington is the last commercial fishing port in Connecticut. In Boston, I visited the USS *Constitution*, the oldest serving ship in the U.S. Navy, old enough to have fought in a campaign against us English, and now used as a training ship for Naval Officers. From here, I travelled north through the multicoloured hues of the golden brown leaves of upstate New York in fall to reach the spectacular Niagara Falls. At this point, I turned back south through the undulating, lush green forests of Virginia, so green that from a distance they appear blue and are consequently named the Blue Ridge Mountains.

A fleet of ships accompanied Somers's flagship *Sea Venture*, which included *Blessing*, *Diamond*, *Falcon*, *Lion*, *Swallow*, *Unity*, *Catch* and a vessel built in another recently failed colony at Sagahadoc by the Popham colonists. Using Planetarium software, it is possible to go back in time to make some interesting discoveries about this particular voyage. As the fleet headed down the English Channel and into the open Atlantic, Somers and his crew could have used the planet Venus as their guiding star; it was gone midnight by the time it sank behind the western horizon. Somers had already made his first mistake, since the fleet had set off for an Atlantic crossing at the wrong time of the year. This was a grave oversight for the seventeenth-century navigator, since it marked the start of the hurricane season - not the time to use the yet undiscovered tradewinds for an Atlantic crossing. The hurricane season runs right through the northern hemisphere summer, and officially ends on the first of November. After seven weeks at sea, the flagship lost sight of the rest of the fleet in thick fog. A fierce storm then developed from the northeast, and winds howled for three continuous days.

One particular crew member, William Starchey scrambled onto the bridge of the ship as it blew along in the fierce storm. He prayed in the howling noise of the wind and rain, asking God to spare himself and the lives of the one hundred and fifty men, women and children aboard *Sea Venture*, all colonists destined for the New World. Each time the ship reached the trough of a wave, the sea would overtake and breach the stern. Water then swamped the wooden decks and ran between the damaged seams that had now split wide apart. Down in the flooded bilges, everyone was taking his or her turn to work the pumps. The ship, weighing three hundred tonnes, was already heavily overladen with provisions for the desperate settlers of Jamestown. She had not been designed to withstand these stresses; the storm threatened to sink her with all hands.

Starchey later recorded the following events and his firsthand account, the *True Repertory of the Wreck and Redemption of Sir Thomas Gates*, dated July 15th 1610, is by far the best of this astonishing voyage to the Americas.

"Saint James, his day, July twenty fourth, being Monday. The clouds gathering thick upon us, and the winds singing, and whistling most unusually, a dreadful storm began to blow from out the Northeast, which swelling, and roaring as it were by fits, some hours with more violence than others, at length did beat all light from heaven; which like an hell of darkness turned black upon us, so much as, in such cases, horror and fear use to overrun the troubled, and overmastered senses of all. For four and twenty hours the storm in a restless tumult had blown so exceedingly as we could not apprehend in our imaginations any possibility of greater violence, yet did we still find it, not only more terrible, but more constant, fury added to fury, and made us look one upon each the other with troubled hearts, and panting bosoms: our clamours drowned in the winds, and the winds in thunder. Prayers might well be in the heart and lips, but drowned in the outcries of the officers: nothing heard that could give comfort, nothing seen that might encourage hope.

"The Sea swelled above the clouds, and gave battle unto heaven. Howbeit this was not all; it pleased God to bring a greater affliction yet upon us; for in the beginning of the storm we had received likewise a mighty leak. And the ship in every joint almost, having spewed out her oakum, before we were aware was grown five foot suddenly deep with water above her ballast, and we almost drowned within, whiles we sat looking when to perish from above.

"On the Thursday night Sir George Somers, being upon the watch, had an apparition of a little round light, like a faint star, trembling, and streaming along with a sparkling blaze, half the height upon the mainmast, and shooting sometimes from shroud to shroud, tempting to settle as it were upon any of the four shrouds; the light stays with them half the night, and suddenly disappears upon the morning watch.

"The superstitious seamen make many constructions of this sea-fire *(an electrostatic discharge also known as Saint Elmo's Fire)*, which nevertheless is usual in storms: the same which the Grecians were wont in the Mediterranean to call Castor and Pollux, of which, if one only appeared without the other, they took it for an evil sign of great tempest. But see the goodness and sweet introduction of better hope, by our merciful God given unto us. Sir George Summers, when no man dreamed of such happiness, had discovered, and cried 'Land-O'.

"We found it to be the dangerous and dreaded islands of the Bermuda. And that because they be so terrible to all that ever touched on them, and such tempests, thunders and other fearful objects are seen and heard about them, they be called commonly 'the devil's islands', and are feared and voided of all sea travellers alive, above any other place in this world. Yet it had pleased our merciful God to make even this hideous and hated place both the place of our safety, and means of our deliverance."

From this account, one can easily imagine Starchey standing alongside Somers on the bridge, cold, wet and fatigued. Somers was responsible for the many lives aboard ship, and if the storm did not abate soon, then the consequences would have been disastrous. He may well have thought back to the time of the Biscay storm after a buccaneering voyage in the Azores. There, he had also been separated from the other ships of the fleet, amongst which was Raleigh, who, on his return to England had presumed Somers dead. Later when Somers' ship also returned safely to harbour, he won the reputation from Raleigh as, "a man of good skill in all passages".

The sky was momentarily litup by forked lightning, followed by a loud clap of thunder, and he may well have realised that this storm was to be a greater challenge. The sea still raged as rigging ripped off the main mast. "It's the land of Bermudaz, we could run her aground, it's our only chance," realised Somers. Another wave crashed over the stern and washed along the deck. This time, rigging ripped off the mizzen. The ship rolled and Starchey almost fell, but retained his hold as a terrifying thought occurred to him.

"The Devil's Islands," he spluttered, "are feared and avoided by all sea travellers alive, above any other place in the world."

"Better devils than storms", replied Somers calmly. He gazed into the night and realised a possible way to survive the storm; the rain continued but now it was hardly noticeable in the raging surf. The island was much closer, with a violent onshore wind blowing. Somers still had the choice either to run aground or take in the topsail. This would check the ships drift leeward and give them sea room to pass the island, but he knew they could never weather the storm. Somers looked up at the remaining rigging and cried, "Let out the topsail". The boatswain implemented the order and the shivering wretched crew pulled on halyards. Somers noticed surf breaking on a reef ahead, and realised they were rapidly approaching the shore.

"Down with the top mast!" The last order meant to ease the ship by reducing weight aloft and make the vessel roll less. After checking the continuing drift shoreward, he could feel the keel skim the bottom. An abrupt jolt in the ship's motion threw everything forward. Planking on one side of the hull split inwards and water flooded the lower levels. In terrified panic, everyone started to scramble for the main deck. *Sea Venture* listed, then crashed through a reef and wedged itself between two large rock clefts off the eastern end of mainland Bermuda. As incredible as it sounds, all one hundred and fifty men, women and children made it safely ashore - even the ship's dog survived! I'm not sure what happened to the dog, but I do know what happened next.

Four centuries later, one wonders how on earth Somers and his crew accomplished this remarkable feat at night, in complete darkness, during a raging storm. Even today, using modern technology such as GPS navigation aids, radar and sonar depth sounders, it would be difficult, if not damn near impossible, to repeat it. Using state of the art astronomical software, I placed myself just offshore from the eastern seaboard of Bermuda on that terrible night and early morning of July 27-28th 1609, and the only possible source of light in the night sky - had the cloud momentarily broken - would have been a very thin crescent of the waning moon rising in the east in the early morning; but even this was not bright enough to show up the silhouette of the island, and may well have not occurred until after the shipwreck.

However, I then realised my mistake; the date is from the old Julian calendar, not the currently used Gregorian one!

The Julian calendar was introduced by no other than Julius Caesar himself, and was chosen after consultation with the astronomer Sosigenes of Alexandria, since it had been known since the time of the ancient Greek philosopher Happarchus that a year was about 365 ¼ days long. So the regular year of 365 days was divided into twelve months, and a leap day was added to February every four years. Hence, the Julian year is on average 365.25 days long. In actual fact, a year is about eleven minutes less than this, so about one millennium and half later, all those accumulated minutes amounted to an error of about ten days. A reform had to be made. The spring (Vernal) equinox now occurred on March 11th, and was moving steadily earlier in the calendar each year. Since the equinox was tied to the celebration of Easter, the reform in the calendar was undertaken by the Roman Catholic Church, and the new calendar shifted forward by ten days was named after Pope Gregory XIII; a papal bull known by its opening words as 'Inter Gravissimas' was signed by him to decree this. The new Gregorian calendar was adopted later that year by a handful of countries, with other countries adopting it over the following centuries.

Britain was one of those countries to adopt this calendar much later, in the middle of the eighteenth-century, when the difference was almost eleven days behind. The reason for this is that since the dissolution of the monasteries by Henry VIII, the British had become Protestant and no longer Catholic, and so had retained the old Julian system. At the time of Somers's shipwreck, the difference was still about ten days behind so, correcting the dates of Starchey's accounts by adding on ten days, we have the correct Gregorian night and early morning of the 6-7th of August and a bright half moon setting in the west directly behind Bermuda, showing the desperate crew of the flagship the unmistakable silhouette of the island. At about the time of the shipwreck, the Moon was in the constellation Virgo, a coincidence since another name given to the Bermudas was Virgineola, a smaller edition of Virginia, the British colony founded a few years earlier and named in tribute to the late Virgin Queen.

The survivors came ashore on Bermuda at a spot known today as Discovery Bay, and in the daylight, instead of finding a haunted island, everyone was astonished at the beauty of the place and the wealth of food and supply that could be found. No sign of devils or ghosts, but there were prickly pears, palmetto berries, wild hogs, birds and several types of fish that had never been seen before instead. Somers alone took enough fish in half an hour from the surrounding waters for everyone to have enough food for the whole day.

The castaways remained on these islands for ten months, and in that time they formed the Bermuda colony, building a church and houses. Somers and Sir Thomas Gates, who was also amongst them, oversaw the construction of two ships, *Deliverance* and *Patience*, from the spars and rigging of the wrecked flagship and local cedar timber. There had been several uprisings by renegades, resulting in a hanging, as well as a marriage and two children being born - a boy and a girl named Bermuda and Bermudas. These little baby Bermudians were born to John Rolfe and his wife, who would later die along with four other colonists from natural causes, including Sir Thomas Gates's wife.

In May the following year, the two newly-constructed ships set sail, with one hundred and forty two castaways on board for their initial destination, where the surviving ships of the fleet had long presumed the death of Somers and others of the Sea Venture. On arrival, they found the Virginia Colony almost destroyed by famine and disease, during what has become known as the 'Starving Time'. Very few of the supplies from the Supply Relief Fleet had arrived; the same hurricane which caught *Sea Venture* had also badly affected the rest of the fleet, and only sixty settlers remained alive. Many of the colonists had perished from disease caused by mosquitoes and brackish waters during that summer. The fort had been constructed three years earlier, but had been reduced by fire a year after.

Today at the Jamestown Visitor Center is a description of what the castaways from Bermuda found at the Virginia colony: "The winter had been a classic, the starving time, cruel to the bone, beyond power of telling, each man an experiment in endurance, each man a gravedigger."

There had even been cases of cannibalism among the desperate survivors; one survivor was put to death for eating his wife's dead body. The main failures of the Jamestown colony had been ignorance and folly. A council meeting was called for, during which Sir Thomas decided to abandon the colony, and Admiral Somers suggested sailing to Newfoundland, where it might be the fishing season. This would also be the most likely time to meet up with other English ships and disperse most of the company for the return to England. As they sailed to leave the Chesapeake, they met the new governor of Virginia, Lord de la Warr. It was only through the arrival of the two small ships from Bermuda and then the coincidental arrival of this second relief fleet commanded by Lord 'Delaware' that the abandonment of Jamestown was avoided and the colony was able to survive. An argument did pursue, however, when Lord de la Warr suggested that they all return to Jamestown.

"It was their patriotic duty as colonists to maintain a foothold in the New World over the Spanish," he ordered.

Once back ashore at Jamestown, situated on a small island in a tributary to the Chesapeake Bay, they sterilised river water to drink simply by boiling it. The problem of mosquitoes was also easily resolved by caking oneself in soap - this acted as an ideal repellent. Soap manufacture was then made common practice amongst the colonists simply by mixing animal fats or fish oils, with beech ash furnishing the alkali. The problem of gathering food was not so easily overcome. The surrounding countryside was still mainly uncharted territory, and full of Native American Indians whose relationship with the strange colonists, who could not fend for themselves, had become very strained once again.

Somers volunteered to return to the Bermuda Isles to get supplies, a distance of twenty-eight English leagues. He sailed in *Patience* and with him sailed Captain Samuel Argylle in *Discovery*, although he lost the Admiral in thick fog just off Cape Cod and a month later he found a great bay, which he named after the new governor of Virginia, 'Delaware.' He eventually reached Cape Charles and discovered the Gulf Stream, a thing of much importance as it would later improve our understanding of transoceanic currents and increase safety and efficiency for future Atlantic crossings using the trade winds. This was also the year that another type of exploration was being made back in Europe, as the great scientist Galileo first used a telescope to view the heavens, and opened up a whole new universe for future discoveries.

Meanwhile, Somers reached Bermuda, but had become weak and ill on the journey and died at the age of fifty-six on his beloved island of Bermuda. His health had slowly deteriorated through the many hardships which he had been through, and medical experts today have diagnosed the illness as a possible form of hepatitis, caused by unhygienic conditions, and which can result in fatigue and tiredness, with the liver becoming unable to produce sufficient antibodies. With George Somers was his nephew Mathew Somers, who then inherited the title of Captain of *Patience*, but he lacked the leadership qualities, authority and charisma of the Admiral. Morale amongst the crew became low after his death, and some odd decisions were made. Mathew appears to have insisted on returning to Jamestown with supplies of fish, fowl and hogs, but it was now winter, and after all this time Jamestown must have found alternative plans. So the decision to return to England was made. One today wonders if Mathew's decision was influenced by his needing a body to verify his uncle's death for the benefits of a will.

Whatever the reason, Captain Matthew Somers embalmed his uncle's body and they took it back to England. On the last day of May 1611, a gentle southwesterly breeze blew *Patience* across the English Channel and into Lyme Bay. Fishermen at the Cobb in Lyme were the first to see the weather beaten pinnace, with its unconventional sails, appear through the morning mist as it slowly approached the harbour. The crew looked on eagerly at the approaching land of green pastures and forests that capped the dark cliffs surrounding the bay. As *Patience* approached closer, boatmen at the Cobb recognised the voices of some of its crew, also natives of Lyme. It had been two years since they had left England, and many locals had assumed the worse, never expecting to see any of them again. The excitement was uncontrollable as news of the mysterious vessel spread throughout the shops and homes of Lyme. After the ship docked, the fate of the Admiral also reached the townsfolk. It was hard for them to accept that their most cherished son had died. The crew carried a cedar wood casket onto the Cobb. Following traditional seafaring custom, the remains of the Admiral were taken ashore first, and he was later interred with military honours, allegedly inside the church at nearby Witchurch Canonicorum.

At about this time, William Starchey's accounts of this voyage would reach the ears of a close playwright friend and used in his new play where a reference is made to Bermuda: "We are such stuff that dreams are made of and our little life is rounded on a sleep... Safely in harbour is the king's ship. In the deep nook where once thou called'st me up at midnight to fetch dew from the still-vexed Bermoothes, there she's hid."

The founding of a permanent English colony in the New World, and the establishment of its first Crown colony on Bermuda, certainly was the stuff that dreams are made of. On the first day of November, following the return of *Patience* at the Cobb, Shakespeare first performed *The Tempest* at the Globe Theatre in London, and it may well have even been his favourite play, as he took farewell of the stage as the magician Prospero in his last ever performance. It is a humbling thought that this little fishing village on the south coast of England, which I had adopted as my home, had played such an important role in helping to lay a foundation stone for the most powerful nation of all time - the United States of America.

It's interesting to note that the fictional *Star Trek* classics that I enjoyed as a child (okay then, also as an adult!) was originally an idea created by Gene Roddenberry, influenced by the first colour science fiction film called the *Forbidden Planet*, which was an adaptation of Shakespeare's *Tempest*, which we know was based upon the exploits of Admiral Somers, whose own career was no doubt influenced by Lyme, with its little harbour. It may be a tenuous connection, but it did so impress me during my own career as a charter boat captain when I realised that the idea of Captain Kirk can be connected to the Cobb, proving that, at times, fact can be stranger than fiction.

While researching the archives of the Dorset History Centre for this book, I came across three signatures of George Somers from court records during his term in office as mayor, and shortly after. It is interesting to note that the last signature is on a Borough Council document, and the date indicates he was in Lyme less than four months before his shipwreck off the coast of Bermuda. An examination of this signature by a graphologist indicated something interesting about his personality: "The first noticeable handwriting movement in this signature are the full and inflated letters 'G/g' and 'S' that enter the zone below the baseline. Here we enter the lower zone sphere of strong instincts in the form of food, money, security, deep roots. The first letter 'G' resembles a money bag. All basic instincts are usually associated with this zone, including the subconscious and thoughts below the surface. The large inflated top part of the 'S' suggested someone with a very strong imagination. The letters are somewhat difficult to read taken out of context. The illegibility seen with the large(r) capital letters indicates a proud but enigmatic and private person, one who did not wish to disclose much of his inner self to others. The signature appears to be more simplified and less ornate than others on the same page. This would indicate a person who was not so attention seeking, and therefore possibly more reserved. The writing is also on the small side indicating someone who did not seek attention; he was probably rather shy. Smaller handwriting can indicate a high degree of concentration, realism, sometimes intentional understatement, a distaste for boasting. Some of the letters are connected with an 'angular stroke', indicating a hard-worker with critical ability, someone not always flexible who could be uncompromising. Pointed tops to the letter 'm' indicates a penetrating, fast, and intuitive thinker, one who sizes up situations and grasps facts instantly. The right slanted writing belongs to the sociable group. This person was a good communicator and he possessed drive and was active, goal-minded with the desire for progress. The connected letters indicate logical thinking and the clever linking of letters suggests an innovative way of problem solving. The letters seem wide rather than narrow indicating someone who was both open and broad-minded."

This brief analysis based on handwriting movements of today was provided by the graphologist Margaret Webb and, although not familiar with copybook writing of the seventeenth-century, she assumed that the few people in those days who could write endeavoured to keep to the way they were taught in school, and any deviation from this style at the time would indicate courage and originality. Our illustrious Admiral left behind no original painting of himself, and this is the only evidence we have to date where we can glean anything about this particular merchant venturer's personality.

In 2010, Phil Street, who, I believe as Town Crier had exemplified his duties second to none as an ambassador for Lyme Regis, included this information in a time capsule for the four-hundredth anniversary of Somers' shipwreck and the founding of this country's first crown colony. It is ironic that after months of research to bring to light new information about our illustrious knight and Admiral, information that had remained in the dark for four centuries, a copy has been returned to the dark for another four... Ah, such is the price we pay to preserve our history!

The Jamestown colony was later moved further inland to Williamsburg, and the oldest continuously inhabited British colony in North America, which was also the second successful settlement after Jamestown, was founded by John Carver and English Dissenters seeking religious freedom. These became the settlers of the Plymouth Colony in Massachusetts and are better known today as the 'Pilgrim Fathers'. From the outset, the expedition almost ended in complete disaster as two vessels, *Mayflower* and *Speedwell*, set sail from Southampton. Some of the crew of *Speedwell* deliberately caused their ship to leak, allowing them to abandon their year-long commitments. The ship's Master and remaining crew transferred to *Mayflower*, which set off across the Atlantic with a hundred and two passengers in September 1620.

Halfway through the voyage, *Mayflower* nearly sank in strong winds and storms which had caused a main beam to crack. They even considered the possibility of turning back, but the colonists managed to repair the damage using house construction equipment. A passenger was washed overboard in the storm, but miraculously caught a rope and was rescued; another passenger and a crew member died of disease; while a child was born and named Oceanus during the sixty six day voyage.

Once ashore at Cape Cod, it was imperative for the survival of the colony to make peace with the native Indians; it was now winter in North America and they would need their help to obtain food and survive the harsh weather, if the mistakes at Jamestown were not to be repeated. Exploratory parties found recently cultivated fields and some old buildings which were native-built and some European-built, but they failed to find any natives. Fearing starvation, they borrowed baskets of corn and beans they found in abandoned huts and near Indian graves, which they intended to plant and repay the natives once they had made contact.

By December there was still no contact, and by now many were ill from the effects of scurvy and too weak to search for the natives; also, ice and thick snowfall had restricted exploration efforts. By the end of this first winter, almost half of the colonists would perish. On December 6th (Old Style)/December 16th (New Style), an expeditionary party used a shallop to sail along the cape where they first spotted natives ashore. As the party landed and approached them, they ran away. Remaining ashore overnight, the colonists could hear cries near the encampment. The following morning, they met the Indians, who fired arrows upon them, so the colonists returned fire using the much noisier and more effective firearms they had, then chased them off. This was to be the only contact with the Native Americans for several months to come.

When contact was finally made, the surviving colonists had the shock of their lives as the solitary native Indian who approached them not only spoke fluent English but, as amazing as it sounds, in a familiar London Cockney dialect! His name was Tisquantum, who today is known better as Squanto. It is possible that Native Americans had purposely kept their distance from these new colonists until this English speaking native could be traced for first contact.

Can you just imagine a modern day equivalent of Del Boy from the British sitcom *Only Fools and Horses* meeting the Pilgrim Fathers?

"I heard on the Dog and Bone down at the Nag's Head that you had arrived. Lovely jubbly!"

The disused European-style buildings that the colonists had recently discovered had indicated an earlier contact with Europeans, and the locals were already familiar with the English, who had intermittently visited the northeastern seaboard for fishing and to trade, but in the Cape Cod area relations between the American Indians and the English had been strained by a visit from Thomas Hunt, who ironically had once been a lieutenant to Captain John Smith. Hunt kidnapped people from Patuxet (currently New

Plymouth), and elsewhere to sell them into slavery in Europe. One of these was Squanto, who was sold in Spain for twenty pounds. Some local friars realised what Hunt was doing, and so bought all the Indians to instruct them in the Christian faith. Squanto managed to convince the Friars to let him return home, and he managed to work his passage to London on a fishing boat, where he was then employed for a number of years by John Slany, a shipbuilder. This is how Squanto learned to speak English with his distinct Cockney accent.

Squanto was part of Slany's crew on a failed expedition to North America, where he had the opportunity to return to his homeland. Sadly, he discovered that the Patuxet, along with other New England Native American Indians, had been wiped out by a plague epidemic, possibly smallpox introduced by Europeans. The isolated Indians of a separate continent had no immunity to infectious European diseases. Other Indian tribes, such as the Pokanoket, had also developed a hatred for the English after one group came in, captured numerous people, and shot them for no apparent reason. At this time, there had also been many reciprocal killings in places like Martha's Vinyard and Cape Cod, so it is a wonder that Squanto chose to help the colonists, but he did. Squanto taught the pilgrims how to increase food production by fertilising crops and the best places to catch fish and eels. Had it not been for the interventions of Squanto, and Pocahontas earlier in Virginia, then it is extremely unlikely that permanent English colonies in the New World would ever have been established.

Even though James I despised tobacco smoking and was the first to ban it in public places, this would be the export commodity that would finally establish a permanent colony in Virginia. Despite James' opposition to tobacco, a tactful move by the Virginia Company and its Jacobean colonists in naming Jamestown after him may have been one of the main political reasons to make the colony survive. Raleigh had strove to bring about a permanent English colony in the Americas, and had been one of the earliest to take up tobacco smoking. James, on the other hand, was Raleigh's nemesis, having no interest in a New World colony, preferring instead to make peace with the Spanish. The easiest means of doing this was not to get involved in any New World power struggle.

Today, both here and in the Bible Belt of the Deep South of the States, this monarch is better known for the printing and wholesale distribution of the King James I version of the Bible. By the early seventeenth-century, printing had even arrived in Lyme, and demonstrates that not all of its seafaring community were such gentlemen as the illustrious George Somers, as a printed court order still survives that reads that one "John Bonner, Mariner… has lately in a violent manner beaten his wife!", and was to be arrested and gaoled if he refused to attend the Borough Court to answer to this charge. Paper manufacture would also become another major commodity to finance the American colonies.

The dense virgin forests of Virginia were cut down at an alarming rate to clear land for the tobacco industry. The wood was not only used for the construction and shipbuilding industry, but later for paper mills. When tobacco ripened, it was cut and graded for use in smoking, chewing and sniffing. It was then easier to cut down more woodland than to return nutrients to ground, as there appeared to be an infinite stretch of it to the west. The first frontiersman were woodsman, and as the lush green of the forests shrank towards the west, so the desolate landscape of burnt tobacco stumps grew in the east, blackened by the tar and charcoal. The expanding frontiers produced the Carolinas, named after the term 'carolinus' – 'of (King) Charles (I and II)' - and then Georgia, named after King George. Today, a part of this region of the States is still called the 'Tar Hills', whose hillbilly inhabitants speak a form of English dialect that is almost incomprehensible.

"Honey, take that goddam cigarette outta ya mouth! How on earth do ya expect the limey to unnerstan' a word ya saying?"

"No, no, that's fine," I replied. "Tell him to keep the cigarette in his mouth, as I still wouldn't understand what he's saying!" I replied to the girlfriend of my new-found hillbilly friend, who wasn't herself from the Tar Hills and so could interpret American hillbilly English to American English so that I could 'unnerstan'', then translate back again. Through my interpreter, I established that tobacco was harvested in the summer months and woodcutting was undertaken to a certain extent in the winter. The wood was known as 'plushwood' and used in the paper mills. This had been a long traditional way of life out here and it was a hard one that aged you quickly and shortened lifespans... and does so even today! But nevertheless, it was a life, and back in the seventeenth-century, life was much harder and shorter than it is today. The oaks of the USA are different to ours, having smaller leaves and acorns, but logging would soon become a much bigger industry than here, and was starting to make the colonies very prosperous places indeed, with wood and tobacco being exported all along the eastern seaboard of New England in exchange for imports of cattle, horses and slaves for the newly-formed cotton industry further south and the sugar plantations in the Caribbean.

From Virginia, I managed to hitch a long distance ride with a trucker all the way to Mobile, Alabama. It had been two years since I was last here, and as I stepped out of the truck, the familiar smell of wood pulp from the surrounding paper mills brought with it many fond memories of my career as a yardman in the rich downtown area. From here, I travelled along memory lane – specifically, west again on the I-10 to Baton Rouge. I couldn't have timed my arrival any better, as cash was low again (the story of my life!) and the Louisiana State Fair had begun, so I started yet another new temporary career, this time as a carnie! The interview was most strange, as I answered questions as honestly as I could - no formal qualifications, no experience and no fixed abode, and above all that I was a migrant with no work permit!

"With an accent like that, son, you got yourself a job," replied my new employer, and I walked off wondering what he meant by 'running the BB joint'.

I spent the duration of the fair showing rednecks the virtually impossible task of shooting a red star out of a piece of cardboard with a ball bearing gun! Years later, while working at another carnival (fairground), I would meet my trusted friend Andy, a Welshman who had spent a decade on the road as a carnie, and who told me every trick of the trade at these game shows, an experience that made one feel like a member of the elusive 'Magic Circle'.

About two weeks later, when this particular fair had ended, I walked over the tall bridge on I-10 that spanned the great Mississippi and looked down at the city spread out below, with its many oil refineries along its river banks. I had got the wanderlust once again, and it wasn't long before I got another lift with a trucker, this time to Corpus Christi in Texas, where I spent the night on the beach watching the winter constellation Orion the Hunter rise, with Jupiter shining brightly in Taurus the Bull. Earlier that evening, before sunset, I visited the harbour and someone pointed out Al Capone's wooden cruiser bobbing up and down on its mooring, which I believe he used as a rumrunner in prohibition days. It was still in the same pristine condition as it was when he was avoiding the Internal Revenue Service, and walking around with dodgy contents in his violin case.

The following morning, after a breakfast of freshly-caught fried shrimp from a kiosk near the fishing port, I was on the road once again, and got a lift with a Catholic Priest through a desert of giant cacti towards the Mexican border near a place called Zapata, which incidentally is Spanish for shoe - why it should be named so was beyond me, although I did notice many poor Mexicans illegally shoeing it across the boarder for a better life in the States at Lerado. Here, I crossed the Rio Grande by bridge to Nuevo Lerado in Mexico, in the opposite direction to the wetbacks that openly swam the river. Enroute, I befriended a Mexican going in my direction, who worked as a computer operator in San Antonio and was commuting home to his wife in Mexico. He invited me back and I accepted, to find that home for most Mexicans was in a shanty town; this particular one was in the suburbs of Monterrey.

The next day, I walked through the depressing landscape of breeze block homes with rusted corrugated roofs and open pit sewers with piles of burning rubbish and plastic, half-starved dogs barking and scrawny cockerels crowing. Eventually, the slums disappeared, followed much later by the rubbish-strewn streets typical of shanty town suburbia. I had reached the open desert once again, and my next lift was with a very drunk Mexican who zigzagged his way along a metalled road in the middle of what could only be described as 'nowhere'. We finally stopped at a red brick building in 'nowhere', and I was delighted to discover that it was an old traditional tequila distillery.

Technically this was a refinery of Mezcal tequila, an alcoholic beverage that was first produced just a few decades after the conquest of Mexico by the conquistadors, and is North America's oldest distilled drink. This is modern day tequila's grandparent, named after a small town in a valley in Jalisco state. The word 'tequila' is said to be an ancient Nahuatl Indian word meaning 'the place of harvesting plants'. Agave, the plant from which tequila is distilled, also produces a hemp-like fibre used to make rope, mats, clothing and paper. My drunken amigo introduced me to his amigo who worked at the refinery, and who was more than happy to show me how they produced Mezcal, which nowadays is shrouded in many urban myths.

For a start, tequila is not made from a cactus, but from the sugar-rich part of the agave bulb, called the piña. The plant is cut down and the piña is dug up and hacked up with a machete into chippings, which are baked in a rock-lined pit oven over charcoal, and covered with layers of Agave fibre mats and earth; this gives the Mezcal its distinct strong, smoky flavour. The chippings are washed in an open stream which, in the refinery I visited, ran to a huge vat as large as a modest-sized room. At one end, a tap dripped the final product of Mezcal tequila, just like heavy water production for a nuclear bomb. This was no watered-down version with its touristy worm that dumb American college kids drank in sports bars while whooping on their favourite team in a ball game… This stuff was for the cleverer American college graduates, who no doubt used it for rocket fuel when they became astronauts. Its colour was grey from the charcoal chippings, and it tasted like smoke-flavoured moonshine. The stuff was dynamite and it sold for about two dollars a bottle, so I decided to purchase two of them - one for the road (so to speak), and the other to transport back home and introduce real tequila to Europe.

From 'nowhere', I travelled southwest on up into the hills, where the scenery changed into woodland of dense pinewood forests with many sawmills. It was now evening and I found a spot to sleep just off Highway 40, about two hundred and fifty miles from Durago. I slept literally like a log after just a couple of capfuls of Mezcal, which was enough to make me completely comatose. In the days that followed, the scenery gradually changed again as I descended the highlands along sharp hairpin bends with breathtakingly steep sides, where the occasional burned wreckage of a car, lorry and even a bus could be seen and crossed the Tropic of Cancer into beautiful subtropical jungle that ran almost the whole distance to the beach at Mazatlan. First time at sea level since Texas, I had crossed three of Mexico's principal mountain ranges - the Sierra Madre Oriental, the Altiplano, and finally the Sierra Madre Occidental. What a strange place Mazatlan was, as that night I sat on the beach sipping tequila and watched two moons rise!

If there is anything harder than trying to understand a ferry timetable, then this must have been it - a ferry timetable in Spanish! After a considerable time, I fathomed it out - no pun intended - and purchased a ticket from the ferry terminal office, only to find out that the timetable was out of date and completely wrong. As I walked across the parking lot, clutching my ticket for the next day's voyage, someone called out,"Hey gringo!"

I looked around at some grey-haired old boy stepping out of a British MG sports car, of all things. "You got any idea how that goddam ferry timetable works?"

This was my introduction to Alec Shilin, an eccentric retired American of Russian descent; his grandfather was once the chauffeur to the Tsar, and little did we know it at the time, but Alec was about to be mine back into the States. He was heading home to Sacramento, California after a vacation in Mexico, and had also been completely flummoxed by the timetable. After helping Alec get his tickets for the ferry crossing to the Baja California peninsula for his drive north, he returned the favour in the nearby Senor Frogi's bar, and introduced me to the tequila cocktail that it is famous for – a Margarita (as if I needed the encouragement with the amount I had already had). Amongst the noise of music and the table dancing by both Mexicans and American tourists, we swapped life stories, and I learnt that Alec was an active septuagenarian, who had retired from a lifetime career on the railroads but still enjoyed travelling. It was his suggestion to keep a travel diary to record my experiences, a diary that finally evolved into this book.

The following evening, the Sea of Cortez was like a mirror as the setting sun reflected off its still surface. The ferry pulled out of the dock, and I assured Alec that we were in for a smooth passage. I couldn't have been more wrong, as a storm blew up that night and I had one of the roughest sea voyages of my life. The bow of the ferry crashed through each wave and had its cargo of cars and trucks not been firmly chained to the deck of the hull, then the resultant damage caused by this rolling would surely have sunk us.

The next morning, once safely ashore at La Paz, we drove about five hundred miles non-stop north on Carretera Federal one, the main highway that runs through scrubland desert with giant cacti. The highway itself runs all the way up the Baja peninsula to the US border, a distance of about eight hundred miles. By evening, we were looking for a motel for the night and ended up on a dirt track that ran east back towards the gulf. The Gulf of California is only named Cortez locally, and is one of the most diverse seas in the world, being home to more than five thousand species of macro-invertebrates. The mainland is known as Baja California, and has the second longest and most isolated peninsula in the world, with varied wildlife, including buzzards, pelicans and coyotes. As evening approached, I watched a myriad of fireflies dancing amongst the brush for the first time. I've heard stories back home from the previous generation to mine of children once catching these insects in jam jars and using them as a nightlight; but pollution in the UK has now completely eliminated them.

Baja, California was initially thought to be an island and depicted on early maps as the 'Island of California', making it one of the most famous cartographic errors in history. It was one of the men who had mutinied during an exploratory expedition of the conquistador Hernán Cortés, who accidentally discovered the southern part of the 'island'. The legendary island had been thought by the Conquistadors to be the Garden of Eden, its location having long since been moved a substantial distance further east across the Pacific than at the time of Columbus, and it being now believed to be inhabited by a tribe of black Amazonian women. It is interesting to note that some early cartographers had correctly joined the Baja peninsula to the mainland, such as the Dutchman Joannes Janssonius in 1613; although later, in 1680, another Dutchman Frederick de Wit had decided it must be an island and therefore disconnected it again. At this time, it was even postulated that the Sea of Cortez may even be the fabled Northwest Passage. Needless to say, neither cartographer had ever left their offices in Amsterdam to travel to California to confirm their suspicions, but had relied only on secondary sources instead.

We came to a fork in the dirt track road, and the route we chose came to a dead end at the ghostly ruins of a whaling station, for here in the bay is the nursing ground for the grey whale that migrates between here and Alaska's Bering Sea. Parts of the old and rusted corrugated roof flapped in the cool evening breeze. The discovery that the Sea of Cortez was the nursing ground much sought after by commercial whalers almost brought the species to extinction back in the early twentieth-century. Had whaling not been banned under the Endangered Species Act, then almost certainly none would exist today.

Back at the fork in the road, we took the alternate route in a second attempt to find the main highway. For many miles we drove through a landscape of ranches, until we arrived at a solitary building which looked like an old-fashioned saloon bar; we assumed it must also be a motel, which in a sense it was. We pulled up on the dusty parking lot, got out of the MG, and walked through the swing doors like lost cowboys. Inside the old wooden building, we were both instantly transported back in time. Chickens ran out of our way across the dirt floor, old fans hung from the ceiling rotating blades in a cloud of cigarette smoke and many glamorously dressed *senoritas* came over to greet us; this sort of place is better known in this part of the world as a 'cantina'. In a nutshell, we had accidentally stumbled across a brothel for local farmhands, but it is worth mentioning here simply for being exactly as you would expect a cowboy saloon to have looked like a century ago! You could easily imagine Wyatt Earp and Doc Holliday playing cards at one of the tables.

The metalled roads that we had traversed were so bumpy and the midday temperatures so hot that, to my dismay, the reserved bottle of tequila that I was hoping to take back home exploded in the trunk of Alec's car. He was equally dismayed, as you could smell the stuff on everything for the rest of our journey. The landscape changed again as we continued north through scrubland desert, then mountains, and into sierra once again. We crossed the border at Tijuana, the notorious border town where I had caught the bus and got myself robbed on that first trip to the States. Our adventure together across Baja, California came to an end at San Diego, when Alec dropped me off in downtown before carrying on to his home in Sacramento. We swapped addresses and I promised to pay a visit to meet his family the next time I was in the area, but on this trip I had purchased a round-the-world air ticket, and was planning Australia next.

In San Diego, I was soon back to my former occupation as a yardman, and I even acquired accommodation by house sitting for a realtor company while the property was up for sale. It was a huge middle-class American home with its own swimming pool and a patio that overlooked the Pacific Ocean, and all I had to do was keep the place tidy for the occasional visiting prospective buyer.

The property was above Ocean Beach on Saratoga Avenue, not far from the Point Loma lighthouse. Nearby is the Cabrillo Monument and it was from this spot that, on Christmas Day, I watched a herd of grey whales about three miles offshore migrating back from Alaska, almost certainly towards Baja California. I thought of Alec and that crazy drive through Mexico. We kept in contact and the following summer, both him and his son Danny visited me in England. After my trip to Australia, it took two consecutive bad seasons on the boats in Lyme before I decided to take a year off and travel the North American continent, and the first thing I did was to visit Alec in Sacramento.

I again flew into New York and, once through immigration, sent Alec and his family a postcard to let them know I had arrived safely on the continent for a grand tour of the States, and keeping to my promise I would be visiting them at some point. The majority of the research for this book was about to begin, and it wasn'tlong before I was walking west through the Big Apple, with the standard backpack slung over my shoulders, to a truck stop on the outskirts of the city. A police car passed by with the cop remarking through his mic, "Keep on walking, you transient bum!"*And you have a nice day too*, I thought. With that sort of reception, how easy was it going to be to research this book?

Now this was just a simple case of mistaken identity; how were they to know I wasn't some transient bum? I certainly looked like it; I had the backpack to prove it, something which immediately stereotypes you as a homeless, unemployed person here in America. How could they possibly know I was a low-budget British traveller, over here to explore America and write a book about my adventures, unless they had actually stopped and asked?

When the police had gone, I thought back to Lyme and the two bad seasons I had just experienced on the boats. Even then, it was a case of mistaken identity, as the other boatmen assumed I had poached the few customers who had visited Lyme and blamed me for causing the decline in tourism. At the time, I thought the hostility and anger towards me was generated by jealousy. I was the youngest boatman at the Cobb, and the most proactive, with new ideas for getting customers on boats and for advertising these trips. I'd even created a tripping boat tour, which included a commentary on the local history of the area, something that had never been thought of before, but even this generated hostility. I'd had enough of small-town politics and so decided to get out of it for a year.

I couldn't have picked a better time, as the real reason for this decline resulted from a combination of factors, such as bad sea and weather conditions during the peak season, and the opportunity of cheap package holidays abroad, where families were virtually guaranteed good weather. Lyme was in for another equally bad season; the third in a row, which was about to see almost every business at the Cobb sell up and change hands - not just the boats, but pubs, hotels and restaurants would all be affected by the summer of '93, which was about to be another 'summer' that never happened.

Even when I returned after a year away, the jealousy never abated, and it wasn't until I started researching Lyme's historical archives that I found out the real reason why, and the terrible secret that Lyme was hiding. As crazy as it sounds, it was not jealousy from other competing boatmen that was the reason I was having such a difficult time but rather because most of the population of Lyme did not want me delving too deep into the town's past, because they all had something to hide. It was going to take a few more seasons before I found out exactly what this was all about.

On top of the decline was the bad publicity that was about to be generated from the Lyme Bay Canoeing Tragedy and the death of four teenagers. It's ironic but on the day of this disaster, I was leaving Lyme for my year off to America. I had gone down to my parents' burger bar on the seafront to say my farewell and best wishes for the season to come, which was also to be their last before they retired, when I noticed the bosun to a privately owned outdoor activities centre looking out to sea, wondering where a party of canoeists had gone. The wind was offshore, and the sea flat calm near the coast except for the direction in which the bosun was looking, to the east where the Charmouth Funnel blew. I suggested that maybe they had continued up into the river Char; he shrugged his shoulders and agreed, as it was the most logical conclusion. I found out months later that sadly, as I was leaving Lyme, the group of eight schoolchildren and their teacher, accompanied by two instructors, had headed out into the direction of this easterly wind and, as a result of a series of errors and circumstances, the party had run into difficulties just offshore from Charmouth as one kayak became swamped. The group was swept out to sea by the easterly blowing Charmouth Funnel, where all the kayaks were quickly swamped, resulting in the four drownings.

In less time than it took for the postcard to reach Alec and his family, I managed to hitch the breadth of the American continent from New York City to Sacramento. In record time, I travelled along Interstate 80 through Pennsylvania, Ohio and Indiana to a huge truck-stop at Gary on the outskirts of Chicago, Illinois; then another ride took me across the prairies of Iowa, Nebraska, Wyoming, the deserts of Utah and Nevada and through the Rockies at the Donna Pass to Sacramento, California. The second truck driver drove so fast that we covered a thousand miles in just thirteen hours; he was so high on crack cocaine, which he smoked through a pierced soda can that he used as a makeshift pipe throughout the journey.

I stayed for a while with Alec's family, and when funds got low I found work aboard a New Orleans-style paddle steamer, of all things! Unfortunately not as the Captain but at the slightly reduced rank of 'bus boy', cleaning tables in the restaurant for a percentage of the waitresses' tips, which varied depending on how fast I cleared away the dirty crockery and wiped the tables. The beautiful *Matthew McKinley* was a tourist boat that did a return trip every evening from the 'Old Town' along the Sacramento River. I was told by the crew that one of its previous owners was none other than John Wayne, the Duke himself, who had used it in the film *Blood Alley* with Lauren Bacall, although I was unable to verify this story during my research for this book. Anyway, even if it isn't true, it was a nice thought to have as I would have my break halfway through the cruise, sitting out on the rear deck, smoking a cigarette and watching the paddle splash though the water beneath a spectacular star-lit night. Despite it being diesel powered rather than the traditional steam powered stern wheeler, and thus not having had the history of an original, it was still like something out of Mark Twain's *Life on the Mississippi. Matthew* was also used for longer trips to San Francisco, which captured what it must have been like to make such a journey in those Wild West cowboy times of the nineteenth-century.

The old town is also famous for its cowboy connections, particularly the Pony Express, the first transcontinental mail service that began here - or rather ended, depending which way your mail was sent across the continent - and also the California Gold Rush, whose gold-seekers were also called the 'Forty-niners' referring to 1849, the year that it all started. Alec once drove me to a spot famous for panning gold. I can't say that I caught the gold fever, but I did find a minute little speck of the stuff panning the Sacramento River, using a borrowed hub-cap from his MG sports car.

My local bar was the Back Door Lounge, an original cowboy saloon, not like the cantina Alec and I had found in Baja, but more updated for the tourists who frequented the old town. It had an upstairs balcony where, allegedly, a cowboy had been lynched for cattle rustling, and to this day a pianist, whom I befriended, still plays away at one end of the bar. We joked one night about the saloon being a great film set for *Casablanca* - I even mimicked Bogart with an English accent; "Play it again, Sam! Play it." From that moment onwards, every time I walked in through those swing doors, he would suddenly change whatever he was playing to a rendition of 'As Time Goes By'.

It was here in Sacramento that I went to my first Star Trek convention, and the only way I could get to the Masonic hall where it was held was by using the city bus. No way was I going to dress up as Captain Kirk for the convention and use public transport, so I arrived normally dressed and stuck out like a sore thumb. There must have been over a thousand Trekkies at this convention, from every walk of life and every age group, from young Vulcans and Klingons - one of which was still in the pram - to an old man who must have been in his nineties dressed as a Starfleet Admiral - and me as the only one not in a costume. I met the beautiful Grace Lee-Whitney and got a signed photograph from her. She is better known for her role as Yeoman Rand in the original Star Trek series and to non-Trekkies as the stunning leggy blond who is said to have started the 60s miniskirt craze in her small, tight-fitting uniform.

One evening in the downstairs saloon of the Back Door, a beautiful girl walked in with jeans and cowboy hat. Well, that was enough for me, and before I knew it I was talking in accentuated English again. Her name was Lisa and she introduced me to Manhattan Ice Tea, after several of which I took her upstairs to the lounge bar with the pianist; and sure enough and as regular as clockwork, as we walked in through the swing doors, "… You must remember this… A kiss is still a kiss…"

Nicely timed, I thought, and tipped 'Sam' to play it again. It worked, and it wasn't long before the cowboy hat came off and she looked me in the eyes and asked, "I always wanted to know how an Englishman kisses…"

… Anyway, I'm not going to bore the reader with any of my conquests in the States, but rather how, on this occasion, it came very close to prompting my downfall, and thus serves as a warning for any single Englishman travelling the States.

From the Back Door, we went onto the Saturday night line-dance with many cowboys and cowgirls in a night club the size of an aircraft hangar, something I had never experienced before and I was amazed how everyone kept in perfect step. Little did I know in those days that they spent the rest of the week practising! In California, it is still legal to carry a firearm as long as two thirds of it is uncovered; in the nightclub, I noticed many with pistols in holsters. At the pool table I was still chatting to Lisa with an accentuated English accent, which definitely works for me, but is very bruising for the male American ego. As we shot a game and I explained the difference between British and American rules, two very tall, wiry built cowboys, each with a pair of pistols came over. One leaned down, stared me close in the face and barked, "Duth you knowth whath I duth for a livingth?" I looked up at a nose flattened across the face of the meanest looking cowboy I had ever seen.

"Line dancing," I quipped.

Well, you can imagine his reaction to that little thigh slapper. I'm obviously using artistic licence, as I certainly would not be here writing this today if I had made such a comment. The truth is I nervously shook my head and said nothing.

"I ride boollths bareback!"

Ouch! *That's one hell of a thing to do for a living*, I thought. Then, realising my present predicament was more dangerous than his while on a wild bull in a rodeo straining its genitalia with a rope reign, I had to think fast, as his ego had been bruised because I was chatting up the pretty blonde at the pool table. I had to quickly turn things around.

"Wow! You're the first real cowboy I've ever met. I'm from England and we don't have them over there," I replied, sounding impressed with my British accent.

He returned a toothless grin and I was relieved that his ego had been restored. This was my first encounter with an Okey, a cowboy from the state of Oklahoma, mainly descendants from Scandinavian immigrants. Tough, tall, of wiry build and probably the nearest thing you can get today to the original of Steinbeck, who wrote of them and their plight in his *Grapes of Wrath*. Set during the Great Depression, the story focuses on a poor family of sharecroppers, the Joads, driven from their Oklahoma ranch by a terrible drought that destroyed crops and laid waste to the Midwest. This economic hardship was also due to changes in the agriculture industry that coincided with this dust bowl, and many thousands of Okey families just like the Joads set off in an almost no-win scenario to California in search of land, jobs and dignity.

Steinbeck had a strong passion for what happened and in preparation for this novel, he wrote, "I want to put a tag of shame on the greedy bastards who are responsible for this [the Great Depression and its effects]". He won a large following amongst the working class population of America, and later the Nobel Prize for Literature. For an insight into American life in these times, I have always strongly recommended reading both Steinbeck and Twain, even to Americans; in my opinion, they definitely wrote the best guidebooks.

Sacramento is situated in the middle of a desert, and therefore it is of no surprise that summer was scorching hot. In July, I headed north along Highway 101 through the Humboldt Redwoods State Park, also known as the 'Avenue of the Giants' for its impressive giant redwood trees, which are the tallest in the world. The sequoia can live for over 2,500 years and it was a humbling thought that most of these trees were around when the Romans ruled the known world.

The '101' became a coast road at Eureka, the town named after that famous exclamation by Archimedes on making a discovery, in this case no doubt gold during the Gold Rush; and from here onwards the landscape, with its backdrop of ocean, was spectacular. I soon forgot about the ugly cities of Southern California; north of the Golden Gate is far better, I decided. I went through Washington State via Oregon, and the scenery suddenly became more mountainous. It was here that I took time off hitchhiking to properly hike the Cascade Mountain Range. From a peak overlooking the Coldwater Lake I could see Mount St. Helens in the distance, made famous for its catastrophic eruption in 1980. I remembered as a school kid back in the UK seeing glorious red sunsets after this eruption, because so much debris had been ejected into the upper atmosphere – incredible.

Washington State must be the last true frontier of the North American Continent, with its endless wilderness of open fields not yet converted into farmland. I crossed the border into Canada and continued through the logging country of British Columbia. At the bar in a log cabin roadside pub, I met a very old man drinking and smoking and chatting away to the regulars. Not so surprising, you might think. Until, like me, you find out that he's over one hundred and ten years old! Both the town I was in and his name escape me, as my records on this particular trip into Canada were destroyed in the inclement weather to come. I do remember him being a bit of a character, and a well-known local icon. We soon struck up a conversation and in between sipping our beers, I asked the obvious, "What's the secret to your longevity?"

"Never do anything strenuous first thing in the mornings, especially when you haven't quite woken up properly!"

"How do you mean?" I enquired.

He took a long draw from his cigarette, then exhaled the smoke and replied, "Well it may not seem stressful at your tender age but as you get older, the most ordinary and simple things can put an unforgiving stress on the heart, and the heart is the most vulnerable organ when you first get out of bed. You wouldn't believe how many end their lives on the toilet seat first thing in the morning!"

For days after meeting the wizened old man, I was determined to reach Alaska, and even though it was now August, with over twenty hours of daylight, the climate had changed to a continuous deluge of rain. It had been pouring for many days in British Columbia and just ten miles from Alaska's border I gave up, as everything I possessed was soaking wet - even my sleeping bag and dry clothes. I was cold, wet and miserable as I turned back in a torrential downpour and hitched south again, eventually coming back into California and camping for a while at the foot of the beautiful El Capitan in Yosemite National Park.

Back in San Diego, at Point Loma Marina, I gained temporary work as a deckhand on a tuna sport fishing boat. Not only was the vessel much larger than anything I had experienced back in Dorset, but again the American way of doing things was also very different. The head decky was a crazy Vietnam war vet with an attitude who seemed to have the idea that he was back fighting that war, rather than on a mere fishing trip. This would be my first and last trip on a Californian sport fishing vessel, but it was certainly an experience, especially when the customers arrived all dressed in combats as if going to war. You guessed it - most of them were also eccentric, gung-ho Vietnam war vets! On our second day out, we started catching blue- and even rarer yellowfin tuna, and as I learned later, this would be an above average catch.

The film *Jurassic Park* had recently been released, and the Captain so named this rich fishing ground after the film. The coastline near Lyme is famous for its Jurassic age fossils, and from the sport fishing captain's nick-name for this tuna ground, I coined the phrase Jurassic Coast when I returned to the UK. Later on that afternoon, while drifting over this *Jurassic Park* feeding frenzy somewhere off the Mexican coast, some anglers started reeling in the occasional full-sized tuna that had been bitten clean in half. Then, all of a sudden, I watched as one particular angler struggled to reel in the largest tuna one could possibly imagine. I grabbed a long pole gaff and was about to hook this beast as it struggled to escape at the surface when 'Rambo', the head decky, pushed me out of the way, making me miss the gaff. I soon realised why he had done this, as a giant hammerhead shark breached the surface and snapped the fishing line. It had also been joining in the feeding frenzy, snapping at the readily caught tuna.

Even though I had enjoyed myself in the Wild West, the pace of life was just a little too fast and hectic for me, and I missed the slower more laid back style of the Deep South; soon I was back at an Interstate truck stop hitching for a ride east. My first lift actually took me north on I-15 to a place called Barstow in the heart of the Mojave National Preserve. At the time this seemed a good idea, as I was now far enough north to cross the Midwest without passing through Texas which, from previous experience, I had found tediously long to get from one side to the other. I walked from the junction at I-40 where I was dropped off to the next truck stop, which was a bad move, as I was just south of Death Valley and it was about midday in August. The hottest place on Earth! I couldn't have walked more than a mile when I seriously started to overheat. I found a bar just in the nick of time, staggered into the cool air-conditioned environment and ordered a Coke with as much ice as possible. I was shaking so much from hypothermia that I very nearly collapsed at the bar. I sat down and dropped my head into my arms from sheer exhaustion. Moments later, when I had cooled down enough to stop shaking, I looked up and a Native American met my gaze, smiled and said profoundly, "There ain't no stop sign at the end of your road."

He was right - my road is endless and it is impossible to reach such an end, let alone there being a stop sign telling me when I have. I could spend a whole lifetime travelling the States, it was so huge; maybe even several lifetimes, and still not see all of it. In that year alone, with the exception of Alaska, Hawaii, the Dakotas and Maine, I had visited all the others states, forty five in all, and to date I still haven't been to those last five.

Before the end of that month, I was broke and in downtown Mobile, Alabama. Once again, things had got that desperate on my journey here that I had even sold blood plasma at the Louisiana State University in Baton Rouge. Something Brits could do back in those days, until it was banned because we all contracted 'mad-cow' disease. On Government Street, I passed the Attorney's office where I had started my career as a yardman on my first trip to the States, and noticed two construction workers replacing part of the wooden panelling. I asked them for work but they didn't have any, and as I walked off they had second thoughts and called me back. These two Alabama boys were Jim and Kevin, both carpenters who had more than enough work - not here in Mobile but on the Gulf Shores, the Alabama coast that was rapidly being converted into a Florida-style tourist resort. I spent the rest of that summer working for them on a luxury holiday home they were building which, incidentally, still stands to this day after an earthquake and two hurricanes!

From here, I travelled on through Florida, finding any work I could, and ending up in Key West once again, this time painting a hotel ironically named the Trade Winds. Early the following spring, I headed north towards New York and my flight home, via the Jamestown National Park and the foot of the John Smith statue.

On my way up to New York, we crossed the Potomac River, and the truck driver told me the urban myth of George Washington throwing a dollar coin across this river as we crossed over the Interstate 95 Bridge at Washington DC. The river was at least a mile wide at this point. The end of the French and Indian Wars here in the former British colonies had been a costly affair, and King George III and his government wanted to tax the colonists to recoup this expense and also to re-establish control over the increasingly independent colonial governments.

Such actions as the Stamp Act, the levies imposed by the Townsend Acts and then the Boston Massacre, only agitated the colonists, and strained relations with the mother country. Parliament retracted all taxes on the colonists except for a small tea import duty tax, which they cleverly retained in a bid to exercise their right to tax the colonies. As the colonists had no representation in Parliament, they rightly believed that even this small taxation was unfair.

The struggling East India Company was given the monopoly by the British government to import tea into America at a greatly reduced duty, which the colonists would have to pay for the imported tea - the idea being that if the colonists paid even this small duty on tea, they would be accepting Parliament's right to tax them. They had wrongly assumed that the American colonists would rather pay this tax than deprive themselves the pleasure of a cuppa.

The Americans were not fooled by this, and so refused the East India Company to land tea at the ports of Philadelphia and New York. In Charleston, the ships were allowed to land their cargo of tea, but it was immediately confiscated and remained in a warehouse for three years, until it was sold by the patriots to help finance the revolution.

The Boston Tea Party was the fuse needed to ignite the explosion that would lead to America's independence. With the arrival of three tea ships in Boston Harbour, as many as seven thousand angry patriots milled about the wharf where the ships were docked and a mass meeting was held at the Old South Meeting House, where a decision was made that the three ships were to leave harbour without paying any duty. A selected committee then took this message to the Customs House, where the Collector of Customs refused the ships to leave without paying this duty. The committee reported this back to the Meeting House and that night, two hundred men, disguised as Indians and whopping war cries, marched to the wharf, boarded the three tea-laden ships and dumped their cargoes into the harbour.

George Hewes was a member of this band of 'Indians', and his recollection of the event was published a few years later. We now join his account of what happened that evening when they marched to the wharf and boarded the British ships: "It was now evening, and I immediately dressed myself in the costume of an Indian, equipped with a small hatchet, which I and my associates denominated the tomahawk, with which, and a club, after having painted my face and hands with coal dust in the shop of a blacksmith, I repaired to Griffin's wharf, where the ships lay that contained the tea. When I first appeared in the street after being thus disguised, I fell in with many who were dressed, equipped and painted as I was, and who fell in with me and marched in order to the place of our destination. When we arrived at the wharf, there were three of our number who assumed an authority to direct our operations, to which we readily submitted. They divided us into three parties, for the purpose of boarding the three ships which contained the tea at the same time. The name of him who commanded the division to which I was assigned was Leonard Pitt. The names of the other commanders I never knew.

"We were immediately ordered by the respective commanders to board all the ships at the same time, which we promptly obeyed. The

Commander of the division to which I belonged, as soon as we were on board the ship, appointed me boatswain, and ordered me to go to the Captain and demand of him the keys to the hatches and a dozen candles. I made the demand accordingly, and the Captain promptly replied, and delivered the articles; but requested me at the same time to do no damage to the ship or rigging. We then were ordered by our commander to open the hatches and take out all the chests of tea and throw them overboard, and we immediately proceeded to execute his orders, first cutting and splitting the chests with our tomahawks, so as thoroughly to expose them to the effects of the water.

"In about three hours from the time we went on board, we had thus broken and thrown overboard every tea chest to be found in the ship, while those in the other ships were disposing of the tea in the same way, at the same time. We were surrounded by British armed ships, but no attempt was made to resist us.

"... The next morning, after we had cleared the ships of the tea, it was discovered that very considerable quantities of it were floating upon the surface of the water; and to prevent the possibility of any of its being saved for use, a number of small boats were manned by sailors and citizens, who rowed them into those parts of the harbor wherever the tea was visible, and by beating it with oars and paddles so thoroughly drenched it as to render its entire destruction inevitable."

America gained its well-earned independence, and also inherited a terrible legacy from the British. When in the next century Lincoln met the frail and elderly Harriet Stowe at the outbreak of the American Civil War, he is reputed to have said, "So you're the little lady who started this big war". Even Queen Victoria was moved to tears after reading this little lady's novel *Uncle Tom's Cabin.* She was certainly not amused, and God bless her majesty's little cotton socks for being so, since the use of slave labour for both the cotton- and tobacco-growing industry is exactly what the story is all about, and it was the British who had started it all. The book was the bestselling novel of the nineteenth-century and second only to the Bible as the bestselling book. The anti-slavery theme focuses on the character of Uncle Tom, a long-suffering slave, around whom the stories of both other slaves and slave owners revolve.

Harriet and her husband had a very religious upbringing and both supported the 'underground railroad', a network of secret routes and safe houses used by escaped slaves to reach either the free states or Canada; they even housed several fugitive slaves in their own home. When Congress passed the Fugitive Slave Law, prohibiting assistance to fugitives, Stowe presented her objections on paper and the forty-year-old mother of seven children sparked a national outcry. The country became divided along the Mason-Dixie line, with free states to the north and slave states in the south. This, along with other economic and political factors, such as the abolition of slavery and the unification of all states, escalated into the American Civil War. Britain, having vested interests in the slave and plantation industry, initially erroneously sided with the south, but Queen Victoria opposed this - possibly after reading Stowe's work.

It is interesting to note that one of the first skirmishes that led to the American Civil War involved another Washington, this time the grandson of that first President. Britain came very close on two occasions to being at war with the Union. The first was the Trent Affair, when Confederate diplomats to Britain and France were seized and arrested aboard the British merchant ship *Trent* by Union agents. This triggered anti-Union feeling amongst the British, which led to both eleven thousand British troops being deployed in Canada, and the Royal Navy ready on standby to capture New York City. The situation was assuaged by both Victoria's husband Prince Albert, who intervened to calm the situation, and Lincoln who, realising that it was not of any advantage to the Union cause by entering into war with Britain again, ordered the prisoners released. The second mistake, this time on Britain's behalf, was caused by the British shipyard John Laird & Sons, which built two warships for the Confederates, despite strong Union protest, one of which was the CSS *Alabama,* which caused so much damage that Britain was forced to pay fifteen and a half million dollars compensation, and apologise to the American government after the war for the destruction caused by these ships.

The most enormous casualties occurred when Grant drove on Richmond, which resulted in a death toll in excess of one hundred thousand men. Several smaller battles are also notorious for their casualties, such as at Franklin in Tennessee, when General Hood's

Confederates lost over six thousand of a total army of twenty one thousand, mostly within the first two hours of battle. The Battle of Gettysburg resulted in the greatest losses in any Civil War battle, with the Twenty Sixth North Carolinas having the greatest percentage loss of any regiment in the war; seven hundred and fourteen out of a total of eight hundred men, almost ninety percent. On the first day, this regiment reported five hundred and eighty four dead and wounded, and at roll-call for G Company the following morning, the Sergeant lay on a stretcher with a severed leg and only one man answered, because - lucky for him - he had been knocked unconscious by a shell burst the previous day. Experts have pointed out that the famed Charge of the Light Brigade at Balaclava resulted in a loss of thirty seven percent of its men, while at least sixty three Union regiments lost as many as fifty percent in single engagements. Confederate records are not so accurate because of their loss or destruction during and since the war.

One is left speechless after researching this bloody war and thinking of that idiom 'the pen is mightier than the sword', because it was such a terrible and wasteful loss that had developed from the pen in that little old lady's hand. Passions ran extremely high on both sides during the war, with relatives fighting against their own families, and in some cases fathers fighting their own sons, resulting in a death toll of over six hundred thousand Americans, with some modern day experts estimating a figure closer to seven hundred thousand. Either way, both figures are far greater than the total loss of all American lives in every campaign they have ever been involved in since. This includes each World War, Vietnam and those continuing today in the post-9/11 campaigns.

CHAPTER 4

'For whosoever commands the sea commands the trade; whosoever commands the trade of the world commands the riches of the world, and consequently the world itself.'
- Walter Raleigh

Four days I spent skulking around 'Muelle Deportivo', the marina in Las Palmas used for visiting yachts, asking boat owners for work crewing to any destination across the Atlantic. Eventually *Lady Luck* found me, in the form of a forty-foot 'channon class' built in Rhode Island. The owner of this yacht and his single crew member were both retired American physicians.

"Have you had any experience?" asked the owner, John.

"A little. I almost completed six seasons as a charter boat skipper back in the UK."

"A little! That seems quite a lot," he replied.

I grinned modestly and he suggested that it would be a good idea for us to all meet back at the boat tonight, when he would take us out to dinner, where we could talk about it and see if I was suitable for the job. That evening I met John and Bill aboard *Lady Luck* and we proceeded to walk to the restaurant in the old town, just to the south of the marina.

"Have you ever been around the old town?" asked Bill.

I tried to impress them with my recent visit to the Casa de Colon.

"Yes, I went and had a look at the house Columbus lived in before he set off and discovered your own country," I replied coyly.

"Yeah, they have one of those on nearly every island around here. We have the same thing back in the states with a little plaque that says 'George Washington once slept here'," replied John.

We all started laughing, and I felt very much at ease with these two, the ice seeming to have broken.

After that, the evening went very well, as we joked and laughed about the differences between American and British senses of humour during our meal of grilled mullet and slightly saline 'papas de gris', better known as fish and chips to us Brits - and it was the best meal I'd had for weeks. Little did I know at the time it was to be the best meal I'd have for months to come! At the end of the evening, as we left the restaurant and walked back to the marina, John told me to come back to the boat tomorrow, and he would let me know the outcome of the interview. *Interview!* I thought. *I didn't realise it was one, as we had spent the whole evening cracking jokes!*

The following morning, I met John and he was pleased to inform me that I had passed the interview!

"If your references check out okay, you can come with us, to the Caribbean, or even as far as the States if you so desire. If you should decide to get off on any of the Caribbean islands that we visit, I will pay for your flight back to the UK, or to any destination in the world that you wish to visit."

I was speechless - in fact, I had to go and sit down on the end of the Muelle to recover from the shock. Meanwhile, John went and phoned my referee. Wow! *I had really landed on my feet this time*, I thought. My references checked out okay and then a thought occurred to me.

"But you haven't even asked me about my experience or looked at my tickets," I told the doctor, who gave a wry grin and replied, "You told us you had experience as a charter boat Captain and so I assume you don't suffer from sea sickness - anything else you need to know we will teach you. Once we're in the trade winds, there's no stopping or turning back, whether you like it or not – you're on a one way ticket!"

Trade wind sailing is very trying for any vessel with the wrong shaped sails, such as yachts! The triangular design common to most vessels is fine for tacking, coming about or sailing close hauled to the wind, but in the trades this shaped sail is next to useless as the wind comes constantly from astern. I could only recall a handful of vessels of all the hundreds at Las Palmas that intended to trade wind sail the Atlantic which had the correct sail design - these were the square rigged, tall ships. Most noticeable to me was *Astrid*, a youth training ship from Weymouth, not far from Lyme.

On Tuesday 29th October, 1996, we first set sail from Las Palmas marina to the much smaller marina Pasito Blanco on the south coast of the island. We used the time to recharge the batteries of *Lady* by running the engine, and also towed a dynamo. I made myself busy by washing mud off the foredeck from the hauled anchor, and then spliced a frayed rope. Both John and Bill seemed experienced sailors, having already sailed the Atlantic, bringing *Lady* to the Canaries from the States via Portugal.

Lady Luck's owner, John, had bought the boat twelve years previously and even though the forty-four foot length was too big for what he really needed, he had got it for a good price. The previous owner had died at only forty years old from a heart attack, and his wife wanted a quick sale.

Bill, being an ex-Naval Officer, was also a skilled diver and both were retired physicians. John held a professorship, which he liked to keep modestly quiet, and had recently had an article accepted by a yachting magazine. This had described part of their voyage across the Atlantic, which had been on almost the same return route as one Columbus took back from the New World. We cut the engines and then hoisted the jib in a northerly force three and sailed around the island on a beat, as the wind appeared to follow us; probably a local activity and not necessarily the trade winds.

At Pasito Blanco, the wind blew due east in the direction of the trades. The plan was to stay here for a few days before the big jump across the Atlantic to the Caribbean. On Friday we took a ride on a safari jeep up into the mountains, in the hope of learning more about these volcanic islands. This turned out to be a disastrous move, as it was a tourist gimmick more suited for young kids on an 18-30s vacation than two retired doctors.

The time spent over the weekend was a bit more constructive, as we replenished our food supplies for the crossing, mainly with fresh fruit and vegetables. Further inland, the main agricultural products such as tomatoes, onions and potatoes could be found on the island's middle elevations and tropical fruits such as bananas, avocados and papayas on the lower levels could be had for a song. I learnt to pick wild figs by finding the plants that sprouted up near any little oasis which sprang up in the area of an underground stream or reservoir. The soft green ones tasted the best, as they were the ripest and contained a dark red kernel. All of this was grown in the rich top soil of these volcanic islands. It is also because of the minerals in the ancient volcanic ash that causes the marine life about the islands to be abundant, and subsequently the fishing is very good.

Once you are away from the tourist ghettos of the coast, the Canaries are truly beautiful islands, with their fauna of wild rabbits, hedgehogs and lizards, while in the air can be seen osprey, turtle-doves, partridges and the fittingly-named canaries. It must be said that these islands are named after the Latin for dog – literally, the 'Isles of Dogs', or as in the case of the Gran Canaria, the Big Dog. Whether early navigators had likened the appearance of these islands at sea to those of resting dogs, one can only speculate.

When I wasn't doing the normal chores of washing dishes, cooking or cleaning, I spent my time studying a Reeds Almanac and a US Naval Training Command Manual to brush up on my astronavigation. I was surprised how quickly it all came back to me. Within a few days, I could confidently determine my latitude and longitude from a meridian passage using a sextant. How accurate I would be was to be discovered in the next few weeks, as we had arranged for two sets of logs - one for John and me to record our position from the use of the sextant, and a copy for Bill to keep a true record of our position by using the GPS navigation system. Each day, when we needed to determine our exact position, only he would know, but he would let us know how far out the both of us were from our calculations.

One evening in the Tiki hut bar in the marina, I met a fellow Brit called Pete, who had lived on the islands for many years and was a skipper to a large sport fishing boat registered in Guernsey, but originally from Miami. It was owned by a Spanish millionaire who also had a third-share ownership of this very harbour. Pete was quite a character and told me the story of how he had recently taken his boss on a fishing trip to Madeira and helped him catch a thousand-pound marlin - so he told me!

On Tuesday 5th of November, 1996, and according to the GPS our initial position was latitude 27 degrees 44.83 minutes, north, and longitude 15 degrees 37.44 minutes, west. *Lady Luck* produced a small wake of ripples as she cut through an almost mirror-like sea. 'Ship-shape and Bristol fashion', as the expression goes, a saying which originated not in Bristol, Rhode Island, but near my hometown, where it once referred to the tightly compact mooring of vessels in the relatively small, yet once busy, major seaport of Bristol docks. After spending almost the whole day waiting for a delivery of diesel fuel and cooking gas to arrive for *Lady*, at 15:20 GMT we departed the marina in the late afternoon sun.

"I must down to the seas again, to the lonely sea and the sky,
"And all I ask is a tall ship and a star to steer her by,
"And the wheel's kick and the wind's song and the white sail's shaking,
"And a grey mist on the sea's face, and a grey dawn breaking."

We may have left in calm seas, but that night the story was vastly different, as the wind picked up; for the first time in my life, I was feeling seasick. Within the first twenty-four hours we covered a distance of 124 nm, and had sustained a broken topping lift, making it difficult to use the boon and therefore the mainsail. The wind was now a fierce easterly force 6, gusting 8, and we decided to reef the jib. On the second day, late in the afternoon, the wind had dropped enough for us to use the auto-helm; although I still hadn't been sick, I was feeling so ill that I refused to take my turn at cooking. Bill joked to John that it was mutiny, but shortly afterwards he was throwing up over the side, and John did not look too well himself, as his face went as white as a ghost.

"I must down to the seas again, for the call of the running tide
"Is a wild call and a clear call that may not be denied;
"And all I ask is a windy day with the white clouds flying,
"And the flung spray and the blown spume, and the sea-gulls crying."

It was then decided that we would first head for the Cape Verdi islands to repair the mast and to break the journey up across the

Atlantic, especially if it was going to continue to be this rough - we still had at least another 2570 nm to cover before Barbados. We decided to split the watch into four-hour shifts and my first watch was 8pm till midnight (GMT). Alone on the helm at night became the most enjoyable part of the voyage for me, a time to practice my Astronav and to reflect on my past. The wind had now dropped right away, and the gentle wake created by *Lady* in the pitch black sea agitated the photo-plankton, leaving a vapour trail behind us of sparkling lights. As the night sky grew darker, it too lit up with countless myriads of stars. The view was spectacular, as the band of the Milky Way arched overhead across our direction of sail. The planet Jupiter shone brightly in the west as our 'evening star', and in the early dawn Venus would be our morning one. I scanned the breathtaking view of the constellations that can never be appreciated, and much less seen, with the naked eye until you are this far out in the ocean, away from human light pollution.

"I must down to the seas again, to the vagrant gypsy life,

"To the gull's way and the whale's way where the wind's like a whetted knife;

"And all I ask is a merry yarn from a laughing fellow-rover

"And quiet sleep and a sweet dream when the long trick's over."

I first determined the 'Square of Pegasus' directly above the three bright stars of the 'Summer Triangle' of Deneb, in Cygnus the Swan, Antares, in Aquila the Eagle and Vega in Lyra, the lyre to my starboard. As Jupiter set, so the constellation of Orion the Hunter could be seen rising to port; the brightest of all the winter constellations and the most recognisable by non-astronomers. The story of Orion is one of the oldest surviving works of Greek mythology. Described by Homer as the son of the sea god Poseidon, Orion became a great hunter, boasting to the goddess Artemis, with whom he hunted, that he could kill every animal on Earth. Mother Earth objected - proving even the ancient Greeks had a green policy! - and sent a giant scorpion to kill Orion, in which it succeeded, since he was half human. After his death, the goddess asked Zeus to place Orion among the constellations. Because he was such a great hunter, Zeus agreed, and placed him on the opposite part of the sky to that of the scorpion, which has constantly chased him about the heavens ever since.

Astronavigation is no longer the complex subject it once was in the days of inaccurate time pieces known as chronometers, when long laborious calculations had to be made using spherical trigonometry and mind-numbing rules such as those of the Cosine-Havesine law. Today, all you need is a GPS. I can hear some bright spark saying, 'yet even that cannot be relied upon all the time; suppose, for example, your electrics fail?' A good point, considering I once had a GPS and two handheld back-ups fail me at the same time!

Latitude has always been relatively easily to calculate, and was even before the days of Harrison's accurate timepieces of the Regency period. The altitude of the Pole Star above the horizon is the same as your latitude in the Northern hemisphere. Here, we are lucky enough to have an observable bright star almost in line with the northern axis of the Earth. Our antipodean counterparts are not so fortunate and have to rely upon the motion of the Southern Cross constellation to determine their position. This can be proven without going into any complex mathematics. For example, if you stand at the North Pole on a clear night, you will see that the Pole Star is directly overhead at all times. The Pole Star has an altitude angle of 90° above the horizon, and your latitude is 90° north. At the equator, the North Star is always on the horizon and consequently its altitude is 0° the same angle as your latitude. At all other northern latitudes, the Pole Star will have the same corresponding altitude.

Longitude is a little more difficult to work out, but nowhere as difficult as it used to be. Basically, you need a watch accurate enough to always give the time at the Greenwich Meridian (a major problem in the past), and an almanac, a table giving the times that all the brightest stars and planets (including the Sun and Moon) pass overhead at Greenwich (the Meridian). Greenwich in London has been designated as 0° West Longitude - not that it has any special reason to be so, other than the fact that Harrison, who invented the first accurate timepiece, was a good old Brit, and London is its capital. Greenwich Observatory was purposely moved to its current position when light pollution from the city obscured observation of the heavens.

Now, the earth can be divided up into twenty-four hourly time zones, corresponding to a total circumference around the earth of $360°$, which is the same as saying that a difference in one hour to Greenwich Time (GT, the same as Universal Time UT and British Winter Time BWT, just to confuse matters!) corresponds to a longitudinal difference of $15°$. For example, if a particular bright star or planet is due to pass over Greenwich at 9pm on the same day that you are sailing the Atlantic (and your three GPS navigation aids have all failed!), you notice that the same point of light passes overhead (your Local Meridian) two hours later, indicating that you are exactly two time zones west of Greenwich, which is the same as saying your position is $2 \times 15° = 30°$ West Longitude. Obviously, the skill is to be able to measure this exact point in time using a sextant, especially at night in rough seas, but a bit of practice can get a measurement within $3°$ which puts your exact position within, give or take, two hundred miles! By continuously repeating these measurements with different celestial objects over a period of many nights and days using the Sun or Moon, you can reduce this error, but it takes practice, and lots of it.

With the stars shining above and the illuminated plankton below, it was like flying in a spaceship, and is probably the nearest you can get to space travel without leaving the Earth. That night, we made visible contact with several freighter lights in the far distance - possibly a shipping lane somewhere off the coast of Morocco. Basking in the early morning twilight, the Moon rose just before Venus as a waning crescent, and in that twenty-four hour period we had covered 246 nm.

The guide did not seem to mention much about the Cape Verdi islands, other than the fact that they were once Portuguese colonies and had recently obtained independence. There also doesn't seem to be anything plentiful for supplies except fish! The commentary for the Verdes in this particular copy of navigation text is about as thorough as the section about Earth in *The Hitchhikers Guide to the Galaxy*, where it simply states, 'mostly harmless'!

John had decided not to visit these islands, since a halyard was being used in place of the snapped topping lift. It's a pity, as I would like to have seen the islands and their people. They are supposed to reflect Africa very much and has not yet been over commercialised by tourism as the Canaries have been. According to the chart, we had now crossed the length of Morocco and the southwestern Sahara. I noticed some familiar place names of towns that I had visited back in '86; Agadir, Sidi Ifni and Laioune. That was the first time I had travelled outside of Europe.

My popularity as a boatman at the Cobb far exceeded my expectations. It was during the Thatcherite regime of the eighties that I barely graduated with a degree, in astrophysics of all things. The country's mass unemployment was miserable, and combined with the closure of the pits and the end to the British industrial revolution, poll tax riots and a process of privatisation from which our postal, rail and telecommunication networks would never recover. I took to the boats and the sea literally like a duck to water, and yet my popularity as a boatman with anglers and tourists on fishing trips was to be my own undoing, as other boatmen became envious of my efficiency and hard work - so I suspected at the time.

After my first trip to the States, I decided to travel further afield and the following winter saw me in Southeast Asia. I had bought a cheap return flight with Aeroflot to Bangkok. This was back in the days when such a place had only been heard of as a venue for the World Chess Championship, when Kasparov won the world title from Karpov. I was inspired by Conrad's *Lord Jim*, which is supposedly set in this part of the world, and my plan was to travel as far south as Singapore to find work on a yacht as a crew member.

The whole trip was a disaster from the outset. Within the first few days of arrival in Thailand, I went down with severe food poisoning, and for a month I laid ill in bed in a dingy Bangkok hotel room. The part of the city I was in was known as Kaosan Road by the locals and as 'Shoestring City' by the veteran travelling backpackers. When I finally recovered, I travelled down through Malaysia, which was beautiful, with over eighty percent of its jungle dedicated to national parks and onto the sterile, concrete jungle of Singapore. There, I was one of the last to see the old Chinatown before it was pulled down to make way for even more sterile high rises. Even the world-renowned Stamford Raffles Hotel, of Singapore Sling cocktail fame, was closed for refurbishment.

I finally reached Singapore harbour to find work as crew, only to discover that I was out of season. Trade wind sailors tend to follow a designated route when sailing around the world, as they have to be in certain places at certain times of the year to use the connecting trade winds. For example, after spending the summer in the Mediterranean basin, yachts congregate at places such as Gibraltar, the Azores or, as we did, the Canaries in order to use the trades around October/November time to cross the Atlantic. From here, it is traditional to spend Christmas in the Caribbean, then proceed through the Panama Canal to pick-up the Humboldt Current to cross the Pacific, pick up the roaring 40s across the Indian Ocean, and then head back up through the Suez Canal to spend the summer again in the Mediterranean. Known as the 'Millionaires' Commuter Line', there are many variations to this basic route that the very rich take on their voyages around the world each year. Yachts therefore tend only to congregate in certain places at certain times to await the different trade winds for this mode of transportation.

After my failure to find a crewing job, I headed back to Bangkok to use up the return on my Aeroflot ticket for a flight home. While in a bar back in Kaosan Road, the locals tried explaining something to me, which, at the time, just did not seem to make any sense: "Wall down… No more Communism… Russia gone!"

Had there been a nuclear war during my long absence, or had the locals been taking too much heroin? I wondered. When two excited Thais left the bar and returned a moment later with an English-speaking newspaper, I realised what had happened, as splashed across the front page was that famous picture of the Berlin Wall coming down, signifying the end to Communism. I remember thinking, *Wow! We do live in interesting times!*

The flight home with Aeroflot was the most enjoyable part of my journey to Southeast Asia - it was complete chaos. First, we landed to refuel in Delhi, but could not take off because of adverse weather conditions due to high winds. So everyone was taken off the plane and put up in a hotel for the night. The following morning, we all piled back on the plane and landed in Karachi, Pakistan to refuel, but were then refused permission for take-off and had to wait on the runway all day until permission was granted.

By the time we reached Moscow, passengers had missed connecting flights throughout Europe by at least two to three days, and so again all of us were taken off the plane. This time we all had a special transit visa issued to us so we could all be transported across the city to be placed in a top hotel near Gorky Park for the night. We must have all been the last Europeans to have been issued such a visa, and to have a first-hand view of the former Union of the Soviet Socialist Republic. It was like something out of a Cold War spy novel, with KGB guards marching around everywhere.

The following morning, we had a luxurious buffet breakfast of rich Colombian coffee and bread rolls, with as countless a choice of every type of meat, sausage and cheese that you could possibly imagine. I glanced out of the window as I ate my breakfast, and was shocked to see the long shop queues of poverty-stricken locals. They patiently waited in the freezing cold streets of depressingly grey refrozen sludge for a single loaf of bread, then joined another queue for something equally essential, such as a pair of secondhand shoes.

On Saturday morning, I heard a conversation on the yachty sideband radio between a Brit and one particular yacht that had just entered the Atlantic from the Gambia, whose accent sounded Australian.

"I heard on the radio yesterday that there had been a Coup in Gambia," said the Brit.

"Well, I've just been about thirty-five miles upriver, and I saw nothing; in fact it was very peaceful. Where did you hear that?"

"On the BBC," said the Brit.

"Well, that explains it then," laughed the Aussie.

That night, while I was on watch looking at the luminous plankton and revising the names of various stars, I noticed the occasional flash of lightning far behind in the east, so far away that one couldn't even hear the accompanying thunder. The following day the wind increased from astern, and so we hoisted up three sails - the main, mizzen and Genoa - and our speed improved. We also used the steering weather vane, which is a pendulum device attached to the rudder, and acts like an autopilot. Our speed had been as much as six knots at times, and we must have been averaging five. Our present position after exactly four days out from the Canaries was lat. 24 5.39N and long. 21 46.47W.

Night watch on the helm became my favourite part of the voyage. The blistering heat of the day at last finished as a more comfortable cool night air fluttered through the sails. I sat alone on the helm in complete control of our destiny across the Atlantic. Every now and then I would check the compass and make the appropriate adjustments to keep us on our course. The stars would shine above and a school of dolphins would play alongside, agitating the photo-plankton and occasionally criss-crossing beneath the hull leaving behind torpedo-like trails. It was during these placid moments that I would think back over my life and reminisce.

After a tedious fourteen hour flight from Los Angeles, we arrived in Australian airspace and through the port window I watched the crystal blue of the Pacific break upon the golden sands of the Australian coast just before we flew into Sydney and touched down on the runway. I felt cheated on my journey around the world as I had crossed the date line and lost the second day of 1991, which was now only to last a total of 364 days. But my travel through time and the loss of a mere day were justifiably compensated for by visiting this fantastic country. I had just spent four months hitchhiking around the USA and now thought of myself as some veteran road warrior. An Aussie Customs Official was most perplexed when he checked my luggage; a small solitary backpack containing a sleeping bag, one worn-out pair of Levis, half a bar of soap, a toothbrush, and three quarters of a bottle of that notorious tequila.

"Just for medicinal purposes!" I quipped, as he held the bottle up to the light to inspect its contents.

"Are you Australian?" were the first words muttered to me by an Aussie in the land down under.

"No, British; I just get out a little bit more often than most of the others."

The summer of 90-91 turned out to be one of the hottest since records began and the deserts of the continent's interior were not the place to be for some fresh-faced, naive pommie (Pomegranate, Melbourne rhyming slang for immigrant). So I spent the first half of my visit hitchhiking north up the Australian east coast, and what a great time I had. The beaches were beautiful, as were the Australian girls that frequented them, and knew how to dress in their sexy summer attire - and everyone was so friendly. Everything produced or manufactured in Australia, such as food and drink, was so cheap, and only things that had to be imported were expensive, such as materialistic products that I could easily get by without.

Just as the seventeenth-century had been the English Golden Age of exploration of the Americas, Spain having dominated the sixteenth-century, so the eighteenth-century would be that of British antipodean exploration. It can be argued (which I'm going to do!) that this all started with the great astronomer Edmond Halley, who had suggested a way of measuring the dimensions of the Solar System, which was then thought of as the major part of the universe and not some miniscule and obscure corner of it. This high-precision measurement of the distance between the Earth and the Sun could be achieved by timing the transit of the planet Venus. But alas, just like the returning comet bearing his name, the next transit would not occur until long after his death, and then only on the other side of the world.

The talented Halley was involved in many scientific discoveries and inventions beneficial to further exploration of our world, ranging from a theory on tradewinds to an early version of the diving bell, in which an underwater atmosphere was replenished by way of weighted barrels of air sent down from the surface. In a demonstration, Halley and five companions dove to sixty feet in the River Thames and remained there for over an hour and a half. Halley made improvements to his invention over the next few years, and later extended his underwater exposure time to over four hours, suffering as a result one of the earliest recorded cases of middle ear barotrauma. At a meeting of the Royal Society, Halley introduced a rudimentary working model of the first magnetic compass to use a liquid-filled housing to damp the swing and wobble of the magnetised needle during an ocean voyage.

Not many people know this, but Halley was even made a temporary captain by the Royal Navy because of a dispute that had arisen amongst naval officers resentful of being under a civilian's command aboard *Paramour*, on the first purely scientific voyage of discovery by an English naval vessel. This resulted in a series of voyages by 'Temporary Captain Halley' into the South Atlantic to research the laws governing magnetic variation of the compass, no doubt using his new wobble-free invention instead of the standard naval version. Halley was also involved in the promotion of Harrisson's extremely accurate timepiece, which was essential to measure longitude accurately enough to save the lives of many crews from shipwreck. However, Halley is probably most famous for realising the genius of a young Cambridge student; he even paid for the student to have his work published on mathematics. This was no other than Sir Isaac Newton himself. Ah, Captain James T. Kirk 'eat your heart out', as in any future world I bet they will never have such great captains of exploration as Halley, and certainly not with the legacy that he left behind.

As vast as the Australian continent is, I was surprised to learn at Surfers' Paradise that the Japanese were buying up the beaches at an alarming rate to reclaim land from the sea for the construction of prime real estate seafront properties – crazy! That night, a few miles north of Sydney, and in a cool sea breeze, away from the profusion of insects and mosquitoes, I slept on the beach with my case of 'stubbies' and saw the Southern Cross constellation and Magallanic Clouds; the satellite galaxies to our Milky Way for the first time, named after the great explorer Magellan and only visible in the Southern hemisphere. Throughout the night, I could hear many small crabs burrowing in the sand.

Just up the road, as the Australians say, at Airlie Beach - well over a thousand miles away! – my night on the beach was not as tranquil, as I was mugged while cocooned in my sleeping bag. The two cowardly thieves only managed to relieve me of my spare pair of Levi's. As I had learned in the States, one of the advantages of travelling light is that everyone thinks you are some poor homeless bum – including thieves. I had come here for a reason, and the following day I sailed as a tourist out to the Whitsunday Islands, just off the Great Barrier Reef, on the beautiful tall ship *Golden Plover*, featured in such notable films as *Blue Lagoon* and *Dead Calm*. As I stepped aboard, a placard hanging above the gangplank bore the inscription, 'All who sail in her, fall in love with her'. So true, as that was the highlight of my two month journey along the Australian Gold Coast.

Three decades after Halley's death, the Royal Society hired Captain James Cook to record and take measurements of Halley's predicted transit of Venus. Cook was then a talented young midshipman and cartographer, who was promptly promoted to lieutenant and named as commander of the expedition to the other end of the Earth. This expedition sailed from England in 1768, rounding Cape Horn and crossing the Pacific to reach Tahiti on the transit date of April 13th of the following year. The results of the shore-based observations may not have been as conclusive or as accurate as the scientific community back home may have wanted, but the expedition gave Cook and his crew the opportunity to map the whole of the New Zealand coastline, and that of southeastern Australia, making them the first recorded Europeans to encounter the Australian Gold Coast, and securing Cook's fame forever. During the previous century, the Dutch had already become quite familiar with the Australian north coast, while traversing back and forth to the Spice Islands in South East Asia, and had already named it New Amsterdam.

Another captain made famous by studying the works of Halley, and who would much later be denied the real credit that he deserved, was William Bligh, whom Hollywood made the villain of the notorious *Mutiny on the Bounty*. Not only did Bligh's achievements outshine those of others of his time, showing that he was another great sea Captain, but he also had the mentors to prove it. Bligh joined the Navy at the tender age of seven, since in those days it was common practice to sign on as a 'young gentleman' simply in order to acquire the necessary experience at sea required for promotion. At twenty-two years old, Bligh served as master's mate aboard Cook's *Resolution*, Cook praising him highly for his navigational skills. This was also to be Cook's third and fatal voyage to the Pacific, in which he was sadly murdered by Hawaiian natives.

Bligh was later mutinied on his own ship while trying to transport breadfruit from tropical Tahiti to the Caribbean. He went via the cold, rough Antarctic seas of Cape Horn, where the plants started to die and Bligh's problems with the crew began. The plan was then to transplant breadfruit in an experiment to see whether it could be successfully grown to feed slaves on the sugar plantations. While I completely condemn anyone involved in the promotion of slavery, the incredible voyage of survival that Bligh and the crew that remained loyal to him achieved next cannot be disregarded. Christian Fletcher and the other mutineers provided Bligh and the eighteen of his crew who remained loyal to him with a twenty-three foot launch no bigger than my old tripping boat. It was so heavily loaded that the gunwales were only a few inches above the water line. They were equipped with four cutlasses, food and water for a few days to reach the most accessible ports, a sextant and a pocket watch, but no charts or even a compass. The launch could not even hold all of the loyal crew so the most useful were detained on *Bounty* by the mutineers and were later released back in Tahiti.

Tahiti was upwind from the marooned Bligh and his loyal crew, and may have been the obvious destination of the mutineers, but Bligh had formulated another plan. Many of the loyalists claimed to have heard the mutineers cry, "Huzzah for Otaheite!" as the *Bounty* pulled away. Timor was the nearest European outpost and so Bligh and his crew made for Tofua in Tonga first, to obtain supplies. Here they were attacked by the natives, and one crewman was killed. After fleeing Tofua, Bligh did not dare to stop at the next islands of Fiji, as he had no weapons for defence, and expected further hostile reception. Cook had been right about Bligh's brilliant navigational skills, and Bligh also knew about Halley's theory of trade currents, which is how he managed the seemingly impossible 3,618 nautical mile voyage to Timor. In this remarkable act of seamanship, Bligh succeeded in reaching Timor after a forty-seven day voyage, and his only other casualties were several men who, after surviving this ordeal, died from malaria in the Dutch East Indies port of Batavia while waiting for a ship to return them to Britain.

I tried to hitchhike into the outback in an attempt to reach Ayre's Rock, which I never did reach, as we were cut off in a small town because of rain and river flooding – here, those travelling through were put up in a school as emergency accommodation, but in these parts the red spot spider is prolific and has a bite which is deadly within minutes; we were all told where the antidote was kept, just in case! I then travelled back over the Great Dividing Range, where I was introduced to the enigmatic call of Ding Dong birds, and onto the Twelve Apostles rock outcrop on the Australian south coast. Eventually back in Sydney, I ran out of money and so became a door-to-door cold sales window cleaner once again. I met Errol Flynn's mother; born Lily Mary Young, she was a direct descendant of Fletcher Christian of *Mutiny on the Bounty* infamy, and must have been a hundred years old, if not more! I cleaned her windows while she made me a cup of tea, and afterwards we sat talking in her living room. Then she told me who her famous son was and on the wall hung a picture of the actor; apparently he was a 'nasty little boy' and his father could not have been much better, as she broke the marriage long before his acting career began.

It was 47 degrees centigrade in the shade on my last day in Australia and -3 back in Lyme. After the longest possible non-stop flight via Copenhagen, I arrived back in Lyme with the same day's newspaper documenting the Australian heatwave in February, which my parents hung up in the Burger Bar while I was on the frost-covered beach with my kid brother Darren, trying to master the boomerang that I had bought him.

The following morning, back on *Lady Luck*, I noticed a pair of sheer waters flying around miles away from land. They were the only seabirds I had seen since we left the Canaries, so I decided to try some fishing by trolling a plug out of the back of the boat. I caught the first of two bright yellow fish with a long blue dorsal fin and a large forked tail. They were female El Dorado fish, which the Americans call dolphin fish, but are no relation to the mammal. We gutted then soused them, and ate them for lunch. John mentioned this noteworthy action in his log, which is probably today the only proof I have that I had sailed across the Atlantic. I stood up on the bowsprit, keeping my balance by holding onto both stantion wires on each side of me as *Lady* cut through the deep blue abyss before us. We must have been about a third of the way across the Atlantic, and the foam of our wake ran along the hull as the keel pierced into yet another wave.

I thought of Lyme and back to the summer of '92, as overall that season had not been a very good one for the pleasureboat industry and had been the second consecutive bad one summer weather-wise. So, it was the following spring that I decided to take a year off and travel the North American continent.

Jealous boatmen at the Cobb teamed up with corrupt local councillors, and at the start of the peak season of '94 my licence was

'Suspended with immediate effect and thereby preventing him (me) from operating as a boatman for commercial gain.'

The reason for this is that I had committed the heinous crime of letting '...a girl known to him, who worked in a takeaway close by, who was believed to be approximately seventeen years of age, at the helm of the boat with the tiller in her hand. At the time the Appellant Mr Herbert was seen a third of the way along his boat putting out a fender as the vessel entered the Cobb and the Appellant, at about 3:15 pm on the 31st July 1994, was informed by the harbourmaster that, in the interest of the public, he was suspended of his licence and told to cease tripping.'

As early as the 11th of January 1996 (!), at the next Recreation and Amenities Committee of the District Council, the appellant's application was considered and it was unanimously decided to refuse to grant the appellant a boatman's licence. It was as if I no longer had any human rights, and eventually I took the Council to court at Dorchester on the fittingly named 'mayday' of that year, but my appeal was rejected by the court without cross-examining any of my witnesses. The whole affair was very odd, and would take several more years before I finally realised what it was all about. My licence was finally reissued after I threatened to complain to the local Government Ombudsman for retaining a licence for an unreasonable length of time. But by the time it was reissued, I had lost my mooring at the Cobb and had been forced to sell my boat.

To make matters worse, just as the next season was upon us and I could use my licence again as a Cobb boatman, I got involved in a fracas with some drunken, lowlife scum over a vicious unprovoked attack on my brother Darren. Seeing him with a broken nose and blood streaming down his face was like waving a red flag to a bull, and I went berserk. I beat the thug to the ground and pounded his face with my fist as hard as I could; his head dragged along the ground and beneath a railing and, ouch! I hit it with full force and snapped my wrist. The thing is that it never even hurt until I tried to set the break myself afterwards, but at the time, had the police not got involved, I was going to finish the thug off with my left fist. I hope to this day it will be the first and last time in my life that I ever lose my temper like that.

Darren and I ended up in the emergency ward of the local hospital that night, Darren with a broken nose and me with a broken arm. I looked at Darren with his bulbous nose and he looked back at my decrepit arm.

"You know, there's a lesson to be learnt from all this."

"Wath dat?" he replied.

"Well, you're too young to fight and I'm getting too old."

We were both crying with laughter at my pathetic joke when the doctor came in to check us over. Both of us had been drinking, and it's normal procedure for our National Health Service to administer painkillers for brawling drunks; it tends to soften them down with a killer hangover! When the nurse enquired of the doctor why they had made the exception this time, he retorted, "Because, nurse, I happen to know the other brother and he's a doctor!"

That was Mark, the brains of the family, and twin of my sister Debbie. This doctor was also smart, as he knew not to mess with us Herberts.

For six bloody weeks I wore an external metal brace screwed into the bones of my arm, but I made a miraculous recovery. When the screws were finally removed, it took every effort I could muster to lift an orange at arm's length during that first week; it was like trying to lift a cannonball singlehanded. Yet within five months, I was sailing the Atlantic and operating the 'coffee grinder', the winch to the main mast in all seas without any feeling in the last three fingers of my right hand.

Looking down at the sounder on *Lady,* I could see that our depth ranged from between five to six thousand feet. This colour of the sea could only ever be seen in British coastal waters on one of those rare hot August days, when the wind had not blown for a couple of weeks and disturbed the silt on the sea bed. The forty-three foot ketch must have been making six knots and the moderate breeze blew from astern. I looked down at the reflection of the mid-afternoon sun as it glistened across the waves off the port bow, and then looked up at the few wispy white clouds in the bright blue sky above, reminiscent of giant cottonwool buds. This east-to-west direction of the wind was a good indicator of the North Equatorial Current, and the trade wind that would eventually blow us across the Atlantic. I remember feeling great; this was real freedom and real adventure, this was what life is all about.

I spent a lot of my spare time reading, as the library of books aboard was very good. Within days I had read Voltaire's *Micromegas*, Salinger's *The Catcher in the Rye,* and *The Great Gatsby* by F. Scott Fitzgerald. Reading is so important on these sorts of trips, since there is not much else to do after cooking, eating, washing-up and the occasional reef or change of the sails. Bill and I tried to play chess, but the board was not one of those magnetic ones. The whole thing was a wasted effort, as the pitch and roll of the boat just threw the game into the air, and we spent the next half hour on our hands and knees trying to find all the lost pieces.

During the next few mornings at twilight, as the sun was just beginning to light up the deck, we found dead flying fish on the boat. It reminded me about the adventures of Thor Hyerdall's Kon Tiki expedition as he and his crew sailed the balsa wood raft across the Pacific. They became so used to flying fish decking themselves that they would even catch them in the frying pan as they prepared breakfast, and then carry on cooking as if it were one the most normal things in the world. As the days progressed, the flying fish became a more and more common sight for us, and it was not unusual to watch whole shoals of them jump up out of the water as the bow of *Lady* disturbed them. Fried flying fish tasted very similar to mackerel. Manx shearwaters could be seen often skimming across the sea, sometimes extending their little feet, and performing a sort of run across the crest of a wave.

The wind had increased the previous night, and our average speed was now about six knots. Bill and I had this standing joke that whenever anything went wrong, such as wrapping fishing line around the battery charger which we towed behind the boat, or drinks knocking over and spilling across the galley table in a rough sea, we referred to it as, 'the romance of the sea!' He had a good sense of humour and was great company, and I would while away many a long hour listening to his stories about his time in the Navy. He was once in an experimental diving unit back in the late sixties and early seventies based in Key West, in the barracks that once stood in the Truman annex, very near to my once local, the Green Parrot, when I had spent a winter there. I knew of the place before it was pulled down. He had a senior officer who had a very pale complexion, and always wore a black cape. His nickname became Count Dracula and whenever he did cabin inspections, someone would always hide a rubber bat behind a locker or pipes for him to find.

The funniest story he ever told me was about when he was serving on an aircraft carrier just off Cadiz. He was standing on the bridge with other senior officers on the first ship of a whole fleet. Just as the order was given for the fleet to go underway, a small fishing boat, with its smoking diesel engine, chugged into view and across their bow. On the helm stood an old Portuguese fisherman with a pipe in his mouth, his fat wife dressed in the traditional black robe sat on the thwart of the boat and a dog peering over the gunwale. As seen from the bridge of the carrier, the little boat just disappeared beneath the giant vessel, and everyone on the bridge held their breaths for what seemed like ages, until the little vessel reappeared with its nonchalant fisherman still puffing his pipe with not a care in the world. The Captain on the carrier repeated the order again that they were underway and, without looking up, the fisherman removed the pipe from his mouth, casually stuck his finger up at them and shouted, "Fuck you, Yank!"

Our course was 260 degrees north, magnetic. The Earth's magnetic field slowly migrates and is therefore not aligned with its axis. This difference, known as 'magnetic variation', can be quite large, enough to affect our position over a long enough distance. The difference between true and magnetic North at this particular point in the ocean was about 17 degrees west, decreasing by about three arc minutes per year according to the chart. Our present course was compensated for this difference and was enough, we hoped, to get us to the Caribbean and far enough away from the dreaded doldrums. At night, I noticed that the shooting stars, which are mainly dust particles from the vapour trails left behind from comets, have the least angle of dip here in the tropics. They momentarily leave behind a vapour trail path that is very nearly parallel to the horizon as they burn up in the atmosphere, as opposed to straight down nearer to the poles. I even have a theory for this and that is that they are charged as they heat up and therefore follow the Earth's magnetic field lines, which are also parallel to the horizon at the equator.

Early one morning I finished my turn on the 'Dog Watch' and climbed down into the cockpit, unclipped the lanyard, and passed it to Bill who took over. I sat at the chart table and wrote the log for that watch. In the clammy darkness, I recorded our estimated position and noticed we were about halfway across the Atlantic. I took another look at the chart and in the silence something struck me that I can only describe as a revelation. Here I was, one of three crew in a forty-three foot vessel on a one way ticket across the Atlantic, in a depth of water that was currently over five miles deep, and I was over a thousand miles from the nearest land in all directions. It suddenly hit home exactly what it was that I was doing… and it wasn't taking Mum, Dad, the kids and granny on a one-hour mackerel fishing trip around the bay!

The wind dropped completely one morning, and we were stuck in the doldrums for a few days. When the wind picked up again, on the American celebration day of Thanksgiving, I was the first to see something we had not seen for twenty three days.

"Land ahoy," I shouted, last seen on the fifth of November, ironically the day of the British celebration of Bonfire Night.

It was a Sunday and the first day of December when John returned from the bank, which surprisingly was open. A cool sea breeze blew across the balmy beach as I sat with my backpack waiting for him at the Boat-Yard, the famous Tiki hut beach bar that specialised in Bacardi rum cocktails. Today was the day I had chosen to leave *Lady* and her crew and it was also the day of my big pay-off. We exchanged addresses, and I said my goodbyes to Bill and John. They left me at the bar, never to be seen again. I stuffed the thick bank roll of Barbadian dollars into the pocket of my beach shorts, and ordered a Bacardi and milk. I was trying to be clever as it was about the only rum mixed drink that wasn't advertised on the extensive drinks board. I looked out across the turquoise blue sea as it broke on the shore of a pure white sandy beach and listened to the palm trees rustle in the gentle breeze. On the horizon I could see the tall ship *Astrid* sailing away into the glorious sunshine. At least I had got this far in my life, I thought, and to think just three months ago, I was lying in bed with a broken wrist and a metal frame that externally pinned my whole arm into a fixed position. *Now*, I thought, *if I should die tomorrow, I shouldn't have any complaints.* The barman returned and poured copious amounts of rum with milk over a glass of crushed ice, then looked me straight in the eye and asked, "Would sir like cookies with that?" Teach me to be so damn clever!

The bus took me to the north of the island on my exploration of Barbados. Passing sugar plantations and many brightly coloured chattels, home to the native Barbadians, the bus stopped in some strangely English-styled village, with its quaint little church, landscaped lawns and, cut into a field of sugar beet, a cricket green where a match was taking place. I circled the island and doubled back towards Bridgetown, passing old colonial homes and a military barracks with the dormant old rusted cannons of the long departed British Army.

At Speightstown a massive modern day seafront construction was in progress. This, I was told by a fellow passenger, was a new marina designed to win back yachts and tourists from the other Caribbean islands, which had proper marina facilities. Even ARC now sailed to Saint Lucia instead and, as Barbados is the most easterly of the Windward Islands, if it is not visited first then the chances are that it will not be visited at all. At Six Man Cay, I sat at a drink kiosk, talking to the local friendly fishermen. All along the seafront, colourful little wooden boats had been hauled up the beach after the previous night's fishing. I was told that the flying fish are caught using surface nets at night, with lanterns hung over the side of the boats to attract them into the nets. An ex-fisherman, now a local gardener, worked on the grounds of a nearby stately home, frequented by the British Royal Family during visits to the West Indies. He told me of how he had the honourable job of cutting down all the recently sprouted coconuts in the tops of the palm trees, in the unlikely event that one might fall on top of Princess Diana during her visits – now, after the princess' untimely demise, I suppose the gardener has gone back to fishing!

"I don't have a return flight to Britain. I sailed across the Atlantic in a yacht," I explained again to the pretty Barbadian girl at the reception desk, as she stared at me with her big beautiful brown eyes.

"I'm sorry, sir, but I cannot issue a ticket on this without the Captain's permission".

I waited for a white-uniformed gentleman to arrive and noticed the gold and black braid on his shirt – it was the Captain, and he looked the spitting image of Peter O'Toole! I explained to him my circumstances as he flicked through the pages of my passport.

"Can you show that you have enough money, such as a bank card, when we arrive at Trinidad?"

I pulled out a bankcard from my wallet.

"I think we can risk this one, Purser," said Captain O'Toole, as he handed the girl my passport.

"Thank you, Captain,"

"You're not clear yet; Customs will probably give you a difficult time when we arrive!"

The tangerine-painted hull of the aptly named *Trade Winds* cut through the dark blue sea, as its wake of lighter blue burst into white foam. *It felt very different under power than under sail*, I thought, as I watched Barbados slowly disappear over the horizon. The apparent wind blew from the north, and after a little mental vector calculation I worked out why, as the trade winds were still blowing a northeasterly and our direction of travel was to the southwest, towards Saint Vincent. I stepped inside the ferry and down a flight of stairs to the main reception room, and over the ships music system wailed, 'Noel... noel... born is the king of Israel'. *Christmas*, I thought, *is so out of place here in the hot Caribbean.* It just didn't seem like December. This had only been my second reminder; the first had been the other evening with some flimsy bit of tinsel subtly hung up in the Boat Yard. *Strange*, I thought, *since back in the UK, pubs tended to advertise the Christmas dinner specials the moment the last tourist has said goodnight at the end of the August bank holiday weekend!*

Later that day, the island of Saint Vincent had come into view, and I had struck up a friendship with two fellow British passengers.

"I know a good bar that's famous for its rum punch for when we arrive," said one of them, and I winced at the thought after my heavy night back at the Boat Yard. He told me he was a writer and lived semi-retired on Trinidad. The other Brit was on a mission; he wanted to trace someone who may have known his father when he was serving in the British Army back in the colonial days. When we arrived ashore, he said he would catch us up. We walked through the streets of the downtown part of Georgetown, as I was guided through buildings far more colonial-looking than the chattels of neighbouring Barbados. We finally arrived at a wooden structure not dissimilar to an old cowboy saloon bar. We climbed some stairs to a veranda bar that overlooked the main street of Georgetown. We ordered a rum punch each and the cocktail arrived with the full works of umbrellas, cherries, crushed ice and a fancy straw, and we sat watching the bustling street below.

A certain famous yachting guide to these islands had described Saint Vincent as looking similar to a West Country village. I couldn't have disagreed more strongly - from my vantage point, I could see many locals going about their daily lives on foot or bicycle and no sign of any cars. Reggae artists sold their beautiful wares of pottery and paintings on the boardwalk that ran parallel to the red mud street. High above Georgetown and in the distance could be seen a mountain that pierced up out of the lush green jungle, and strange sounds from an array of tropical birds could be heard as they flew high above. No matter how much rum I drank, I still couldn't see any resemblance to a West Country village. After our third drink, the Brit on his mission caught up with me. He was very excited because he had found someone who had known his father. *Fast work*, I thought; we had barely been on the island two hours! He introduced us to her, she was certainly too young to have known his father, and looked more like a working girl to me, but I said nothing. Who was I to spoil his adventure?

As the afternoon wore on, I was starting to feel quite giddy from the many rum punches, and we only just made it back to the ship on time, with a very impatient and angry-looking captain waiting for us. I don't think I helped matters by telling him how much he resembled Peter O'Toole as I staggered up the gangplank; it certainly didn't seem to cheer him up much. We sailed away from Saint Vincent into the evening twilight aboard a ship freshly laden with so much cargo and passengers that we had a problem finding somewhere to sit. We eventually found room on top of a stack of boxes packed with bananas. Here, we spent the rest of the night drinking beer with a Canadian who had joined us at Georgetown. The last thing I remember that night, just before I fell asleep atop of my cardboard box of bananas, were lights shining on the distant horizon in the darkness as we passed the islands of the Grenadines.

The following morning, I had a hangover that could have given a whale brain damage. I wearily climbed down off the stack of banana boxes, and noticed that I had the lower decks of the *Trade Winds* almost to myself, since all the other passengers had gone up to the main deck as we passed the north coast of Trinidad. The islands here were even more beautiful and less populated than the ones I had seen earlier. A manta ray breached up out of the sea not far from the ferry as hundreds of pelicans flew alongside us, and all with a background of a dense jungle coastline. We passed many smaller offshore island rock stacks with arches and caves, and it didn't require much imagination to entertain the thought of some old buccaneer's treasure being hid in them somewhere!

Moments after the main springer mooring rope was cast ashore at Port of Spain, I was in the queue on the dock to exchange Caribbean dollars for Trinidad and Tobago dollars; the rate worked out at about one for three Trinidad, at this time about three Caribbean was equal to one pound sterling. I then joined the second queue through customs.

"What is your address here in Trinidad?" The serious-looking Customs Officer flicked through the pages of my passport and stopped at the page showing my Australian visa.

"I'm not sure, as I haven't arrived yet!" was my reply.

"Then where is your outward ticket from Trinidad?" He had now turned my passport sidewards to look at my old South East Asia visas.

"I don't have one yet; I'm on my way to Venezuela." It was a stupid reply as this only added to the confusion.

"Then where is your outward visa from Venezuela?" he asked, now looking at my Canadian visa.

"I haven't got it, as I haven't arrived in Venezuela yet... I'm eventually going to travel to the States, then fly home to the UK from there."

"Then where is your return ticket from the USA?" He was now looking very irritated.

"I haven't got it yet as I haven't arrived!"

The Customs Officer then exploded. "Sit down over there; I will see you later!" He pointed to an inverted wooden crate and threw my passport down on the collapsible blue vinyl-covered table that stood between us. I waited ages as the long queue from *Trade Winds* slowly dwindled down as they all passed through immigration.

At long last, the irritated Customs Officer turned to me and, after a lot more questioning and showing him my money and bankcards, he reluctantly stamped my passport. The other Brit, who had been on the mission at Saint Vincent - and was now looking very exhausted after a night with his father's long lost lady friend! - came over and asked the Customs Officer if he could also have a stamp in his passport, even though he was only in transit back to Barbados. The Officer, in his fury with me, just turned around and, without even batting his eyelids, stamped his passport, muttering something about crazy British before breaking into a smile. The whole thing then ended quite jovial as he asked me for a cigarette, and the three of us all had a good laugh about the situation.

The other Brit, who lived in Trinidad, gave us a quick guided tour of Port of Spain as we walked down Independence Square, which isn't a square but a long corridor of many squares, forming one long street bordered by big commercial banks run by Asians and a variety shops run by the Afro-Caribbean. We paused at a neon-lit sign to a fast food joint beneath a palm-strewn roof, and in the centre of the road stood the statue of the legendary cricket ace Brian Lara. At the end of our tour we parted company, with the Brit guide leaving me with a warning.

"Be careful, Glen; this is a nice country, but remember this city is a cross between Harlem and Seville."

For just two Trinidanian dollars I caught the bus to the Trinidad and Tobago yacht club, just a few miles west of the city on the shore of the Chaguaramas Bay. I was looking for a boat to get me across to Venezuela and mainland America. This was a typical yacht club, just like so many all over the world – nice decor but no one goes anywhere in case they blemish the gel-coat of their aquatic status symbols! But they do have committee meetings to elect a new commodore and hold the occasional social event. It was here that I discovered the two main classes of Trinidad's citizens; the poor, working-class black descendants of the once-rife slave trade of these parts, and the richer, upper-class of Asians who seemed to run an economy based on oil.

I did not stay for long, but headed along the coast to the neighbouring Peake and Powerboats Marina. This was more like the place I was looking for, with its many international yachts, mainly from the States, but also British, Dutch, German, French and Australian. Boats ranged from transatlantic racing yachts with their boy-racer crews, to the smaller vessels carrying mum, dad and the kids - and also the pet dog. Most of them had just crossed the Atlantic, and it was traditional to spend Christmas in the Caribbean before heading either north to the States, west to the Panama Canal or to South America, and through the Magellan Straits, or, for the more adventurous, around the Horn on their world voyage back to the Mediterranean for the following summer. Many of these people would pick up work en-route to pay for expenses; some families had been away from home for years, while others could afford to live in the lap of luxury and would jet back and forth for home at each leg of the journey. As if the marina wasn't full enough with yachts, right across the bay as far as the eye could see were many more.

It was now a scorching 30 degrees plus in the shade, as I sat beneath a palm tree that looked out over the marina and the bay. Around me, yachties from all classes of society went about their daily lives, buying provisions, visiting the laundromat, getting a much needed hair-cut or just lazing around in a hammock over near the open-air Tiki bar.

English was the official language here, although local speech had its own rich idiom. For example, 'to lime' was to spend time talking, laughing, drinking and watching the local pretty girls walk by, and seemed to be the main pastime. My favourite expression was 'a freshwater Yankee', who was someone who returns home with foreign mannerisms after just a short stay abroad. It made me laugh to think of the Brits I had met over the years who, after a two week trip to Orlando, no longer went 'shopping' or filled a 'car' up with 'petrol', but went to the 'store' and filled the 'automobile' with 'gas'.

That night, I watched fireflies darting about amongst the jungle, as I roughed it on the boardwalk of the marina. The following morning, I decided to put out a message on the 'net' asking for passage as crew to Venezuela. The 'net' was a social VHF broadcast that went out to all the yachts every morning at eight on channel 68. It was on this day that I met Michelle, a pretty, young girl from the states, and owner of the yacht *Wooden Shoe,* who told me an amazing travel story. She seemed honest, and as we spoke she never once came across as a person who exaggerated, which made the story even more interesting.

She had been in Trinidad for five months and had sailed single-handed since her boyfriend had died from diabetes. She was probably one of the most experienced sailors I had ever met, and wanted crew mainly as company. I would have accepted her offer had she been going my way and not back the direction I had just travelled. She had sailed the Pacific a number of times and once sailed with an Australian couple to a group of remote tropical islands near Fiji, whose location I promised not to reveal. The natives here had never seen a white woman before, and the sea temperature varied erratically due to recent underwater volcanic activity. At one particular island clouded in a thick mist, her two companions decided to swim ashore, leaving her to look after the boat. A few hours later they came back aboard, exhausted from the swim and looking very worried. She asked them what the problem was, and one of the Australians described seeing creatures roaming around the island that he could only describe as prehistoric, as he climbed over the rails of the boat and slumped to the deck with shock.

In complete disbelief, Michelle went back with them to the island once they had recovered to take a look at exactly what it was they had seen. They reached a virgin sandy beach, which looked as if it had never been trodden on by humans before, and then clambered up a bank of thick jungle to a clearing at the top of a hill. Sure enough, there appeared giant reptile-like creatures feeding on the leaves of trees. In terror the three of them hid in the bush and watched a whole 'herd' of these dinosaurs walk by with their young.

"It was unbelievable!" exclaimed Michelle, with real conviction in her voice. "It was just like something out of *Jurassic Park."* The three of them returned to the boat, very bewildered and confused about what they had just seen. A while later, a white patrol boat raced up alongside them and one of several park rangers asked in an Australian accent, "You ain't just been on the island, have you?" Michelle and her companions denied they had just swum ashore, thinking that they had stumbled across something they shouldn't have.

"It's just that this particular island is off-limits – it's a nature reserve for the last giant land iguanas in the world!"

I had an interesting morning talking to Michelle, as we sat in the shade of a palm tree near the Tiki hut, sipping ice-cold sodas. I asked her why none of the yachts seemed to be going to Venezuela, which was unusual as it seemed so close; the mainland could even be seen from the marina on a clear day. She told me that most yachts had already visited the mainland or, like me, had just crossed the Atlantic, but further south to avoid the doldrums and the normal route from there was north, to follow the Windward Antilles, the chain of Caribbean islands that ran around in a giant arc to Cuba and the Bahamas. I was, in fact, going against the grain, so to speak, by going to Venezuela, said Michelle. My only other chance of getting to the mainland was by catching the ferry *Trade Winds*, but that would have meant waiting over a week.

Over the next few days, I decided to pass the time by doing some sightseeing and went to visit the Maracus waterfall. I caught another bus across the northern range of Trinidad, and spent the day listening to the radio. I heard about the imminent eruption of a volcano on the island of Montserrat, and the predicted thirty-million tonnes of hot ash and lava being ejected into the atmosphere, and the ensuing tsunami of a height of at least fifteen metres - high enough to reach as far south as Trinidad, said the newsreader. I thought about Michelle and her lone voyage north on the *Wooden Shoe*; I doubt if a volcano would have perturbed her, as she was already used to them – very brave.

On my arrival at the small village of Maracas, it was starting to get dark. The local villagers advised me that it was dangerous enough to visit the falls alone and even more so at night. The surrounding countryside was rife with banditos waiting to prey on unsuspecting tourists. I ran into a nearby bar as a tropical downpour commenced in order to avoid the deluge, which always looks as if it is going to last for hours, but stops as abruptly as it starts. I asked the barman if he knew of a cheap hotel, and he directed me back down the valley to the Scarlet Ibis hotel - at US$13 per night, it was a bargain compared to the US$80 plus nearer to the marina, something the Trinidad tourist board never bother to mention!

"I don't need a guide!" I said, but whether I wanted one or not, I had one and I wasn't sure if I felt more secure with or without him.

I looked down at the little nine-year-old boy, dressed in a torn T-shirt and biddims. He carried a machete, which was almost his own height.

"What's your name?"

"Keron."

"What's the big knife for?"

"Snakes," he replied, with a mischievous grin that showed off his brilliant white teeth.

"What type of snakes?" I asked, as I walked up the mountain pass, with my little black guide running behind to keep up with me.

"All sorts, mon – I wod bitten by dem once." He paused to show me a scar on his ankle.

I told him I only had one and a half TT dollars - about 15 pence - which I gave him, hoping he would go away but no, that was sufficient payment, and the act of offering the money only sealed the contract. Whether I wanted a guide or not, I had one!

He seemed happy enough with the loose change, and all the cigarettes he could scrounge off me for the day's hike. Goodness me! He was only a child, yet smoked like a real trooper. On the two-mile trek up the muddy track to the waterfall I had to keep pausing so he could catch up as he stumbled along with his snake sword. We passed an evangelical group of women and children on the roadside chanting,

"Jesus is coming, Jesus is coming, oh, Lord Jesus is coming!" They lit colourful candles and placed them alongside our path. Needless to say, I never met him as I reached the waterfall, and I know it wasn't for the help of my guide that I didn't have an early visit to my maker. He had slumped down on the bank of the river in exhaustion. My clothes were drenched in sweat from the climb in the humidity. I stood beneath the little waterfall, and marvelled at the simple beauty of the place.

A cool breeze blew down from the top of the fall as many blue butterflies and hummingbirds no bigger than my thumb flew around us. I slung my backpack to the ground and then stepped beneath the 200 foot high fall and let the cool spray shower me. I've seen bigger waterfalls, such as that at Niagara, and probably even more spectacular ones, such as those in Yosemite Park, but this one was just as wonderful in its own way, and this will be how I will always remember Trinidad - the island that Columbus named after the Holy Trinity. After hiking back down to the main road and returning my invaluable guide to his waiting mother, I hitchhiked back to the hotel. An Asian couple gave me a lift, and I asked them about paying local fishermen to take me across to Venezuela. They said that it was possible if I went down to the city dock, but to be careful, as the south seas of Trinidad are still infested to this day with pirates. The maxi-taxi back into Port of Spain played a new version of an old Christmas carol on the radio, 'I'm dreaming of a black Christmas... just like the ones I've always known'. The Caribbean lyrics fitted in well with the sound of steel drums. The news reported sixteen inches of snow in New England, and I correctly surmised that they wouldn't be having much of a 'black Christmas'!

At the city dock, I felt like Papillon escaping from the French Guiana prison, as I looked down at the small dugout canoe that was to take me across the Bocas Del Drago, again named by Columbus, since 'the mouth of the dragon' had been the place where he had lost one of his ships on a subsequent voyage to the New World. At the junction of the Atlantic, Caribbean and the Orinoco River, the seas here can be unpredictable and very dangerous, and a possible reason why I had not seen a yacht make the crossing. I would have to rely on local knowledge, and this came in the form of two Venezuelan boatmen, Juan and Lois, two brothers who, after a bit of negotiating, agreed to take me across for US$25. A miserable old woman in the import/export hut said that I could get away with murder at such a low price! I had to pay her 75 TT departure tax, and then she tried to extract a 50 TT boarding tax, which I refused to pay.

The city dock of Port of Spain is exactly how one would imagine a boomtown port to be, with many suspicious and poor-looking characters hanging around boats and offloaded cargo. I felt very uneasy there. After waiting for six hours, our papers were found to be in order and we could leave. Juan pulled the starter cord to the fifty horsepower outboard, and the motorised dugout named *Magdalia* cut out into the bay. The sea was a dark grey in colour, with much flotsam of palm tree branches and coconut shells. This was possibly debris that washes down the Orinoco after each tropical downpour that momentarily floods the river. We passed many offshore islets with beautiful large houses; obviously the homes of the more wealthy Asians. I looked back and in the distance, I saw the marina with its many yachts. As we entered the Bocas del Drago, a squall blew up and we had a downpour of warm tropical rain. This didn't seem to bother Juan or Lois, so I didn't let it bother me. I was more worried about being robbed, having my throat cut, and then my corpse being tossed overboard by these two poor Hispanics - who would ever know? I then noticed that the name of the dugout was written inside my passport along with my exit visa from Trinidad, which was a relief, since my name would also appear on their export documents as a passenger, and would have a difficult time with the Venezuelan authorities if they arrived without me.

Juan dodged the floating debris very skillfully, and we motored close to the Venezuelan mountainous coastline - *maybe a little too close*, I thought at times, so close I could distinguish different types of birds and plants at times in amongst the dense jungle. By sunset we entered the Golfo de Paria and it grew dark very quickly, a phenomenon that is normal the closer one is to the equator. Juan steered even closer to the shore as Lois stood up on the bow as lookout. They then explained to me why they were doing this, which was the first conversation we had had since leaving Trinidad. We passed many small whirlpools swirling in a clockwise direction the further we headed out to sea, and this was why we motored so close to the shore - to avoid them; the strange undercurrents were treacherous to small boats if you happened to get caught in one, and the job of avoiding them was becoming even more difficult now that it was night. By 6:30pm it was pitch black, and of course *Magdalia* had no navigation lights. Juan then abruptly steered towards the shore, and I could just make out a dim light flickering in the jungle. We were now several miles west of the oil terminal at Puerto de Hierro, the only other lights I could see, but it was now impossible to travel any further tonight.

Lois called to the shore, and in the darkness I heard a voice call back to him. He then turned towards me and explained in his broken English that this was his other brother Don's place, and we would spend the night here at his house and continue the journey tomorrow because it was now too dark. As we approached the shore, using the dim light as our guide, I heard the engine cut and then the anchor drop and could just about see the silhouette of Juan feeding out more anchor rope so that we drifted in towards the beach. A young boy came running up to us, holding an oil lamp which he used to show us the way. As I waded ashore in the shallow water and then stepped onto the beach, I realised in the darkness that I had now stepped on every continent on Earth except Antarctica. We followed the flickering oil lamp to a small shed of concrete blocks and a thatched roof of dried palms - Don's home.

I was given the best bed in the house by my kind hosts, the only hammock in the place, and it hung from the rafters. Juan cooked scrambled eggs, which he got from chicken somewhere from behind the hut. The water used to boil some yams came from a plastic container used to catch rainwater. It started to rain again, and I could hear the water splashing on a corrugated sheet used as a lean-to, as well as the run off for the fresh water supply. Before the boiling water was used for the yams, it was used to make coffee, which we all drank from the single communal cup. I pulled out a bottle of rum and gave it to *mon capitan* Juan, more out of guilt than good will. There I was earlier in the day, expecting these people to mug and kill me and here they are now sharing what little they have with me! I covered myself with insect repellent as I started to hear the male mosquitoes buzzing around my ears searching for the females that bite, a precaution I had learned long ago. Lois smoked the hut out for me by burning dried coconut shells when he realised the mosquitoes were bothering me, who until then seemed oblivious to them.

The meal of scrambled eggs with boiled yams and chilies was probably the best meal I ever had, not for its culinary delight, but because it was from my newfound friends who had very little but were prepared to share the very little they had with me. I wonder how many people in the Western world could learn from this. The meal was served to me in an old margarine container, and my hosts insisted that I use the only piece of cutlery - a single spoon that had been used for the cooking – while they ate theirs with their fingers. It was at this point that I would have gladly given them more money if I had it.

What I had paid seemed a very small price for all the kind service I was getting. That night, the three brothers chatted and laughed while I tried to sleep in the hammock, but I had sweated so much during the day that I had terrible cramp in my legs and it kept me awake. I dared not complain, as the three brothers were huddled together on a cardboard sheet on the dry mud floor.

The following morning we arose at first light for the final leg of our journey to Guiria. As I repacked my backpack just outside of the hut, the brothers introduced me to their mother, who mysteriously appeared from nowhere in the jungle thicket, with a piping hot cup of sweetened black coffee for me. I assumed she lived in another hut not far from there.

A beautiful red sunrise welcomed us as we motored out into the Golf de Paria, along with more black clouds and - you guessed it - more rain. After the rain, a thick mist enveloped us and eventually, as the mist cleared, a vast mountain range appeared ahead - this was the northern tip of the Andes, and it was beautiful as the dawn sun reflected off its highest peaks. Finally, by about midday, we arrived in the port of Guiria and moored up against a long row of brightly-coloured wooden fishing boats. Once ashore, Lois bought me breakfast at a little cafe used by the fisherman as we waited for customs.

The Customs Officer arrived and he was very friendly and jovial – I'd never met one like that before. He checked the cargo of *Magadalia,* then stamped my passport with no questions asked and I didn't even have to negotiate a price for the visa as it was free. I shook hands with everyone including the Customs Officer and, having said my farewells to Juan and Lois, hiked west on the dusty track of hard-baked mud of highway nine. The intense heat of the sun had turned the muddy track rock hard, but it wasn't long before I was soaking wet again, this time with sweat from the dense humidity.

In amongst the town of concrete black walls and corrugated rooves, I found a bank. I exchanged $55 into 26,000 Bolivares, which was such a large amount in this part of the world that the bank cashier did not have enough cash and had to go to another bank to borrow the money. *Christ!,* I thought, *it was barely thirty quid!* The pile of notes was lain on the counter in front of me, and it was so thick that I had trouble folding it and had to separate it into two piles and squeeze each pile into my pockets. I walked out of the bank with such a gait it looked as if I had a displaced hip joint! Other customers stared at me as if I had just withdrawn a million dollars in cash.

I then hitched a ride on an open-top truck driven by some farmhands who drove me to Carupano. It rained twice more that day and the sun reflected off the many-shaded green leaves of the tropical vegetation. On the roadside, the base of palm trees were painted with a red and white stripe – I suppose this was to contrast the edge of the road from the lush green jungle. We drove up into the mountains, where I saw birds that I thought were condors gliding high above on warm air currents. We drove back down to sea level, and then I got dropped off near a beach, where I spent the night. Luckily, my sleeping bag was waterproof, as it rained almost all night as I roughed it. I felt terrible the following morning as I hitched into the downtown area of Carupano; my plan was to reach the Pan-American highway and hitchhike all the way to the States, but someone told me on my last lift that the Colombia/Panama border was closed and impossible to pass.My money was low and it was less than two weeks until Christmas, plus I was homesick.

Here I was in the land of the Conquistadors, which may well have once had the wealth so richly portrayed by the early Spanish, but today all I could see was poverty, with many poor rural fishermen and farm labourers and their families going about their daily lives. They call such places the Third World, yet technically it is not. In Third World countries, food and material items are difficult to acquire, unlike the Western First World countries. South and Central America have their own category, a type of Second World, although that usually refers to Communist or Socialist countries, which is a category that some, although not all, Latin American countries fall into. There, material items such as a new telly or a car may be difficult to acquire, but food is cheap and plentiful - probably more so than in the West. It is even free if you know where to find it, as a vast array of fruits and vegetables grow wild on the roadside all year round and, having improved my fishing skills for the Tropics during the crossing, I could easily balance my free vitamin diet with protein.

At the city bus terminal, I found I could buy an ice cold bottled beer at the bar for the equivalent of 30 cents. Homesick or not, that soon cheered me up, and before I knew it I was on the overnight bus to Caracas and managed to get a good night's sleep en-route for the first time in days. The following morning we entered this vast, crazy city with its bustle of traffic jams, and from here I caught a second bus to the border town of Cucuta in Colombia. This was an extremely desperate place for a gringo, as a group of unlikely-looking Government officials attempted to relieve me of my back-pack at the bus station near the border. That night, I roughed it on the banks of a river that was a tributary to the Orinoco. The following morning a jogger came by and, realising I was a gringo a little off the tourist-beaten track, he stopped and warned me with the words, "*guerrero… guerrero!*" pointing in different directions. He then ran off. I rummaged through my backpack for my Spanish dictionary and looked up to see what it translated as: 'warlike!'

As I got to my feet, another person - this time a very scruffy-looking urchin - came strolling by and stopped to make conversation. Before I could reply, he attempted to steal my bag; we both pulled on the straps and he let go. With lightning speed, he snatched the watch off my wrist instead – this boy was a professional! I panicked and backed off as he came towards me again; I grabbed a rock and struck him over the head as he attempted another go for the backpack. He ran off whining, with one hand over a cut gushing with blood, and my watch in the other. I was now shaking with adrenaline and fear – I was in an extremely bad area of Cucuta, and ran from this ghetto back towards the main streets of the downtown area, passing through a large deserted plaza with a statue of some grand old forgotten Conquistador on his stallion, covered in graffiti. The streets were covered in litter and stank of urine, with more graffiti and paint peeling off all the buildings.

Back at the bus station, the poverty and desperation of the people wasn't much better, as many eagerly offered help, eyeing my backpack and clothes with envy. I quickly got on a battered but brightly-coloured bus with paintings of saints and a portrait of Jesus above the dash facing the driver. This is the most common form of public transport here in Latin America – old American Blue Bird school buses, which are no longer safe enough to transport First World children, but perfectly fine for the poor, albeit that I was now in a separate category all of my own.

The bus journey turned out to be quite an experience, as we bombed along the hot, dusty and bustling streets, as the driver's young companion, no more than about nine or ten, hung out of the door shouting our destination to the crowds in the busy, mid-morning streets. Every now and then, an exceptionally attractive young lady would get on; elegantly dressed, but not overdone with jewellery, except for a cross about her neck, which she would kiss and make the sign like a priest as we passed a church – *this was going from one extreme to the other*, I thought.

I soon found the correct bus heading west out of the city and then south to Bogota; to my surprise, we entered a beautiful landscape of lush, green valleys and palm-strewn roads. Every now and then, we stopped at a road junction, where many sellers entered the bus or dashed to the windows outside trying to sell their wares – mostly food. Here in the tropics around midday you get a deluge of rain, which quickly dries up in the afternoon heat of the sun. My plan was to reach the Pan-American Highway (Route 45) and head north after a brief trip to the capital, which took me over the eastern branch of the Andes, then down into the valley of the Magdalena River. I soon got chatting to the locals as we bombed up along the mountain passes of Route 55. Many seemed completely bewildered that a 'Europa gringo' should be travelling this part of the world on his own. Many women would ask me if I had an *esposa* (wife), and when I told them I had not, they found it doubly strange, some even asking if I was sexually normal. Well, I think I must have been, as the next beautiful *senorita* that entered the bus and sat next to me caused a stirring in my groin. God, I couldn't now even remember the last time I had sex; it had been another world and seemed such a long time ago!

We finally reached Bogota, and I had been chatted up by beautiful women almost throughout the whole trip from Cucuta. Colombia was indeed a great country with, I think, the most beautiful women in the world. At Bogota, I saw the ugly and violent side of the country again. The homeless in the poorest slum areas are reduced to unshaven, unwashed tramps rummaging in trash cans for cardboard, which they sell for recycling, and the meagre change they make is used to buy cocaine, which is even cheaper than alcohol. An alcoholic is a luxury here, with the entire tramp population consisting of hard drug addicts. I did not stay for long and soon returned to the bus station, getting on another bus north towards 45, the Pan-American Highway.

The battered Blue Bird buses seemed to stop everywhere. It felt like it took forever to reach the main highway. Once we did get to it, I had already decided to get off the bus and try my luck hitch hiking a lift with northbound truckers. I managed to get a lift with a trucker heading high up into the western branch of the Andes, to the city of Medellin. His name was Ernie, and he drove like a bat out of Hell, but with great skill, around the mountain passes. Even when we hit the fog and rain, it never seemed to slow him up. This may have been typical good driving by the Colombians, but it did not mean accidents did not happen, as I saw the results of two fatalities, with burnt-out car hulks at the foot of hills looking like crushed matchboxes. I even witnessed one very near miss as another truck towing a car braked too quickly then accelerated to avoid a newly formed mud slide. The trucker actually caught his own tow line which snapped, resulting in the car careering off into the valley abyss. Luckily, the driver was on the mountain side not the valley side when this happened, and he came to a grinding halt.

Later that evening, high up in the Andes, we temporarily stopped when nature called, and in the freezing cold, it started snowing – snow at the equator, whatever next!? Later that night, as we entered the city, it was breathtaking. Medellin was lit-up with Christmas lights, and looked like a galaxy of stars as we trundled around the sharp bends of the mountain passes high above the city; each bend we rounded would reveal another sparkling spiral arm to this magnificent galaxy of city lights. I got dropped off at the city bus station and that is where I roughed it for the night – I couldn't imagine any trouble here, as there were so many soldiers and police about, many of them sleeping on the floors themselves as they waited for buses; it was like an airport which for some reason or other had many delayed or cancelled flights.

The following morning, I walked out into the open air and had another shock – the whole city lay in a huge mountainous valley, a *caldera* if you like, with the bus station at the base of the bowl. It was impossible to get lost here, as all you had to do was look upwards for an obvious landmark such as the cathedral, and you immediately knew roughly where you were in Medellin. From there, I took another bus out of the city, then hitched at truck stops north along the Pan-American.

The road twisted down through the valley of the Cauca River, crossing many bridges and waterfalls. I was told that it was possible to cross into Panama and Central America at the port of Turbo, so that was my destination. The human history of Colombia had started over 13,000 years ago, and since that time, many Andean and Caribbean cultures have occupied this area of South America. The Spanish Conquistadores arrived at its northern coastal areas in the early sixteenth-century and it became Spain's chief source of gold, subsequently being named after Columbus (Colombo). The coastal city of Cartagena, and its current capital Bogota, were founded later in the mid-part of that century. The Spanish, like the British, increased taxation on their colonial cousins and this sowed the seeds of revolution. By the early nineteenth-century, the national hero Simon Bolivar and his armies defeated the Spanish, and an independent republic was formed, which included the lands of present day Ecuador, Colombia, Panama and Venezuela. Within the next two centuries, this association split up, and Colombia became its own country. Since that time, this beautiful and mysterious land has been rife with Government upheaval, political assassinations, drug cartels and civil wars.

Along with the beautiful women and scenery, this was all I knew about the place at the time, and what I was unaware of is that Colombia had the highest rate of homicides in the world, peaking to 74 people for every 100,000 of the population by the end of the very year I was there. The statistics are quite staggering, but there were 3,173 people killed for political reasons, beating by a fraction the number of murders during the whole seventeen-year regime of Chile's Pinochet dictatorship!

The major cause of this violence is the disparity of wealth, with three percent of the elite owning seventy percent of the arable land, resulting in fifty-seven percent of the poorest Colombians subsisting on just three percent of the land. Some forty percent of the whole population are considered to live in absolute poverty, meaning they cannot meet basic needs, while a further eighteen percent are in absolute misery and cannot even meet basic nutritional needs. This has resulted in a society that has a large power structure to maintain this disparity, with frequent uprisings and guerrilla warfare from the many poor. A peasant farmer at this time could earn up to $2,500 for each hectare of cocaine he grows, as compared to about $100 for plantains or other agricultural products. Couple this up with the powerful Colombian drug barons, financed mainly by the West's markets, and dodgy politicians, and it results in one hell of a volatile situation and a Colombian military with the worse human rights record in the world.

I listened to the football commentary on the radio as the truck driver tore along the Pan-American, splashing through large puddles from the midday rain as a giant lizard the size of a dog ran across the road in front of us. Another goal had been scored and the commentator went crazy, as they do in Latin America, where football is almost treated as a religion. Not that I have any interest in the game - far from it, I actually hate it - yet it was about to save my life. I was only listening to it because I had no choice other than walk all the way to Turbo and to try to pick out any words I recognised to improve my Spanish; as no one seemed to speak English, I was in an ideal situation to learn the language which I had always wanted to speak.

The driver dropped me off during another deluge of rain and turned down some muddy farm track on the outskirts of a poor Indian village, some hundred miles south of Turbo. The rain was quite refreshing after the tropical heat and I stood on the side of the road, showering in it fully clothed. The rain stopped as quickly as it had started, and a woman in her mid-thirties came out of her hovel of a home and walked up to me, pleading, "*plata, plata.*" I looked at her, bemused, as she looked me up and down then pleaded again to do anything for *plata, plata*– money. She looked again at my worn-out clothing and backpack, then shook her head in disbelief, looked nervously around, then quickly went back inside. The odd thing about this is that she didn't seem to be a prostitute, just an ordinary peasant farmer's wife.

Moments later, on the brow of a hill, appeared three silhouettes – they were armed! *Oh God*, I thought, *don't panic… don't do anything hasty.* I sat motionless on my backpack at the side of the road. As they approached, it reminded me of that famous gunfight scene in *The Good, The Bad and The Ugly*, but they were much more heavily armed. One, a belt of bullets slung around his shoulder, was carrying a general purpose machine gun, while the other two had an array of grenades and throwing knives strapped to their arms and were carrying rifles. These weren't Hollywood's version of cowboys; these guys were battle-hardened guerrillas.

One of them walked straight up to me, while the other two stood back in the shade of a palm tree. *Always make the most of a bad situation,* I thought, and here I had the perfect example of one. He appeared a giant of a man as he loomed over me and pointed an Israeli assault rifle down to my head; the safety catch was off and his finger gripped the trigger. Shit! This was it. That's why the other two stood away. I was about to have my brains blown out, and they did not intend messing their combats. In the blazing heat I squinted, and with my left eye I watched a bead of sweat slowly run down the rim of my nose and drip to the floor, leaving a tiny splash mark on the tarmac surface...

CHAPTER 5

"The walk to the Cobb, skirting round the pleasant little bay, which, in the season, is animated with bathing machines and company; the Cobb itself, its old wonders and new improvements, with the very beautiful line of cliffs, stretching out to the east of the town, are what the stranger's eye will seek, and a very strange stranger it must be who does not see charms in the immediate environs of Lyme, to make him wish to know it better."
 - Jane Austen

My travels have taken me around the world and, navigating at sea by way of the stars, it could be argued that it has even taken me across the universe. I have even been to the world of an alternate universe, and I don't mean McCulloch's version of an English village in Arizona, but rather in my imagination; I've been to that of the Mappa Mundi. Now wouldn't it round things off just nicely by adding yet another dimension to travel? If only one could travel through time to any point in the past that one chose!

The brilliant intellect Carl Sagan, a prominent founder of SETI (Search for Extra-Terrestrial Intelligence) and author of *Contact* (which is certainly the best book I've ever read), asked the equally brilliant Kip Thorne to work out the mathematical equations for a time travel voyage through hyperspace to the star system Vega so that his book's heroine could meet a super-civilisation of extraterrestrials (as you do!). Thorne later recalls in his own work *Black Holes and Time Warps* that Sagan always posed the most challenging questions and had phrased it, "How could an alien society of infinite capabilities achieve this?" While a critic noted, "With terrestrials like Sagan who needs extras?" not only did Thorne calculate the mathematical equations for this, but even worked out the possible physics for such a thing to happen and - would you believe it? – while driving his wife and children along the Californian Interstate! It makes you think those bloody clever Americans don't do anything by halves!

If a mere mortal - and, as you may have noticed, a rather stupid one at times - like me, could have got his head around such a thing and used it to dip back through time, then he would have. But alas, such things will not be possible in the immediate future, and it may very well be anything up to a million years before this sort of technology is developed, if indeed we should still exist by then, which seems unlikely as no time traveller from that distant future has yet come back to visit us. It all has something to do with stretching a 'wormhole' out of some incredibly small stuff called 'quantum foam' but, just like Columbus with his two guide books, any potential time traveller interested in this subject should start by consulting Sagan and Thorne's pieces of work.

A problem with time travel is known as the 'Grandfather Paradox', and this effectively observes that, if someone could go back in time and kill their own grandfather before either of their own parents were conceived, the question arises as to how s/he could have existed in the first place to go back and commit the crime? The problem was superbly overcome in the cartoon *Futurama*, when Fry manages this and becomes his own grandfather! In other words, if anyone did travel back in time, then the future world they came from would instantly be changed; a new timeline would have been created.

Given the opportunity, who would not want go back in time and kill some megalomaniac like Hitler before he came to power, creating a new timeline and saving the lives of millions? Now, here is the twist; I have dipped back into the past like a real time traveller and, although I did not eliminate evil as bad as Hitler, the consequences may be the same, as I may have changed our future world by doing what I did.

… So, just like Captain Kirk aboard the USS Enterprise, I zipped around the Sun and time-warped back to the Earth of yesteryear to save humpback whales from extinction, or whatever else they do in the *Star Trek* universe… Actually, because I just don't happen to have a starship with warp drive capabilities, the way I did it was slightly different.

Before I could set off on my own time-travel voyage, I had to imagine that I was the person I mentioned in the second chapter, born about a century before myself and lived to be eighty. With this in mind, I decided to travel back in time to the place that I thought I knew best, my adopted home of Lyme, and boy, was I in for a few surprises. With the local knowledge that I had acquired as a boatman at the Cobb, and with the help from a few other resources, I chose to start my voyage by going back in time to the mid-nineteenth century.

Other resources that I used were old maps, such as tithe maps, and most notably the town survey commissioned by the mayor and local merchant John Drayton, showing all town properties belonging to the Corporation of the former borough. This survey had survived from a time when council property had to be remortgaged to raise funds to repair the Cobb from storm damage. The lifelong research of two local historians, Roberts and Wanklyn, were of invaluable help, along with a visual interpretation of those glorious times gleaned from a new invention which, fortunately, was used extensively in the Victorian era - photography.

The Colway Manor house of Lyme was badly damaged from the Civil war, and later, in the nineteenth-century, its ruins were described by the historian Roberts as, "the property of the Henley family, who lived there in great style for many years. The house was large, and a road between two rows of stately trees, which have been long since cut down, led to the church, to which some affirm there is now a subterraneous passage. The house is gone to decay - some of the ruins are visible at the back of the present farm-house. No courts are held, nor any symbols of a manor preserved."

This secret passageway still exists today! Nothing like the dramatic to get the reader interested - but then I suppose time-travel is (and I should know, as I'm the one who is now in Regency Lyme). By the beginning of the next century, this tunnel will be realigned with red brickwork and used as a conduit for the town's water supply, transporting up to 12,000 gallons per day from a source further uphill at the borough reservoir near Rhode Barton Farm. The tunnel has its entrance at the seaward end beneath the Davies Bath House, which someday will become the Marine Theatre. It runs underground via the church for one nautical mile north along the eastern bank of the River Lym, to an exit point beneath the third slab in the garden on the left hand side of the porch to the Colway Manor House.

Now, isn't that strange? A secret subterraneous passageway that runs from the seashore to the church, and then inland to the former home of Lord Cobham. Many stately homes throughout the country have such old secret passageways in the grounds of their estates that connect to the local church, but Lyme's is different. According to the Domesday Book, the Colway Manor was a three-hide estate with salt workings held by Glastonbury Abbey. It is difficult, if not damn near impossible, from the surviving Cotton records to connect this estate across four centuries of the Dark Ages to the suburbs of the Roman City of Moridunum, but it may have once been part of a larger salt-producing Roman estate. The secret passageway is certainly not this old, but could date back to the times of Abbey ownership, when Colway was a lazar-house, a type of hospital used for lepers. The resident monks may have once used this route to connect it to Saint Michael's church, to transport their contagious patients underground away from public view.

A far more plausible explanation is that this secret passageway was used for smuggling, and may have once connected to another harbour, one that predated the Cobb and existed nearer the river estuary, possibly the one destroyed in the fourteenth-century. We know that Lyme was notorious for smuggling as early as Cobham's time, since the Virginia explorer Ralph Lane was sent here while still a Customs Officer to investigate gold bullion smuggled out of England. He carried a special warrant to search ships, which resulted in a riot amongst the locals; the warrant was destroyed and his deputy thrown overboard from the ship they were inspecting!

With its own charters, Lyme had similar privileges to the Cinque Ports and was able to self-govern, which no doubt led to council corruption and smuggling, especially prevalent at the time in this part of the country, making it Lyme's most dominant industry. A maze of tunnels can also be found around the river estuary near the location of the former custom house, as smuggling became an organised trade by the eighteenth- and nineteenth-centuries. In fact, it was probably the only trade that ever kept Lyme alive, and when that declined, so did the town. Tourism, as well as the cement works at the Cobb, would later become the new industry that would help revive the town from the moment that I'm in now. Not only did the ancient smuggling tunnels shape the layout of Lyme, but also its long history of political corruption.

Again, in his own time Roberts recalls the town's resourceful smugglers: "A tub carrier, who ran into a senior official of the custom house, reputedly exchanged warm greetings and put the tubs down at the officer's feet, telling him 'The excise man axed me to take these two tubs to you, and gied me two shillings for the job; but damn him! If I had know'd they'd be so heavy, and would ha' cut my shoulder so, I'd seed unto the devil afore I'd ha' touched o' 'em.' Whether or not the Officer believed the story is unclear, but unable to carry the tubs himself, he eventually gave the man a further florin to carry them back to the Custom House, and strode off to await their arrival while the tub carrier 'rested'. As soon as the Officer rounded the corner, the man's exhaustion left him, and he effortlessly shouldered his burden and made off."

So, what types of goods were being smuggled into the area? A page possibly torn from an old Lyme Custom House account book, dated a century before Roberts' recollection and during the heyday of smuggling, lists: "Goods in the King's warehouse to be condemned before his Majesty's Justices of the Peace as soon as possible for the advantage of the King as well as the Offices."

This included two gallons of rum seized in the house of Henry Symes at Burton Bradstock, four gallons of brandy seized in the house of John Forse, concealed in a cave underground, having no permit for the same, and 110 gallons of brandy. "10 gallons of rum were seized being in the sea sunk at a raft near Seatown, by sweeping on suspicion of being there sunk."

In Roberts' time, the Lord of the Manor was Henry Holt Henley, who was also Lyme's parliamentary representative with a long line of Henleys having been representatives right back to the reign of Charles II. Secret passageways once ran from the cellars of the Custom House to various locations in the town, including his manor house. The Custom House stood in Beaufront Street to the rear of the fish market, now Bridge Street on the east bank of the river, and is today the site of the local hardware store. Between here and the sea stood Cobb Gate, where imported goods from the harbour were inspected after being transported along the seafront by packhorses. Henley held land to the rear of the custom house and the passageways led from the custom house cellar to the original Three Cups Hotel nearby (someday to become the Golden Cap Restaurant and then a bookshop), and somehow to the other side of the river into the main passageway. Standing here on the fourteenth-century Buddle Bridge, one can see how smuggled goods could get across the river without being seen using an older bridge covered by a cottage further upstream. An undated sketch by Wilfred Stephens even names this residence as 'The Smugglers' House'.

"If you wake at midnight, and hear a horse's feet,
"Don't go drawing back the blind, or looking in the street.
"Them that ask no questions isn't told a lie.
"Watch the wall, my darling, while the Gentlemen go by!"

A lot of contraband was just sneaked in under the noses of the understaffed Custom officials, who were also handicapped by unhelpful local bylaws about where their jurisdiction ended; cargoes unloaded at the Cobb could not be inspected until they had been carried half a mile east along the seafront to the Cobb Gate Custom House. From the Custom House, contraband could be despatched across the river by those very same Custom officials, out of the jurisdiction of the Cobb and into the cellars of the nearby corporation-owned properties such as the George Hotel, Golden Hart, or even the church that connected to an even larger passageway that ran up to the local manor house.

This longer passageway may have once been wide enough for ponies to transport the goods this extra distance. Not only was smuggling at this time a very organised industry in Lyme, but everyone was making a tidy profit from it. Boatmen, fishermen, government officials, and - no surprise - politicians; even the Lord of the Manor is replenishing his coffers. This was not just happening in Roberts' time, but certainly as far back as the medieval ages. What percentage of imported cargo was actually smuggled in Lyme may always remain unknown, but I bet it was high.

"... Five and twenty ponies,
"Trotting through the dark -
"Brandy for the Parson,
"'Baccy for the Clerk;
"Laces for a lady, letters for a spy,
"And watch the wall, my darling, while the Gentlemen go by!"

Throughout the eighteenth- and early nineteenth-centuries, as import duties increased, so did smuggling. The Napoleonic Wars had a dire effect on the trade, because French ports were closed to British shipping, but things soon picked up again after the war. In fact, smuggling became such a prosperous industry here in the West Country, that for many it became a way of life, not just for smugglers but also for the customs and preventive officers. Each knew one couldn't survive without the other, and so a fine balance had to be struck. As long as the profits from the contraband seized would satisfy the collector and the Board in London, and did not put the smuggler out of business, everyone was happy.

One of the most famous smugglers in the area during the eighteenth-century was Isaac Gulliver, nicknamed 'The Gentle Smuggler' because he claimed that he had never killed anyone during his smuggling career. Born near Trowbridge in Wiltshire, Gulliver bought North Eggardon Farm, not far from Lyme, with his ill-gotten gains. The farm was on a high enough position adjoining Eggardon Hill, which could be seen from the sea. He planted a circle of trees to act as a landmark for incoming smuggling boats from the bay. It is said that his gang were noticeable because they wore white wigs as a trade mark. Eventually, revenue men cut down the trees, and Gulliver continued his career at the other end of Dorset. Gulliver's Lane leading from the hill still exists today and whether it continues to be used for its intended purposes remains a mystery.

The most well-known of the next generation of smugglers was John (Jack) Rattenbury because he kept a diary of his exploits and then published a book entitled *Memoirs of a Smuggler*, which was still essential reading when I was a Cobb boatman! Nicknamed 'Rob Roy of the West', Jack had a very long and colourful career. He was born in nearby Beer, and as a child his father went away to sea and was never heard of again, so his mother had to support them both by selling fish.

Jack first went to sea when he was only nine years old, first on his uncle's boat and then as an apprentice to a Brixham fisherman. By the age of sixteen, he was well travelled and had started his smuggling career which he recorded as "then being plied very briskly in the neighbourhood!"

At the age of twenty-two, he married Anna Partridge, a Lyme girl, and still to this day has descendants in Lyme, Beer and Brixham. He described his occupation as a fisherman, pilot, seaman and smuggler. At the time, many clergymen were involved in these illegal activities, and John Smith, Pastor of the Unitarian Congregational Church of Colyton was the one who wrote Jack's diaries for publication.

Jack was forever having brushes with the law, being caught and then escaping, not just from the preventives but from the press gangs of the Royal Navy, and a reward for his capture was soon issued. His luck only changed when he helped in the rescue of a boat in distress that was carrying men of the Prince of Wales' Volunteers Regiment, who obviously had friends in high places, and it wasn't long before Lord Rolle had seen to it that all charges were dropped against Jack and that he received a reward for his daring rescue.

With such good fortune he tried to change his career, and at one time opened up a pub, became a boat dealer and even used his connections with Lord Rolle to attend the House of Commons in London to forward a case for the construction of a harbour at Beer. But just like all 'those who go down to the sea in boats'–types, he caught 'sea fever', an incurable virus that always brings one back to the sea. It's a difficult thing to explain, but as a former boatman I can well understand how Jack missed the excitement of his former employment, and it wasn't long before he was back smuggling and in trouble with the law.

After several more stints in gaol, he decided to hang up his cap for good and end his smuggling career at fifty-five, yet by this time, his son William was continuing the family tradition. Jack died ten years later and is buried in Seaton's churchyard; although the exact grave is unknown, his cottage is still standing in Beer. He still lives on in fiction in Falkner's *Moonfleet* as the Dorset smuggler Elzevir Block, who apparently has a striking resemblance to him. Jack is also the only one of all the great seafarers that I have mentioned that has a day of remembrance named in his honour on - would you believe? - 'Rattenbury Day', which is the sixth Friday after the first Monday in August.

Many argue that the most famous sea Captain that can be associated with the Cobb is Thomas Coram, the son of a local mariner and a native of Lyme. Although I have a passion for Somers and other merchant venturers, I am forced to agree with this argument. Coram spent much of his early life in the American colonies, where he operated a ship building business in Taunton, Massachusetts. He helped promote New England colonies, including sponsoring one in Novia Scotia for unemployed artisans. He made his fortune trading with America and supplying stores to the Navy, and it was while he was in London working for the Admiralty that he was horrified by the fate of many - often illegitimate - young children who were left abandoned to die on the roadside. He is famous today as the philanthropist who created the first Foundling Hospital, situated in Brunswick Square, Bloomsbury. Hogarth and Handel were two artists among his many supporters, and he spent the rest of his life developing this hospital, spending his entire fortune in the process and ending his days as a pauper himself. In 1749, two years before his death, Lyme made him a freeman of the borough.

It was during Coram's time that the disparity in wealth between rich and poor started to diminish, especially for sea merchants, with some poor mariners earning immense fortunes in trade with the American colonies, becoming Captains and even ship owners in their own right. Many of the older and larger buildings seen around Lyme today were built by these working-class merchants made rich from trade with America.

Not all the famous of Lyme need be associated with the Cobb. For example, Andrew Tucker was the uncle of Sarah Andrew, who was destined for his son. This is the beautiful Sarah that the novelist Henry Fielding fell in love with and attempted to abduct. She lived with relatives in the Tudor House across the road from Long Entry, next to the Wesleyan Methodist Chapel, a beautiful old Gothic building that was pulled down in 1979, and the graveyard desecrated to make way for a sterile looking block of flats. As a teenager, I watched in disbelief as old leather coffins were unearthed, bundled onto the backs of lorries and driven off to the crematorium!

The house is not of the Tudor period, but is actually named after a Mrs Tudor who had it built in the early seventeenth-century. It was for many years a hotel, but now also converted into - you guessed it - another sterile block of flats. One Sunday morning, Fielding, along with his servant, had planned the abduction of Sarah as she was on her way to church but, being heavily chaperoned by the jealous Tucker family, things did not quite go as he expected. After a scuffle, and a harsh exchange of words with the Tuckers, Fielding was chased off. He only made matters worse by getting himself into further trouble after pinning behind a note before leaving Lyme for good:"This is to give notice to all the world that Andrew Tucker and his son John Tucker are clowns and cowards – witness my hand, Henry Fielding."

He travelled to London, and this is where his literary career began. One likes to think that Sarah was his inspiration for Sophia in the satire *Tom Jones*, which is among the earliest English prose works described as a novel. Fielding was an old Etonian, and through frequenting Lyme had established a lifelong friendship with William Pitt the Elder; this contact inspired a career writing political satires. His consistent anti-Jacobite stance and support for the Church of England rewarded him with the position of London's Chief Magistrate. He even went on to help found the Bow Street Runners, England's first police force. Later described as one of the best magistrates in eighteenth-century London, he did a great deal to enhance the cause of judicial reform and improve prison conditions. Not a bad achievement for someone who started out on the wrong side of the law after the failed abduction of a Lyme girl.

According to a map of Dorset at this time by Emanuel Brown, "Lime Regis is a noted seaport town, is very much improved of late in trade and commerce; the harbour below it call'd the Cobb and Pier, is the best and largest in England."

This notwithstanding, Roberts seems to disagree, as he believed that from about this time the Cobb started to decline in commercial importance and Lyme was becoming a fashionable watering-place, at a time when spar towns such as nearby Bath were places for the 'taking of the waters' for health reasons, so now bathing machines became more popular at coastal towns like Lyme. In fact, it was Ralph Allen, the 'Man of Bath', who first used such machines on a commercial basis and was Fielding's inspiration for Squire Allworthy in *Tom Jones*. Allan was also responsible for the founding of a post office in Bath, one of the earliest postal systems in the country. If the port was declining in maritime trade as Roberts suggests, this could well have been compensated for by the creation of tourism by people like Allen.

At this time, the Henley family owned most of the parish of Lyme, which had a total area of 1,600 acres, with the borough owning just 40 of them! Henry Cornish Henley sold Cobham's warehouse to the libertarian philanthropist Thomas Hollis, from nearby Halstock; this building was situated near the river estuary and was to become the Assembly Rooms at the Cobb Gate end of town. He purchased several other properties along the seafront which he restored, including land at the eastern end of the walk, which today is the Marine Parade, greatly improving Lyme for a tourist resort.

It was this Hollis who donated the first town Bible to Holliston, Massachusetts, which was named after him and, like his father - also called Thomas - was a benefactor of Harvard University. In 1764, a disastrous fire swept through Harvard's Massachusetts Hall and destroyed all of the college's scientific instruments and most of the library, which was now more than a century old and the largest in British North America; its loss was a grave blow to the New England Colonies. A third generation Hollis - also named Thomas - sent books, money, scientific equipment, and funds for scholarships, and became Harvard's most generous benefactor, even though no Hollis had ever set foot on American soil. As a Baptist, he was concerned about the perceived intolerance of New England's varying Protestant beliefs or toleration of the Catholics, and agreed to endow a Professorship of Divinity at Harvard, provided the professor had communion with either one of the three Protestant denominations, Congregational, Presbyterian or Baptist. The Board of Overseers missed out Baptists until Hollis threatened to remove Harvard from his will and this was quickly amended with the promise to: "Observe religiously the will of ye donors & benefactors to ye said College in all disposal of their donations."

This was just as well, as the Hollis benefactors were not only republicans but dissenters in religion and Whigs in politics, and hence were great supporters for the most dissenting academy in the New World. Many of the donated books contained texts of political resistance from the seventeenth-century English writers who had been affected by the English Civil War. On his death, he bequeathed a fund to continue buying books, helping to make Harvard University the largest and richest educational establishment in the world today, thus indicating the consistent close links for over one and a half centuries between places like Lyme and the Americas.

He lived at Urles Farm in Corscombe and owned the Corscombe and Halstock manor houses. He left some property, including that leased from the Church as part of the Prebend lands of Lyme and Halstock, to his travel buddy Thomas Brand, provided he changed his name to Hollis, thus creating another generation of Thomas Hollises who continued the tradition as Harvard benefactors. This last Hollis would rename the Dorset farms that he had inherited to Harvard Farm, popularised the philosophy of John Locke (Locke Farm), admired satirist Andrew Marvell (Marvell Farm) and urged the acceptance of his fellow transatlantic republicans Liberty Farm. On Thomas Brand's death, some of his estates were left to John Disney - no relation to that of Mickey Mouse fame but – would you believe? – a direct descendant to none other than Lord Cobham.

Hollis is also reputed to have persuaded the Earl of Chatham to bring his sickly son to the town for the sea air. This was to be the future William Pitt the Younger who, at just twenty-four years old would become Britain's youngest ever Prime Minister. His time in office was dominated by the French Revolution and the Napoleonic Wars, and he was known as William Pitt the Younger, whose father, the Elder, was the same good friend and contemporary at Eton of Fielding, and after whom Pittsburgh, Pennsylvania was named when he became the British Secretary of State. The Younger, often referred to as a Tory, or 'New Tory', called himself an 'Independent Whig' and became a friend of William Wilberforce, the politician and philanthropist, who started one of the earliest movements to abolish slavery.

Near my birthplace in the little village church of Affpuddle is a unique piece of American history. After the dissolution of the monasteries, the village became an estate of the Lawrence family, and the coat of arms on the north wall of the chancel is identical to that on the signet ring worn by none other than George Washington. The stars and stripes, technically known as the bars and mullets, of the Washington family joined the crusader cross of the Lawrences after the marriage of Edmund Lawrence and Agnes de Wessington towards the end of the fourteenth-century, who were ancestors to the first President of the United States. More examples of the Lawrence coat of arms decorate Steeple church on the Isle of Purbeck, and are thought to have been the inspiration for the American flag and the Great Seal of the United States.

Modern conspiracy theorists suggest that this Great Seal was influenced by Freemasonry during the founding of the United States. George Washington was certainly a mason, and this was dramatised in the film *National Treasure*. However, the first use by masons of the pyramid, with its 'all seeing eye' was years after the creation of the American Great Seal. The eye is actually supposed to be that of God and not that of Big Brother watching over us, a fairly common Christian motif throughout the Middle Ages and during the Renaissance. The thirteen levels of the Pyramid indicate the original thirteen states, as do the red and white stripes on the American flag, and not the various levels of 'enlightment' of the 'Illuminati'. On the single dollar bill next to this symbol it reads 'In God We Trust' and I have often heard Americans follow this up with, "Everyone else has to pay!" I thought I should clarify this point, as I would someday discover a national treasure of my own that links to Freemasonry.

Hollis' Assembly Rooms had by now become the social centre for Lyme. Referred to as the 'Rooms', it had a ballroom large enough for an orchestra, with three chandeliers. The public nights were every Tuesday and Thursday, with an extra ball night during the summer season. Gentlemen could retire to billiard rooms or even one for cards, and several daily newspapers, along with most of the country's newspapers, could always be found here, delivered on a regular basis by a mail coach from Axminster, so any news of the outside world was first heard of here.

A plaque today marks Jane Austen's accommodation near the Shambles market place, and Bay Cottage on the Walk, not far from the Assembly Rooms, had a fictional resident, Captain Harville from *Persuasion*. She even wrote to her sister, telling of the delights of bathing machines, walking around the Cobb, and dancing at the local Assembly Rooms. One can easily imagine an ideal, twee society of sea-bathing, tea and cakes on the lawn with the provincial airs and graces of the locals, and Austen dancing the night away with her imaginary Mr Darcy from *Pride and Prejudice*. Yet, the reality of the time was far different, and any daily delivered to the Rooms would be a constant reminder.

These were violent times, and things had hardly changed since the Dark Ages. The Napoleonic war was already in its fifth year when Austen visited Lyme; while she was here, old Boney would declare himself Emperor of France, and war would rage not just across Europe, but throughout the colonies as well. The Christmas Ball at the Assembly rooms that year 'to commemorate his present majesty's accession and birthday' was for the 'barking mad' George III, during whose reign the Americans rightly won their independence from the greedy, overbearing British Government. American trade had built up places like Lyme by crumbling away the disparity of wealth that had previously infested our society and prevented poor, working-class sea captains from becoming the rich philanthropists that they now were. With the loss of the American colonies and trade with the 'New World,' recession was about to set in, not just here in Dorset, but right across the country.

These were hard times indeed for anyone who had not gained from American trade, and mainland Britain suffered intense economic depression and much social unrest because of it. Here in Dorset, the workers had been waged labourers and small tenants with very few rights; in some places, little had changed since medieval fiefdom. There was now little work, and the first food riot happened some two decades before the American War of Independence. Some women worked as button-makers, one of the main industries here in Dorset for over a century. At first, the buttons were made from a disk of Dorset sheep horn, covered with cloth and fine tracery. Later, metal rings manufactured in Birmingham were used instead of horn, and button-makers could earn reasonable wages. Women workers, often the sole breadwinners, averaged two shillings a day for making six or seven dozen buttons, which was much more money than farm labourers made, and in better conditions, even if it was just enough for tea for two at Lyme's Rooms.

If conditions were bad on land, then you can be sure that worse things happen at sea, as no less than one hundred and eighty six Dorset men - of which at least five were from Lyme - fought at the battle of Trafalgar, including the most famous captain at Trafalgar, Thomas Masterman Hardy of the flagship HMS *Victory,* from Portesham. Spain was already a sympathiser with France, and the Dutch also sided against the British. Austria and Russia were our only allies, since the American Revolution had ended too recently for any support from the former colonies, and the war of 1812 with America was still in the future. A single man-o-war or the larger seventy four gun ship-of-the-line - which was French designed, by the way - needed around three thousand tonnes of wood for its construction. This is roughly equivalent to the same number of fully-grown oak trees, and could clear away anything up to one hundred acres of forest.

Nelson and Napoleon may have had their differences but they actually agreed on something - the preservation of woodland. Napoleon even went as far as banning all tree felling without authority, and every tree felled was to be over one hundred and fifty years old and replaced by a new oak, leaving behind a legacy today of the finest and largest oak forests in all of Europe. Britain, on the other hand, never listened to Nelson, and all the great forests that we once held have long since gone. Even during Trafalgar there was a shortage of wood, Britain having relied heavily on its import from the former American colonies.

One day, while seated on the large admiralty anchor placed on the seafront near the spot where the Assembly Rooms once stood, I struck up a conversation with a passer-by, who asked me about Hardy's monument, which can just be seen in the distance from this spot. *Another inquisitive grockle,* I thought, as I tried to impress him with my knowledge of our beloved Captain Hardy. After a long and tedious lecture on Trafalgar, with which I could have bored the pants off Lady

Hamilton, I asked him why he was so interested and was left speechless with his nonchalant reply as he walked off.

"Oh, it's just that I'm one of his descendants."

Sir Richard Spencer, a distinguished Post Captain, who was to become another local resident, had served under Nelson and, after his Naval career ended, he married a local lass, Ann Liddon Warden of Langmoor Manor. They lived near the Cobb, where nine of their ten children were born. Here, Spencer became acquainted with the young historian Roberts, who transcribed old borough documents for the captain. While at the Cobb, it is contended that Spencer was inspired by the 1824 hurricane to invent a new type of lifeboat using buoyancy tanks. However, concerned about his future employment and that of his many children, he decided to emigrate to Australia, where he was appointed the position of governor of Albany in Western Australia. Unfortunately he died suddenly, leaving his wife, now Lady Spencer, to bring up their large family. The family name can still be seen on the old tithe maps, with land belonging to Lady Spencer in Lyme, and adjoining land on the Devon and Dorset border in Uplyme held in trust for the deceased Captain.

The Manor of Uplyme had once been vested to Glastonbury Abbey, and during the Dissolution, many realised that the crown was about to confiscate all this monastic property, so the church made the best bargain possible by selling monastery land to local gentry before the King's commissioners arrived. They were then able to raise some funds on which to live, in addition to the small pensions which were granted to many of the dispossessed monks. In the case of Uplyme, the farmland belonging to the former Newenham Abbey was sold to John Drake of Ashe, from nearby Musbury.

Francis Drake was distantly related to the Drakes of Ashe, and recent research by genealogists has linked the two families to a common ancestor in the early thirteenth-century, Ralph Drake of Worcester. The thirteenth-century was a period of growth and prosperity in the West Country and this could explain the migration of the Drakes further south. At this time, a new suburb in Lyme, known as Lyme Abbas, was being created on the west bank of the river Lym, and a grid-plan for its sister port at Melcombe was also being developed. In fact, it was at Melcombe that during the next century the

Black Death arrived aboard a Gascon ship, which brought so much devastation to the country.

Sir Francis Drake and Sir Bernard Drake were on friendly terms. Sir Francis loaned money to the Drakes of Ashe, and he mentioned Richard Drake of Esher, brother of Sir Bernard, in his will, calling him 'cousin'. Richard Drake, in turn, named his son Francis in honour of the famous Admiral. Apparently there was a dispute over this loaned money when Francis Drake was refused the use of the family coat of arms. The Drake family coat of arms included a red wyvern, an eagle-legged dragon and apparently, when this dispute came to blows - Sir Bernard having boxed Sir Francis on the ear - Queen Elizabeth intervened and created a new coat of arms for Francis. This coat of arms depicts the *Golden Hind,* the ship in which he circumnavigated the Earth, with its own red wyvern, this time hanging upside down from the masthead.

A descendant to the Ashe Drakes, Lord Marlborough, who also lived in Musbury, married into the Churchill family, and this explains why the Churchill family coat of arms is also quartered with this red wyvern. Today, a monument to the Drakes of Ashe can still be seen in the little church at Musbury, and is well worth the visit if only to remind you of this quaint and possibly true story. As we know, Sir Walter Raleigh was a friend to Lord Cobham of Lyme, and it is interesting to note that the two most famous Captains of the golden age of exploration both had connections to this small, remote part of the West Country.

Another seadog worth mentioning, who also adopted this part of the world as his home, is a young midshipman whose career began under Nelson aboard HMS *Boreas.* His name was John Talbot, and he worked his way up through the ranks aboard many Naval ships, including HMS *Victory* at Portsmouth and HMS *Windsor Castle* under Dorset's Samuel Hood in the Mediterranean. Talbot's final command was aboard HMS *Victorious,* and he was dispatched to the Adriatic, to intercept the French ship-of-the-line *Rivoli,* recently constructed in Venice. Talbot found this ship with a small escort on her maiden voyage, and immediately engaged. The ensuing five-hour duel inflicted heavy casualties on both sides, including on Talbot, who was badly wounded in the head by a large splinter. When *Rivoli* finally surrendered, half of her four-hundred-strong crew were either killed or wounded. Both battered ships were returned to Britain, where they were repaired, and *Rivoli* joined the Royal Navy. Talbot miraculously recovered from his wound, and was presented with a gold medal for his bravery and achievements.

When the 1812 war broke out with America, he took the repaired *Victorious* to the West Indies and then up the eastern seaboard of the United States, spending the next two years cruising the New England coastline, blockading the port of New London in Connecticut and preventing its use by American shipping. Later, the *Victorious* was sent into the Arctic Circle to defend whalers in the Davis Strait from American privateers. During this service, *Victorious* was badly holed by a rock and was forced to return to Britain. With the end of the Napoleonic Wars, *Victorious* was paid off and so ended the thirty-year naval career of this forty seven-year-old admiral, the Honourable Sir John Talbot Knight Commander of the Order of the Bath, as he would later become.

But the one thing I found most intriguing about this particular seafarer's life is the legacy that he left behind ashore. For in his retirement, he acquired a large country estate called Rhode Hill in the village of Uplyme in Devon, becoming Lord of the Manor and owning land which had once belonged to the Drakes of Ashe. The admiral had married Juliana Arundell, the daughter to James Everard Arundell, ninth Baron Arundell of Wardour, who just happened to be the largest landowning Catholic in the country.

The Arundell peerage had started with Thomas 'the Valiant' Arundell, grandson to Margaret Howard, sister to Queen Catherine Howard, the fifth of King Henry VIII's six wives and a cousin to his second wife, Anne Boleyn. I believe this strong Catholic lineage is where Juliana's dowry came from, which provided the finances needed to purchase this large estate rather than the bounty acquired from Talbot's naval days, as modern historians would have you believe. Even Nelson himself, the most predatory and by far the best of all these battle-hardened seadogs, never acquired enough bounty to purchase this amount of land.

Further research in my own future time would reveal that the marriage settlement of Sir John Talbot and Juliana Arundell was the

Delvin plantation on the island of Montserrat in the West Indies with all negro slaves. Here the slave owning - and many white slave - inhabitants were Irishmen who, in the early part of the seventeenth-century, had been banished by the English of Virginia, and later by Cromwell in Ireland for their Catholic faith. Land in Uplyme and Lyme that had originally been vested to the Catholic Church had become Catholic-owned once again, three centuries after the Dissolution of the monasteries, albeit through profits gained from the repulsive commerce of the slave trade.

It was this particular Arundell whose niece Isabel later caused a scandal by marrying a Protestant, the greatest of all the Victorian explorers, Sir Richard Burton, famous for not only introducing the Kama Sutra into Victorian society which, in those times, must have been deemed equally scandalous but for seeking the source of the Nile and his visit to Mecca during which he 'browned up', learnt Arabic, circumcised himself, and thus became the first - and perhaps only - non-Muslim to have taken part in the Haj pilgrimage.

The Arundells have an interesting and colourful history, with their family seat at Old Wardour castle in the adjoining county of Wiltshire. During the Civil War, it was besieged by over a thousand Parliamentarian troops, while the second Lord Arundell, a staunch Royalist, was away with the King in Oxford. His wife Lady Blanche, with only twenty-five fighting men, managed to hold them off for nine days before they surrendered after some vicious hand-to-hand combat, which lost them their family seat. Lady Blanche's son, Sir Henry Arundell, the future third lord was, as you can imagine, not too pleased when he returned home to find it overrun with Roundheads. If he couldn't have his family seat back, then he was dammed if he would let the 'Roundies' have it, and so besieged his own castle.

After three months of heated battle and constant bombardment by cannon fire, he recaptured the castle ruins from the Parliamentarians. It remains today as it was after its recapture, except that the eighth Lord Arundell employed Capability Brown to landscape the area, with the castle ruins becoming a folly next to a lake in the beautiful surroundings that still remain. It was this particular Arundell who sold the manor of Chideock near Lyme to his cousin Thomas Weld of Lulworth, and the Talbots of Axminster even adopted the Arundell surname when this lineage became extinct after the sixteenth Baron, a 'Bachelor Baron' was killed in action during the Second World War. Arundell is a proud family name that none could part with easily.

After the long Napoleonic Wars, militia service ended with the demobilisation of about a quarter of a million soldiers and this, together with the start of mechanisation, began a serious economic crisis right across the country. In Dorset, riots started, with farm labourers going around in gangs destroying threshing machines to try to force rich landowners to raise wages. Although the riots achieved a measure of success, it was short-lived. The government was ruthless in meting out punishment, and appointed a special commission of three judges to try prisoners in five counties, including Dorset. Of the many prisoners who were tried, twelve were sent to Australia and Tasmania. The threshing machine became a symbol of misery for the people of Dorset, as portrayed in Thomas Hardy's novel, *Tess of the D'Urbervilles*. It was soon to be joined by the button-making machine. Near-starvation hit many families across the county, with hundreds either emigrating to America or ending up at the workhouse. The British legal system at the time had few human rights for the poor, if any, as an old stone bridge not far from Lyme and similar to many others throughout Dorset proves, by bearing the warning, 'Any person wilfully injuring any part of this county bridge will be guilty of felony and upon conviction liable to be transported for life by the court.'

I have often wondered what would happen today if someone took a sledgehammer to one of these bridges to test the applicability of such laws, and thereby gain a free world cruise aboard a tall ship! In a court hearing you could always argue that this had been the punishment meted out previously and, if that should not have been the case, then maybe the court should consider compensation to the many poor families that had been subjected to this! Since, after America achieved its independence, Britain still needed a place to transport these poor desperate people, of which most could hardly be termed criminals in this day and age, the lot fell upon the newer colonies of the antipodes – Australia and Tasmania. After sentencing by the Dorchester Assizes for petty crimes such as stealing bread or a chicken, or damaging an old stone bridge, a potential convict could expect the standard sentence of seven years' transportation, which in many cases meant life.

Today, as you drive east from Dorchester along the A31 between Wimborne and Bere Regis, near a place with the illustrious name Winterbourne Zelston, you will come to a crossroads with an unusual red signpost. The original red post signified to prison guards in an age of high illiteracy the direction of Poole harbour, where convicts were marched in chains from Dorchester gaol for transportation on the awaiting ships. Turn right at this red post, and you arrive at the ruins of an old red brick barn at Botany Bay Farm. Today, this old historic building is used for paintballing. How things have changed! After a day's walk from Dorchester gaol in heavy chains, convicts would spend the night here before the next day's trek, before being loaded onto ships like cattle, and then enduring an eight-month journey to the other end of the world. It is an ominous place indeed, as one can still see the chain rings where convicts were shackled, and for many it would have been their last night ever on British soil. Further east, one arrives at the equally ominously named Botany Bay and World's End pubs.

Here again we are back at Morden village and my birthplace, so I can officially claim to have been born near the World's End when my father was a poor farm labourer before he joined the Army. The rich landowning gentry at Charborough House, the Drax family, are the direct descendants of those who used it for Monmouth's Revolution House, and my great-grandmother would later be a servant to them. Currently, the incumbent is the Right Honourable Richard Drax MP for South Dorset, whose ancestors also include a former mayor of Lyme. My own family name is French in origin and, because it is so uncommon, it can be easily traced as far back as an Officer under the command of William the Conqueror. Now, while travelling in Australia, I came across a statue dedicated to the first convicts landed at Botany Bay, where eleven ships of the first fleet came ashore with their 'human cargo' of around seven hundred and eighty of Britian's poor outcasts. I was ashamed of our barbaric history, but proud to see my family name mentioned on this statue, no doubt ancestors of this Right Herbert!

In direct response to these hardships and the food riots shortly before the point in time that I am going to travel to, the men of nearby Tolpuddle village instigated a 'Friendly Society of Agricultural Labourers', vowing not to accept any work for less than ten shillings a week. Unfortunately, six members were arrested on a charge of making an unlawful oath - even then an outdated and irrelevant law - and were transported to Australia for seven years. They were the brothers George and James Loveless, father and son Thomas and John Stanfield, James Brine and James Hammet. This caused a public outcry, resulting in thirty thousand demonstrators marching with a petition to the Home Secretary; the six martyrs were finally pardoned. It took a long time, but the actions of the 'Tolpuddle Martyrs' led directly to the creation of the Trade Union. In 1934, the Trades Union Congress, who meet every year in Tolpuddle, built six memorial cottages in their honour, and the conditions of Dorset's farm labourers are improving, albeit slowly... Very slowly!

One cannot finish describing this period of Lyme's history without mentioning the famous palaeontologist, Mary Anning. Her career also started early, when she and her brother Joseph found a skull protruding from the cliffs. Over a period of months, Mary painstakingly uncovered an almost complete skeleton of a 'crocodile'. The specimen was bought by the land owner Henry Hoste Henley for £23, and was passed on to William Bullock for his Museum of Natural Curiosities in London. This brought Mary's reputation to the attention of the scientific community. Henley must have had a keen interest in fossils, as an ammonite was named after him, *Liparoceras Henleyi*. The specimen that Mary found was later named *Ichthyosaurus*, the 'fish-lizard', by scientists de la Beche and Conybeare. At just twelve years old, she became synonymous with palaeontology and the children's tongue twister, 'She sells seashells on the sea shore...', is reputedly based on her. Another local fossil collector had a table made from a slab of inlaid coprolite - dinosaur shit, to us laymen - which is known today as 'Buckland's dinosaur poo table'! His son Francis remembered this table in his father's drawing room, where, "It was often admired by persons who had not the least idea what they were looking at!"

As early as the thirteenth-century, Lyme was such an important market town that it was represented by two seats in Parliament. For instance, in the first year of King James I's reign, its parliamentary representatives were the Knight Sir George Summers and John Hassard, Esquire. Later, John Drake, the distant relative to Sir Francis, would also hold a seat, as would the rich landowning lords of the manor Henry Henley, John Henley and Henry Holt Henley, and then from the Charlborough estate Henry Drax. We even had our very own Winston Churchill in the early eighteenth-century, an ancestor to the one that we all know better. The Churchill family were actually neighbours to the Drakes in nearby Musbury, and John Scrope, who shared one of these two seats with Churchill, had been an MP for Bristol, but lost his seat because he supported Walpole's unpopular Excise Bill.

As a Whig, Scrope was invited by the Henley family to help represent Lyme in Parliament, sharing the seats with Henry Holt Henley. His nephew was the Bristol merchant Francis Fane, and this is how the Fane regime entered the Lyme political arena, representing both seats when the Henleys retired from politics in the mid-eighteenth century. It is worth noting that Scrope had once disguised himself as a woman to spy for Monmouth when in Holland, and it was this espionage work that had decided the Duke's landing place because of his popularity amongst the locals - that's Monmouth's popularity, by the way, not Scrope's when dressed as a woman!

The Fanes built up a certain overwhelming majority on the Council. They did this for two reasons; the mayor was the returning officer at elections, and also, the Town Council made 'freemen', and in these times only freemen could vote for Members of Parliament. It had been realised that whoever commanded the Town Council commanded two seats in Parliament. Unlike Walter Raleigh in times gone by, 'the Fanes did climb and did not fear to fall', as an unbroken lineage of this corrupt family represented Lyme in both seats of the house for the next eight decades, and rarely visited the town or showed any interest in the place.

The official decline in trade at the Cobb during the first half of the nineteenth-century that Roberts described obviously brought about a corresponding decline in the unofficial trade of smuggling. I must be careful what I say next, as I believe the historian George Roberts was one of Lyme's greatest intellects. He was the local schoolmaster and well versed in Latin and Classics, which helped immensely in translating ancient manuscripts. Later on, he became mayor and had access to the 'unexplored' borough archives, resulting in a priceless piece of work that took a lifetime to complete; all the historical research was his own - a truly remarkable Renaissance man. He was no doubt the best authority on the Georgian era of Lyme, but he unfortunately lived in a time when even recent history could be wild conjecture or, at the very least, inaccurate.

Or did Roberts know a little bit more than he let on? He certainly admits to being aware of local smugglers when he recalls an account of them in the first edition of his work. This book was dedicated to his benefactor, the Right Honourable Earl of Westmoreland, who is none other than the sixteenth Earl Anthony Fane, MP for Lyme. It is interesting to note that the latter Edwardian historian Cyril Wanklyn was puzzled as to where the fortune of the Lords of the Manor, the Henley family, had come from. As incredulous as this may sound, he even conjectured that it was from sheep farming, as they had held so much land for generations, but that it had mysteriously dwindled to nothing by the start of the twentieth-century, when a butcher purchased the country seat of Colway on the strength of a rumour that the Henley fortune was buried in its grounds. He never found anything, and is said to have spent a larger fortune looking for the family jewels than what they may have actually been worth, had they existed. More Henley land can be found to the rear of the old Custom House and, as I covered earlier, if smuggling was occurring in the cellars beneath the Custom House, then it was obviously the result of a cover-up from the top, and a nice little perk for the Henleys, then the Fanes.

Now, the reader may wish to know why I have chosen to travel back to this particular point in time. Just prior to this time, the High Wall of the Cobb had 192 feet of it breached during a storm in 1817 and, due to lack of finances mainly caused by the country being virtually bankrupt from the Napoleonic Wars, nothing much could be done to repair it, and this is how it remained when another storm struck seven years later. At the time, two important things happened to help preserve the Cobb and the town of Lyme Regis. The first was the renewal of the Cobb Act in 1821 after the original Elizabethan one, and the second was the genius of Colonel Fanshawe, Captain Savage, and the men of the Royal Engineers who repaired the Cobb.

This new amended Cobb Act, 1 & 2 Geo IV, was "an act for maintaining and improving the harbour, Pier or Cobb, at the Port and Borough of Lyme Regis" by funding the repair and maintenance of the harbour from new rates placed on merchandise. Back in my own future time, the historical records of our realm are held mainly in the National Archives, which are immense. For my home county alone, there are over six miles of shelving at the Dorset History Centre. Historical records relating to the Cobb and Lyme consume quite a large proportion of this, with even more related documents spread throughout the archives of other counties. Yet no copy of this 1821 Cobb Act can be found, and only recently, with the power of such tools as the Internet and the Freedom of Information Act, has it been possible to piece together a history that is far more concise than any previous historian, such as Roberts, Wanklyn or even Fowles (had he tried), could have imagined.

Back in my own future time, I obtained a copy of this Georgian Act from the House of Lords Parliamentary Archive Record Office, and in the margin of the second page were listed the various acts that had been used over the centuries to amend it. One was the original Elizabethan Cobb Act, which did not exist in Parliament's Long Calendar of Acts, and during my research of Roberts' work I came across a description of this earlier act officially titled '27 Eliz I', since it was created in the twenty-seventh year of Elizabeth the First's reign, 1584. I then realised that I had seen a copy of this Elizabethan Act in the National Archives in Dorchester. Someone had gone to a lot of trouble to separate the Georgian Act from the original Elizabethan one, but why?

Some further research revealed that a total of fifty-eight Private and Public acts are missing from the Parliament's Long Calendar of Acts. The earliest one is from a time just after the War of the Roses in the reign of Henry VII, and the rest during each monarchy up to and including the Restoration of Charles II. Most are missing from the time of Henry VIII, with an obvious one being the 'Private Act, 23

Henry VIII: An Act against Payment of First Fruits to the See of Rome; Missing: not in the original Parliament Office Long Calendar of Acts'. One can easily imagine a temperamental Henry tearing that one out during the conflict with the Pope that resulted in the Dissolution of the Monasteries. Eleven others are also similarly categorised, while forty-one are 'missing for several centuries', and the remaining six are just 'missing'.The Cobb's original 'Act 27 Elizabeth I' is a Private Act categorised as 'missing: not in the original Parliament Office Long Calendar of Acts'.

The official definition for each type of 'missing' from Parliament's original authoritative list of original acts is that the first volume of missing acts was compiled in 1608. This means that any acts dating from before 1608, which are missing from the Long Calendar, were missing when they compiled the list in 1608, while 'missing for several centuries' simply means that they've been missing for a very long time, but Parliament can't be sure how long. There are some historic lists from the mid-nineteenth century of 'missing acts' and Parliament believes the acts regarded as 'missing for several centuries' are the ones on these lists - i.e., recorded as already missing in the mid-nineteenth century. 'Missing' simply means they're missing and Parliament doesn't know exactly when - presumably since the mid-nineteenth century.

I blinked, read the email that I had received from Parliament explaining this to me a second time, and again realised that none of this made any sense. The Act of 1584 that I had returned to Parliament had been officially missing since 1608, but had continued to be used as a legally binding document for two centuries for the upkeep of the Cobb until it was amended in 1821. The whole thing was now becoming as complex as a hunt for some national treasure, with clues woven into the complex fabric of the Cobb's history, and only a time travel voyage would reveal the answer.

The Royal Engineers had started work on the Cobb seven years after the High Wall was breached, when unfortunately a second storm struck and washed away all the scaffolding and equipment needed for its repair. This is the hurricane that inspired Spencer to design a new type of lifeboat, and that had also thrown up a shingle bank and taken the status of 'island' from Portland, as it was now permanently connected to the mainland. Even under these conditions, Fanshawe and his men went on to complete the repair of the Cobb in record time and under budget at a cost of £17,337.0. 9¼. Who could ever vouchsafe doing something under budget and ahead of schedule in my own future time?

The High Wall of the Cobb was designed to be sacrificial, as a mostly hollow structure with very little mortar; it is ironic that hydraulic cement would become its major export for many years after from the works on the adjacent Monmouth Beach, yet very little was ever used in its construction. The landward end of this wall was lower and acted as an over wall sluice to self-sluice the harbour. The work was completed within a year, using masonry blocks running in courses and each block bound to the next one by wooden dovetails; this was preferred to the previously used iron cramps because if any part of the wall shifted in respect to the rest, it could easily be disassembled and the block work realigned by Cobb masons using a gin crane housed in the gin shop in a section of the hollow wall.

In my own future time, a bricked-up doorway at the beginning of the Cobb marks where the original ginshop used to be. In Victorian times it was moved to where the future seated alcove exists further along. On top of the High Wall between the two of them, if you know where to look, can be seen the year 1825 carved into the masonry work, indicating when construction had been completed. Further along, a compass rose is also carved on the curve of the wall, used to lineup the beginning of the harbour wall with magnetic North of that year. This was something I would work out for myself while bored of touting for boat trips on one of those hot, balmy days far too early in the year for any tourists. Below this is the whispering gallery which, just like the one in Saint Paul's Cathedral, has strange acoustic properties.

Captain Savage found that a ratio slightly less than two to one of sand and 'Lyme lime' made the best mortar. During storms, the hollow sections inside the High Wall between the cow-stone (the siliceous nodules of the upper greensand, as an expert informed me!), extracted from the town quarry with occasional bonding courses of capstone, would fill up with seawater to reinforce the wall, and behave as a buffer against the next wave. As the storm abated and the tide ran out, so did the sea through the narrow half-inch gaps between the masonry works; the reverse happened at the next high tide. This method was so efficient that the Victorians would later drill holes around the top of the wall so it could fill up with water much faster during high tides and storms.

At about this time, trade at the Cobb had been on the decline, due to competition from the larger seaports of Southampton, Portsmouth and notoriously Liverpool, after the *Liverpool Merchant*, its first slave ship, set sail for the American and West Indian colonies via Africa, making Liverpool prosperous from the 'Slave Triangle' which resulted in its control of eighty percent of Britain's slave commerce, and over forty of Europe's.

Roberts states that the number of vessels which entered the Cobb from foreign parts just after the High Wall was rebuilt was thirty-four British, and four foreign; the number of those which cleared outwards thirty-two British, and four foreign. Sixteen vessels were built and registered here the year that rebuilding started, six in the year work was completed, and eight the year after; about this time, there were belonging to the port thirteen vessels of more than one hundred tons burden, and twenty-six of smaller size. By 1831, the number of vessels which entered and cleared with cargoes inwards, outwards, and coastwise, was 629, the aggregate tonnage of which amounted to 44,930; two years later there was a drastic drop with the number of vessels at only 201, and the corresponding tonnage 11,877. This was at a time when trade with France, Spain, and the West Indies had greatly declined, and only a few vessels were fitted out for the Newfoundland fishery, and a little trade with the Mediterranean ports.

"Indeed, the harbour appears chiefly valuable as a place of refuge for small vessels during bad weather, as it is the only safe shelter between Lyme Regis and the Start Point of Portland."

A House of Commons paper for the same year of this drastic decline appears to be the result of the Royal Commission of Lord Grey's enquiry for the Municipals Corporation Act and describes: "The property in the possession of the Corporation consists of divers lands and tenements situate within the borough of Lyme Regis; the greater part whereof is leased for 99 years, determinable with the decease of three lives, under small conventionary rents and heriots;

and acquired by grant from King Charles I, in the tenth year of his reign *(1634)*, upon condition of maintaining the pier and harbour, called the Cobb, and seawalls, and other tenements acquired by grants of individuals; the whole producing an income communibut annis of 230/., subject to repairs and taxes. The pier or Cobb granted to the mayor and burgesses, with power to receive tolls or harbour dues for vessels with their cargoes entering the Cobb, averaging about 450/. a year, to be applied to the maintenance of the Cobb, but which is so very inadequate to the repairs of that building, which has suffered so much by repeated storms and tempests of the sea, that the Corporation have exhausted their funds on account of the repairs of the Cobb and sea walls, and have been obliged to mortgage all their property for the preservation of the Cobb, leaving a very inadequate provision to carry on the municipal government of the town."

In other words, the newly amended Cobb Act was issued too late to provide sufficient funds for the proper maintenance of the Cobb from duty levied on its shipping. Consequently, all property owned by the Corporation of Lyme had to be mortgaged to finance the repair of the High Wall, and this is the reason for the survey map commissioned by the mayor John Drayton when the Royal Engineers started work on the Cobb. The money was borrowed from John Frederick Pinney, whose family had, since the seventeenth-century, been involved in the slave trade on their Caribbean sugar plantations. The family received more than £30,000 in compensation when slavery was abolished, while the freed slaves received nothing. It's ironic that something as appalling as slave commerce had purchased the Talbot Estate of Lyme and Uplyme, been a contributing factor that had brought about the decline of the Cobb as a major seaport and compensation paid to slave owners when slavery ended was used for its recovery.

In the year that work on the Cobb was completed, it was estimated that the duty levied at the Cobb was on average £400 per annum, which was barely enough to cover the interest on the money borrowed. So the government ordered the Corporation to sell off some of its property to raise the cash for this deficit. This may explain why the Pinney family are suddenly the largest property owners after Henley on the 1841 tithe map for Lyme.

To complicate matters further, a dispute had broken out when the current Lord of the Manor, Henry Hoste Henley, brought a lawsuit against the Corporation because seawalls were found to be defective, after a storm which left his land inundated with seawater. The case was heard at Dorchester and Henley won a £100 settlement. The Corporation, run by the Fanes, appealed and Henley won again. The Corporation continued to appeal, and the whole case was carried on to the High Court. After almost eight years of litigation, for a matter that could have been settled for £100, Henley won again and the lawsuit cost the town £3041 and 10s.

The case heard in the High Court had a very interesting twist, as the Corporation, in its defence, stated that the funds granted by the new act had been inadequate and that is why they could not possibly have repaired the Cobb before the 1824 storm had struck. Henley argued that the charter created on the 20th June 1634 in the reign of Charles I (10 Car. 1) had already provided the adequate funding for the Cobb's repair, by relieving the town of more than eighty percent of Royal Fee-Farm, a type of tax payable from renting out Corporation owned properties for the Royal Borough. A copy of this charter still exists in my own time in the Dorset archives; beautifully inscribed in Latin, it translates as a confirmation by Charles I for the relief of 27 Marks out of a total of 32 Fee-Farm paid each year forever, provided it is used for the Cobb's proper upkeep and repair. A single Mark is the measure of eight Troy Ounces of gold, making this relief in my own time equivalent to about a quarter of a million pounds per annum, proving that the unique Cobb is a very expensive structure to maintain properly. For generations, these two families had been close acquaintances and then suddenly the case of Henley versus the Mayor and Burgesses of Lyme (the Fanes) seemed almost like a game that left the town in recession.

Lyme had a small electorate that was used by the Fanes to gain undue and unrepresentative influence within Parliament; this fits the definition 'rotten borough' perfectly well, but reform by Lord Grey's Municipals Corporation Act brought about change, and Lyme was now represented by a fairly voted single Member of Parliament. This was Colonel William Pinney MP, a Whig whose father had been the mortgagee of a staggering £4,000. The interest on this figure alone was a further £336 and 10 shillings per annum. The total owed by the corporation at this time, including costs, now amounted to £5,300, a very large sum in those days.

Now, the interesting thing that resulted from this case is that the Cobb charters could be used to raise money for the repair of the Cobb, even though it was no longer a major seaport, by investing money in property and renting them out for both the locals and a new type of import – tourism. Thus, one could argue that it was from this point onwards that tourism really started in Lyme and became its staple industry. The Corporation not only paid Pinney back his money, but started investing in more inns, hotels, holiday villas, shops and offices to maintain the Cobb as it transformed from seaport to tourist resort.

Despite the decline in maritime trade in the early nineteenth-century, Lyme has become a relatively prosperous place, with extensive cloth manufacturing by the firm Glyde and Company in Mill Green on the banks of the river Lym, once the site of the Elizabethan Court. Every Tuesday and Friday, a market was held at the Shambles and down at the Cobb, pleasure boats could be hired by visitors with excursions along the cliffs, and larger vessels sailing to Guernsey or Jersey every ten days. The London Constant Trading Company has three eighty-tonne ships, one of which transported passengers every fortnight to and from the Cobb to Carpenter and Smith's wharf, London. Other vessels were owned by local merchants and used for its main import of coal, which incidentally sold at one shilling and four pence for a double bushel, a volume equivalent to a sixteen gallon bucket.

The streets were badly paved and not at all lighted, and the principal thoroughfare was so narrow that the safety of foot-passengers was said to be endangered. Open water courses flowed down Silver, Broad and Church streets at this time, with many complaints about the annoyance of pot water. The fish-market, which was in front of the Custom house, was held in the best part of the town at this time, and regarded as a nuisance, as was the butchers' Shambles further up the main street. This market was founded in the late-sixteenth century and was a messy place indeed; here, meat was cut up and hung for display, hence the expression 'it's a right shambles!'. It was known as the Cornhill until the end of the century. It had a bell tower with a clock which perished in the fire of 1844, and would never be replaced - only the bell survived and would someday be on display in the Corporation museum.

At 'Top O' Town', the road divides, and on the left hand fork the historian Cyril Wanklyn recorded in the next century that, "The most interesting of all the houses in Pound Street is the Lawn, which was once the tavern attached to the old bowling green, or occupies the site of it. The house had a licence in past times, and is constantly mentioned in old records."

According to the Drayton survey, this was part of the Corporation estate, and it was here that the townsfolk first sighted Monmouth's ships prior to his landing. A place called South Cliff had recently been built on the old bowling green by the Town Clerk, Henry Franks Waring. He gave the name to Lucy's Jetty on the seafront below, after a boat of that name that he used to keep moored there. The jetty was the creation of pioneer geologist Henry de la Beche, who grew up in the town and was one of the leading scientists of his time. Not only was he the first to realise the talent of Mary Anning, but also that a well-positioned groin would restrict longshore drift, thus creating a small beach area along the seafront using shingle build-up that had been sluiced out of the Cobb.

Further uphill at the junction of Cobb Road is Belmont, also part of the Corporation estate and the future home to novelist John Fowles. From here to the bowling green, it was known as 'The Island' and all of it is Corporation property. The road down to the Cobb is nothing more than a rubble track at this time, and from here I can see the masts of several ships berthed in the harbour. This was once a toll road named after the Coade family, who had also leased Belmont. It has now been renamed 'New Road', since it was given to the town by John Stein, the owner of the last shipbuilding yard in Lyme. He lived further uphill at High Cliff Lodge, and once owned the prestigious High Cliff across the road. These two buildings are in wide-open fields with very little tree cover, Stein having used up all the wood for shipbuilding many years previously.

1833, and the last day of July, the first steam ship to arrive at the Cobb opened up a new era of maritime passenger transportation. The steam packet HMS *Messenger* towed the royal yacht *Emerald* into the bay, which had arrived to collect two important passengers - a young Princess called Victoria with her mother, the Duchess of Kent. The royal party had spent a couple of days at Melbury House, and were escorted over the hills to the Cobb by the Earl of Ilchester's yeomanry. They were met at the harbour on the 2nd of August by the mayor, John Hussey, no doubt with the town's brass band blurting out 'God Save the King' as the royal party passed through a double file of coastguards to ascend the Crab Head steps onto a floating platform. This part of the Cobb was later renamed Victoria Pier in honour of the future Queen. No doubt the young Princess 'was amused', as the steps are so narrow they can only be negotiated by walking sideward like a crab. The steam packet ferried the party and their carriages out to the *Emerald,* which weighed anchor at 3pm and sailed southwesterly for Plymouth. Boatmen had a field day, as every vessel in the harbour was full of people at one shilling a head for that brief one hour; it was Victoria's only visit to Lyme.

Sole visit or not, Her Majesty had set a precedent, since by the end of her reign, two large, steam-operated passenger vessels, with the fitting names *Victoria* and *Duchess of Kent* regularly ferried visitors to and from the Cobb. The ancestor of a friend of mine was the cobbler and town crier George Legg, who used to be the agent for the steamer operators Cozens & Company, which had an office in Silver Street. The summer day trips aboard these vessels reached many beaches, piers and ports, from as far away as Torquay or Bournemouth. Local boatmen would ferry passengers back and forth when the tide was too low to berth the larger vessels, and these visitors generated an extra income for the locals.

The Cobb had become a bonding port, where dutiable goods could be received in bond. John Drayton had built the 'Bonding Yards' for the reception of his timber and erected a very extensive warehouse, later used for the accommodation of the public. Just recently, the north wall of the Cobb had been moved further eastwards, to increase the number of moorings. At this time, a new Custom House was being erected nearer the harbour on land purchased by the Corporation from Colonel Pinney; had the Free Trade year and the passage of Peel's Act been foreseen, the new Custom House would never have been built or the north wall moved, because the days of the Cobb being a major seaport were numbered. The Custom House would become leased housing, known as Cobb Lodge and, when the Borough Council was abolished after the 1974 government reorganisation, this became one of the few government properties to be legally transferred and was eventually purchased by my parents. What happened to the rest of the Corporation estate is a point I am about to raise.

On Christmas Day, 1839, creaks and rumbles could be heard to the west of Lyme at a place known as the Undercliffe, likened to thunder by farm workers and artillery fire by the veterans of Waterloo. The ground then shuddered and collapsed on Boxing Day. This was to become known as the 'Great Slip' and became very famous because it was well-documented by the two famous geologists Buckland and Conybeare, who just happened to be in the area when it happened. A large tract of land below Bindon Manor and Dowlands Farm slipped, creating the features now called Goat Island and the Chasm. It took with it an area of sown wheat field, which remained sufficiently undamaged for the wheat to be harvested, and the slip became a popular visitor attraction.

My journey through time takes me to the moment when ship building had almost finished. We have a new Custom House erected on the site of the former shipyard, the bonded store and warehouse still remain on Drayton's land, and at the other end of the seafront, there are the skeletal remains of the burned out old Custom House and marketplace, a result of the fire that had also destroyed the Shambles Market bell tower. The charcoal remains of buildings in Coombe Street and Lyme Abbas, the oldest part of the town, can also be seen, along with the former George, once famous for its smuggling; now all gone. This may not have been such a bad thing, as this part of Lyme had become the slum area with constant problems of pot-water being flushed into the river.

Piles of collected sedimentary rock can also be seen, as they can in my future time, on mid-nineteenth century plans of the Cobb belonging to the Harvey, Hutchinson, Osborn and England family firms. These are stored in the lagoon to await transportation at low tide to the cement works, and are used to fire the lime kiln furnaces on Monmouth's Beach for production of its main export of cast hydraulic cement bricks. Quarried from the nearby cliffs, the Blue Lias rock was transported by the 'stone boatmen' to the Cobb come summer or winter, for crushing and heating in the kilns. One assumes that the imported rock and finished product were transported back and forth from the kilns by horse drawn carriages, along a rail track around the Cobb.

It is low-tide, and the small coasters *Glencoe* and *Masterman Hardy* can be seen aground beside the Cobb warehouse, with their hoisted sails drying out in the sun while awaiting a cargo of Lyme lime-made cement. Surprisingly, a recent plan had been proposed to extend the High Wall of the Cobb around to Cobb Gate Jetty, near the burnt-out remains of the old Custom House, which would make the harbour large enough to accommodate the newer, larger shipping that were now plying their trade elsewhere. Had this happened, then Lyme would surely have been able to compete with the larger ports of Liverpool, Southampton and even nearby Weymouth, and maybe back in my own future time, we would have a vast yacht marina on the scale of Plymouth's or Dartmouth's.

In the next decade, the Chard Road and Lyme Regis Harbour Railway Company was formed and put forward another revolutionary idea; scaled plans to build a new twelve-and-a-halfmile rail link from Westford, the Corporation owned property in Thorncombe, to link Chard Junction and Lyme with a terminus in Monmouth Street near Saint Michael's Church, and a further three-quarter mile extension around the seafront to the Cobb. Had these two ideas been merged into one, then it is possible that the Cobb would have remained a major seaport into the 21st century. Imagine visiting yachts and cruise ships arriving at a supersized marina, with a steam train link for its new import of tourists to the rest of our rural and beautiful West Country. Whoever said the 'olden ways were always the best' may well have been right!

In the previous century to the one I am in now, George III's inspector of inland letter carriers was a Frederic Festus Kelly, who created the first Post Office Directory for London, which is now extended to cover the whole country. All editions of Kelly's Directory can still be viewed in my future time in the London Guildhall Library, and from the mid-nineteenth century onwards, it is possible to trace all privately owned residences throughout the country, including places like Lyme.

By 1875, the Post Office Directory shows that a Major-General Sir Percy Herbert, Bart., KCB, MP, had his private residence at Holmelea House in Lyme, which can still be seen on later Ordnance Survey maps as a building on the site of the old Cobb Road toll gate of the previous century. Sir Percy Herbert had a distinguished military career, notably during the Crimean War. I'm only mentioning him in passing because it's the only other Herbert that I have ever been able to associate with my adopted home during my time travel voyage, and he's not just any old 'Right Herbert', but a Right Honourable one at that!

On towards the closing years of the nineteenth-century, and Lyme can be associated with such notables as the artist James McNeill Whistler, the authoress Beatrix Potter - who used views of Lyme and the surrounding area for *The Tale of Little Pig Robinson*, which is obviously beyond the scope of this book – and the surgeon Dr Joseph Lister, who lived at the Highcliff. Influenced by Pasteur's germ theory of disease, Lister used carbolic acid as an effective antiseptic agent, and introduced it to the surgical process. The Listerian system dramatically reduced the number of patient deaths by infection, and was quickly adopted throughout Europe and America, becoming the standard mode for surgical procedure. It was said that prior to his time, a person had a better chance of surviving the battle of Trafalgar than as a patient under the surgeon's knife. He became the first physician to be made a peer and sit in the House of Lords. He took the name Baron Lister of Lyme Regis which, incidentally, without a male heir was to be the first and last time any person held that title… Hmm, I wonder.'Baron Herbert of Lyme'… No, no, on second thoughts, I still much prefer to be a Right Honourable Herbert instead.

Being a former boatman at the Cobb, I now arrive at a point in time that is my personal favourite, as surprisingly I find it is the heyday of the pleasure boat industry, with anything up to forty boatmen taking visitors on trips around the bay in rowing boats or by sail. Not so surprising is the bloody mindedness of the local Council - talk about history repeating itself.

The competition must have been fierce amongst the boatmen, as a dispute concerning overloading with passengers had arisen. A memorandum to the borough, dated 11th June 1895, from Charles P. Wilson, the assistant secretary of the Board of Trade Surveyor's Office, described various formulae to calculate the maximum safe number of passengers, depending on a vessel's length, breadth and draft. The problem was that each port around the country had a different formula. A sailing boat with a length of twenty-four feet, breadth eight feet and a draft of two feet at the Cobb is about the right size to negotiate all states of the tide for tripping.

At Yarmouth, the life-saving appliances rule was followed, which meant about fifty passengers for that sized vessel was used; far too many - imagine trying to come-about in a force six with a full boat load! Maldon had twenty-nine, Sheerness nineteen, Tynemouth fifteen, and rowing boats in Scarborough with a length between twelve to seventeen feet held six to eight passengers, including crew. The whole system for licensing pleasure boats was in chaos. For example, at Redcar, it was noted that, 'The person employed to fix the number of passengers is the master of a steamer, who uses the rule of the life-saving appliances for section A boats (Statutory Rule made under the Merchant Shipping Act of that year), with the result that too many persons are assigned'. At the other extreme, in Barrow, it was noted that, 'the inspector is a retired printer and knows very little about boats'!

The Cobb Act had given the borough the power to enact its own bylaws, and in 1898 Henry Sprackling, a local police officer, was the inspector for pleasure boats. This must have been a good season, as his report to the Council states, 'That no accident in boating was reported during the year, notwithstanding the fact that, during certain periods of the summer, the Watermen (boatmen) were taxed to their fullest capacity.'

The number of licensed watermen was thirty-two, with thirty licensed rowing boats and nine sailing although, 'There have been two prosecutions, and two convictions under the Pleasure Boat Bylaws during the year. With these exceptions the Watermen generally, I am pleased to say, show a willingness to carry out the Council's Bylaws.'

In present times, I've never known the Cobb to have more than fourteen licensed pleasure boats in a season, and most of them have never been taxed to their fullest limit (in any season!), but this is more to do with the current local politics than good or bad summers. The competition between boatmen was as tough then as it would be in my own time, but with far more of us then, as seen in Mr Sprackling's report for the final season of the nineteenth century, when the Cobb had twenty-six licensed watermen using twenty three rowing boats and nine others under sail: 'One Waterman has been proceeded against for carrying a greater number of persons than his boat was licensed for [*depends which formula you used!*], and ordered by the Magistrates to pay five shillings towards costs. I am glad to be able again to report loyalty on the part of the Watermen generally in carrying out the Pleasure Boat Bylaws, and the fact that no accident in boating has occurred during the year. I regret to have to refer to the loss by death (*natural*) of an esteemed Waterman in the person of the late W. Rattenbury [*this is the son of the smuggler Jack Rattenbury – William, then in his late sixties or early seventies, had no doubt like his father continued the family trade but it certainly had not been 'plying as briskly' as in his father's time!*].

'There is one matter I wish to lay before the Council to order upon for future guidance viz:-

'On the occasion of one of Messrs Cozens and Co's steamers bringing up off the pier at low water, various watermen were engaged in taking passengers to and from the vessel. The last fare was brought off from the steamer by Edmund Gratton [*the person who will lease my local, the Royal Standard, from the Corporation and the great uncle to Nick and grandfather to Jim, other good friends of mine!*]. Several had unloaded passengers and one being alongside the steps. As Gratton came up, the former moved off to allow the latter to discharge his fare. At the moment of disembarkation, another fare came up to be put aboard the steamer. Gratton took this fare off amid the protest of the boatmen ['*Not Fare, they cried!*']. It would have been the moral right of the boatman who courteously moved off to have conveyed this fare to the steamer [*What about the moral right of the fare being fed up waiting and the moral right of Gratton realising the market for this?*]. I was appealed to by the latter and I promised to submit this point of dispute to the Council which I now beg to do [*Today we call it 'competition', which is encouraged for market growth*].

'As the Bylaws do not affect such a case, I would suggest that in future if any dishonourable conduct such as this be noticed, the boatman in fault should the following year have his licence suspended for such a period as may be determined by the Mayor [*Don't you just love it? And to think, my whole livelihood was taken away for something just as petty!*]'

The following year, Henry Battrick, another local bobby, became the pleasure boat inspector, as I suspect Sprackling had by now realised his moral right of not getting involved in 'Cobb politics', and one likes to think he changed his career to that of a printer! The new inspector noted to the council meeting on the 15th July, 1901, that during the previous season: '…several licensed Watermen has allowed persons to embark in Licensed Rowing Boats for hire without a competent person being in charge of the boat (*hardly rocket science, rowing a dinghy!*).'

This problem continued, since in 1901 we have twenty one licensed watermen with twenty-five rowing and eight sail; the following season has twenty-three licensed watermen, twenty-eight rowing, nine sail; then the season after that, Inspector Battrick finally got his mathematics right when he issued an equal number of licensed waterman and rowing boats, at thirty-one and ten for sailing when not rowing, so everyone lived happily ever after... Not! In 1907, Parliament issued a statutory instrument that empowered councils with the right to issue pleasure boat licenses, which is not only confusing but unfair, since corrupt councillors still had the power to issue licenses as they deem fit (as in my own time, and even to this day, this Act has not once been amended). For a seafaring nation with a long maritime history, our legislation for licensing small commercial craft is poor. One thing we can learn from our American 'cousins' is that every private or commercial vessel must be licensed and insured just like a motor vehicle, regardless of its use or size.

On Henry Hoste Henley's death, his Sandringham estate was sold and came into the hands of Queen Victoria, becoming the royal residence that it is today. His son, John Henry Henley, still owned much land in Lyme, as shown on the tithe map, but the bulk of the Henley chattels were later sold off by a Henry Cornish Henley. He left no male heir and his sole daughter, Florence Hoste Henley, married into the Torbock family. Torbock, an iron-ore dealer during the late nineteenth-century boom, married into what was then regarded as high society, and they subsequently moved to Crossrig Hall in the Lake District.

Their sons, Henry Cornish Torbock and Commander Richard Henley Torbock, became the sole grandsons of Henry Cornish Henley, and both passed away in 1994. Neither of them married. Henry was extrovert and devoted much of his inheritance to his chief pleasures in life which were gardening, social life, music, painting, shooting with friends over his grouse moor, and that most manly pursuit of flower arranging! He was educated at Eton and was the first boy to be allowed leave to attend the Chelsea Flower Show!

Henry fared better than his brother Richard, who, as a captain during the Second World War, was ordered to arrange the deportation of a group of White Russians, knowing that in Russia they would face the death penalty. He played for time by repeatedly bodging the forms; for example, under 'Racial Origin' he entered 'Neo-Georgian', until the order was rescinded some weeks later. In all fairness, one cannot fail but have admiration for him and his obituary reads,

"Commander Richard Henley Torbock, RN, of HMS *Chaser*, who lived at Penrith, Cumbria, left estate valued at £3,336,232 net."

A substantial enough figure that could have almost purchased half of the Mappa Mundi, but a rather pitiful amount considering the vast estates that the Henleys once held.

The future world in which I write is a time that leaves the Henley family thin on the ground, with a couple of white game hunters in Africa and a smattering of cousins around the world comprising all that remains of Lyme's most distinguished family. It is interesting to note that records as late as 1953 show that Richard Torbock was the High Sheriff of Westmorland. Now, where have we heard of this place before? The fifteenth Earl of Westmorland at this time was no other than David Anthony Thomas Fane! These two families had retained close links for three centuries, back at least to the time that Francis Fane's 'dear old' uncle Scrope was invited by the Henley family to help represent Lyme in Parliament. Virtually a century of political corruption and smuggling ended with a battle over the Cobb Act and its royal charters that had left Lyme bankrupt.

Freemasonry is the obvious link that connects these families, and one cannot help but think again of that George Washington crest in the little church at Affpuddle. Overall, I don't hold anything against the Freemasons, as some great people have been masons, including Winston Churchill, the actor John Wayne, even astronauts John Glenn and Edwin Aldrin, the second man on the moon; let's face it, history would have been so much duller without the likes of them included in it. But sadly this secret fraternity, that was supposed to bring like-minded intellectuals together, whether artisans, doctors, engineers, soldiers or politicians has, over the years, become so corrupt that in my own future time in Dorset they have been reduced to a mafia-like organisation no different to what I had experienced in war-torn Colombia.

The other rich landowner Admiral Talbot, Lord of the Manor of Uplyme, had a typically-sized Catholic family of two sons and five daughters. The eldest, and heir to the estate, was John Reginald Francis George Talbot, who married a reverend's daughter, Sarah Eliza Jones; they had a further four sons and five daughters. His heir, the Admiral's grandson John Reginald Charles Talbot, married into more money by taking the hand of Lady Maria Josephine de Stacpoole, daughter of George Stanislaus de Stacpoole, third Duke de Stacpoole, a prelate to no other than the pope. De Stacpoole had recently purchased the former home of Pinney, which Maria converted into the Alexandra Hotel.

In 1887, all this land and housing in Uplyme was placed in a trust for the marriage of the Admiral's grandson, and four years later a conveyance to this trust included Henry Cornish Henley's Estate in Lyme. An annual court was held at the Talbot Arms public house in Uplyme to collect rent from the tenants, even though the estate had now spread over the border into Dorset, including the Colway Manor House in Lyme. Rent money from the tenants was used to pay off the interest on the numerous mortgages that the estate had now accumulated. After the death at just forty-eight of the Admiral's grandson, this estate was split up into thirty-seven lots and went under the hammer at auction two years before the outbreak of the First World War. The majority of the lots including Rhode Hill never reached a minimum value, and consequently only twelve of the smallest lots were sold.

The Admiral's granddaughter Annette Mary Laura Talbot married Alban James Woodroffe, the county High Sheriff, and a founder of Dorset County Council. He inherited the nearby Rhode Barton, Lower Barton, Harcombe, Lane End and the Uplyme Mill farmlands, and two smaller lots which were sold to the council, to create a road to the east of the town that contoured around the steep Timbervale Hill, making it easier for horse drawn logging carts to haul timber up out of the town from his woodland. At this time, the estate was mortgaged at £14,000 for an unusual term length of three thousand years. By all accounts, Woodroffe was a very energetic and forward thinking person. Not only was he the founder of the town's first 'modern' grammar school, but he also introduced electricity into Lyme, making it the first town in Dorset to benefit from it. He was also the mayor when Lyme was shocked by first-hand experience of the First World War.

Five ships of the Royal Navy have been named HMS *Formidable,* and the fourth ship of that name was the first British battleship to be sunk in the First World War by a German U-Boat. Under the command of Channel Fleet Commander-in-Chief, Admiral Sir Lewis Bayly, while on exercise in Lyme Bay with two light cruisers, the *Topaz* and *Diamond,* HMS *Formidable* was struck by two torpedoes. Even though submarine activity had been reported in the area, it was believed that the seas were too rough for any threat from them. Early in the morning of New Year's Day 1915, the first torpedo from the German sub U-24 struck the *Formidable's* number one boiler port side.

Her captain, Noel Loxley, thought that she might be saved by reaching the shore, but within minutes of being struck, she was seriously listing to starboard, and so Loxley gave the order to abandon ship. Launching life-raft pinnaces in thirty foot swells proved difficult enough, without the second torpedo striking shortly afterward on the starboard side. The two light cruisers came alongside and managed to pick up eighty men in rough seas before the *Formidable* capsized, rolling onto many men already in the freezing waters. Brave Loxley remained on the bridge with his fox terrier Bruce, calmly overseeing the evacuation and going down with his ship.

Provident, a Brixham trawler off Beer Head, skippered by Captain Piller, managed to rescue one pinnace shortly before it also sank, saving the lives of a further seventy-one crew. The other pinnace, with seventy more crew, eventually made it ashore at Lyme the following night, by bailing sea water out with their boots, but only forty-eight of them were still alive, the rest having perished from exposure. Of the original complement of seven hundred and eighty crew, seventy percent lost their lives, and Admiral Bayly was relieved of his command for negligence. Many bodies of the crew washed ashore at Lyme, and old black and white photos show the funeral procession for the crew of the *Formidable,* with the whole population of Lyme turning out, dressed in their 'Sunday best'. A cross in the local churchyard marks the spot where some were interned.

Captain Loxley's dog, Bruce, was also washed ashore and was later buried in a marked grave as a war dog at nearby Abbotsbury Gardens. In Lyme, another canine hero would also emerge from this disaster - a cross-haired collie named Lassie. The Corporation-leased Pilot Boat Inn at Lyme was temporarily used as a makeshift mortuary and one sailor, John Cowan, was laid out to rest with the dead, when the landlord's dog, Lassie, kept licking his face and miraculously revived him. This particular incident is said to be the inspiration for the Lassie books, films, and television series.

One of the most extraordinary veterans of this war is also associated with Dorset and possibly Lyme. His name is Colonel Thomas Edward Lawrence, CB, DSO. He was living at Clouds Hill near Wareham when he died in a tragic motorbike accident. As an Oxford History graduate he studied crusader castles, which lead him on a thousand-mile trek across Ottoman Syria. On the outbreak of war he was a leading authority on the Middle East, and consequently was sent as an archaeological smokescreen for a British military survey of the Negev Desert. He eventually became involved in a campaign of internal insurgency against the German-backed Ottoman Empire in the Middle East, which has forever immortalised him as 'Lawrence of Arabia' ('El Orens', as the Arabs call him). It is said that he helped with the construction of a slipway at the Cobb while in obscurity during his latter RAF days, but I have found nothing yet to confirm this!

After the Great War, as did the rest of the country, Lyme suffered economic hardship during the Great Depression of the thirties; a far cry from the rich Elizabethan trading era when, according to the original court book where I had found a copy of George Summers signature, merchandise to and from the Cobb would pass through Mill Green on pack horses, that being its economic centre and the location of two large water mills, the town hall with a leet court, so named from the channel (or leet) used to transfer water from the river to the mill wheels. This was now the town's slum area, and if Lyme had any prosperous times during this next period of its history, they were short-lived.

The morning weather in Lyme Bay on a Thursday in July was just what you would have expected for an ordinary English summer's day. The coastline from Portland Bill to Start Point was covered in exceptionally low cloud cover and in places a cool thick bank of fog rolled in off the sea. A pilot of the time would later recall:

"Oh! I have slipped the surly bonds of Earth
"And danced the skies on laughter-silvered wings;
"Sunward I've climbed, and joined the tumbling mirth
"Of sun-split clouds, — and done a hundred things
"You have not dreamed of — wheeled and soared and swung
"High in the sunlit silence. Hov'ring there…"

This was not to be just some ordinary summer's day, as it was 1940, during the darkest hours of the Second World War. The thick fog would have made flying impossible without radar, and the Luftwaffe had decided to strike along this part of the coastline first; for many British pilots, it would have been the first time that they would have ever seen the role played by the Junker Eighty-Seven 'Stuka' dive bomber. Just like those brave souls at Trafalgar or the Somme, with an endurance and courage unsurpassed by any human today, it was again for the defence of this realm that this same breed took to the skies.

"…I've chased the shouting wind along, and flung
"My eager craft through footless halls of air…
"Up, up the long, delirious burning blue
"I've topped the wind-swept heights with easy grace

"Where never lark, or ever eagle flew-"

Radar had picked out a blimp in the region of Portland Bill, which turned out to be a formation of Junkers (nicknamed 'Stukas' from the German *Sturzkampfflugzeug*, or 'dive bomber'), so six Spitfires, single-seater fighter aircraft of 609 Squadron from Middle Wallop were vectored into this area.

The fog was burned off quickly by the morning sun, as 609 entered Lyme Bay and approached the observable enemy. The Stuka was a two-seater ground-attack aircraft, first used by the Luftwaffe's Condor Legion during the Spanish Civil War, and easily recognisable by its inverted gull-like wings and the infamous wailing siren known as the 'Jericho Trumpet'. Its poor manoeuvrability, lack of speed and defensive armaments required the Stuka to have a fighter escort to operate effectively. This is exactly what had been arranged, as the Spitfires were pounced upon from the upper rear by three Staffels of Bf 109s; cloaked by the low cloud cover, they must have seemed to appear from nowhere.

Also known as the Messerschmitt Bf 109, the first true modern fighters of the era were produced in greater quantities than any other fighter aircraft in history, and were the core of the Luftwaffe. It was used as an interceptor, bomber escort, fighter bomber, day/night-all-weather fighter, bomber destroyer, ground-attack aircraft, and as reconnaissance aircraft. Its primary weakness was its lack of agility in the air, but this made no difference as 609 immediately lost its Flight Commander in the ensuing dogfight, and another Spitfire was shot down over the bay.

A Stuka attack on Portland later incurred slight damage, but nothing else was achieved until the arrival of Hurricanes from 601 Squadron based at Tangmere. The Royal Air Force's casualties list for that day reads depressingly, in its methodical and unemotional dialogue:

'0800 hrs. Hurricane P2485. 501 Sqn Middle Wallop. (Aircraft lost at sea)

'Sgt F. J. P. Dixon. Drowned. (Hit by gunfire from Bf109 of 111/JG27 ten miles off Portland. Baled out but search failed to find any trace of pilot)

'0805 hrs. Spitfire L1095. 609 Sqn Warmwell. (Aircraft lost at sea)

'P/O G.T.M.Mitchell. Drowned. (Shot down in combat by Bf109 over Channel off Portland protecting convoy. Body later washed ashore at Newport, Isle of White)

'0810 hrs. Spitfire L1069. 609 Sqn Warmwell. (Aircraft lost at sea)

'F/L P. H. Barran. Died of burns. (Shot down in combat by Bf109 over convoy in Channel off coast at Portland. Baled out. Pilot was rescued but died on rescue boat).'

The Spitfire, with its elliptical wing and thin cross-section, allowed a higher top speed, resulting in two Stukas finally being shot down. Later, two Messerschmitts also suffered the same fate and the enemy decided to abort its attack here in the bay, and just like that sea battle with the armada 352 years previously, the whole affair continued east up the Channel as a sporadic fight, this time made by Junker 87s and Heinkel 111s, with various targets west of the Isle of Wight. The 'Dog fight over Lyme Bay' may have finished, but the first major campaign to be fought entirely by air forces had now begun - The Battle of Britain.

"…And, while with silent, lifting mind I've trod

"The high untrespassed sanctity of space,

"Put out my hand, and touched the face of God."

The failure by Germany to reach its objective of destroying Britain's air-defences and thus forcing Britain into surrender is considered its first major defeat, along with that of Stalingrad on the Eastern Front - the crucial turning point in the war. If Germany had gained air superiority, Hitler would have launched Operation Sealion, a simultaneous amphibious and airborne invasion of Britain. Even in my future time, all along the south coast one can still visit the remnants of the combined allied defences in preparation for such an invasion, with pillbox-shaped gunning posts along river valleys and military bases on the surrounding clifftops.

Some three centuries after leaving its shores from places like Lyme, the descendants to those early American pioneers returned home to help defend Britain. 'C' Company of the Sixteenth Infantry Regiment of the First U.S. Infantry Division, whose commanding officer was Captain Victor H. Briggs, had their headquarters based here. On D-Day, they took part in the assault landing on Omaha Beach, Normandy, then fought their way across Europe, ending the war in

Czechoslovakia. This is a proud regiment, whose history dates back to some of the hardest fought battles in the American Civil War, including the Battle of Gettysburg, where they took significant losses from a position between the Wheatfield and Devil's Den. During the First World War, this was the first American regiment to take combat casualties and engage German forces, which resulted in them twice earning the Croix de Guerre, France's highest military honour. Even in my future time, the soldiers still wear its symbol on their uniforms.

The remaining companies of the Sixteenth had landed in North Africa and taken part in the invasion of Italy, where my grandfather had fought alongside them as part of the joint British Allied Forces. His wife had died prematurely during the war, and his children were placed in an orphanage. My grandfather never recalled much of the war, although I know he was involved in some of its toughest fighting. My father, on the other hand, as a 'Barnardo's Boy' in Dorset, fondly recalls the kindness of American soldiers when they threw a Christmas party for all the kids at the orphanage. They were taken onto the American base and presented with a chest full of candy that was poured out in front of them - those poor, astonished kids had never seen so much chocolate before in their lives.

An American camp was also located near the World's End pub, and before the invasion, this was frequented by American troops. One can easily imagine a Saturday night dance here, with American soldiers dancing with English girls and Glen Miller music blaring out; a similar location to where my great-aunt Doris had a date which resulted in making her a GI bride. While here the American troops tastefully covered the ceiling in graffiti, but unfortunately the building caught fire in the 70s, resulting in the loss of a little piece of American history here in Dorset. A young inventor who lived a few miles away at Bridport would also help to further curtail the Nazi holocaust. His name was Barnes Wallis, and the Bouncing Bomb would later complete its sea trials just off Dorset's Chesil Beach.

Having been born two decades after the end of the Second World War, it is difficult - if not damn near impossible - to imagine what it must have been like during those dark times. I remember in my youth leaving British soil for the first time and hitch hiking around France and coming across an American war cemetery. Its location was a valley with white gravestones, spread out from horizon to horizon in regimental rows as far as the eye could see - it was huge. I walked along a single row and read the inscriptions. The names I've now forgotten but not their ages; seventeen, eighteen, nineteen and twenty - on average my own age at the time. This is school-leaving age - time to go out and begin a career and a life, but not for it to end! Those very names on the graves could have so easily been my classmates in my own time, and I was both shocked and humbled to stand next to those that had selflessly given away their lives, so that future generations like mine could have one. So many of them did it in both world wars!

Ironic how times have changed since, in my own future world, we have many German tourists who visit Lyme possibly more than any other foreign nationality, and what a friendly bunch they are. Over the years I have made many German friends, most notably the Melichar family of Cologne. Sabine and her younger brother Mike and their parents have visited the place so often that Mike virtually grew up here, and after logging up so many sea hours, he even became a licensed boatman. Just as I had set my own new standards by being the first to pass my boatman's test by going aground, so Mike, with his poor English, would set his.

He passed the verbal part of the exam not only by answering every single question wrong, but also by not having a blinking clue as to what the examiner was asking of him, even after being told the correct answers! Mike left the exam room so confused that he could only put his good fortune in gaining his tickets down to the fact that all us English are crazy! I later found out that the examiner was not only a high ranking ex-Naval officer, but also a Second World War veteran, who no doubt had taken pity on Mike and realised he was intelligent enough to pass the exam, but lacked the English to prove it.

Back in my local a few nights later, Mike was being teased for his nationality with the old, 'You have to get to the beaches before the Germans for the towels', and so I had to interject.

"Don't listen to them Mike; my grandfather used to visit Cologne quite often."

"He did?" asked Mike, looking up at me with his big innocent eyes.

"Yeah, in a Lancaster bomber!"

This banter continued for many years, and on a return trip to Germany to visit the Melichars we took a guided tour of the beautiful medieval castle at Magdeburg with its stunning views overlooking the Rhine Valley. At one point, the guide paused to show us the damaged section of the defences, bombed during the war by no other than a Lancaster bomber!

Mike couldn't resist the quip, "Would that be your grandfather, by any chance?"

Coincidentally, while both of us were on a boat trip later on in Lyme during 'Lifeboat Week', the last Lancaster bomber made a fly-by over the bay and again Mike got his own back.

"Ah, I see your grandfather has finally found his way back home!"

But now, back to the last part of my time travel voyage, and it's 1941, the year that the National Farm Survey was commissioned to assist the war effort by assessing Britain's ability to feed itself during wartime. At the time, this survey was hailed as the 'Second Domesday Book', being a 'permanent and comprehensive record of the conditions on the farms of England and Wales'. The data was gathered through questionnaires covering farming types, cropping and stocking, machinery, farm size and structure, land ownership and farm buildings, labour and even the physical condition of the farmers. All the questionnaires, together with a complete set of maps showing the boundaries of about 320,000 farms over five acres in size, became available to the public in 1992 after a fifty year closure period due to the restraints of the Official Secrets Act. The survey was also integrated with the census for the same year, which is helpful in determining the names and addresses of landowners and tenant farmers, information that would not normally be available until the year 2041, due to the even stricter restraints for the closure period of a national census.

By comparing the 1912 Rhode Hill sales particulars with that of the 1941 National Farm Survey, one can see that most of the Lyme/Uplyme estate, including its 3,000 year mortgage for the marriage settlement of John and Maria Talbot, had been inherited by Alban Woodroffe. This estate was now held in trust by the estate agents Rawlence and Squarey of Sherborne, and included the former Henley Estate of Lyme held in trust by R. C. Snell of Axminster.

Woodmead Farm had become a housing estate above the west bank of the River Lym, known as Hachett, the Colway Manor Fields became the Talbot Road estate and Whites Farm was used for building land for the rich spacious homes of the Somers Road and Westhill Road housing estates where Cobb Houses Ltd were based, indicating a link between Corporation estates, the town's royal charter and its harbour.

Although trade at the Cobb no longer occurred at this time, the Cobb Act and its charter are still used to raise funds for the proper maintenance of the harbour, by leasing Corporation owned properties. But now, the Corporation not only owned and leased farmland and individual homes and shops in the older parts of town, but whole housing estates, which included hotels, holiday villas, public houses, offices and schools, including the one that Woodroffe had founded, with housing not only for its boarders, but also for teaching staff.

As post-war austerity eased, and before airliners opened up new horizons and brought foreign holidays within easy reach for everyone, tourism in Lyme started to peak. This 'feel-good' factor of post-war Britain is superbly portrayed in the film *All Over the Town*, directed by Derek Twist and filmed in Lyme during the summer of 1948, starring Norman Wooland and Sarah Churchill, daughter to the one we know better!

An RAF pilot returns to his job as a newspaper reporter in the seaside town of 'Tormouth'. He questions the importance of writing about small-town politics, but after unexpectedly becoming a partner of the newspaper, he decides to use his elevated position to improve the community. He falls in love with the woman who filled his job while away at war. The film is a true masterpiece and is one of my favourites; it really gives the town a feel of what it used to be like and how it should be in my own time. The characterisation of the locals is superbly written and acted, with a dry sense of humour running throughout the film, especially by the local undertaker. The comically corrupt Council are coincidently similar to the real thing of my own time, especially when it comes to proposals to develop the seafront! By the end of the film one is left wondering, 'how on Earth did they know that this sort of thing was ever going to happen all those years ago?' If, like me, you're a fan of *The Avengers*, you can spot a young

Patrick MacNee in a small role as one of those corrupt Councillors, the only time I can ever recall him playing the part of a villain.

My voyage to Lyme's past is now complete. I'm beamed back to the present and just like a 'real' time traveller, my trip has created a different timeline, and therefore an alternate future. What really happened is far different as, of course, I never physically travelled through time - I just researched the town archives and only visited the past in my imagination - but the consequences are the same. This research into Lyme's past has revealed a flaw in its history that stems from the local Government reorganisation of 1974, just two years before my family and I moved to Lyme. Revealing this will change not only our present, but consequently the future timeline that many expected Lyme to have. Effectively, my journey to the past has indeed changed the future.

With the exception for properties such as Rhode Hill, which became Government-owned by the Second World War, other properties sometime between Woodroffe's death in 1964 and local Government reorganisation in 1974, when the Lyme Regis Borough Council was dissolved and became Government-owned. This is when many of the town's historical documents had been 'roped in' by a local firm of solicitors, who have since been liquidated and the deeds associated with this documentation disappeared! The unusual mortgage for the Talbot estate was paid off and became a charity using taxpayer's money, but instead of being officially inherited by the Government, this estate was broken up and sold to certain individuals with profits siphoned off into the ether. In other words, the large estate that once encompassed East Devon and West Dorset, including its royal charter properties, was broken up and leasehold deeds fraudulently converted into freeholds, then illegally sold off.

Effectively, in an attempt to change our history, this fraud could be covered up. This sort of thing has happened before, most notoriously when Nazi Germany held its Kristallnacht on the night of November 11th 1939, when fanatics attempted to change history by destroying everything of the Jewish faith. In a single night, they burned books by Jewish authors, smashed the windows to their synagogues, shops and businesses. The streets became littered with broken glass, hence the expression 'Crystal Night'. The persecution of people of the Jewish faith had started, an excuse for Nazi empire building had begun and, as we know all too well, this resulted in a war that devastated our world, leaving over fifty-five million dead.

During the first week of April 1974, right across Britain, we had our very own 'Crystal Week'. During the hiatus of local Government reorganisation, many historical documents that should have been transferred from old Borough Council archives to the newly-formed District Councils, or placed in the National Archives for safe keeping went missing. I was even horrified to learn from an archivist that in some places around the country, whole skip-loads of documents had simply disappeared!

This fraud was finally uncovered using the power of the Internet and the British Freedom of Information Act (a much more diluted version of its American equivalent), neither of which had been dreamed of when all this happened. I managed to thoroughly research the archives, not just for copies of the records I know exist, but also for clues about the ones that I know should be there, but are missing or altered. Examples of these are leasehold deeds belonging to the Corporation-owned estate, its Cobb Act, and evidence that leasehold funds were used for the proper maintenance of the Cobb as decreed in its royal charters.

Take away the money from leasing this property and how else can you obtain funds for the Cobb's proper upkeep? Well, you cannot! Which is why, shortly after 1974, ballast in the form of giant boulders were connected to the ends of the Cobb walls and the over-wall sluice has since been blocked off in an attempt to restrict longshore drift and silt up the harbour! The reason for this is to convert it from a commercial seaport into a breakwater, making it easier and much cheaper to maintain. But this is not working, as attrition action by the sea and shingle, built up from the restriction of longshore drift on Monmouth's Beach, are undermining the foundations of the High Wall, which has started to slump, resulting in the Cobb being slowly destroyed, and it is only a matter of time before it is gone!

One should not speak ill of the dead, but try to convince yourself that the local historian and author John Fowles knew nothing about this. His home, Belmont, has been leasehold property belonging to the former Corporation estate on every historical document that I have seen, which is typical of the many other properties throughout Lyme, used to raise funds for the Cobb's proper maintenance. Fowles was a Freemason, and he may well have been trying to tell us something out of guilt when he used the names of the former major landowning families, Woodruff (Woodroffe) and Talbot, as fictional characters in his novel *The French Lieutenant's Woman*; the family names of former property that had become Corporation-owned and leased out, to raise funds to protect the Cobb during the publication of his novel, then illegally converted into freeholds and sold off shortly afterwards.

Looking back after all these years, I found it equally amazing to discover that I have another account of 1974, in the form of my own childhood diary, and on the day when the history of Lyme Regis was being ransacked, a twelve-year old elsewhere in Dorset was ill off school, in bed with flu, reading Jules Verne's *Around the World in Eighty Days* and dreaming of his own future voyages. I must have made a rapid recovery, because five days later I was on holiday at the family chalet on Mudeford Beach, which my parents sadly sold when we moved to the coast at Lyme at the western end of Dorset. It was in a southwesterly breeze that I flew my kite off Hengistbury Head, completely oblivious to the fact that much of this country's heritage was about to disappear.

So how will making this common knowledge change the future? Well, for the better, I hope. On the small scale it may save the Cobb and take, for example, Lyme's beaches, which have never once obtained Blue Flag status. In fact, they were recently categorised by English Heritage as some of the most polluted beaches in the country. With the rediscovery of the ancient smugglers' tunnels beneath the town, I was advised by a friend, who is a hobby geologist and potholer, to obtain a plan of the underground asset information from the local water board. Since water, with the help of gravity, takes its natural course through the bedrock, it would be possible to elicit a map of this maze of tunnels. With this information, I realised that the tunnels had once been used as the town's water conduit in the early part of the twentieth-century. I also realised that the outfall locations of unverified sewer pipes were running into the river and polluting the beaches. Making this information public knowledge meant that it wasn't long before these outlets were sealed and Lyme now waits for that Blue Flag.

On the larger scale, other dodgy dealings in Dorset, due to ignorance of missing historical documents, have also been gleaned from something as simple as an application for a farmers' market. Circular 08/44/CP of the minutes to a meeting of the Lyme Regis Town Council Community Plan Implementation Committee, held in 2008, states that a Farmers' Market was being held up by legal issues surrounding the use of Gun Cliff Walk, but Prince Charles, the District Council and the local Member of Parliament had been engaged to resolve the issue so that a farmers' market could take place there in the future.

Now, excuse me, unless I have gone completely bonkers, but does that seem a rather strange statement? Why on earth should the heir to the throne, of all people, be consulted - if ever he was - about such a minor issue as a farmers' market in Lyme Regis? Perfectly good legislation for a market in Lyme has existed since medieval times, and even the former borough's royal charter makes it clear that the town mayor is clerk of the market, so why not let the mayor decide? Oh, and what happened to those various plots of land, with all those nice big luxury homes built on them - and have you seen the current property market value for these? Ouch!

On a nationwide scale, this problem may even be more severe, and the answer to this strange puzzle lies not here in the West Country but in the southeast, specifically Kent. At Canterbury Cathedral, we must delve back in time again to when Cobham's Cobb was first constructed and the Hundred Years War, for here lies in state Edward the Black Prince, the first Duchy of Cornwall. The title was created by his father, Edward III, for his first son and heir to have his own kingdom within a kingdom to generate his own private income, before he became king himself and passed the title onto his own heir. The Duchy was originally created as a charter and was a collection of private estates, mainly in Cornwall. The only part of Dorset mentioned as Duchy property at this time was Canford Heath, then a salt marsh probably very similar to the Lyme of the Cotton Records. Kent is also the Freemasonry county that is presided over by the Grand Master of the United Grand Lodge of England, no other than the Duke of Kent himself, always chosen as the uncle to the Duchy of Cornwall, which links the two.

Edward, Prince of Wales, was named the Black Prince after the black armour he wore during campaigns. He was a popular military leader during his life, although he died a year before his father, and therefore never became king. The throne passed on to his son Richard instead. Later, a charter was drawn up by Henry IV for his heir, Prince Henry: 'We have made and created Henry, our most dear first-begotten Son, Prince of Wales, Duke of Cornwall and Earl of Chester, and have given and granted, and by our Charter have confirmed to him the said Principality, Duchy, and Earldom, that he may preside there, and by presiding, may direct and defend the said parts.'"

In the late-eighteenth century, the Anglo-Irish statesman Edmund Burke sought to curtail further the power of the crown by removing the various principalities which existed.

'... the five several distinct principalities besides the supreme... If you travel beyond Mount Edgcumbe, you find him [the king] in his incognito, and he is duke of Cornwall... Thus every one of these principalities has the apparatus of a kingdom... Cornwall is the best of them...'

However, his Parliamentary Bill failed, due to the fact that the current duke, the future King George IV, was still a minor.

The Land Registry website shows today that Duchy land at Poundbury in Dorset has increased in area since the National Farm Survey. Has illegally acquired Government land from local Government transition been added to it? If not, then why are those on behalf of the Duchy showing such a keen interest in Lyme land, which we now know has been illegally acquired?

Burke had a great philosophical mind; he also opposed the French Revolution, becoming the leading figure within the conservative faction of the Whig party, which he dubbed the 'Old Whigs' in opposition to the pro-French-Revolution 'New Whigs', as was Lyme's William Pitt the Younger. He had also expressed his support for the American colonists under the government of mad King George, and even made a speech to repeal the infamous tea duty that was about to lead to the American War of Independence: 'Again and again, revert to your old principles—seek peace and ensue it; leave America, if she has taxable matter in her, to tax herself. I am not here going into the distinctions of rights, nor attempting to mark their boundaries. I do not enter into these metaphysical distinctions; I hate the very sound of them. Leave the Americans as they anciently stood…The Englishman in America will feel that this is slavery; that it is legal slavery, will be no compensation either to his feelings or to his understandings.'

The following year during the war, Burke even gave another speech for reconciliation with America: '… the people of the colonies are descendants of Englishmen... They are therefore not only devoted to liberty, but to liberty according to English ideas and on English principles. The people are Protestants... a persuasion not only favourable to liberty, but built upon it... My hold of the colonies is in the close affection which grows from common names, from kindred blood, from similar privileges, and equal protection…Slavery they can have anywhere. It is a weed that grows in every soil. They may have it from Spain, they may have it from Prussia. But, until you become lost to all feeling of your true interest and your natural dignity, freedom they can have from none but you.'

Burke was appalled by celebrations in Britain, due to the defeat of the Americans in New York and Pennsylvania. He claimed the English national character was being changed by this authoritarianism. In Burke's view, the British government was fighting 'the American English... Our English Brethren in the Colonies; with a German-descended king employing 'the hireling sword of German boors and vassals' to destroy British colonists' English liberties and later on American independence. Burke wrote: 'I do not know how to wish success to those whose Victory is to separate from us a large and noble part of our Empire. Still less do I wish success to injustice, oppression and absurdity.'

I may have diverted away from the point I was originally trying to make, but if it proves to be the case that illegally-acquired government property has also been used for the Duchy of Cornwall's estate, which future historians may reveal from a careful study of the National Farm Survey, then we may well have a scenario very similar to that under Charles I, which brought about Civil War, and it will again seriously call into question the purpose of this country's royalty. If that should be the case, then we will certainly need America's help if we are going to choose to rid ourselves of any future sovereign and reunite with that 'large and noble part of our Empire'.

Today, the British economy is based on the housing market, and some of the most expensive real estate in the country can be found in the Oxfordshire countryside, where old farmhouses have been converted into luxurious homes. Take another look at the National Farm Survey and you will discover that when this was drawn up, the land here was uneconomically farmed, and hence requisitioned by the Government. If, like Lyme, most of the associated deeds have since been falsified, then the whole country is in for some very serious economic problems. If Freemasonry is undermining our country's royalty, then it needs to stop, since royalty is what this country is all about - unless, of course, we choose to become a republic and the fifty-first state. I may be wrong on this particular point, and I certainly hope I am, but one thing is for certain; land and property belonging to the corporation of the former borough of Lyme Regis, under its Charles I Charter, including land belonging to the Talbot Trust charity, has been illegally acquired. A legal graphologist report could easily confirm if a deed has been falsified, and it would not surprise me if this included most of Lyme Regis and Uplyme.

I know now that, from the very start when I chose to pursue a career as a boatman at the Cobb, I never had a chance. Everyone involved in this property scam was against me, and I feel I have been duped for that part of my life. Yet, the one thing I have learned from this Pandora's Box that I have now opened is that at the bottom of it all there is hope, and that hope is the Cobb which can help resolve the mess that has been made. The Cobb will be destroyed if its act and charter cannot be properly adhered to, and they can never be used or amended without revealing all this illegality. Remember also, it did not just happen in Lyme, but throughout Britain. No wonder this country has had so many recessions since the mid-seventies, and is now displaying a growing disparity of wealth between its few elite rich and its masses of poor. It is this 'Second Dissolution' that has caused it, and the new timeline that will now begin is certainly going to be an interesting one. I profess not to be an author anything like Steinbeck, but like him I also wish, 'To put a tag of shame on the greedy bastards who are responsible for this'.

CHAPTER 6

"If in doubt, do nothing."
 - Arthur C. Clarke

In the corner of my right eye I could see his finger on the trigger... Those few seconds seemed to last an eternity, but unlike a dying man's last thoughts, I had no flashback over my life. As crazy as it may sound, all I could think about was that blasted game of football, and with an adrenaline level running so high I wasn't even nervous, just wary... Very wary.

"*El futbol es bueno...* Colombia uno, Venezuela zero... *es excellente*," I spluttered out in the best pidgin Spanish I could muster. Those well-chosen words temporarily broke the ice; as I noticed his finger lift slowly off the trigger, I sheepishly grinned and carefully handed him my passport.

"Ah, *Ingles*... err... How you say... err...My Commander, he speak *Ingles*... and he teach me," grinned Rambo, patting his chest as he admired the passport cover. "Yo... I... err... I am Colombia militia... Welcome to Columbia!"

We shook hands.

The young Officer was the first person I had met in ages who spoke English... Okay, an English that was far superior to my Spanish. The three soldiers wanted to know why I was here, and when I explained that I had sailed the Atlantic and was heading overland to the States to fly home, they couldn't do enough to help me. However, the three of them seemed rather surprised I was going by way of the notorious pirate haven of Turbo. But Turbo it was and they assisted by waving down the next vehicle that came by... at gunpoint! It was a coach load of passengers and they ordered the driver to take me along. The militia guided me aboard, and I was quickly offered a seat by the best working air-conditioning unit. As the coach pulled away, I smiled and waved to the meanest looking, battle-hardened soldiers one could possibly imagine, as the other passengers looked at me, then at each other with very curious expressions.

A two-tier class system seems to be prevalent throughout South America with an extremely rich minority of white descendants from Spanish colonists who are the major landowners, and a huge poor working class of Native American Indians, whose ancestors had migrated here towards the end of the last Ice-Age some fourteen to thirty millennia previously. New scientific evidence suggests that the Paleo-Indians' first widespread colonisation of the American continent occurred during the late glacial maximum, after crossing 'Beringia', a giant land bridge that was about a thousand-miles wide which, at that point, joined modern-day Alaska to Siberia at various times throughout the Pleistocene ice ages. The Beringia was not a glaciated bridge as previously thought, since snowfall at this time was very light due to the warm southwesterly Pacific currents. It was most likely a grassland steppe that had expanded further to the south, along with its human inhabitants as the American glaciers melted at the end of the 'last' ice age - or should I say 'the most recent', as it will someday return. Today, the bridge has long since gone, having been replaced by the ice-cold Bering Sea.

The migration of these so called Paleo-Indians south across the American continent resulted in many different cultures, all of which may have descended from the same human colony long before the first Europeans arrived - including the Vikings or Romans, if this last theory of pre-Columbian transfusion should ever prove to be true. The impact of European influence post-Columbus was completely disastrous for these many indigenous tribes of Native Americans. The most tragic episode in human history, during the establishment of the world's first superpowers, had its roots buried deep within the silk and spice trade, and an early-fifteenth century Portuguese prince named Dom Henrique, better known as Henry the Navigator. The son of King João, he became famous for financing voyages of discovery that eventually led ships rounding the African continent, first by Bartolomeu Dias, who established a sea route to India for Vasco da Gama and monopolised the spice trade for Portugal, from that of the overland route to Venice.

As I covered earlier, the voyage of exploration by Columbus to the West was followed a year later by the division of the world for the two greatest seafaring nations, the Spanish and the Portuguese. From this point onwards, an astonishing chain of events would reshape the Americas, resulting in the complete annihilation of most of its indigenous native population. The age of the conquistador had begun, one which resulted in the destruction of a whole culture in just a fraction of the time that it had taken to establish it.

Just as the biblical 'O-T' maps relied upon a symmetrical shape for the known world, so new world mapmakers used this symmetrical idea for an extended world map after the discovery of the Americas. If the world consisted of four continents - Euro-Asia, Africa, North and South America, with a southeast passage around Africa - it was reasonable to assume for the purpose of symmetry that passages must also exist at the other three corners of the world - around South America, Northern Russia and the top of Canada - and that they must all lead to the Spice Islands.

The first of this chain of events were the actions of one of this larger-than-life character, the conquistador Hernando Cortez. He sailed as a teenager to the island that Columbus mistakenly thought was offshore to Japan, Isla Hispaniola, now the headquarters to the Spanish West Indies. Both a soldier and a farmer, Cortez was one of the earliest European settlers, and shortly afterwards sailed with Diego Velasquez to help conquer Cuba. There, Velasquez became the governor and Cortez was promoted to the mayor-judge of Santiago. Seven years later, when the news of the discovery of mainland Mexico reached the ears of Velasquez, he chose Cortez to build another colony there. Velasquez soon rescinded this decision, suspecting that the headstrong Cortez would go beyond his orders. Unfortunately for Velasquez it was too late, as Cortez had already assembled men and equipment and set off for Mexico.

He sailed around the Yucatan Peninsula and landed on the coast of what is known today as the state of Tabasco. The Aztec Indians he met attacked the conquistadors, but were no match for the Spanish and their firearms, especially the Harquebus, an early portable gun with a long barrel, supported on a tripod. Compared to modern day firearms, they were practically useless, being tactically limited by the lengthy reload time and logistical difficulties - but they were a formidable weapon for the Spanish simply because of the noise, flash and smoke, which terrified the natives. Also, the heavily armoured and battle-hardened Spanish, with their swords of steel, proved to be much more effective militarily. A Spanish sword made of Toledo steel was considered the finest mark of craftsmanship, and to a Spanish knight it represented chivalry, dignity, and devotion to Christ. A well-trained conquistador would have been an awesome opponent, and not someone one would want to have a disagreement with - a bit like the Colombian militia of today, I suppose.

With his small army, Cortez took many prisoners, including a young princess who became his interpreter. He then sailed further north up the coast and landed somewhere near today's Veracruz, where he famously burned his ships to prevent any thought of retreat by his men. He rightly guessed that they were invincible against the relatively peaceful Aztecs, and left just a small force on the coast before heading inland with the rest of his army to Tenochtitlan, an impressive city built on stilts over a lake, long since overlain by present day Mexico City. Even a warlike tribe of natives, outnumbering his army by three hundred to one, were unable to repel them en-route; when Cortez finally reached the city, he was greeted by the Aztec emperor Montezuma, who had, no doubt, already heard about this invincible, almost godlike army that appeared to come from another world. 'Godlike' not only in the sense of being invincible, but also because these shining metal clad aliens could pass on a curse that left many for dead just a short time afterwards, without any physical contact. Unknown to Cortez and his army, they carried a smallpox epidemic that killed many of the non-immune natives.

At Tenochtitlan, he learnt that the Aztecs had attacked and killed the men he had left behind on the beach where he had burnt his ships. Outraged, Cortez arrested Montezuma and forced him to hand over the attackers, whom he subsequently executed. Meanwhile, back in Cuba, Velasquez had decided to send a posse of fourteen-hundred soldiers to arrest this subordinate, but they were defeated, and most of the survivors joined Cortez instead. The Aztecs were angered by Montezuma's submission to the Spanish, and so started an uprising in Tenochtitlan, which Cortez suppressed with an army of 100,000 men, of whom only two percent were Spanish; the rest were from many different Indian groups, who despised the Aztecs for their barbarity.

At one point in the battle, Montezuma tried to pacify his people, but they stoned him to death. Soon, the Spanish Army was surrounded and losing the battle. In the confusion, Cortez and three others managed to kill the new Aztec chieftain, whose army then retreated due to this apparent 'miracle.' With less than five hundred of his men still alive, Cortez retreated from Tenochtitlan back to his Indian allies. He later attacked the city again, this time by ship, and the next Aztec chieftain, Guatemoc, surrendered. The many centuries old Aztec empire had come to an end.

The smallpox epidemic and others like it, which the Spanish brought with them, would continue to wipe out far more natives than all the brutalities ever inflicted by the conquistadors in the New World. Recent DNA analysis of deceased Native American Indians have suggested that as much as eighty five percent of the indigenous population may have died in this way. The conquistadores may well have been formidable, larger-than-life foes, but it would be microscopic pathogens that would destroy the many different societies that had evolved from the migration of the Paleo-Indians across the American continent all those centuries previously.

Cortez spent several years working towards peace amongst the Indians of Mexico, and developed mines and farmlands to establish the Spanish colony of Nueva Hispaniola. He eventually returned to Spain, where he was warmly received and honoured by Charles V. On a later mission to Mexico, he explored the Baja Peninsula of California, where the sea is named after him, as I know only too well from the roughest sea crossing I've ever had. For many decades after its discovery, California was erroneously depicted on New World maps as an island. Had Cortez only explored a little further north into what is now the present American state of California, he would have realised this error. Cortez went on to lead an expedition against the

Mayans on the Yucatan Peninsula, and then returned to Spain for the last time to fight the Barbary Corsairs. He died near Seville in 1547.

There is an interesting story about Cortez during his retirement. While he was drinking in a bar in Seville, a young man asked him, "What is Nueva Hispaniola like?" Cortez took a sheet of paper, screwed it into a ball, then flattened it out on the table and replied, "It looks like that!" Until you have actually travelled Mexico and seen it at first hand, it's difficult to understand what he meant. In the south are lush green tropical rainforests, and in the far north, sandy deserts. Yet most of Mexico is a country of undulating hills of rich farmland, where the grassland browns in the summer, which does indeed give the appearance of creased parchment. But what I think Cortez meant is that Mexico was an unspoilt and uncharted country, with a similar climate to Spain, but four times the area. Just the challenge needed for any young Spanish adventurer! A story it may well have been, but add to this the rumours of undiscovered riches of gold, silver and pearls, then it is easy to understand how these stories would inspire the imagination of the next generation of conquistadors.

I finally arrived at Turbo, a port town on the inlet of the Uraba Gulf and Colombia's most northerly harbour. Unknown to me at the time, this was also the centre to border clashes with drug cartels and guerrilla groups. Most of the population here were poor Afro-Hispanics, whose shantytown homes were built on stilts for protection against flooding from the daily deluge of tropical downpours. A young white security guard stood near the port office with a rusty old Kalashnikov. I walked past him hesitantly after my recent experience with the local militia, and into the port area of town. Here, I struck up conversation with various skippers of single outboard engine canoes, similar to the one that had brought me across the Boca Del Drago. I needed to get to Panama, and one of them offered to take me for a hundred dollars, which seemed a reasonable rate, except that I was now beginning to run drastically low on them. Back at the port office, a motor launch advertised a ferry service that ran every morning to the island of Capurganá, stopping off at other islands in the region.

That night I roughed it on the boardwalk of the working pier, immersed in the strong smell of diesel and rotten fish. Lights from the town reflected off the water, and I could see military vehicles, including a tank on manoeuvres, as if in preparation for a battle. I don't recall sleeping that night, as I had to remain alert, hoping no one would find me hiding from the dire poverty of the place and its paranoid militia. Dusk and dawn happen very quickly near the equator, and daylight appeared almost instantaneously, as if someone had just switched a light on. At the first sound of cock crow, I rushed along to the port office, where I bought my ticket and boarded the motor launch. I was not sure what was going on here, but I knew I needed to leave as soon as possible, since more militia now seemed to be patrolling the docks.

Before long, other passengers clambered aboard, then the engines burst into life and we sped across the bay to an island named San Francisco. Here my passport was stamped with a Colombian exit visa by government officials who appeared from an old worn-out wooden shack, while the ferry refuelled at the depot next door. Some passengers disembarked and cargo was unloaded before we continued our voyage further north to our final destination of Capurganá; a strange tourist ghetto in the guise of a shanty town, if one could only describe it better.

At this poor man's paradise, I met a German named Hanz from Hanover, the first European I had seen since Trinidad, which now seemed such a long time ago. He was married to a beautiful Colombian girl and told me he had resided here since '83. He was in the construction industry, and I wondered just how much work could be generated from the poor locals living in their worn-out old palm thatched huts. He offered me a coffee, and we sat on the porch to his home as he pessimistically recalled how notoriously difficult it would be to cross the Darien Gap and reach Panama City. After what I had just been through, it was the last thing in the world I wanted to hear.

Children ran around playing on the dirt track which was the main street through the village, as their parents stood patiently at kiosks, waiting for the odd tourist to pass through and buy their wares of beach balls, yo-yos and, of all things, Panama hats, which just served to remind me of my unobtainable destination. The jungle around us came to life with the squawking of parrots and the song of other tropical birds. After another deluge of rain, the sun broke through the overcast grey cloud and as quick as the sunrise, the sky turned blue once again. Everyone was walking around in T-shirts and shorts as if they were tourists on Spain's Costa del Sol. It was only six days until Christmas, and I could not have possibly been anywhere with a less festive feel to it.

Back at the shore, I met another boatman who ferried passengers to the border in his small outboard canoe, and we negotiated a fare of two thousand pesos. The next landing was at Sapzuro, still in Colombia but a short walk to the border over a steep incline to a white stone monolith, with two simple shields on either side of it. One represented Colombia and the other Panama. No customs, no immigration and no militia touting old rusty Kalashnikovs - just an open frontier and the gateway to a most beautiful, yet notoriously hostile place.

Soaking with sweat, and out of breath after the uphill trek, I rested at the base of the monolith. After continuing downhill to the next bay, at the village of Miel, I was now officially in Panama but still a long way from the city. When I reached the village I noticed more wooden shacks, this time populated by even poorer, mixed-race locals. They were friendly enough though, and told me that the only way to the city was either by walking through hundreds of miles of dense jungle or for just fifty bucks, I could fly by air taxi from the next village, which stood above the fourth bay further along on the Caribbean coast. With restored optimism and a spring in my step, I continued on with my journey.

I can only describe the walk to the first bay as an unspoilt tropical paradise of dense green foliage, with colourful parrots and macaws flying around the branches making strange sounds. At dusk I reached another bay, full of the roar of the sea smashing against an offshore rock outcrop, and the hiss of surf receding down the beach. I had never seen anything like this before - it was spectacular, it was heaven! Had the Columbian militia, those modern day conquistadors, really killed me? If not, then this was exactly how I imagined the place beyond the Pearly Gates to be. I fell asleep on the beach that night, and for breakfast the following morning I had a couple of scones covered in peanut butter that I scooped from a large jar that I had purchased back in Venezuela. After breakfast, I used a small bar of complimentary hotel soap to wash my dirty clothes in seawater. The combination produces slime instead of foam which, I knew from my sea voyage, works just as well. Just like some Robinson Crusoe on his marooned paradise island, I now realised just how little a person needed to subsist in life. I hung my washing over a palm-thatched sunshade used by the natives to dry wild corn, or the palm bark that they used for rope making.

Further along the beach, I came across a heap of coconut shells, dried by the natives and used for fuel, and a pile of beach-combed glass bottles - nothing around here seemed to go to waste. Running parallel to the sandy bay was a dense thicket of palm trees that leaned slightly towards the southwest, away from the prevailing northeasterly trades. Beyond the beach, the palm trees blended into the even denser green of the Darien, which itself ran to the foothills then smothered the mountainous terrain of the interior. A native back at Miel had advised me to look out for a large mountain at the end of the third bay, emphasising, "*grande, grande montana*". High above me condors drifted on the air currents as I searched for the mountain, but all I could see were palms that disappeared into the green haze. By the time I got to what I thought was the third bay, it was getting dark again, so I spent another night on the beach.

When Cortez was still a farmer on Hispaniola, there were two traders named Vasco Núñez de Balboa and Rodrigo de Bastidas, also inspired by Columbus - I mean, which Spanish explorer wasn't in those days? They heard from Cortez that pearls could be found on the north coast of present day Venezuela. They had traded European goods for a large amount of these pearls and gold, but on the return voyage home, their ship had struck a leak. They pulled into port here but had their rich cargo seized by Velasquez, the greedy governor of Cortez's dispute. Completely broke, Balboa tried to survive here as a farmer, but a farmer he was not - rather an explorer and trader -so in sheer desperation and heavily in debt, he stowed away with his pet dog aboard a supply ship sailing to Panama, and helped to establish its first colony.

It was here that Balboa first became friendly with the Coiba Indians, and even married the chieftain's daughter. Just as Smith would befriend Pocahontas a century later further to the north of the continent, in Virginia, so an alliance was created between the natives and the Spanish colonists in Panama. Balboa further befriended Comogre, the chief of another group of Indians, who promised to show him the route to the fabled Southern Sea, proving once and for all that the 'New World' was another continent, if only Balboa would help him defeat one of his tribe's enemies. Balboa agreed, and marched an army of one hundred and ninety Spaniards and about a thousand Indians through the dense jungles of Panama. Amongst this army was Balboa's first mate from a previous sailing voyage, who had helped him establish the Panama Colony. This man, Francisco Pizarro, was a relative of Cortez, whose inspiration would lead him to become the most infamous of all the conquistadors.

Balboa and his men fought the enemies of Comogre all the way through the densest rainforest in the world. After his victory, Balboa and his men were advised by Comogre to ascend a mountain range in the middle of the Panamanian peninsula and, true to his word, they became the first Europeans to clap their eyes upon the Southern Sea, later to be misleadingly named the Pacific Ocean because it appeared so calm. This discovery was of major significance at the time, because it effectively doubled the known diameter of the earth. Columbus had died thinking the West Indies were some offshore islands to Japan, and Amerigus had discovered the mainland, but until now no European had crossed the continent and seen the ocean that separated it from Asia, just as the Atlantic separates Europe from America.

Looking back at my journey log years after that first trip into the Darien, the memories come flooding back as if it had only been yesterday. On the morning of December 20^{th,} 1996, I again awoke to the roar of the sea smashing against the rocky shore, realising it was caused by a making tide. This time I also noticed a footpath at the far end of the bay that ran into the jungle, and as I entered the thicket the disturbance alerted hundreds of land crabs which scurried up the trunks and along the branches of the nearby teakwood trees. The path started off as a well-beaten track and appeared to ascend the '*grande, grande montana*', but twice that morning I lost the footpath and ended up following streams and tributaries down towards my starting point back in the third bay. I was not lost, I just could not find the right footpath - but looking back and thinking about it now, it is the same thing!

So while I'm trying to find the correct route through the Darien, it might be a good opportunity to occupy the reader with the story of Pizarro, although I must admit that at the time he was the last thing on my mind. Born into a distinguished Spanish noble family, and a second cousin to Cortez on his father's side, he was an ambitious young man who won favour with the jealous Pedro Arias de Avila by arresting Balboa, who he succeeded as the newly appointed governor of Castilla de Oro in Costa Rica. Those cutthroat conquistadors were always trying to outdo each other, and poor old Balboa was subsequently beheaded. In case you are wondering, as in the case of Summers after his shipwreck a hundred years later, I can find no record as to what happened to his dog either!

But I do know that for his loyalty, Pizarro was made mayor of the recently founded Panama City, coinciding with the first attempt to explore the western half of the America continent by Pascual de Andagoya. The native Indians that Pascual encountered in South America told him of a gold-rich territory called Pirú, no doubt an early version of the fabled El Dorado, except that this one was for real. Named after the river that flowed there, it was later corrupted by the Spanish into Perú. Pascual travelled as far south as the San Juan River on the present day border between Ecuador and Colombia, but here he fell ill from tropical disease, and so returned to Panama City. It was here that Pizarro heard the story of El Dorado de Perú.

This information, in combination with his elevated position in the New World gained by betraying Balboa and the inspiration from the success of his cousin Cortés in Mexico, was exactly what made Pizarro the wrong person in the wrong place at the wrong time - an ideal example of how one man can change the world for the worse. The first two of Pizarro's expeditions penetrated into the Tombes Region of northwest Peru, and it is here that they encountered the incredible riches of the land, where the native homes were decorated in silver and gold. Pizarro and his men were the first Europeans to see the Peruvian llamas, which Pizarro called 'little camels'. But gold and other treasures were of far more importance to conquistadors than little camels, and they could be acquired as easily as taking candy from a child from the friendly and peaceful Incas, whose god was the sun and who erroneously called the Spanish 'Children of the Sun', due to their fair complexion and brilliant armour.

Pizarro returned to Panama to equip for a final third expedition but the new governor of Panama, Pedro de los Ríos, a typical conquistador, was constantly paranoid of being surpassed by his peers and so refused permission. Pizarro's men convinced him to leave for Spain and appeal to the sovereign in person. Pizarro sailed from Panama back to Spain and King Charles I heard of his expeditions in South America, a territory the conquistador described as very rich in gold and silver, and which he and his followers had bravely explored 'to extend the empire of Castile'. The king was impressed at the accounts of Pizarro, and promised to give his full support for the conquest of Peru, and Queen Isabel signed the Capitulacion de Toledo, the licence which authorised Pizarro to proceed with this conquest and the start of the destruction of paradise.

What happened next is the most tragic episode in the history of the New World if not world history, as Pizarro, with his new army of conquistadors, returned to Peru. They advanced upon Cajamarca, the capital of the Inca Empire and requested an audience with its emperor, Atahualpa. Just as for the Aztecs with Cortez and his men, a strange fatal illness seemed to befall many of the Incas just days after meeting these 'Children of the Sun'. The Incas had at first believed the Spaniards to be gods who wished to befriend them, but they now became suspicious of them due to their greed for gold. Pizarro and his men were confronted by an army of about 50,000 Incan warriors in the town square but they did not attack. Pizarro convinced them that they had come in peace, and again requested an audience with Atahualpa, accompanied with his unarmed body guards. Atahualpa agreed, which was a fatal mistake, that would lead to the complete demise of the Incan Empire and its culture.

Pizarro knew that if he captured the emperor, he would have the entire Incan Empire, and all the gold which it held. Shortly after meeting with Pizarro, Atahualpa's gold crown was pulled from his head and, with the help of cannon fire, Pizarro's men slaughtered all of the Incas within the square, an event known today as the massacre of Cajamarca. Atahualpa tried to bargain with Pizarro for his life, offering him the famous room filled with gold in return for his release.

The room measured roughly 17 feet by 22 feet by 9 feet, and gold from all over the empire was brought forth to fill it; another two rooms were filled with silver. Shortly after Atahualpa gave Pizarro the rooms full of treasure, the deceitful conquistador had him executed by garrotting.

Not only was this the largest gold haul in history but a much worse fate was to befall the Incan Empire. During the late-sixteenth century, 200,000 Spaniards emigrated into South America. Rapidly the landscape of the southern continent of this paradise began to change, with imported plants, large sugar plantations, vast estates, and imported animals overtaking the native landscape. Bureaucracy and government also took hold quickly in South America. The Spanish established the *encomiendas*, where the Government granted conquistadors the right to employ groups of Indians. The encomiendas in truth were a form of legalised slavery. Relegated to practical slave labour within sugarcane plantations and mining caves, the native population of Peru declined from well over a million to 600,000 within the next half century.

The same thing happened to the Aztecs, and although slavery played the largest part in the decimation of the Incas and Aztecs, disease by no means played a minor part within this timeframe. Widespread epidemics of smallpox and other imported microbes were not uncommon, and claimed the lives of millions. On the psychological front, historians and psychologists have offered another reason for the decimation of the Incan and Aztec populations; namely, the Indians lost the will to live. This, accompanied by the pressure of Christian missionaries and later the Inquisition, who created laws preventing the practice of any form of native religion on pain of burning at the stake, finally annihilated both the Aztec and Incan cultures.

Historians have often compared Pizarro's and Cortés' conquests in North and South America for their similarity in style and trajectory. Pizarro, however, faced the Incas with a smaller army and fewer resources than Cortés, at a much greater distance from the Spanish Caribbean outposts that could easily support him, which has led some to rank Pizarro slightly ahead of Cortés in their battles for conquest. Based on sheer numbers alone, Pizarro's military victory was one of the most improbable in recorded history. For example, Pizarro had fewer soldiers than Custer did at his last stand at the Battle of Little Big Horn, while the Incas commanded forty times as many soldiers as Crazy Horse and Sitting Bull put together - on top of which, Custer and his men were armed with repeating rifles, whereas Pizarro and his conquistadors were armed only with muzzle loading muskets! Though Pizarro is well known in Peru for being the leader of the Spanish conquest of the Incan Empire, a growing number of Peruvians today rightly regard him as a kind of criminal, as many native North Americans do Custer and his men for the cowardly act of killing women and children. Pizarro is also vilified for having ordered Atahualpa's death, despite his enormous paid ransom, which was later split among Pizarro's closest Spanish associates.

By taking advantage of the natives, Pizarro ruled Peru for almost a decade, and initiated the decline of Inca culture. The Inca religion was replaced by Christianity, and both Quechua and Aymara, the main Inca languages, were reduced to a marginal role in society for centuries, while Spanish became the official language of Peru, Ecuador, Bolivia and Chile. The cities of the Incas were transformed into Spanish, Catholic cities. It had never been the intention of Queen Isabella of Spain for anything like this ever to happen. Having funded Columbus' expeditions, she had created a law when she discovered that the New World was already populated that prohibited the arrest or capture of her new children, even stating that no harm or evil was permitted against their person or possessions.

Now, how were god-fearing, fortune-hunting conquistadors expected to obtain the free labour necessary to mine gold, if they could not enslave the native population? A creative solution was needed and 'cannibalism' was to be that solution -part error, part bigotry, part religious zeal, part cultural arrogance, but mostly human greed and propaganda. No different to the Nazi persecution of the Jewish faith as an excuse for empire building. It was an answer that made enslavement of native people legally possible for the conquistadors, and religiously palatable to their Queen and benefactor. This resulted in the native groups who aided the conquistadores, and who were considered potential converts to Catholicism being designated as peaceful Arawaks, while those native groups who resisted, or who did not advance Spanish goals, were decreed warlike Caribs, the cannibals who deserved enslavement for their sins.

On my next attempt along the footpath, I ended up in a jungle thicket so tangled that it took forever to make any headway. I even used my backpack as a projectile in an attempt to clear my way through a wall of creepers. Then the ground started to fall away, which sped up my progress a little – until, that is, I impaled my good hand into spiked tree bark, slipped, and tumbled down a steep muddy incline, landing with a splash in a small pond, surrounded by brightly coloured poison dart frogs. These amphibians are so named because the local natives once used their toxic secretion to poison the tips of blow darts. The most deadly is *Phyllobates Terribilis*, the Golden Dart Frog, which is actually bright yellow in colour - and I was in a pool full of them! The indigenous Indian population's blow darts were so deadly that just a smear of it in the blood system can kill a human within seconds. Even Pizarro recorded the deadly accuracy of the natives with these darts, and never again did the powerful conquistadores come anywhere near the place, leaving it as wild and unspoilt today as it was then.

I held my badly cut hands up in the air, as far away from the poisonous frogs as possible, and waded to the far end of the pond. There were hundreds of the little yellow buggers, and just a microscopic smear from any of their sweat glands on my open cuts or grazes would have been enough to kill me almost instantly. I clambered out of the pond and stumbled on through the dense jungle, up along an arête to what I hoped was '*grande, grande montana*'. Both my hands stung equally badly with pain, my broken right wrist still on the mend and now a recently impaled left hand.

I staggered out into a small clearing, where tiny hummingbirds fed on the nectar of what appeared to be flowers to banana palms. I had lost my mosquito repellent and so sat down in the clearing and caked my face, arms and legs with soap. I had also long run out of sterilising tablets, and so used small amounts of toothpaste to sterilise my drinking water, the fluorine having a similar effect to bromide. These two substitutes of soap and toothpaste may well have guarded me from malaria. I carried on through the jungle for another twelve hours with a very heavy backpack, sodden wet, not just from my tumble in the pond, but also from frequent tropical downpours. I was beginning to suffer from exhaustion, and the next time my water ran out I collapsed, shaking with hyperthermia.

As I started to cool down, I could make out the faint sound of trickling water in the distance and so I struggled to my feet and carried on in that direction. I found another tributary, where I replenished my water supply and then rested again as my back ached terribly. I used my penknife to scoop out more peanut butter, then struggled to swallow as it burnt the roof of my mouth, indicating the bad diet I had been subjected to in the last few days. I noticed that the spot where I was resting had recently been cleared with a machete. *This looked promising*, I thought, as I could not be too far off the beaten track, since palm leaves were often collected for roofing by the natives. I then noticed elongated piles of them, to be used for fuel once they had dried. No doubt whoever had done this would be back to finish the work, and I could ask for directions, as the airfield couldn't be that much further. I fell asleep for the night waiting for them.

It must have been past midnight when I woke up and watched fireflies dancing about in the undergrowth. Suddenly, the lights grew bigger and I realised they were torches flashing - and they were approaching me. Two poor black natives carrying backpacks appeared from behind the lights, and I quickly stood up. We all seemed equally astonished to see each other. I greeted them and asked for directions to the airfield. 'It wasn't too far away', they said, pointing their torches along a track not far from where I had been sleeping. They both wished me luck and disappeared back into the night. The following morning I thought it had all been a dream, but when there was enough light, I could see the path. Feeling very weak, I got to my feet and followed the track, occasionally doubling back so as not to lose it again, as I had on previous occasions.

Every five minutes or so I had to stop and rest, but after rounding two more headlands, I saw a welcoming sign piercing through the jungle canopy. A white tower with a flashing beacon light - the airfield at long last. Now barely able to walk, I staggered further and met a wood chopper with his son. I asked again how far to the airfield, and the father told his son to guide me. We entered the small village and I virtually collapsed on a log seat at the perimeter of the airstrip. I gave the boy my penknife as payment, which he keenly accepted and returned to his father - it would no doubt serve him better than it had me as a peanut butter scoop.

In the village of Obaldia, I startled the customers at a Tiki hut cafe as I staggered in and seated myself at a table. They gaped in disbelief at this alien, as if it had survived the crash landing of its spacecraft. I wore a dirty pair of cut-offs and a T-shirt that had been soaked with sweat so many times that it had tide marks, and that covered a scrawny, sunburnt body bearing scratch marks and insect bites. As obvious as it was that I had just barely survived the jungles of the Darien, I acknowledged the poor locals in the shade of the hut with a joyful *"buenos dias"*, then ordered a coffee as if it were the most natural thing in the world. A black coffee arrived and I winced with pain as I picked it up with my impaled hand.

A police officer clad in khaki carrying an M16 with an attached grenade launcher also arrived as I poured loads of sugar into the cup, then stared past him at the airfield where more khakis toted the same weapons, while a small aircraft taxied on the runway. I took a sip, and without looking up told him to wait until I had finished. I slowly took another sip and noticed the launcher was loaded, so I added sarcastically,"... and I suggest you don't go using that thing in here or you'll kill both of us!"

It wasn't needed, as the officer was only doing his job and I was led away through the little village of run-down palm-thatched homes, where poor black natives hung about, as others walked around with those long machetes. Whatever they did for a living required a means to hack their way through the dense jungle. At the police station, the meagre contents to my back-pack was emptied out onto a desk and I was searched. Everything was damp and stunk of mildew. Behind the desk, another officer checked my passport and behind him hung a rack of machine guns.

Once the police realised I was just a daft gringo who had barely survived the Darien, and not some guerrilla trafficking drugs or firearms, I was speedily processed. From here I was escorted to another hut further down the street, where scrawny chickens pecked away at the dirt floor. This was the immigration office, and after a lot of convincing and pointing at my bank card, as I was almost completely out of cash, I was issued with a Panamanian visa.

At a palm-thatched seating area on the beach, I hung out my wet sleeping bag and clothes. I had exactly 2,000 pesos left which I exchanged for U.S. dollars, the currency used in Panama, and after purchasing a packet of cigarettes, I was left with the grand total of 55 cents. The first visitor at my Tiki home was a pretty female employee of the air taxi company, who came up to ask when I would be flying out. I told her, "*no dinero*", and that I would have to wire money over from Britain to pay for the flight once I arrived in Panama City. We both went to check with the company to see if that was permissible, but back at the office there was no communication with the city. Whether the radio link was down, or because it was a Saturday I wasn't sure, but in any event I was given a seat on the plane and would have to pay the $50 airfare when we arrived.

I spent the rest of the day recuperating by watching fierce emerald green rollers break on the seashore. I was never short of guests to my new home, as old men and women came in smiling and joking and sat down in the shelter, while their young grandchildren played on a grass verge scattered with discarded coconut shells. The pace of life was so different, and if it weren't for the odd plastic waste amongst the flotsam and jetsam washed up on the beach, you would never have thought life existed anywhere else beyond Obaldia. Here, the old looked after the young while the parents worked, and I was astonished to find out that the rate of pay here for a day's toil in the heat and humidity was a mere dollar a day. Farm labouring or forestry were the only occupations I could imagine in the Darien, except for the obvious drug running and arms dealing, which these poor people just couldn't have been involved in. The children played without toys, and so I gave them the rubber exercise ball I had for my broken wrist; having literally nothing, they were elated.

An old man carried a pile of coconuts to a little clump in the grass right by the shelter. He laughed and joked with the natives inside, and proceeded to cut one open with a long machete and shared it with us. With a skilled chop of the machete, he sliced the stalk off the coconut at an angle, much like flipping the lid off a bottle. He then passed it around and we all had a turn drinking the milk. Once it was empty, he split the nut into slices and used the stalk as a spoon to scoop out the meat. The roof to my mouth burnt and blistered from the juice after the dehydration I had experienced in the jungle, but it was still the best meal I'd eaten for ages.

The locals are used to the gringos who fly in and out of Panama City before taking a boat to or from Columbia, as it's the only overland route through the Darien Gap. Panama seceded from Columbia in 1903 with backing from the United States, and promptly signed a treaty for them to complete the failed French construction of the canal. Technically, Panama is in South America, but has the reputation of being the 'Crossroads of the Americas' because of its privileged position of joining the North and South America continents. The isthmus connecting these two massive continents has an incredible diversity of flora and fauna, with almost a thousand different bird species alone - the most for any single place on earth. The word Panama actually means 'abundance of fish', reflecting the country's reputation as a paradise for fishing and other water sports. It also has many indigenous tribes that are still thriving and living in the same ancient manner as their ancestors; this creates an exceptionally rich culture.

Because of its long border closure with Colombia, the jungles of the Darien are a dense vegetation of no-man's land and I could see now why the air taxi was the only practical form of transport. Despite this, a local told me that a road still existed between El Real and Chepo which ran through the jungle, and that a guide could get me to it for just ten bucks. After my recent experience of the jungle, I decided on the flight instead. On the morning of the flight, I awoke to a piping hot cup of coffee being proffered to me while still in a hammock in my borrowed Tiki-hut home. It was from the kind old man with the coconuts and his home was right next door to mine - we were neighbours. Many of the homes near the village square, including his, were brightly painted in pink, yellow, blue and lime green - a sharp contrast to the dull grey sunbleached homes further off in the jungle.

The airfield was a runway of cracked and potholed concrete that stretched from the high watermark on the beach to a clearing of felled trees on the perimeter of the jungle. The control tower was a tall shed, and next to it was a little wooden kiosk, with a donkey tied to a post on the grass verge between it and the runway. This, would you believe, was the airport terminal. The runway itself was being used by the locals for a game of football, which abruptly ended at nine thirty sharp when the temporary goal posts were taken down and a ten-seater air taxi landed shortly afterwards. It taxied around in the clearing, then came to a halt and out of it stepped a dashing young black captain with a crisp white shirt and Ray-Ban sunglasses, who then assisted the passengers out of the plane. He agreed that I could fly and pay when we arrived in Panama City, and I was allocated a seat directly behind him.

On takeoff, I had a spectacular view of the dense jungle below and a huge tropical storm cloud ahead, which we flew around and then out over an offshore island in the Caribbean. From the air I could see that is was populated by indigenous Indians. Further along the coast we landed at another airfield on the paradisiacal San Blas Bay to pick up another passenger. It was here that I experienced contact with the Kuna Yala Indians, who gathered around the plane while some daringly peered into the cockpit at this strange, magical machine that brought gringos down from the sky. They were covered in homemade gold jewellery. Gold was so plentiful there that even their teeth were capped in the stuff.

We continued on our journey, dodging around more storm clouds until we arrived at Panama City which, in a different way, also provided a spectacular view from the air with its many skyscrapers along the Pacific coast. Once landed, I was allowed to make a call to the British Embassy, and within half an hour, two well-dressed English-looking ladies arrived in their Mercedes to collect me from the airport and take me to the embassy, where I could wire money over from my bank account. One of them was even the vice consul. That's what I call service.

It was a strange feeling to walk into the consul waiting room, with its air-conditioned environment and pictures of London hanging on the wall. They depicted an alien world of Beefeater guards standing to attention outside the Tower; on another, a red double-decker splashed through a puddle in the pouring rain as it drove past Big Ben. The consul himself came out of his office to greet me, a fine gentleman who was a keen sailor himself. He offered me tea and biscuits, and we sat and talked as he asked me about my travels. He told me about the Balboa Yacht Club situated beneath the Bridge of the Americas on the Pacific side of the canal, where it was possible to find work crewing yachts through the canal. I didn't visit it on that occasion, but thanks to the consul, I would return many times to Panama to become a line-handler, helping transiting yachts through the canal and even working temporarily on a tourist boat visiting the nearby Islas Perlas, the beautiful Pearl Islands, just a day's sail from there.

The canal itself is a magnificent technological achievement, and one of the most difficult engineering projects ever undertaken. It is comparable to the Great Wall of China, the pyramids of Giza or even the modern day Large Hadron Collider. The shorter route that connects the Atlantic and Pacific Oceans saves vessels a journey time of many weeks sailing around the South American continent, and negotiating the treacherous Cape Horn. What started as a French construction towards the end of the nineteenth-century was completed by the US Army Corps of Engineers on the outbreak of the First World War.

It is estimated that over 34,000 workers perished from malaria and other tropical diseases during its construction - mostly poor Chinese and Afro-Caribbean migrant workers. Today, in the poor and dangerous downtown areas of Panama City on the Pacific side of the canal, and Colon on the Atlantic side, live the descendants of these canal workers. Many of the women here are exceptionally beautiful, having the best mix of both races, but a very dangerous place for any gringo to visit because of the poverty and deprivation of the area - a word of warning for any young, hot-blooded male traveller. An agreement was signed for the complete transfer of the Panama Canal Zone to Panama from the US, which happened at the end of the millennium. One hopes that these poor descendants will benefit from this.

Panama City was founded in the early-sixteenth century by the Spanish conquistador Pedro Arias de Avila, and it was from here that Pizzaro began his notorious expedition that resulted in the conquest of the Inca Empire and Peru. Panama later became the centre of the Spanish Empire when it became the main trade route across the

Panamanian isthmus. Gold and silver that Spain had taken from Peru was shipped to Panama, unloaded, then transported overland along the Via Real or 'Royal Way' to be loaded onto awaiting ships at the ports of Nombre de Dios and Portobello on the Atlantic side. The original city (which?) was destroyed in a devastating fire, when the British pirate Henry Morgan sacked it in the late-seventeenth century, and it was rebuilt on a peninsula a few miles away. Today, the ruins to the original settlement still exist, and have become a tourist attraction known as 'Panama Viejo'. On my own visit I could still blacken my hands on the charcoal remains from Morgan's torching three centuries later.

It was Christmas Eve when I booked into the Gran Hotel Soloy, had a much-needed hot shower, then made my way to the bar and bought an ice cold beer before phoning home to let family and friends know that I was still alive. I conveniently omitted to mention any of my ordeals. As the beers flowed, I decided on a plan of action and at ten to nine the following morning, I awoke to the peal of many church bells ringing out Christmas Day all across the city. My plan was to catch a dollar taxi to the Bridge of Americas that spanned the canal, then hitchhike the three-thousand mile length of the Pan-American Highway to the United States.

An island just offshore from here is Taboga. Once used as a whaling station for refining whale oil, the smell was so bad that the residents of Panama City would be in uproar when the wind was blowing in the wrong direction. This island is also infamous as a base for the most notorious and ruthless English pirate during the reign of Charles II, Henry Morgan. Morgan worked under the direction of the governor of Jamaica, Sir Thomas Modyford, who was ordered to call in all pirates and privateers in the West Indies after peace was declared between England and Spain. Most refused to be called in because business was so lucrative, including Morgan, and since he worked directly under Modyford, it appears that he was never even officially informed of this truce.

Any experienced pirate of the time would have known that Portobello, on the Caribbean side of the Panamanian isthmus, was the most important port of the Spanish Empire. It was even considered by many as the centre of the world as far as Spanish trade in the Americas was concerned, and the ideal place for looting treasure ships. Even Drake, a century earlier, had ended his days here, dying of dysentery just offshore while waiting to plunder Spanish galleons returning to Spain. A far cry from plundering them in his home waters of Lyme Bay back in the Armada days, yet a pirate he was to the very end. He was buried at sea in a lead coffin, formerly his sea chest, which now contains the bones of the greatest pirate of all. This has become a valuable treasure in itself, which has been searched for by many, but still lies undiscovered somewhere on the seabed of Portobello Bay.

In Morgan's time, the warehouses of Panama City contained the goods and valuables of many wealthy merchants before they were transported overland to Portobello, and then exported back to Spain. Morgan knew this and with an army of fourteen hundred men, he ascended the Chagres River and sacked Panama City, which itself was defended by an army of fifteen hundred men. Considering how wealthy the city was, and how successful Morgan and his men were in sacking it, they came away with very little treasure. Even after torturing survivors for any that was hidden, very little gold was forthcoming from the victims, as most merchandise had been destroyed in the fire and the remaining wealth, including gold, had been removed to a Spanish ship standing offshore in the Gulf of Panama.

The sacking and destruction of Panama City seriously violated the peace treaty between England and Spain. This resulted in Morgan being arrested and sent back to England. But his luck had not ran out since, after proving that he had no knowledge of the peace treaty, but rather was acting in defence of the English Crown colonies, he was knighted and appointed the new governor of Jamaica. This only made piracy in the West Indies more opportune for the English and Morgan became the most colourful and flamboyant of them all.

Later in life, Morgan's health started to deteriorate as he gained considerable weight and a reputation for rowdy drunkenness. He fell out of favour with King Charles II, who had him replaced as governor, and shortly afterwards Morgan was diagnosed with 'dropsy', which may have been tuberculosis that he had contracted while in London; he almost certainly had liver failure as well, due to his heavy drinking. He died in 1688 and was buried in Jamaica. He has since been immortalised as a result of Steinbeck's first novel *Cup of Gold,* and the film *Captain Blood*, which provided Errol Flynn with his star-making role - and, of course, that famous brand of spiced rum is named after him.

The Portuguese-born navigator Ferdinand Magellan was one of the greatest sea captains of his era and, in my opinion, probably one of the finest of all time. Even as far back as the days of Dom Henrique, Portuguese seafarers were considered by far the finest in the world, and even today, fishing vessels such as commercial tuna craft prefer a Portuguese captain for a successful catch to any other nationality. Personally, whenever I hear of a Portuguese captain I'm reminded of Bill's story of the fisherman sticking his fingers up at the American fleet standing off Cadiz to emphasise that well known nautical phrase of, "Foxtrot Oscar Yankee"... That'll learn 'em!

Magellan was born in the late-fifteenth century and, although Portuguese by birth, he later obtained Spanish nationality to serve King Charles V in the search for a westward route to the Spice Islands. If a western route did not exist, then a Portuguese Captain would still allow the Spanish to reach these islands without breaching the Treaty of Tordesillas, since at this time, the only known sea route was by crossing Portuguese waters east around the Cape of Good Hope at the southern tip of the African continent. A similar route to the west around the New World would have been in Spanish territory.

In August of 1518, five ships under Magellan's command left Seville and descended the Guadalquivir River to the port of Sanlucar de Barrameda at the river estuary. This fleet included the *San Antonio*, *Concepcion*, *Victoria*, *Santiago* and Magellan's ship the *Trinidad*, a caravel, while the others were rated as carracks.

They were equipped with supplies to last two years, and amongst the Spanish and Portuguese were several other nationalities, including Italians, Germans, Flemish, Greeks and French, making a total crew of two hundred and thirty seven at the outset. From the very beginning, Magellan was beset with problems; his jealous Spanish captains could not be trusted, and King Manuel I of Portugal had even dispatched a naval detachment to stop him from going. His most loyal crew included the Venetian scholar and traveler Antonio Pigafetta, who recorded accurate events of this voyage in his journal, and Francisco Albo, who also made records in the formal log.

Magellan avoided the Portuguese detachment by crossing the Atlantic via the Canaries and Cape Verdi Islands to reach the coast of Brazil, near present day Rio de Janeiro. Bad weather would keep them here for a while, but Magellan was determined to push south along the coast to find a straight that would lead them into the Southern Sea, as it had been named by Balboa, since it was first located on the south coast of Panama.

They eventually reached a place in present-day Argentina that they named Puerto San Julian where the crew established a settlement until the weather improved. It was at this time that a mutiny broke out, involving two of the five ship captains. The two surviving accounts conflict as to what actually happened, but it appears that the Spanish Captains Mendoza, of the *Victoria*, and Quesada, of the *San Antonio*, had planned to overthrow Magellan and return to Spain because of the hardships they endured due to adverse weather and sea conditions as they headed further south into the Antarctic seas. Magellan tactfully overcame the mutiny and had the mutineers executed.

It is interesting to note that fifty-eight years later, Francis Drake wintered at this very same spot on his own voyage around the world and came across the gallows and skeletal remains of these executed mutineers. Drake also had problems with a potential mutiny, which resulted in the execution of his friend Thomas Doughty, who was beheaded near this place.

As they continued south, Magellan and his men came across the very tall Tehuelche tribe. Ranging between six feet and six feet seven inches tall, they towered high above the short, stout Portuguese commander, who named the place Patagonia – Big Foot -literally 'Land of the Giants', due to Magellan's fascination with their enormous feet. Before resuming the voyage, the *Santiago* was sent south along the coast on a scouting expedition to look for the strait. A sudden storm wrecked the ship, but miraculously, all the crew survived.

Finally the fleet reached fifty two degrees latitude at Cape Virgenes, and because 'the waters were brine and deep inland', the crew came to the conclusion that they may have found the strait at long last. The four remaining ships entered the strait on All Saints' Day, and so named it the Estrecho de Todos los Santos - All Saints' Channel. It was later renamed the Strait of Magellan. As they passed through the strait, Magellan realised that he was at the southern tip of the South American continent, but could see land to his left. At night he could see the camp fires of the local inhabitants, and so he named it Tierra del Fuego – Land of Fire - and mistakenly assumed it was the continent of the legendary Tierra Australis.

So, how did Magellan know that such a strait should exist? The answer, simply put, is that he didn't. However, cartographers of the time, just like their medieval forbears with the 'OT' maps, liked symmetry. Since the world now consisted of a continent in each of its four 'corners' – Euro-Asia, Africa, North and South America - and a passageway existed to the southeast around Africa, it was logical to assume that passageways existed at the ends of the other continents. Magellan had discovered the southwest one, and the British would spend another two centuries looking for a northeast one around Nova Zemlya, north of Russia and, as mentioned earlier, also a northwest one around Canada.

Magellan and his crew met not only giants but many other strange creatures, including a 'camel without humps', a guanaco, the range of which extends to Tierra del Fuego, unlike the llama, vicuna or alpaca, which are confined to the Andes further north; and a 'black goose' that had to be skinned instead of plucked, which was a penguin. When Magellan reached the western end of the strait, he noticed how calm the sea was and so misleadingly named it Tepre Pacificum – the peaceful sea, hence Pacific.

Only three of the four remaining ships had entered the strait, since Gomez of the *San Antonio* had deserted and returned to Spain. It took thirty-eight days to navigate the treacherous strait, and it is said that Magellan wept with joy when they finally reached this calm sea. His fleet accomplished the westward crossing of the ocean in ninety-nine days, but the death toll was high due to the hardships of disease, particularly scurvy and starvation, and by the end, the men were out of food and chewed the leather parts of their gear to keep themselves alive.

By March of 1521, the expedition dropped anchor at the Philippine island of Cebu, just four hundred miles from the Spice Islands. This was the most easterly point that Magellan had travelled on a previous voyage, now making him the first person to circumnavigate the world, albeit on two separate voyages. Magellan met with the chief of Cebu, whom he knew and had helped to convert to Christianity. The chieftain persuaded the Europeans to assist him in conquering a rival tribe on the neighbouring island of Mactan. During the battle, Magellan was hit by a poisoned arrow, and was left to die by his retreating comrades.

After Magellan's death, the survivors, now in two ships, reached the Spice Islands, and loaded the hulls with spice. One ship attempted, unsuccessfully, to return across the Pacific while the other ship, the *Victoria*, continued west under the command of Basque navigator Juan Sebastian de Elcano. The vessel sailed across the Indian Ocean, rounded the Cape of Good Hope, and returned to the Spanish port of Sanlucar de Barrameda four years later in September 1522, becoming the first ship to circumnavigate the globe and, as incredible as it sounds, with just eighteen of the original two hundred and thirty-seven crew still alive.

The full extent of the Earth had been realised, since their voyage was 14,460 Spanish leagues (60,440 km or 37,560 miles). The need for an International Date Line would soon be established, since upon returning they found their date was a day behind, even though they had faithfully maintained the ship's log. This caused great excitement at the time, and a special delegation was sent to the Pope to explain the oddity to him; some had even assumed that God had taken a day from their lives as punishment for circumnavigating the globe. The greatest minds of the time soon realised that a day had been lost because they travelled west during their circumnavigation, opposite to the Earth's daily rotation. Astronomy may have been a new subject in those days, but the two satellite galaxies to the Milky Way, the Magallanic Clouds, which are only visible in the southern celestial hemisphere, were named after Magellan, as was the space probe that mapped the planet Venus.

And so, why should Drake be at the end of the world and traversing the Magellan Straits some six decades later? Well, the answer to this is that he was on a secret mission for Queen Elizabeth to travel to the Pacific coast of North America, in order to lay claim to that part of the New World for the Crown. Drake had set sail from Plymouth in great secrecy with five ships and nine hundred and sixty men, including the flagship the *Golden Hind*. One ship, the *Sao Tiago*, was abandoned at the Cape Verde Islands, where the expedition met two Portuguese ships.

Technically, Portugal and Britain were allies, due to the Anglo-Portuguese Treaty, signed between King Edward III of England and King Ferdinand and Queen Eleanor of Portugal. It is still the oldest active treaty in history, but at that time it was temporarily void due to the Iberian Union, when Spain and Portugal were united, due to the Pope's division of the world between these two nations. Drake being Drake, and with his convoy being one ship down, couldn't resist a prize, and so captured one of the Portuguese ships and gave its command to the ill-fated Thomas Doughty, who would later be executed for inciting mutiny.

As with Magellan, Drake and his fleet ran into violent storms as they headed south along the Atlantic coast of South America, which was enough to incite mutiny amongst the crew. After Doughty's execution, Drake decided to abandon the most damaged and leaking ships, and continue on into the straits with the remaining three ships. The accounts of the *Golden Hind* describe the straits as an ominous place indeed: 'The land on both sides is very huge and mountainous; the lower mountains whereof, although they be monstrous and wonderful to look upon for their height, yet there are others which in height exceed them in a strange manner, reaching themselves above their fellows so high, that between them did appear three regions of clouds.'

Only the *Golden Hind* made it through the straits; the *Marigold* went down with all hands in yet another storm, and the *Elizabeth* was blown so far of course that it was forced to return to England. While in the straits, a total eclipse of the moon occurred on: 'The Fifteenth day of September, fell out the eclipse of the moon at the hour of six of the clock at night. But neither did the ecliptical conflict of the moon impair our state, nor her clearing again amend us a whit; but the accustomed eclipse of the sea continued in his force, we being darkened more than the moon sevenfold.'

When the *Golden Hind* cleared the straits, it was blown way to the south in a Pacific Ocean that was nothing like the 'Peaceful Sea' that Magellan had found. The crew rode out the storm, then headed north along the Pacific coast of South America. Here they encountered the Spanish treasure ship Cacafuego, which Drake captured and stole its rich cargo of gold, silver, and jewels. Drake and his crew may have sailed as far north as the east coast of Canada, but then returned to a bay that they had passed to repair the *Golden Hind*. Known today as San Francisco, Drake claimed this area for England and named it New Albion.

It is here that the crew sighted a mermaid and, as seafaring folklore had long spoke of such things, Drake did not seem too perturbed about what he saw and recorded it in the ship's log quite simply: 'We have seen a fair merry-maid, her long chestnut hair floating like fine seaweeds along the froth, hiding what appeared to be a blue fish tail, singing her songs as plaintively as the waves.'

Although interesting reading, I just wonder how credible Drake's accounts can be, especially when he recalls his attempt to capture a unicorn for the Queen. While fighting a duel with it on the Tuscan coast, as one does when trying to impress Her Majesty, he received a gash in his side and the unicorn pranced away unscathed by Drake's rapier.

But even Columbus had seen such things as mermaids; on his first voyage to the New World while off the coast of Haiti, he entered in his journal that he and his crew had seen three mermaids breach high out of the sea: 'They were not as beautiful as they are painted, although to some extent they have a human appearance in the face...'

This wasn't something new to Columbus, as he further noted that he had seen similar creatures on an earlier voyage off the coast of Guinea, West Africa. Today we know that in these tropical waters are mammals such as the dugong and the manatee that have very human looking eyes – could this be the origin of the mermaid? In colder climes toward the polar regions are seals that bask in the sun on rocks or glaciers, uttering strange cries. Later explorers such as the English navigator Henry Hudson described a mermaid that two of his crew had seen when looking overboard from his ship while on a voyage seeking the Northeast Passage off the coast of Novaya Zemlya in northern Russia.

'From the navel upward, her back and breasts were like a woman's... Her body as big as one of us; her skin very white; and long hair hanging down behind, of colour black; in her going down they saw her tail, which was like the tail of a porpoise, and speckled like a mackerel.'

While the sex-starved crew of the *Golden Hind* were watching mermaids wallowing around in the San Francisco Bay, it must have occurred to Drake where he was heading next. His original plan was not to circumnavigate the world but to return to England by way of the Magellan Straits. He feared the Spanish would be waiting for him after looting the Cacafuego, so he decided to continue west across the Pacific to the Spice Islands, then across the Indian Ocean, stopping many times for supplies, before rounding the Cape of Good Hope and reaching Plymouth three years later on September 26th 1580. In a single voyage, Drake had achieved what Magellan, Balboa and Pizarro had achieved in a lifetime. By circumnavigating the world and returning with a ship loaded with treasure - a fantastic achievement - he was subsequently knighted by Queen Elizabeth.

So, back to that morning when I was standing on the Bridge of the Americas, hitching for a ride to the States. My first lift was with a truck carrying grain. On our way north on the Pan-American Highway, we passed through lush green jungle interspersed with sugar plantations and citrus orchards. Next, I got a lift with a convoy of two truckers, both named Juan, and the one who gave me a lift was an El Salvadorian who had once served in the Panamanian Parachute Regiment. Both drivers were real characters, and boy could they drink! They used every available opportunity to stop and buy a bottle of beer, and then would carry on driving - something you would never get away with back in the Western world. We passed through some beautiful landscape along the Talamanca River Valley, reaching San Jose, the capital of Costa Rica, the following afternoon. Here I changed my dollars into colones; the British sterling was equivalent to about three of them at the time.

Costa Rica means 'rich coast', yet as the southernmost province during Spanish colonial times, its distance from the capital in Guatemala meant that it was once a poor and isolated part of New Spain. Unlike everywhere else in the Spanish New World, the local indigenous population were not used for *encomienda*, forced labor, but mainly left alone by the Spanish Crown to 'develop' on their own. After Spain was invaded by Napoleon's army in the early-nineteenth century, her colonial power was significantly reduced. In the middle of the next century, when most Central American countries were experiencing civil war, Costa Rica was fortunate enough to have a *junta* under Don Pepe, who later became president, and by him became the first country in the world to abolish its military.

These are probably the reasons why Costa Rica has differed from its neighbours so much, and is now an active member of the United Nations and the Organisation of American States. The Inter-American Court of Human Rights and the United Nations University of Peace are also based here, and a main foreign policy objective is to foster human rights and sustainable development as a way to secure stability and growth. Drake had also stopped here on the Pacific coast during his circumnavigation, and nearby I visited the Osa Peninsula, which is said to be the last true jungle wilderness on the North American continent. Whatever one thinks, one thing is for sure; if you want a quiet life in some beautiful tropical paradise, then Costa Rica is the place, because it is so environmentally friendly that it now ranks as the greenest country in the world.

From here, I travelled through Nicaragua, which had been a relatively stable country for three centuries following the conquest, but had been the subject of frequent raids by Dutch, French and British pirates. I passed the spectacular Lago de Nicaragua, a small inland sea with two huge volcanoes, one of which was so high it was permanently covered in cloud, giving the impression that it was still active. As far back as the early Colonial era, a proposal had been put forward to use the lake for a Nicaraguan Canal connecting the Atlantic and the Pacific, and the idea was only discarded in the early-twentieth century after the United States purchased the much cheaper French interests in Panama. The lake was now polluted, and when I reached the capital I found a dirty, ugly city with walls of peeled plaster, faded

Coca Cola signs and streets that stunk of urine. Here I exchanged my currency with a street vendor at a rate of eighteen lempiras to the pound sterling.

Even though the civil war had ended in '91, the signs of warfare and devastation could still be seen all around, as disused machinegun posts, rusted hulks of burnt-out armoured personnel carriers and even the skeletal remains of a tank were sprawled out on the sidewalk. The war had been between the American backed Contras and the Sandinistas, backed by Castro's Cuba, and had only ended in embarrassment for the Americans, when President Reagan's officials attempted to illegally supply the Contras with the proceeds from an arms sale to Iran, triggering the Iran-Contra Affair. I went to an old sacred church advertised in an out of date tour guide that I had found, only to discover a heap of rubble and a huge crater in its place.

On New Year's Eve at about 8pm, I had somehow got a lift that had taken me off the Pan-American Highway and I was lost, walking up a steep mountain pass, hoping it would somehow take me to the Guatemalan/Honduran border and back onto the main route north. I could hear premature firecrackers going off in the distance, sounding like gunfire, as locals prepared for the celebrations. I peeled an orange and ate it as I trundled uphill in the dark. Suddenly, a headlamp appeared out of nowhere and I instinctively put out my thumb. The Toyota pick-up truck screeched to a halt and I got my next lift with José, an optician on his way home from work. He spoke good English and offered me a beer, and before long we were chatting away like long lost friends. He invited me to his home to meet his wife for the celebrations, and I was more than happy to take him up on his offer.

He lived in the small town of La Unión de Copan, a farming community where tobacco, rice, sugar and coffee beans were grown and cattle reared in the fields for the corned beef industry. José was part of that rare Honduran middle-class, and his house was luxurious compared to the many I had seen so far in Central America. His native Indian wife had cooked us a traditional meal of spiced chicken stew with rice and chillies, and I fell asleep in a real bed with clean bedlinen after watching the telly and the ball drop in Time Square, as the whole American continent cheered in a new year.

The following morning, José woke me at 7am and showed me his ranch, where he reared cockerels for cockfighting as a hobby. He even had a specially-made arena where the fights were held. I was quite astonished at this cruel and barbaric behaviour, where competing cockerels would try to peck each other's eyes out. A prize cock could fetch a hundred dollars, and a single bet could be as high as two hundred, a small fortune here in Honduras, and a year's wages for the many poor farm labourers.

After a huge rancher's breakfast of pork crackling, fried eggs, small kidney beans, tortilla with homemade cheese and a coffee, José drove me to a nearby bus stop and paid my bus fare of fifteen lampédes to the border, which couldn't have happened at a better time; I was now becoming very short of money, and was down to my last twenty bucks, and still a long way from home, wherever that might be. At the border it cost five quetzels - about a dollar - at immigration and the officer said with a smile in his best English, "May Krissmas" as he handed back my stamped passport, then shook my hand. I replied, "*Feliz año nuevo*", and he indicated that I was the first to cross the border in '97.

Next, a large family with many relatives travelling in two cars gave me a lift to a restaurant near Rio Montague on the outskirts of Guatemala City, and insisted on buying me dinner. Even though I was almost broke I ate like a king that day, and that night I slept beneath a giant cactus on open prairie grassland. I reckoned I was at the foothills of the mountain range that separated Guatemala from Honduras, and a cool easterly breeze kept the mosquitoes away that evening. The vegetation around me was beginning to change as I travelled away from the tropics. Palms and banana plants could still be found nearer the coast, but no longer in the hills. I had a few tipples of the cheap bottle of rum, and fell asleep with a canopy of stars as my roof once again.

That next day it only took three lifts to reach the Mexican border. One was by a truck driver who doubled as a Methodist preacher, and quoted a lot of the psalms from his Bible which he carried everywhere. He was transporting an industrial roller which was dropped off, and exchanged for a caterpillar digger which in turn was transported to a quarry. He bought me dinner that afternoon, even though I had offered to pay but he insisted and I exchanged my last dollars for 117 quetzels. From here to the frontera was a lift with another trucker travelling through the night, stopping once between midnight and 4am, where I caught up with some much needed sleep by kipping in the back of the truck, amongst cardboard boxes of some unknown cargo. We finally crossed into Mexico at 8am the following morning.

At Tapachula, I exchanged 100 quetzals for 115 pesetas, bought a cheap bottle of tequila for 9 pesetas, and then had a bath and a shave in the river as children played and swam further upstream while their mothers did the washing. I was in a small shanty town with rusty corrugated metal homes amongst the banana and palm trees that overlooked the river. It was depressing to think that I was now poorer than them, and still about two thousand miles from the US border. After my ablutions I felt refreshed, and a thought occurred to me; I had managed somehow to get this far, and suddenly home didn't seem that far away. I just had to stick it out on the road for the next few days until I reached the States, where previous experience had shown me it was better to be completely broke than in the financial position I was in now.

The Panamanian Highway crossed vast plains of coarse grassland savannah, interspersed with scattered tree growth. One lift was with a park ranger who spoke a little English and gave me a detailed road map of Mexico. He then suggested I take the coast road to Acapulco, rather than through the suburbs of the vastly overcrowded capital. This seemed a good idea since the city was shortly to become the largest city on earth, with a staggering population growth of over 2,000 people a day, and getting through the worse of Latin America's traffic jams would only add extra time to my journey.

I left the Panamanian Highway for the coast road, and reached the small village of Santiago Astata Oaxaca, where I befriended the locals who bought me beer in a Tiki bar, and I fell asleep for the night in a hammock strung from the roof – only in Mexico! At sunrise I caught a bus that twisted through a narrow mountain pass with steep drops, where some drivers had wrongly judged the sharp bends, leaving ominous reminders of rusted and burned out wrecks on the steep slopes. The journey was made even more precarious by the many pigs and donkeys that wandered the narrow roads, and that the driver had to dodge. At the end of the bus route, I hitched rides with many friendly people who gave me oranges and tangerines that I noticed sell for five a peso, whereas gasoline was as little as two per litre. At one point I was resting in a street café, sipping a coffee, when the little daughter of the waitress came up to me and started babbling away in Spanish.

"*No español, yo inglés,*" I replied, pointing at myself; she looked puzzled and I added, "*Americano.*"

"*Ah, Americano*" - now she understood.

"*Si, gringo,*" I replied, then smiled and the whole restaurant erupted into laughter as the young girl looked up at me confused and replied, "*No comprendo.*"

Mexico, Mexico, where the people are so friendly and the children have such sweet smiles; this is how I will always remember the place, although my next three days on the road would be extremely arduous. The following night I was down to a handful of pesos and slept on the beach at Puerto Escondido. Next was the run-down, dirty town of San Marcos, just south of Acapulco. On the roads it was dry and dusty, and the lifts I got were in the back of open farm wagons, which blew dust and sand into my hair and eyes. Mosquitoes were everywhere, and I now even had mosquito bites on my mosquito bites!

At Acapulco, I got a free ride on a micro bus from a driver who obviously felt sorry for me in my even sorrier looking state, and I walked a further two miles back onto the coast road to avoid the downtown area of this tourist ghetto. I filled up my water bottle wherever I could in garages, restaurants, shops, and even asked at people's homes. I bought more tangerines, which had now become my staple diet, and sat down on the beach and ate one whilst checking my current food supply, which included a few broken biscuits, a banana and, of course, that bottle of tequila. Back on the road from this point is where I started meeting fellow gringos who I had not seen since Trinidad. The first was Frank, a Brit from Gloucester, who was also down on his luck after being robbed in Cuba, a nice enough chap who bought me a much needed ice cold bottle of Coke and kindly gave me the bus fare to get out of Acapulco.

Another gringo was a Canadian from British Columbia who dropped me off at a small town about 150 miles north of Acapulco, where I slept in a field near an industrial estate in the open wind - but still the mosquitoes bit. About two miles north of Maruata in the Michoacán region, I came across a beautiful rocky coastline, interspersed with golden sandy bays. I must have wandered off the tourist beaten track once again, as there was such little traffic that I ended up hitching for a ride at anything mobile that passed, with some surprising results. The first was a police truck carrying six officers, dressed in a grey uniform with black Darth Vader-like helmets, and then a troop carrier with some fifty soldiers dressed in green khaki and carrying armalite rifles and M15s. The carrier screeched to a halt, and the soldiers beckoned me to catch up and hauled me aboard, then sat me alongside on a case of grenades, of all things.

My best day's hitchhiking in Mexico was courtesy of Jonathan from Idaho, who was also a seasoned traveller. We swapped travel stories all the way to the spectacular resort of Puerte Vallarta. Here we stopped off for lunch at La Kliff, an amphitheatre restaurant that literally clung to the edge of the white cliffs that overlooked the Pacific Ocean. The view over the bay was spectacular, with many yachts and tourist boats bobbing about on the sea. It was the first time since stepping ashore in Barbados that I yearned to be back at sea again. Where I was now was no doubt the new rich man's holiday paradise which had taken over from the older and much run-down Acapulco, which had its heyday back in the early seventies.

A few days later, I was completely out of food and tried foraging for some in vast fields of mangoes, papaya and chilli, but to no avail, as it was past harvest time. A truck driver named Juan came to my rescue and gave me a lift further north to Guaymas, stopping to buy me a meal of scrambled eggs, ham, frijoles and tortilla with salsa. The terrain changed again as the savannah turned into scrubland desert, and the lifts I got covered greater distances the further north I travelled. At the latitude of Mazatlan I started recognissing place names once again, especially from the time I met Alec all those years ago, recalling the fond memories I had, travelling to the States with him in his MG sports car. We passed the glorious mountains of Los Mochis, and then crossed the Tropic of Cancer at exactly 4:50pm local time on the 11th January. A Mexican construction worker then gave me a lift and, realising my predicament, kindly gave me a twenty peso note which, would you believe, in my current financial crisis was like receiving a $100 bill. The construction worker and the many other good people I had met in Mexico had made it possible for me to reach the border of the United States at long last.

In the darkness and pouring rain, I was dropped off in downtown Nogales after my final lift across Mexico. After sailing the Atlantic, and then an extra journey time of almost two months on the road, I had finally arrived at the United States border and, with the exception of Belize, I had crossed not just every country in Central America but also Venezuela, Columbia, Panama and the south Caribbean Islands between Barbados and Trinidad. I looked around at my new surroundings as the streets overflowed with rainwater onto the sidewalk, which could only be seen by the light of the occasional headlamp of passing traffic.

I found out from an irate border official that it would cost to get an entry visa into the States. British subject or not, it didn't matter if I were the Queen herself, I still had to pay $6. I huddled under the tarpaulin of a street vendor and spent my last few pesos on a piping hot coffee. *Life may have its strange twists and turns*, I thought, *but how ironic that I had arrived back at the very same place and in the very same predicament that I had been in eight years previously.* Well, maybe not as bad as that, as I still had my passport and a backpack, but then again, I didn't have Casper the Friendly Ghost come to my rescue this time.

The rain finally abated, and I walked aimlessly around the backstreets that ran parallel to the border, wondering what I should do next. I noticed the bar where I had previously spent my last pesos on a beer and a packet of cigarettes, and the street corner where I had sat contemplating my next move when Casper had found me. I looked up at the tall, new barriers without any gaps in this time. It was not going to be as easy to get across this time. I could hear the echo of children laughing from all those years ago as I ran with them through the hole in the fence and onto the American side. Eight years was a long time, and I smiled to myself, thinking about those children who would have all grown up, with some perhaps even having little Hallowe'en creatures of their own by now.

    I followed the perimeter of sheet metal of the new border towards the outskirts of town, where there was less traffic and a less chance of raising suspicion. In the distance, I noticed the lights to a second crossing, which I suspected was used for heavy goods vehicles and decided to take my chances there. It started raining again and, suffering from sheer exhaustion, I wasn't thinking straight, but somehow I had it in my head to keep walking, as I heard a dog barking in the distance. Beneath the bright overhead spotlights at this second gate I could see no checkpoint or any immigration officials, and even the brightly lit offices all seemed empty, so I just strolled straight on through. Even half a mile down the road in the dark, I was still having my doubts about whether or not I was actually on the US side of the border, but then I noticed the road was freshly re-surfaced - something virtually unknown on the Mexican side with its many old roads of potholes within potholes. Just then, a car passed by and I instinctively thought about placing out my thumb to hitch a ride when I suddenly snapped back into reality and realised where I was. The cop car screeched to a halt, spun around and sped back towards me. It stopped, the driver's door opened and out stepped Judge Dredd. *Shit! Too late!*, I thought, *this is the States*.

    Two hours after I had been arrested, searched and then processed at the local police department. I was placed in a five-by-ten metre cell for the night. I was just so exhausted that all I wanted to do was sleep, and after what seemed just like minutes after I put my head down and shut my eyes, the cell door opened again, and I was taken into yet another room for my fingerprints to be taken. As if I was some common criminal, I was photographed. I was just too tired to take in everything that was going on around me as police officers and immigration officials rushed in and out of various offices, around desks and computer terminals. Meanwhile, a row of about ten Mexican immigrants sat on a bench in front of the main reception desk, all wearing muddy footwear. These poor wetbacks had intentionally crossed the border illegally for a better standard of living. I remembered what the Mexican construction worker had told me just a few days ago; that it was possible to earn a month's worth of wages in Mexico in just two days for exactly the same work here in the States. So, who in their right mind could possibly blame this lot for wanting to do exactly that?

I was starting to nod off to sleep again as a passing police sergeant spoke to me, but I only understood fragments of what he said.

"You pose quite a challenge to some of my officers. They have never seen a form 210 before, let alone filled one out."

This referred to the condition of my arrest, since under American law I had been arrested for entering the country without inspection, which is an unusual thing for a Brit, since we come under the visa waiver programme. The quickest way for me to get out of this mess, he advised, was that I request voluntary deportation. I don't recollect too much that happened next, except filling out more paperwork and being escorted back to my cell.

The following morning, instead of being released for voluntary deportation, I was transferred to another detention centre in Tucson, Arizona. I had a sixty six-seater bus all to myself as I was driven through the desert. *What the hell is going on?*, I thought, as I gazed out at the cold January rain. At Tucson I was searched again, and had my backpack removed from me. My cigarettes were confiscated and shoelaces removed as I was placed in yet another cell by myself, while about sixty Mexicans were crammed into a similar-sized cell next door. They had also arrived from Nogales, but on a different bus and I was confused by the segregation, as, let's face it, we were all illegal immigrants. I could hear them laughing and joking in the cell next door as if saying, "Oh well, we got caught, better luck next time!"

The next day I was transferred to the processing department for illegal aliens in a town called Florence. 'Illegal Alien' indeed; I felt like telling them that not only was I born on this planet but so were my parents! This time I shared a bus with three Mexicans, one of them being Daniel, who explained to me what was happening. It was here that we would stay until the American legal system had decided what to do with us; in my case, I hoped for voluntary deportation.

The first thing I noticed about my new home were the razor wire fences that surrounded the detention camp as we drove through the main gate. A wristband was clipped onto each of us before we were escorted into another cell, which we shared with other detainees -

there was no longer any segregation. I looked at my wristband. It read A* 74-320-829 - *I was now no longer a name but a number*, I thought sarcastically. Next, we were taken out of the cell one at a time, and when it came to my turn, I had to undress, was searched again, then walked down a corridor naked to the shower. I was then given a yellow box which contained blue prison clothes into which I dressed, and a wash kit. I was allowed to get a book and my diary from my backpack which, along with my muddy clothes, was then placed into storage.

A tall, green-uniformed Okey guard noticed the title to my book, *Spanish Made Simple*, and commented, "You might as well learn the language while you're in here as it's the only thing you're gonna hear." We were then given baloney sandwiches, the first thing I had eaten in two days, then escorted to a dormitory which forty of us shared. A sign above the door simply read 'Foxtrot – One.'

"Where the hell are you from, man?" asked one Mexican in an almost perfect American-English accent.

"England," I replied and heard the word '*Ingleterra*" being muttered throughout the dormitory as a blue-uniformed female guard directed me to my bunk.

"What the hell are you doing here?" asked another in surprise.

"I entered the country without inspection."

He walked away, shaking his head. The second person to introduce himself to me after Daniel was a tall black Fijian. It was of some comfort to know that someone else was here from as far away as me. Even the prison guards were astonished to see a fellow gringo, and I later discovered that I was the third Brit to be incarcerated here in the last year. The last one had been picked up in San Diego, and deported back to Britain four months previously,

"How long had he been in here?" I asked.

"Oh, I guess about two months!" was the reply, and with that my heart sank.

I demanded to speak to the British Consulate and a further two days after filing a request form, I was allowed to make a phone call to the British Embassy. There was nothing they could do unless I could afford to pay for my own flight, as I had requested voluntary deportation – which at the time I could not.

I was given a free phone number to call the British Embassy at anytime if I had any further problems; they had advised me that I would get a hearing in court, and if I did not fight the case I would then be deported within a few days. Although the place looked like a prison, it was in fact a detention centre, and the inmates - unlike criminals - were mainly friendly, ordinary folk from all walks of life; construction workers, factory and farmhands, businessmen and, in the case of Daniel with whom I shared the bunk, a Mexican police officer. The inmates were mainly Mexicans, and other Central and South American nationalities but we also had Chinese, Philippines, Iranians and someone from Jordan.

Daniel loaned me $3 to buy cigarettes as mine had been confiscated, and on my third day there I met Cesar, another Mexican about my age, who could have easily passed as a gringo in appearance and spoke perfect American English. He enjoyed singing and would even sing Louis Armstrong's 'Wonderful World' to a black American guard, who found it very amusing.

On my third day there, I had already worked out two possible ways of escaping. One was by climbing a lamppost at the corner of the recreation yard and leaping over the razor wire fence; and the other was through the gaps halfway up two consecutive gates - but the only problem is that either escape had to be achieved at lightning speed after hiding in a portaloo during the count after recreation time.

I started socialising with my fellow inmates by playing a pool tournament - a game which I hate - and suggested chess instead. To my surprise, I discovered that no-one else in Foxtrot knew how to play the game, and so it wasn't long before I was teaching it to anyone who was interested.

Cesar was my main opponent in chess while a Guatemalan nicknamed Buffalo looked on trying to learn the game. Buffalo was a short, scruffy-looking urchin who gave the impression that his brains had been fried on too many drugs. I later found out that he was a political refugee who was trying to escape to the US after a grenade had been thrown into his home, killing his whole family. He had barely escaped with his life. It was befriending people like Cesar, who was my translator, and Buffalo, who taught me a few tricks that helped me survive in the detention centre as its sole gringo amongst two hundred Hispanics.

One particular trick he taught me was how to light a cigarette without the use of matches or a lighter, which were banned. You place two stripped pencil leads into a plug socket, then arc a piece of paper across them which ignites and you quickly light your cigarette. It wasn't long before I was showing all the smokers how to do this, and when the dormitory started to fill up with cigarette smoke, the guards assumed it was a faulty air-conditioning unit.

Tuesday the 21st of January 1997 was my 100th day of travel on this particular journey since leaving my home town of Lyme Regis, and to celebrate it, I was given some hassle by an inmate who obviously did not like gringos, even if they were European and not American. The following day the hassle continued, and another inmate I had befriended, Roberto, reported it to a guard as he was being released. The troublemaker was transferred from Foxtrot to Alpha, the problem section of the camp, where inmates are distinguished by wearing orange jackets instead of blue, and are placed in solitary confinement.

Each day started at seven with breakfast call, and everyone got up and dressed in their blue uniform, then lined up in the television room next door to the dormitory. We were all then marched in single file into the still pitch black morning to the perimeter fence, and then in double file across the recreation yard to the canteen, while the darker blue-uniformed guards counted us out and then back in again after breakfast. If you ate quickly enough, you got time for a cigarette just outside the canteen doors in a small, wired-off smoking area.

'Chow' is the expression for meal times, which occur again at midday and 5pm, when the same procedure is repeated. While I was there I noticed that no-one tried to escape, but everyone patiently awaited their court hearing date in the faint hope of being able to enter the USA to work and live a better life than they had in their own country. I must have been the exception - as much as I like the States, I had by now enough of adventure and travel for the time being, and wished to get home to the UK as soon as possible.

The food there was very good, mainly Mexican burritos with fijole beans and chilli, which is my favourite. In the evenings i was television, draughts and, of course, the chess club, which I started in Foxtrot. A library was available, and I spent a lot of my time reading science-fiction. Food was not allowed to be taken back into the dormitory, and it had become a game amongst the inmates to try and smuggle something back from the canteen. If caught, whether it was a carton of milk or a piece of fruit or a packet of biscuits, it was automatically confiscated by a tiresome-looking guard, and nothing was ever said. If you were lucky enough to get a job, the pay was a single dollar a day, whether it was cleaning toilets, working in the kitchen or laundry room, or the cushy job as a librarian; it was enough money to keep you in cigarettes.

Inside the television room were two drinks machines that took quarters and a candy machine that took 55 cents. One day, while Cesar and I were playing chess, we noticed that Buffalo was not observing the game, but instead was picking the machines with a piece of wire attached to a long piece of plastic. We carried on playing, pretending to be oblivious to all of it, as candy and drinks were freely passed around the dormitory, right under the guards' noses. Just prior to this an engineer had arrived to try and fix the 'faulty' air-conditioning unit, and shortly after the machines had been relieved of their contents, Cesar nudged me with his foot under the table and nodded in the direction of the confectionery man, who had just arrived to empty the machines.

With a broad grin on his face after seeing that each machine was empty, he opened one up, expecting it to be full of money and his jaw dropped at the discovery of the meagre content instead. At this point Buffalo had re-joined us and was intently studying our game of chess, while in the background we heard, "Hey! Summin's wrong here", then the rattle of just two quarters and a solitary nickel lying at the bottom of the tray. Then, after a little thought, "Hey someone, been taking stuff outta the machines!"

At the same time, the engineer had taken the whole air-conditioning unit to pieces, and was staring at it while scratching his head and wondering why it had been giving off so much smoke. I was now trying not to laugh and had trouble making my next chess move as my eyes welled up with tears.

"Herbert… Herbert, has anyone seen Herbert?" asked a female guard as she walked through Foxtrot. I put up my hand.

"You have to go for a plant."

"What's one of them?"

"You have to go for a T.B. inoculation."

I walked along with several others who had arrived there at about the same time as me two weeks previously. The female guard wasn't the sharpest tool in the box, and it wasn't long before she lost some of us on the way to see the medic, and we had to keep having recounts. At one point, Daniel managed to find his way into a clothes storeroom and decided he would have a few more blue T-shirts. Meanwhile, I had established that the two short Chinese immigrants, Zhi and Chan, that I had befriended while teaching chess had already had the inoculation. I was the translator - not that I could speak Chinese, and Chan could not understand a single word of English, but Zhi could understand a bit of my English but not American English. Zhi was a cobbler by trade and always made me laugh when he tried explaining this to anyone, "Make shooo, make shooo", and demonstrated this with the tapping of an imaginary hammer. He was very clever and easily picked up the game of chess, beating me every time after the first few games that we had.

I explained to the female guard that both Zhi and Chan had been inoculated, and as I made eye contact with her, I noticed Daniel trying to get out of the clothes store immediately behind her. So as a distraction I whispered to Zhi to explain to her what he did.

"Make shoo, make shoo…"

It was a perfect distraction, giving Daniel the opportunity to squeeze unnoticed back into the crowd, wearing his collection of many new T-shirts, and the guard just staring at Zhi in complete bewilderment as he demonstrated tacking with an imaginary hammer. I made the translation: "He says he and Chan had the inoculation a week ago."

She raised her hands in the air and exclaimed in a Southern drawl, "I jus dun unnerstan' a word y'all saying!"

It turned out that the T.B. inoculation was in fact a test to see who had contracted it, and my test proved positive, which was a bit of a worry - not for having the illness, since it can easily be cured with a course of antibiotics, but because under the American legal system, they could not deport an immigrant held in custody if they had T.B., and further, they could retain me for a maximum of six months, or until my test showed negative. The doctor who examined me was a nice man, explaining this to me and that, "If ever you have read any of your Charles Dickens, T.B. was then known as consumption, since it caused a great weight loss as it appeared to consume your body."

I would need to have a chest X-ray in the next few days, and if that proved okay, then I could be deported home within a couple of days after my court hearing – I hoped.

I had not seen Buffalo for a while, and met him again in the rec. yard a few days after the T.B. scare. He told me he had been in the 'Hole' – a solitary confinement cell in Alpha block – because a guard had found him with his wire contraption for extracting candy from the vending machines. Not only was this incident with the A/C and the vending machines the funniest moment of my incarceration, but Buffalo had taught everyone the greatest survival trick of all – a sense of humour - and from then on, everyone in Foxtrot used it as a means of survival.

Cesar and I always queued up together for chow. Even though he was teaching me Spanish, I still needed a translator and he was my ears in this place and a good friend. One day after chow, Cesar clicked his fingers at one of the guards, as if he were a waiter in some expensive restaurant and asked for his cheque. I started laughing, and the guard assumed it was me who had put him up to this. The next time we entered the canteen in single file, the same guard cut the queue by placing his arm between Cesar and me in an attempt to separate us. Cesar pretended to place his jacket over the guards arm as if he was the maître d', and ordered Chardonnay with catfish at a candlelit table by the window!

Later on, while having a cigarette in the compound, I overheard the same guard speaking to an orange-coated inmate, and asking him if he could rough up the limey to teach him a lesson for being sarcastic and a trouble maker. The orange coat turned out to be Buffalo and I heard the reply, "No one touches the limey in here – no-one!"

A new inmate joined Foxtrot and our group of chess players. His name was Frank and he was a tall, thin, black Haitian. We must have looked a motley, multinational crew with a Guatemalan, two Mexicans, two small Chinamen, a tall lanky Haitian and a gringo. Eventually our group started to split up as our court dates approached and everyone was either given US citizenship or deported. Except for Cesar, who continued to appeal the court's decision to deport him back to Mexico in a bid to enter the USA to marry his American girlfriend in Indianapolis. Soon, it was to be my turn to have a court hearing.

"This court then has no choice but for immediate deportation to your country of residence." The hammer struck the bench and the next defendant – a fellow wetback - stepped forward. I quickly raised my hand before the handcuffs were on and I was forced back to my cell.

"You have a question?"

"Yes, sir." I knew middle class Americans liked to be addressed like that. I lookedaround at the sterile whitewashed walls of the court, and realised that if politeness was ever to count in my favour, then now would be a good time.

"I happen to know there's a flight leaving for London this Wednesday night. Would the court see it fit to get me on that one?"

The only real colour in this place except for the faded blue uniform of the detention camp inmates was the starred and striped flag which stood proudly over a crest of the American eagle at the end of the room. The judge, dressed in a black gown, peered across at the other judiciary, more in surprise at the impertinence of the question than anything else. Here was a cocky Brit being deported for vagrancy and requesting when to have his free flight, paid for by the American tax payer.

He nodded.

"Yes, I think we can arrange that."

"Thank you, sir."

"You're welcome."

Now I was the one surprised, and almost expected him to follow it up with, "and have a nice day!" Suddenly, a guard motioned me back to the direction of my cell as even more wetbacks crammed themselves into the courtroom, and the mass hearing of those who had been nabbed crossing the Rio Grande for a better life reverted back into Spanish.

The old rickety Bluebird school bus had been converted into a prison wagon, and I was its sole occupant as we drove towards Phoenix International Airport during that cold winter night. When we arrived, I was allowed to have one last cigarette before I was handcuffed between two ex-marine guards who escorted me through the airport. This was just so embarrassing, as tourists arrived in the opposite direction, some even from Britain, and glared at me as if I was some dangerous criminal. I was the last to get on the flight, and just before I entered the aircraft, the two marines decided to take off my handcuffs.

"We aren't supposed to do this until you are seated on the plane, but we know you ain't trouble and we don't want to embarrass you any further," they justified it in pity for me.

I stepped onto the British Airways plane and official British territory as the cabin crew stood waiting for their last passenger. A beautiful air hostess came up and hugged me.

"This brings out my maternal instincts," she exclaimed.

"At least you are better looking than these two ugly mugs," I whispered, and indicated with a nod the two guards glaring at me.

Another of the flight crew member commented, "I always said they should do away with passports so that we can all travel without any hindrance, regardless of nationality." Never a truer word spoken, I thought.

"Excuse me, sir! Your documents are up in business class!"

I awoke from my drunken slumber and suddenly realised where I was - about thirty thousand feet above the Atlantic. Must be almost home! I turned around and said my farewell to the American beauty that I had been allocated as a seating companion, and followed the equally pretty air hostess along the gangway to the stairwell, ascending up into business class. I must have looked a comical sight amongst the Saville Row suits and attaché cases in my ragged T-shirt and jeans with a busted zipper, still caked in dry mud from the border crossing.

"We did not wish to embarrass you in front of the young lady," smiled the hostess as she lead me to one of those big luxury seats, then handed back my confiscated passport and skipper's licence now that we were back in British territorial airspace.

Well, nothing quite like this had ever happened to me before, *but there's always a first time*, I thought, as I ordered breakfast on my free flight home – well, not quite free; it had been paid for by the American taxpayer and, little did I know at the time, I would be paying them back five times the price in the years to come, proving that there really is no such thing as a free lunch. I peered through the window, sipped a glass of champagne and gazed out over the British West Country in the early morning dawn.

After passing through customs, I was escorted to a waiting area where I met another suit and in it, holding another attaché case, was a British immigration representative. I'm not being prejudicial about people in suits; it's just that it all seemed so bizarre, as it only seemed a moment ago, I was a dirty penniless urchin in rags with no apparent human rights. Now, everyone seemed to be issuing me rights I didn't even know that I had. The gentleman seemed a nice person and explained that it was part of his job to interview Brits in my position to find out if human rights had been breached in the process of deportation.

"Being detained for three weeks seems an unnecessary length of time."

I shrugged my shoulders and restrained any sarcasm, as he appeared concerned.

"Were you mistreated?"

"No."

"Do you wish to issue a complaint?"

"No, not at all. I was treated very well; it was all just an unfortunate incident."

That was probably a lie but why make a fuss and what would it achieve?

CHAPTER 7

"The future just isn't what it used to be!"
  - Unknown graffitist in the Florabama restroom

Lyme and the adjacent beaches are famous for their fossils, specifically those from a geological time known as the Jurassic Period. The area is popularly known today as the Jurassic Coast, a phrase I had originally coined while a deckhand aboard the tuna sport fishing boat in San Diego back in the days when the film *Jurassic Park* was released. If only I had registered the bloody name, as the phrase is used today to advertise almost everything, from fossil walks and cream teas to bus trips and even bleeding boat trips along the bleeding 'Jurassic Coast'. I had made a similar mistake in Lyme back in the early days of the Internet, when everyone was after the 'correct' domain name such as '.co.uk' or 'gov', until I pointed out that '.com' comes up first on a search engine, and the idea was snatched away from me in no time. I hope this time it will teach me to keep my bleeding mouth shut - at least until I can implement any new ideas.

Just as the Jurassic Coast ends at Lyme, where there seems to be little life these days, so too did the Jurassic Period come to an abrupt halt, and most of its life forms became extinct. This happened after a giant rock in space tumbled towards the sun as a result of an earlier collision with two larger rocks between the orbits of the planets Mars and Jupiter, some 160 million years ago, in a region of our solar system known as the asteroid belt. This created a group of gravitationally bound asteroids. A fragment from one of them, known today as Baptistina 298, would at times come precariously close to the

Earth until, about 108 million years ago our planet's gravitational field ripped it further apart into at least two smaller pieces. One of them collided into the lunar surface, forming the large crater Tycho (... and possibly another reason for twinning it with Los Angeles!). The other piece, estimated over sixty miles in diameter, continued on its close Earth orbit until it finally struck the Earth 67 million years ago.

The impact caused some of the largest mega-tsunamis in Earth's history, reaching heights of three miles. A cloud of super-heated dust, ash and steam would have spread from the crater as the asteroid burrowed underground in less than a second. Ejected material blasted into the atmosphere and heated incandescently upon reentry. This raised the Earth's surface temperature to such a point that any lifeform that was not hidden beneath ground or underwater far enough away from the impact zone would have been incinerated. Colossal shockwaves initiated further earthquakes and volcanic eruptions, with emissions of more dust and particles covering the entire surface of the planet for about a decade afterwards, blocking out the sun and resulting in a nuclear winter. This caused the extinction of at least half of all the species on the Earth, including dinosaurs.

One particular species that survived was a rodent type of animal that I like to think was not too dissimilar to the loveable Scrat in the *Ice Age* cartoon movies... Maybe not, but rodents at this time developed into mammals more akin to those we are familiar with today, rather than dinosaurs. This included primates and, after a further 60 million years or so, even mankind. The details are obviously a lot more complex than this, but one thing is for certain - it is very unlikely that mammals would have survived or evolved as they did if dinosaurs were still roaming around, were this asteroid impact not to have occurred. It's also a nice thought that this flat featureless scrubland desert where I now stood, with its tumbleweed blowing down a hot dusty track, was once the location for the event that resulted in mankind's real Garden of Eden over in Africa, where the evolved Scrat may have given up on his search for acorns, climbed down from the Tree of Knowledge, and started to walk upright! Ironic that the place I'm in now is roughly the location of the Garden of Eden on Columbus's spherical Mappa Mundi.

It has long been a popular theory amongst the scientific community that life on Earth may have originally come from the stars, but if current scientific reasoning is correct, then the most profound and extraordinary event in our planet's history happened here. Many different disciplines of science have been used over the last few decades to build up a clearer picture of what actually happened, and many volumes have been written on the subject. The Spanish inquisition had interviewed Columbus out of concern that he might trespass upon it, and the conquistadors had spent at least a further century searching for it. I now stood in the place they had sought. Notwithstanding that a worn-away asteroid impact zone discovered by a petroleum company is very different to the Biblical version of the Garden of Eden, both have one thing in common; they had created the conditions for intelligent life to evolve upon the Earth.

Chicxulub today is a flat, featureless place in which it is almost impossible for vehicles to negotiate the multi-potholed roads, and where the poor cowboys still use horses as the main form of transport. Its Mayan name is derived from 'Ch'ik', meaning 'flea'. The "ik' part means 'to burn' or 'to sting' and is also the Yucatecan word for Habanero chilli - 'it burns like fire'. Xulub, meaning horn, means that Chicxulub translates more or less to 'the horn flea that stings you like fire' because - like most of the Yucatecan beaches - it is infested with fleas, which can make life a living hell if you're not properly protected with insect repellent, and even then the odd flea still seems to get through when roughing it here for the night.

Further south are the steaming hot jungles of the lower Yucutan Peninsular, where I carefully quenched my thirst and replenished that water spent on sweat or urinating. I had long learned my lesson that drinking too much water can make you sweat more, resulting in salt loss and cramp; too little, and you dehydrate. I had naively assumed that my deportation from the States was for a five-year period and during that time, when not working as a boatman at the Cobb, I had focused my travels on tropical America, where I further crewed, this time for eccentric sea captains.

A year after my deportation from the States, I would return again to Panama after flying into Venezuela and travelling overland, getting lost - would you believe? - for a second time in the Darien Gap. This time, I worked aboard a beautiful forty-foot catamaran owned by an Irishman who used to charter it out to the paradisiacal Islas Perlas off the Pacific coast. The down side to this venture was that the owner was an alcoholic, and as with all alcoholics, any new ideas for such a business never get any further than the next empty bottle.

I decided instead to explore this fantastic country overland, and started by catching a minibus north up the peninsula to Penonomé and a further two more local buses to the small town of El Copé in the beautiful La Pintada mountain region of central Panama. Here, tarmac roads ended, and I caught the Landrover taxi to Las Sabanas up in the Rio Grande valley. It was impossible to sit down, so I stood up in the back of the jeep and clung on for dear life, as the road through the jungle was just a potholed dirt track and very steep in places. It was Christmas, and every now and then we stopped to drop off or pick up other passengers, mainly families visiting relatives. The natives may have been poor, but they were better off than their Colombian or Venezuelan counterparts as families clambered on and off the Jeep with new toys, girls with dolls and boys with bicycles, and everyone in the festive spirit, laughing and joking.

The driver's name was Juan and he spoke a little English. With my bad Spanish we struck up a conversation, and he insisted on taking me back to his home at the end of the journey to introduce me to his cousin, who was staying with his family for the festive period. She was a schoolteacher in the city and always wanted to visit England. *Why not?* I thought – I wasn't in any rush to go anywhere. I was introduced to Juan's beautiful cousin, who spoke perfect English, and unexpectedly his two equally beautiful sisters. They were absolutely thrilled to meet an Englishman, and all were interested to know what it was like back in my own country. The following morning, the three beauties took me on a short trek into the jungle to show me a spectacular waterfall of the Rio Grande, which you had to cross by a rope bridge. It was here that I learned that, although there was no gold here in this particular river, there was plenty over the next mountain range at a place called Rio De Belén.

"Gold!" I exclaimed.

It was the greed for this stuff that had brought ruin to the New World at the hands of the conquistadors. I looked up at the distant mountains that pierced out of the dense foliage and into the clear blue skies, and thought of those San Blas Indians the previous year, who had peered into the air taxi covered in gold jewellery. Pure gold nose rings, necklaces and even teeth caps; the attire of just a single Indian must have been worth a small fortune. Was I beginning to think like the conquistadors who had been driven to insanity in their quest for adventure, glory and that shining metal, burning villages, torturing the natives for its location and even wiping out whole civilisations by reducing them to slave labour to obtain it for themselves by mining?

Even Columbus, on his fourth and final voyage to the New World, came across the stuff when he unknowingly reached the American continent by way of Isla de Pinos, off the coast of present day Honduras, and set foot on the mainland of the New World at a place known today as Castilla, near Trujillo. In his ignorance, Columbus was still convinced he was somewhere near Japan, and spent a further two months exploring the coasts of Honduras, Nicaragua, and Costa Rica searching for the Straits of Malacca that led to the Spice Islands. One place he suspected to have been the strait was off the coast of Panama, where he arrived on Christmas Day, but then realised it was a river estuary and named it the Rio De Belén after the nativity. It is now almost five centuries to the day when he gave it that name.

The local natives had many gold objects for which the Spaniards traded, and were told about another ocean just a few days' march to the south. This convinced Columbus that he was near enough to the strait, and that he had the evidence now for being somewhere in the Far East. Unable to venture far because of storms and contrary winds, he decided to build a garrison fort here to explore the area. Had he and his crew gone on that few days march to the south, they would have discovered the Pacific Ocean a decade before Balboa and his crew.

Columbus took his four ships up the river, as he was also interested in finding the source of the Belén gold, and so the Indians attacked them, thinking that the Spanish were planning to permanently settle there. He took three of the ships out of the river, leaving one to guard the garrison, when a large force of Indians attacked them. The Spanish managed to hold off the attack, but lost a number of men and realised that the garrison could not hold back the Indians for long. Columbus rescued the remaining members of the garrison, losing one of his ships in the process. Beaten off by the natives, the three remaining ships, now badly leaking from ship-worm and commanded by a sickly, ailing Columbus, sailed home from the New World for the last time.

A few days later back at El Copé, I said my farewell to Juan's cousin and two sisters, and got a ride in his Jeep as far north as possible into the jungles of the Parque Nacional General Omar Torrijos. From here, I took a village bus as far as possible again. It dropped me off at a little wooden church that overlooked the valley of the Rio De Belén on the perimeter of the dense jungle canopy. I slept in a field for the night, and early the following morning, I was awoken again to a piping hot cup of black coffee by what appeared to me to be some poor peasant farmer. As luck would have it, he turned out to be a local guide, and just the person I needed after my track record of getting lost in jungles.

I may have seen some beautiful places on my travels around the world, but none have beaten the natural unspoilt beauty of the Rio De Belén valley. As we trekked through the jungle, we passed through a mangrove of wild oranges which we picked and ate while on the move, then moved on to a place where startled monkeys screeched at us from high up in the canopy. Every now and then, we would stumble across a myriad of giant colourful butterflies, and the plentiful avian life ranged in size from hummingbirds the size of your thumbnail to colourful macaws and parrots darting about the branches of treetops. From the little church to the river estuary was a total journey time of two days. The first night we rested at a hut in the heart of the jungle, the home to the brother of the guide, and early the following morning, the brother took me down the river in a dugout canoe. The water was so clear that I could see the river bed at all times, even in depths of three to four metres, and every now and then, something amongst the shingle would glisten - was it gold? The only time I could not see the riverbed was during a glorious red sunset which reflected off the surface, as large fish, disturbed by the wake of the canoe, breached the water.

At dusk, we reached the estuary in a copper-coloured sky that also reflected off the water as the second guide slowly yet skilfully paddled the canoe alongside the riverbank. Poorly clad locals inquisitively crowded around the canoe as this strange gringo stepped ashore and entered the mysterious Second World village of Belen. They would no doubt have suspected me of being yet another gold prospector - why else should anyone visit the place? Over the centuries since Columbus, many prospectors have come here in search of gold, including large corporations from the States, but no sooner have they set up their equipment to greedily extract it from the river, than the daily tropical downpour washes everything away.

Prospector or not, the locals were very friendly and pleased to meet me. I was even offered free accommodation in an old wooden derelict building that became my home for the next few days. It was covered in Chinese graffiti where migrant workers had stayed long ago, or perhaps after working on the canal, but I never met any of their descendants. Had they all perished digging the canal, or had they discovered their fortune here and moved on? Even to this day, I don't know. Gold still exists in the Rio De Belén, possibly as a rich vein hidden somewhere within the mountains higher up in the valley - "There still be gold up in them thar hills!" - and I've even heard that after a tropical storm, so much of it is washed downstream that if one puts one's hand into the silt bar that has built up near the estuary and squeezes out a mud ball, it glistens with flecks of the stuff. I never found any gold during my stay, or witnessed anyone searching for it, but I did accidently stumble across the only modern technology that could be found in the place; small, state-of-the-art mobile water pumps, where I secretly watched some of the locals cleaning the filters and fixing them.

Surprisingly, they appeared to have no concept of money, and it was a while before I found the only shop in the village, a small kiosk where I purchased a cheap bottle of rum. It was still the festive season, and even though I had an ulterior motive, one afternoon I shared the bottle with the village elders who were resting in the shade of a large palm on the beach. It was hot and humid, and the only ventilation was a sea breeze from an unusually stormy Caribbean. I tried to find out more about the gold but unsurprisingly no-one let on anything; even when the bottle was empty, everyone was merrily ignorant. But I did discover that one particular black gentleman could speak the mother tongue.

"Where did you learn to speak English?" I asked, as large rollers broke on the shore and the receding water hissed through the sand and shingle.

"My father came from England."

"Oh!" I said, surprised. "And where in England was he born?"

"Jamaica," he innocently replied, and that to me was worth more than gold.

I had arrived here by canoe and without one, I had only two other possible ways of leaving. The first was the least cost-effective, since it required a Harrier Jump Jet - if only I had pre-arranged one to pick me up after I had cleared away a substantial area of jungle for it to land! The other was literally by banana boat. This second form of transport was obviously the more practical and consisted of a large dugout canoe with an outboard engine. The locals used it as the main form of transport to the port of Colon, including mothers with babies, and a cargo of mainly coconuts and live pigs. Although not quite the same as flying in a Harrier, it was an experience in itself to travel Second World-style. We stopped overnight on the way and I helped to offload the cargo. Not the easiest thing in the world, wading waist-high in a choppy sea while carrying ashore a squealing and kicking pig.

Back on the Pacific side of the canal at the Balboa Yacht Club, which has long since been pulled down to make way for a tacky restaurant, I would spend many long hours at the bar, sipping ice cold beers and gazing out across the canal in the direction of the Rio De Belén, thinking about that gold. Here, nearer to the equator, the days and nights are of equal length throughout the year, with very fast sunsets and sunrises. From the club, you could see a constant line of ships lying offshore waiting to traverse the canal and I once watched the *Q.E. II* pass through the canal to enter the Pacific side.

For insurance purposes, yachts can only transit the Panama Canal if captains have four line handlers and a local pilot aboard before entering the numerous locks going up into the Gatun Lake that connects the Caribbean to the Pacific sides of the canal. The lines are at least forty metres in length of stranded nylon, and are retrieved by four handlers ashore, each throwing a catch line with a weighted end known as a 'Monkey Fist'. Volunteers for line handling can always be found at the Balboa and Colon yacht marinas and you can easily cover living expenses by going back and forth, line handling yachts through the canal, and gaining invaluable experience on different types of yachts. Families would provide accommodation and victuals and, in some cases, the bus fare to return to the opposite end of the canal so that you could pick up and crew on the next available yacht, while richer yacht owners would even pay for their crew.

It was in the Colon Yacht Club, while traversing the Panamanian isthmus as a line handler, that I met my good friend Manuel Reina. A fellow Euro-gringo from Spain, who had been a school teacher in the States and also wanted to become a line handler, I was the experienced seadog at the time and he knew very little about boats in comparison, which is ironic because today we have reversed roles - he is a charter boat skipper and, for my sins, I have become a teacher. It was on his birthday that we decided to go downtown to celebrate and share a very unexpected and frightening experience, for which words alone cannot describe, but involved a giant marshmallow and us running for our lives after accidently entering a strip club for the obese. It's the only time I can ever recall leaving behind an unfinished beer, and paid for at great expense on the pittance of a wage as a line handler.

Several days later I tied a perfect half-hitch using a tossed mooring line from a visiting yacht named *Lucky Lady*.Coincidence indeed, since the name of the yacht that had brought me across the Atlantic had been *Lady Luck*; either way, the name was lucky for me, as the solo captain was so impressed with my quick tying off from the tossed mooring line that he immediately offered me the position as first mate.

The days of Drake and Morgan and their ilk may have long since gone, but you can still find eccentric sea captains looking for crew at the yacht clubs located at either end of the canal. The captain of *Lucky*, with his little Jack Russell dog, was no exception and had a fascination for Magellan, and his circumnavigation of the world. This wirily sea gypsy had a theory that a counter current to that of the Humboldt ran during an El Nino year, which could transport you in the reverse direction that Magellan took on his voyage around the South American continent, by way of the straits that today bear his name.

El Nino is a climate pattern that occurs in the South Pacific roughly every five years when the sea heats up, as opposed to La Nina, the normal, cooler part of the cycle. This was an El Nino year, and so we set off in a southerly direction from the Balboa Yacht Club and Panama, searching the South Pacific for an abrupt change in sea temperature that would indicate the location of this countercurrent. Days later, after sailing across the equator, toasting drinks to Neptune and gazing ashore at the monstrous Andes, we had still found no sign of this mythical countercurrent. This was just like Carroll's 'Hunting of the Snark', and I suddenly realized what a fruitless exercise this was going to be, as no such thing as a Humboldt countercurrent could possibly exist. As the seas got heavier the further south we travelled, so the more this eccentric captain would panic, and breaking point came one night when he ordered me to stick a lifejacket on the dog, which, would you believe, had his very own tailor made dog-lifejacket! We finally pulled into the port of Esmeraldas in Ecuador during a storm with adversely high winds, and sailing the trades in the reverse direction did not help matters. Once safely ashore, I decided to leave while the going was good and I was still alive!

On one particular return trip from Britain, I flew into Mexico City, a sharp contrast to the quite solitude of the tropics. The noise and congestion of traffic jams are something to see to believe, as is a 'Mexico Minute', which is allegedly the time taken between the traffic lights turning green and the hoot of the first car horn – very quick. It was coming up to the end of the millennium, and Mexico City was now officially the largest city in the world. I had to smile at a notice in the hotel lobby which read, 'It takes about forty-five to fifty minutes to drive from the airport to the city centre but avoid rush hour as it can then take all day!' Why people from the States should ever want to retire here beats the life out of me, as it is much more crowded than any American city, and the standard of living is much lower, while everything costs about the same. I had enjoyed those five years travelling Central and South America, but I realised now I'd had enough and I was homesick for the States.

Back at the Cobb, I continued working for turkeys as a freelance boatman and the only time I ever really soared with the eagles again was when I sailed with Brixham John aboard his Hurley twenty-two foot yacht, *Creola*. It was a cloudy Easter Day when we set off from the Cobb across the bay to the Dart estuary, where the sun unexpectedly broke out for an early season warm spell. The deep blue sparkled with sunlight, and it was not too difficult to imagine that I was back somewhere in the tropics. That night we moored at the quay, and in the bar of the Royal Castle Hotel we met some Naval Officers from the nearby academy, who had just completed a training course.

Brixham John looked the part of an old seadog, with his bushy white beard and battered cap, and when it transpired that the highest ranking Officer amongst them was the Commander of an aircraft carrier which we had seen in the bay just before we arrived, John asked him his age. With the response of thirty, he rebuked, "You're still a baby", and with that the Commander's number one spluttered in his pint of beer and replied, staring in his glass, "Never heard anyone call the boss that before!"

I cringed with embarrassment, and to think - I had this stupid sod as a character witness in court when I tried to regain my boatman's licence. Fortunately, the officers found this amusing, and we had a very entertaining night with those fine gentlemen. The following morning, as I stepped onto the pontoon with a hangover from hell, a convoy of about six helicopters flew over, heading towards the aircraft carrier, and I called down below to John still in his bunk, "Hey, Captain Birdseye, come up here and see how they're carrying the baby back to its cot!"

We continued on our course upriver towards Totnes, and spent the second night tied to a mooring at Dittisham, opposite the Ferry Boat Inn, which can only be reached by calling over the ferryman for a lift to the landing stage just outside the pub. The next day we arrived at Totnes and moored outside another pub, the Steam Packet. The moral to this particular story is that if you're going to go on a pub crawl, don't drink and drive, but do it the Devon way and go by boat.

On another trip aboard *Creola,* we sailed off Berry Head to observe the 1999 total eclipse of the sun. It may have been a great disappointment for many, because this long awaited and rare event turned out to be on a cloudy day. But unperturbed, we sailed into the eclipse zone just off the south coast and watched the shadow band of the eclipse sweep right across the bay and turn day instantly into night. Then, in the silence, the whole coastline flickered with camera flashes because everyone ashore in excited anticipation had forgotten to turn them off. After totality, daylight reappeared as quickly as it had finished, and confused seagulls flying towards the land turned around and flew back out to sea after realising it was still daylight.

I may have completed some fantastic sailing voyages around the world, but these shorter excursions from the Cobb will always be as memorable. Brixham John always said he was here for a good time, not a long time. My good friend may no longer be with us, but the memories of those good times will always be with me.

The first summer of the new millennium was my last season as a boatman at the Cobb. More legislation restricting the number of passengers that could be carried on small commercial vessels and the associated bureaucratic bullshit brought an era in my life to a close. That last season was depressing enough, without it ending with the unthinkable happening back in the States. I was actually hitchhiking from Lyme to visit Brixham John when I first heard of the destruction of the Twin Towers and the bastards who butchered all those innocent people. 9/11 will forever go down in history as one of those moments when everyone can remember exactly where they were and what they were doing when it happened, much like the death of Kennedy or Diana. A few days afterwards, I travelled to London to sign the book of condolences and pay my respects at a marquee erected in Grosvenor Square next to the American Embassy. Even after all the media coverage showing the terrible horrors that had occurred on that day, it never quite hit home as to what actually happened until I was walking around the garden of remembrance and noticed something as simple as a bar of chocolate with an attached note from a child – 'For Daddy'.

Not long after this, I had to return again to the American Embassy for an interview to obtain a special visa that enabled me to reenter the States, and exactly five years, four months and six days after being deported for life, I flew back into New York. The first thing I did was visit Ground Zero and pay my respects further; even nine months after that terrible day, the dust from the destruction of the World Trade Center still lingered in the air. Flags of many different nations hung on railings nearby, including a Union Jack with the words scrawled on it: 'I never knew you but I will always miss you'.

This is supposed to be a new millennium and with it a new hope for humankind. So what the hell is happening to our world? I thought in dismay.

Even before man had stepped upon the surface of another world, the scientist and prophesier Arthur C. Clarke, with the help of film director Stanley Kubrick, produced a masterful piece of work predicting what our future world might be like by the start of the new millennium. The film *2001: A Space Odyssey* presented us with an optimistic future of a multicultural society, computers that could think for themselves, civilian space travel and voyages of discovery to the far reaches of the solar system. His ideas touched upon such themes as alien super-civilisations that could travel anywhere in the universe, and even immortality.

During the last few decades of the previous millennium, it became evermore obvious that this future timeline Clarke had predicted was not about to happen, and when this issue was raised with him, he pointed out that the opportunity had been lost in the jungles of Vietnam. In other words, the money and manpower needed to make the sixties' drawing-board technology a reality had been wasted on war, specifically the one in Vietnam which was occurring at that time. Our technologies may have improved even further since then, but our politics have not because, as Clark would phrase it, we are still in the Dark Ages. At the dawn of this new millennium, during an Internet conference to a class of Harvard students from his home in Sri Lanka, the now elderly Sir Arthur had suggested in his native West Country accent to America's next generation of super elite that they must not give up the search for intelligent life on Capitol Hill. What wise advice indeed, and it would do no harm for us British not to give up the same search in Westminster.

The Vietnam War was a terrible and wasteful conflict, with most American conscripts arriving not only completely confused about the reasons for being there, but who they were supposed to be fighting. The problems that had developed in Vietnam had their origins in the end of the Second World War, when the allied victors Britain, America and the Soviet Union, the temporary joint superpowers, all agreed that Vietnam had been part of the French Union before the war, and so it belonged to France.

Just after the war, France was in no position to provide the ships and military manpower needed to retake control of Vietnam, so it was agreed that the British would occupy the south, while China, which had previously disarmed the Japanese forces, should occupy the north. The British, who were hardly in any better position than the French, rearmed the interned French forces, as well as parts of the surrendered Japanese forces to help them retake the south, as they barely had the manpower to do it themselves.

The following year, the Viet Minh won elections in the central and northern provinces of the country, and signed an agreement that allowed the French to replace the Chinese forces, in exchange for French recognition of the Democratic Republic of Vietnam as a 'free' republic within the French Union, the details of this recognition to be determined in future negotiations. In March 1946, the French landed at Hanoi as the British forces departed. During the next eight months, the French ousted the Viet Minh from the city, and this is what split the country, initiating a terrorist campaign against the French.

"The eastern world it is explodin',

"Violence flarin', bullets loadin',

"You're old enough to kill but not for votin',

"You don't believe in war, what's that gun you're totin'?"

Worried about a communist takeover of South Vietnam, the American government sent military advisers. By now, the Communist-backed North Vietnamese viewed this as a war of independence from the French, and later against South Vietnam, which they regarded as a U.S. puppet state. From this point onwards, things got terribly out of hand, as America increased its troop levels in the early sixties, with the first combat troops arriving in the middle of that decade. Eventually, the whole thing became a Cold War-era conflict that overspilt into the neighbouring countries of Laos and Cambodia.

"...and even the Jordan River has bodies floatin',

"But you tell me over and over and over again my friend,

"Ah, you don't believe we're on the eve of destruction."

American involvement lasted until '73, when they pulled out as a result of the Case-Church Amendment being passed by Congress, and the war finished with the fall of Saigon in April of that year. This pointless conflict, which could have been avoided had the new joint superpowers not split, resulted in the deaths of 58,220 Americans. The best estimate posits somewhere between a staggering one to over 3,000,000 Vietnamese military and civilian casualties, on top of about 300,000 Cambodians and 200,000 Laotians, which equates to a body count ratio of an appalling seventy for each American. Not only was this a terrible waste of human life, but this new 'world superpower' game that developed from the end of the Second World War is still having its effects on all of us today.

Kubrick directed films to shock his audience, and his take on the Vietnam War in *Full Metal Jacket* did just that. Being too controversial to film on location, every scene was filmed in England, with the London docklands becoming the destroyed city of Da Nang. Interestingly enough, Dorset was used for the Vietnam countryside scenes, with the help of 100,000 plastic tropical plants imported from Hong Kong, and even the closing titles were accompanied by the British Rolling Stones with 'Paint it Black'.

"I see a red door and I want it painted black,
"No colours anymore I want them to turn black.
"I see the girls walk by dressed in their summer clothes
"I have to turn my head until my darkness goes."

I don't like cities, even American ones, but there are two exceptions: New York is okay for a weekend, and in the Deep South there is a city that I have the greatest fondness for - Mobile, Alabama. Maybe it's nostalgia from that very first trip to the States when I became a yardman, or just good old Southern hospitality, but either way, this part of the world is more home to me than even my birthplace, Dorset. It was the first colonial capital of French Louisiana and gained its name from the native Mobilian Indians. It is known today as the 'City of Six Flags' because it was a colony under the French, British and Spanish respectively, then later became part of the Union with West Florida, and then joined the Confederate States of America, which collapsed after the Civil War. It is now under its own Alabama state flag.

Mobile's colourful history makes an interesting chapter for any treatise on the New World. The original colony was populated with the help of the amorous approaches of the 'Pelican girls', twenty-three French prostitutes, who arrived on the ship bearing that name.

Unfortunately, the passengers also brought along yellow fever which they had contracted on a stopover at Havana, and this decimated many colonists and the local Mobilian Indians. It was also at this time that the first African slave ships arrived, and this atrocity would continue for almost two centuries before it ended and segregation took over, which was not much better. During the First World War, Mobile's economy boomed with shipbuilding and the steel industry. When the city enforced its first segregation ordinance, it was to segregate the streetcars. It is also here at the port that the red fire ants were accidentally imported on cargo ships from South America, where they lived in the soil used as ship ballast. They are also known as Texas fire ants, as the sting feels very much like the burn of a flame, and is a menace for any traveller roughing it for the night next to a nest of them, which I have done on more than one occasion.

By the end of the Second World War, African-Americans rightly stepped up their efforts to achieve equal rights and social justice. Some residents of Mobile had considered the city to be tolerant and racially accommodating compared to other cities in the Deep South, especially as the police force and Spring Hill College were integrated in the fifties. Buses and lunch counters were voluntarily desegregated by the early sixties, and three African-American students brought a case against the Mobile County School Board for being denied admission to Murphy High School. The court ordered that the three students be admitted to Murphy, leading to the desegregation of Mobile County's school system. The Civil Rights Movement, led by such notables as Martin Luther King, then helped to bring about an end to legal racial segregation with the passage of the Civil Rights Act.

I hitched a lift along Battleship Parkway, the old road that passes the SS Alabama and over the original bridge that spanned the Tombigbee estuary to Mobile Bay. It was late afternoon by the time I reached Spanish Fort, where I headed south towards Gulf Shores. It was still hurricane season, and during a light shower I sheltered beneath a tall pine on the side of the road somewhere near Fairhope. As dusk approached, so did the evening feeding frenzy of mosquitoes, so I sprayed on repellent and huddled up in my bivvy bag for the night. Even as I write, I reminisce about the feel of the light misty rain on my face and the smell of damp pine needles. Oh, how much I miss those cavalier days backpacking around without a care in the world. I may have been homeless and penniless again, but experience had taught me that something tomorrow would change that; it always did here in the States.

Fairhope was founded as a utopian single tax colony in the late-nineteenth century. The original colonists from Iowa formed a corporation that had pooled their funds to purchase land at Stapleton's Pasture, on the shore of Mobile Bay. They divided the land into leaseholds, and the corporation paid all government taxes from rents gathered from the lessees, similar to the old borough of Lyme, thus simulating a single-tax. The purpose of the single-tax colony was to discourage a monopoly of productive use of the land by any single individual, and to retain its value for the community as a whole. Its British equivalent today is how I would imagine Lyme to be, had those Masonic vampires not sucked its lifeblood out first. Just imagine it as you drive into Lyme, passing a signpost that did not make a fanfare of some old second hand slogan as 'World Famous Heritage Status Jurassic Coast blah, blah, blah', but simply read, 'Welcome to Lyme Regis, twinned with Fairhope, Alabama'. Wouldn't that just sum up the whole place nicely?

It is here that one of the most unusual maritime events in nature occurs, the Jubilee, when whole shoals of fish beach themselves. This phenomenon only occurs in two places in the world - Tokyo Bay in Japan, and here. A Jubilee is basically caused by the exhaustion of oxygen in the seawater due to a population explosion of micro-organisms feeding on decomposing vegetation washed out into the bay from the marshes and swamps. Crabs, eels, flounders, shrimp and stingrays, stifled for breath, crowd into shallow waters before beaching themselves, and it is not unusual for locals to scoop up enough to fill the flatbed of a pick-up truck to overflowing within minutes when the conditions are just right.

Early the next morning I got up, packed away my bivvy and started walking further towards Gulf Shores when suddenly I had the surprise of my life. A passing car screeched to a halt to give me a lift because the driver had recognised me from almost a decade previously. It was Kevin, who lived in Bay Minette, some thirty miles north of here and who, along with his friend Jim, had employed me while working on that attorney's office in Mobile all those years ago. I went on to help build the house on Gulf Shores, and that is how I got to know the place. What an omen! It was the very same attorney's office whose lawn I had cut on my first trip to the States, and if ever in the future I should need an attorney, I will make sure to use him, whoever he is. Kevin was on his way to work on a construction site and got me a labouring job starting that very same morning.

A month later, I had saved enough pay to finally reach the white sandy beaches of the Gulf Coast, and I looked out across the blue azure sea and sky and realised I was back home at last. The only thing I did not recognise was the wall of giant condos that had been built in my absence. It stretched from Florida to the eastern shore of Mobile Bay. Each step I took squeaked in the sugar-sized grains of sand as the warm October sun beat down on my head. I remember finding this place by accident on my first trip to the States, when there were no condos, just miles of empty sand dunes from here all the way to the Flora-Bama, which, in those days, was just a small liquor store that sold lottery tickets on the state line.

Walk along the beach to a point where you stand looking out to sea with one foot in Florida and the other in Alabama, and behind you stands my favourite pub in the world. Originally constructed in the early sixties, the Bama is now a beach and oyster bar that has become a cultural landmark as America's last great roadhouse. It was now in its heyday, with as many as twenty different bars and anything up to five live bands playing simultaneously. It had the reputation as the place where, "you can have a millionaire sitting next to a Harley biker". The rejuvenation of the Gulf Shores for tourism had only increased this diverse make-up of customers, but its location on the beach on the Florida-Alabama state line was still the major contributing factor to its attractiveness.

It's a destination that I would strongly recommend to any single British male traveller, but remember to accentuate that English accent, because those Southern Belles just love it! Although one time back in my own single traveller days I was darting from one bar to another, trying to avoid the amorous approaches of a rather large lady, when in exasperated desperation I asked two pretty middle class ladies if I could pretend to be in their company just to put this other one 'off my scent', so to speak; I would even buy the drinks!

"You sure can honey, with an accent like that," said one.

"Seems you got yourself a corn-fed heifer," replied the other.

The ladies turned out to be the wives of two prominent senators, who were very close friends to none other than the President himself, just proving that you never know who you might rub shoulders with in the Flo-Bam.

The local favourite drink here is the 'Bushwacker', and is a great nightcap before the traditional staggering out onto the board-walk and collapsing on the beach. The Flora-Bama has become synonymous with one of America's great music legends, the iconic Jimmy Buffett, who composed such classics as 'Cheeseburger in Paradise' and 'I Ate the Last Mango in Paris'. It must be a rare limey indeed to relate to Buffett as a man of his own heart, as he calls nearby Fairhope his home town, and Gulf Shores his imaginary tropical paradise in his most famous song 'Margaritaville' - but this place will always be Margaritaville, if not Bushwackerville, to me.

The co-owners of the bar at this time were Joe Gilchrist and Pat McClellan, and when I had the opportunity to introduce myself to Joe and tell him how much I thought of his place, he was so impressed with this limey down on the 'Redneck Riviera' that I benefited from free drinks all night. The Flora-Bama, having survived the realtors with their wall of condos, is still there today, but only just, as it was mostly destroyed by hurricane Ivan, and during its long-term reconstruction, narrowly survived the BP oil spill.

On a recent visit in August 2014, having almost missed the last ferry of the day from Dauphin Island to Gulf Shores, I not only had a chance arrival to a Civil War reenactment of the Battle of Mobile Bay, but also the fiftieth anniversary celebrations of my favourite pub now fully restored. I even had the good fortune to meet Joe once again, who invited me to his home for a party which included country and bluegrass musicians with such illustrious names as Sandy Britches, Wild Bill Emerson, Tumbleweed Ted Handley and Downtown Larry Brown. If ever I were to create one of those 'thousand travel destinations to see before you die' lists, then the legendary Flo-Bam would certainly be in the top ten.

What I have learned from my travels and research for this book is that I hate corrupt politicians, because I have witnessed them at all levels of government. It has also made me ashamed to be British, except for the single fact that some of my fellow countrymen had helped to found this New World but unfortunately it too has its corrupt politicians. From childhood, I have gone from being a staunch Royalist to a devout Republican as an adult and, after my last season as a boatman at the Cobb, I decided to start a new life here in the States. It was time for a base, and as wonderful as Margaritaville is, it was just too remote from anywhere else, and so I opted for somewhere in Florida.

I had a dream of making a living by crewing yachts, just as I had when I sailed the Atlantic, and the yacht capital of the world was only down the road at Fort Lauderdale. Even the senator's wives had tried to pull strings for me to get an American work permit, and I received an email from Capitol Hill asking me to apply for my Green card, promising that they would expedite the application - but alas! My past must have caught up with me and it was refused. I suppose I was lucky enough to get the special visa that allowed me back into the States after deportation, and so soon after 9/11, so maybe it's best not to push my luck. I should have told the full story of my travels, but to summarise this book would only make me look a crackpot.

Florida as a state in its own right is like no other of the States. It's the home of Disney, the Space Program and the main destination for both American and European tourists because of its boats and beaches. The combination makes the place seem endearingly whacky, and when I returned with a trucker across the state line on I-10, we pulled into a gas station to fuel up and buy an ice-cream. At the vending machine we were stunned as a little pink, fluffy elephant's head popped up and used its trunk to suck up the chosen cornet, while playing music with a loud sucking sound as it transferred it to the dispenser. The Yankee trucker picked up his ice-cream, stared at it, and quipped, "They always have to go that little bit further here in Florida!"

Historically, those horrible British held Florida for a brief twenty years after it was traded to them by Spain, and settlers were recruited by offering free land for export businesses. It passed back to Spain before it became US territory, and in the early-nineteenth century it became a wild and lawless place, a battleground for Indian wars, slave rebellions and border skirmishes. Today, an original Floridian is referred to as a 'Cracker', which has nothing to do with the crack cocaine that is slowly destroying the youth of America but rather Cracker friends of mine have told me that the term comes from the use of bullwhips with which cowboys used to 'crack' cattle while herding, as opposed to the Western cowboys who used lassos, or the Georgia cracker who cracked corn.

By the mid-nineteenth century, the native Seminole Indians were defeated and forcibly expelled, and Florida became an official US state, but remained a rural backwater until the building boom of the 1920s when land that the Anglo-Floridian Crackers had stolen from the Seminoles was sold to real estate developers. Which, in my opinion, is today the ugly side of Florida, with its over-commercialised Disneyworld at the centre, and an enclosure of wall-to-wall condos along its beaches. But as difficult as it may seem, if you can ignore all this, you can still find the beautiful Florida of Ponce de Leon still in its natural state - if you only know where to look.

From the Yucatan to Florida it had taken me almost six months to traverse the perimeter of the Gulf of Mexico, so when I reached Cocoa on that warm February day, I was, as you can imagine, completely broke once again, and actually survived my first day by collecting aluminum cans and selling them onto the local recycling centre. At five cents each, I felt like the penniless Dick Whittington arriving on the streets of London but finding that it really was paved with money.

The first non-native settlement in Cocoa was a family of freed slaves following the Civil War, and a group of local men bought the entire tract of land that comprised this area. It went undeveloped until it was bought out, and a beautiful wooden boardwalk pier was erected later in the sixties and Cocoa Beach became a tourist hotspot for surfers.

Outside, a store hustling for spare change was 'Drunk Jim', a real down-and-out hobo who, like so many seen wandering the streets of North America, are veterans of Vietnam, still unable to cope with reality after the drugs and atrocities they experienced during that weird, psychedelic war. 'Drunk Jim' advised me to ask a friend of his for work, a born-again Christian also named Jim. Why, I wondered, are there so many people called Jim in the States? Anyway, he owned a secondhand appliance store called 'Sonshine Appliances' as in the 'son' of God who shone down on us while we cleaned and fixed up secondhand cookers and refrigerators. Jim was a good man who employed two other workers, and reminded us that we "all worked for God" - and might I just add for the record that God pays six dollars an hour for such work!

And so at the start of the new millennium, instead of embarking on a voyage of discovery across the universe and making first contact with some alien super-civilisation as Clarke had predicted, I aspired to go from being a penniless good-for-nothing hobo to a beach bum, cleaning secondhand appliances for God and living on the beach near the Port Canaveral end of Cocoa Beach. Here I could use the showers and washing machines in the nearby tourist trailer park, and with a purchased secondhand bicycle, I cycled to and from work, stopping off at MacDonalds for breakfast each morning. One always has to make the most of a bad situation in life, and here was an ideal example of a bad situation. The hardships of adventure and travel have long taught me that, with the exception of owning another boat, I no longer needed superficial material things in life to make me happy – just an ice cold beer on a Florida beach at the end of a day's work was enough.

Down at the port, I got to know the local fishermen, most notably an old seadog called Red Beard, who had spent a lifetime fishing the Eastern seaboard of the States down to the Bahamas. From his wise tutelage, it wasn't long before I got work as a deckhand aboard a shark fishing boat. After two consecutive night trips laying a drift net, then hauling it in the mornings, it was enough for me, as I am no fisherman by trade, but a boatman and this just wasn't the work for me. Shark fishing is probably the most environmentally damaging type of fishing you can do. The only part of the shark that is used is the top dorsal fin, which is cut off and used by the Japanese for shark fin soup, which they pay a fortune for, while the rest of the carcass is thrown back overboard. On top of this, a commercial shark fishing vessel is only licensed to land shark and everything else is thrown back overboard, including fully-grown sail fish, barracuda, marlin and rare yellowtail tuna –everything dead. It was such a bloody waste. We even killed a fully grown hammerhead shark, but could do nothing with it as it was the wrong type of shark. The ocean here was abundant with fish, and the captain told me that during a night shuttle launch from the nearby space station over on the cape, all these different species could be seen leaping out of the water, startled by the light from the thrusters.

I noticed many visiting yachts also used the port, voyaging to and from the Caribbean, and decided to look for work as crew. While I waited for my boat to come in, I would bus tables at the IHOP, a breakfast restaurant, for a share of the waitresses' tips. In the evenings I would visit the wooden boardwalk pier and sit at the Tiki bar near a sign that read 'Do Not Feed Catfish to the Pelicans' - only in Florida! I would often talk to the many American tourists that passed through Cocoa; most of them would insist on buying the beers – it was payment for being a travel guide, as I told them my worldly travel stories, and my opinion of the best places to visit here in the States. Another local of mine was the motel bar at 'Fawlty Towers', a name that would tip-off any Limey as to the nationality of the owner from the British sitcom of that name; even the barmaid at the time, Margy, was from Dorset.

At the port there was also a casino ship that left twice daily on a five-hour cruise. It didn't cost anything, as they make their money from the gamblers. I used to go on it quite often - not for the gambling but for the free buffet lunch! It was after such a trip that I first met Danny, a fisherman at the port, and a Nam vet. Danny, Redbeard and I would frequent the local bars, including Fawlty Towers, and swap stories about our maritime adventures. One evening, we heard about a search for a shrimper who had fallen overboard at dusk in shark-infested waters. Miraculously, he was rescued after floating in the sea all night. His name was Chip, and it wasn't long before he joined our group of maverick seafarers.

I managed to get two jobs crewing on yachts touring the Caribbean, both with eccentric Canadian skippers, and both failed trips. For one of them, we only got as far as Fort Lauderdale just along the coast, and the other, I had to meet the yacht in Guatemala and spent a whole month in a marina on the shores of Lake Izabal some twenty miles from the Caribbean. I gave up waiting for the skipper to ready himself for the voyage and headed overland back to the States instead. The Portuguese may make the best seafarers in the world but from my experience - and I hope to be proven wrong - Canadians make the worst.

I was beginning to get disheartened about finding paid work on yachts, as we now live in an age where backpackers are prepared to pay for the experience of sailing to their next destination rather than fly. Danny and I even visited the crew agencies in Fort Lauderdale to enlist. That night, we both drank a little too much at the famous Blondies on the seafront and I got so tired I told Danny I was going to have a nap on the beach. "Don't do that," he warned, "the police will arrest you!" As I staggered off across the beach, I looked back to see Danny slump across a veranda table, asleep. Later that night I was awoken by the gentle prod of someone's foot,

"Wake up you drunken bum, this is the police." In a drunken haze, I thought I was back on the beach at Lyme after a heavy session in the Royal Standard and sat up.

"If you're police then you should be addressing me as 'sir', not drunken b..."

Suddenly, the handcuffs were slapped on me, and I then realised where I was, and more importantly who they were. It wasn't any Lyme bobby, who would not only have known me as a boatman at the Cobb, but most likely would have known me since childhood!

"In that case you have just been arrested, sir," replied the cops.

At that same moment a wide-awake Danny walked over and interjected, "If you're going to arrest him, you might as well arrest me, you drunken bums!" With that they arrested him; intimidated by his size, his arrest was a little harsher than mine, as the two young cops, one white, the other black, slammed him against the police car and then handcuffed him.

"You call that a beating? My grandmother could do better than that!" replied a wriggling Danny as he was roughly manhandled into the rear seat of the police car. I was bundled into the seat next to him as Danny continued, "You rookie bum, just how old are you? I bet I got pimples on my ass older than you boy!"

"Shush, Danny, it will only make things worse," but that fell on deaf ears.

"Just what goddam reason have you got for arresting my Limey buddy?"

"It's for his own safety," replied the white cop, driving and finding Danny entertaining.

"How the hell can it be for his own safety? All he did was sleep on the goddamn beach?"

"Lot a strange people out on the beach at night; he could have been robbed or, worse still, got homosexually abused."

"Too right about the strange people - you just gone and arrested him and now you're gonna put him in a cell with Bubba, whose only gonna homosexually abuse him!"

I gulped as the black cop started laughing.

We pulled into the police station, and Danny was hauled out of the car first, still ranting and raving. When it came to my turn the cops were almost crying with laughter.

"Man, your friend sure is funny."

The handcuffs came off and the processing began. First we had to hand over all our possessions, strip off, and then change into bright orange boiler suits. At this point I noticed my bank card, which I had proffered to the white cop for I.D. just after the black one had handcuffed me, was missing. I complained but no-one seemed to care, as the handcuffs were replaced with plastic electrical ties and our photos were taken. Danny just scowled at the camera and I grinned.

"That's what I like, a sense of humour," said another cop as the camera flashed, and we were taken to a reception desk before being lead to separate cells. Here, two female cops were laughing hysterically like two witches as they watched the CCTV of a crack whore going completely berserk in her cell.

My God, I thought, *the wardens are as bad as the prisoners*.

Danny had a cell all to himself, as they thought he was going to be trouble, but I had to share with about four others, all of them black street vendors who had been caught selling drugs earlier that evening. Thankfully, no-one called Bubba was amongst them. This whole incident just shows how ludicrous the American legal system can be, but I was about to find out how this could be to my advantage, because the bank card that the cops had lost wasn't going to be forgotten.

The following morning each of us had to pay a $25 release bond, and then we were escorted to a room to change back into our clothes. Inside was a restraining chair and Danny told me how he had once been strapped into one and beaten unconscious by the police.

"Danny, what the hell did you do to deserve that?"

"Oh, it was after Nam, when I took drugs and got myself into a lot of trouble; even did time in the state penitential"

Danny was a good person, and the sort of person who would give you his last dollar, but I was beginning to discover what the Vietnam War could do to a person. Within the next few months, I made such a fuss about the loss of my bank card that the Fort Lauderdale City Office awarded me compensation of just over a thousand dollars - more than enough to cover our bail bonds and the fine which I received for sleeping on a municipal beach; I mean, just how wacky is that for a legal system?

Danny had a very cavalier attitude towards life, always ready for a fight, and I was the only one who could ever calm him down, not that I could overpower him in any way - far from it! He was twice my build, and a military veteran at that, but we had this strange respect for each other as Anglo-American buddies, and he seldom lost his temper with me.

Danny and I failed to find work as the age of crewing on yachts, for a living has long since gone, as has the age of sail. I do believe that someday it will return, probably when oil starts to run out. This new age of sail will be very different, as I imagine huge cargo ships will be powered by massive aircraft wing-type sails, or even sky sails, a type of kite sail, of which smaller versions are currently used today on tankers and cargo ships to reduce fuel costs.

Danny's drinking was becoming very excessive, even by my standards, and it wasn't until one particular evening during a share-a-case-of-beer-on-the-beach session with other fishermen from the port that I found out why. The conversation got onto films and the Vietnam War, and I just happened to mention the notorious quote from *Apocalypse Now* about the smell of Napalm in the mornings. That was the only time Danny really lost his temper with me, and then proceeded to tell me about some of the horrors that he had experienced.

"We had to bury ourselves alive in the kill zone just before the F100s dropped napalm, and it would clear everything – jungle, animals and the enemy - and when we were given the all clear, we would dig ourselves out and the smell of burning flesh was forever stuck in your nostrils. It's a distinct smell, just like burnt pork."

Danny's health started to deteriorate rapidly. At first I thought it was his heavy drinking, but then he told me that it was from contracting hepatitis from sharing needles during his time as a drug user, and that he had come back to Cocoa Beach to die. Danny needed serious medical treatment to be cured, and surely the richest country in the world could provide it. I emailed my brother Mark and told him about Danny. He advised that treatment was possible, but it was very expensive. Danny was a war veteran so the government would pay for it, and he was also entitled to a pension even though he had only just turned fifty.

I was so pleased to tell Danny the good news, and so shocked to find out he already knew this but refused to let his own government pay for it. To him, any pension or allocation of money because he served in Vietnam was simply blood money, and Danny would rather die than accept it. When I asked Danny about this he told me the reason, on the condition that I promised I would never raise the issue with him again.

Danny had been in the army as an infantryman during the Vietnam War, and had been involved in much of the frontline action and atrocities associated with war. As the statistics show, for such a high body count ratio, the atrocities must have been very high. Danny and his company had been ordered to execute every man, woman and child in a village, even though he knew they were all innocent. His protests fell on deaf ears, and refusal to carry out this order by his commanding officer would have been a court martial offence. When Danny told me this I completely understood and respected his wishes, and never mentioned government money or a cure ever again, even when I spoke to him for the last time on his deathbed before he passed away.

The fighting and atrocities in Vietnam came to end for Danny when he was wounded in the leg and he arrived back in the States on crutches. As he walked through the airport terminal, there was no bunting or waving of the American flag, no heroes' welcome, but an antiwar protest and many people swearing at him, accusing him of being a baby killer and even beating him with placards. Danny refused a military pension and the finances to pay for his treatment for fighting for his country in the Vietnam War because, had he accepted it, he would be indebted to his country. By refusing it, the United States of America will always be in debt to people like Danny, and those poor innocent people that he was ordered to kill for his country.

I have shown that both sides of the Atlantic have 'skeletons hidden in the closet'. Events that had occurred in my own childhood during the early seventies still personally affect me today. Whether it was my good friend Danny fighting for his country in the jungles of Vietnam and being forced to do things that he could not live with afterwards, or in my own country where the government have stolen from the crown, which may well lead to civil unrest if not another civil war, it means I have become part of a lost generation that have no rights, because I am not part of this neo-masonic society that has now evolved back home in Dorset.

The last man to walk on the moon had barely left when all this was still going on and, for a very brief moment during this time, it seemed that human society had finally emerged from the Dark Ages, only to plummet straight back into it. I agree with Arthur C. Clarke; we are still in the midst of a Dark Age and I further believe that we will always remain so unless, of course, we can learn not to make these same mistakes again. Human history tends to repeat itself, and it seems it is all about greed and empire building. But there is hope at the bottom of this Pandora's Box that we live in, as all of us alive on the Earth today stand before the dawn of a new era, with an opportunity for empire building, unlike anything we have ever experienced before, and it may well eliminate greed, giving us the opportunity to finally emerge forever from this Dark Age.

The idea of a space lift for cheap commercial space travel even for civilians is not new. In the Victorian times, the Russian scientist Konstantin Tsiolkovsky was so inspired by the Eiffel Tower that he considered a tower so high that it reached all the way into space. The tower would have to be 22,238 miles high to reach the height of a body or satellite in geostationary orbit, an orbit that a body circumnavigates the Earth at the same rate it spins on its axis, much like a Sky television satellite. This space station would remain above the same fixed point on the Earth's surface at the equator, and would keep the tower erect by the centrifugal force due to the Earth's spin. Except for diamond, no other material existed at the time that was strong enough for such a monstrous construction, and its use is obviously not practical because of its rarity.

What is newer is the discovery of a material that is strong enough; the fourth allotrope of carbon known as carbon sixty, the other three being charcoal, graphite and diamond. It is also named Fullerene or Buckyballs in homage to the engineer Buckminster Fuller, since its molecular structure is similar to the geodesic domed buildings he designed, similar to a leather football. Connecting the domes together forms cylindrical tubes, which not only have a high tensile strength because of the diamond type of bonding at the atomic level, but also an interesting technological application in electronics. The molecular-sized tubes are in the order of a billionth of a metre in diameter, a measurement known as a nanometre, and therefore called nanotubes. These tiny tubes could, in theory, be used to develop electronic circuits a thousand times smaller than the microchip, hence nanochip.

Nanotechnology really is the stuff that dreams are made of - just imagine someday entering a spaceport somewhere at the Earth's equator and taking the space lift up this huge tower. I've flown back and forth across the Atlantic ten times in the course of a year, which would be the equivalent distance up this cosmic elevator. The maximum safe speed would be about half that of a commercial flight, equating to a journey time of about two weeks to reach Earth orbit, but at a fraction of the cost of conventional rockets. With similar constructions on the Moon and even Mars, space travel in the future could become as common as taking a cruise or a flight around the world today. The problems for such a construction are immense; imagine the technology needed to lower a cable of this length from geostationary orbit to the Earth's surface, then tethering it off and protecting it, not just from the ravages of time and weather, but any terrorist attack. If this tower were ever to collapse, just imagine the carnage it could cause, crashing through cities as it wrapped itself around the planet! We must be well out of our greedy warmongering period before such engineering feats like this are ever going to happen, and I believe the other uses of nanotechnology may well achieve this.

A nanochip could, in theory, be like a microscopic factory of electronic circuits that can replicate itself, a bit like bacteria cells reproducing. The first nanochip of the production line will be so expensive it would probably cost the Earth, but as it reproduces clones of itself, so the price of the chip will diminish. What would be the good of this, you may well ask? Well, take for example a commercial product such as a can of Coke. Most of its cost is in the packaging, such as manufacturing the aluminium can and painting on the logo; the actual drink itself costs very little in comparison, as it's just carbonated water and sugar. Now, if we can produce a nanochip that can not only convert bauxite, which is aluminium ore, into aluminium, but reproduce itself so that billions of the chips can do the job to create the container, we have suddenly reduced the cost of manufacturing the can. The more chips produced, the cheaper the can. Other types of chips could design the logo on the can and produce the ink from raw materials fed into it and so on, until you are producing a package that is much cheaper than the contents.

Next generation nanochips could produce tiny electronic chips so cheap that you could eventually incorporate audio chips on the can that advertise the product, similar to the talking birthday cards that we have today. Then eventually, as the technology improves, disposable miniature video screens fixed on the surface of the can advertising other products from the same company - and this still being cheaper than its content and getting cheaper as the chip continues to increase production. The microchip may have given us extremely cheap access to two dimensional products such as the ultimate library of the Internet, but the nanochip will add an extra dimension, and provide three dimensional material products that will increasingly become cheaper until they are no more expensive than the price of their raw materials. Imagine nanochips producing house bricks from sand and clay to build a home, another to build a car, and next generation chips building anything we so desire, such as our own jet plane or even that dream desert island to get away from it all. Suddenly, personal wealth will have become obsolete, greed a thing of the past, and we may have emerged from these Dark Ages.

To me, the space program is that hope for humankind, not only for its spin off technologies that could make this dream a reality, but also because it gives us all the opportunity to pool our resources and learn from our past mistakes, regardless of race or culture, so that we don't mess things up a second time around on all those other strange 'new worlds' that we shall someday visit. Will such technologies ever happen and furthermore, will our politics ever allow it? Maybe, maybe not, but as my father would always say, "one thing that is for certain; time will tell."

It is an optimistic thought, since pessimistically, with no more shuttle launches, the NASA space programme finished in 2011. However, the following year my girlfriend Jan and I were on vacation on Cocoa Beach, and we were fortunate enough to meet Jack King in the Lagoon Lounge Bar. Known by the locals as Jack-the-Voice, as he was the person who did the Apollo countdowns - 10... 9... 8... – and was on first name terms with all those who had ever set foot upon the surface of the moon. A few days later, Neil Armstrong would sadly pass away, but he told us (and I quote), "The space program has not finished, it's just currently in the Doldrums." It is a lovely thought, Jack, and I do hope you are right for all our sakes.

The sixties American sitcom *I Dream of Jeannie* was also filmed on Cocoa Beach, and has a street named in its honour. Not far from it is the Pig and Whistle pub, and a few years ago, I sat there talking to an interesting middle-aged couple about the space program. I had now spent over six years of my life travelling around the States, and I joked with them that I've always missed a shuttle launch in Florida as I'm usually elsewhere in the country, and always seem to be in Florida when they land the shuttle in California. It turned out that the husband and wife couple were NASA engineers from over on the cape, and I was bowled over when they offered me a VIP pass to go on the base to watch the next shuttle launch. It was *Atlantis*, the last shuttle to be launched, and the grand finale for NASA.

"Limey, you will see it as close as any civilian can get - not even the President himself is allowed to get any closer," they told me.

On the day of the launch, I had prearranged to meet them at a certain time at the Kennedy Space Center's south gate and, as good as their word, four NASA personnel were there to meet me in a four-wheel drive. I was issued a special credit card-type pass and even the engineer joked, "Hand that back to me when we leave, Limey, and if you lose it I will shoot you!" My palm sweated every time I handed over the pass at each security checkpoint as we drove further onto the base, and into the heart of the American Dream. The final security guard looked like a *Star Wars* Storm Trooper in his body armour, and carried a weapon that I had never seen before - it looked like some futuristic raygun. Meanwhile, I listened to the husband talking as we drove onto a peninsula of land adjacent to the shuttle on its launchpad.

"You can never beat the good old days when they launched the Saturn Five rockets."

"No you certainly can't," agreed the first rocket engineer, as they reminisced.

"Remember when they had to replace all the cracked windows in Titusville just from the noise of each launch?"

They both chuckled and I smiled to myself, thinking back to the time I met the person who became rich replacing those very same windows.

We pulled up on a makeshift parking lot on the sandy beach, then got out and joined many other NASA personnel with their families waiting for the launch. Some even had deckchairs and picnic coolers and behaved as if it were a normal day on the beach since, at this time, the shuttle was being launched almost every other month to assemble the International Space Station. Along the peninsula were a row of speakers fixed up like lampposts so that everyone could listen to ground control and the astronaut com-traffic. All - whether parents, children or the odd Limey - stood around nonchalantly as a voice came over the intercom,

"10…9…8…7…6…, go for main engine spec, 4…3…2…1…, 0 and lift off…and space shuttle *Atlantis,* with Destiny, the science laboratory for the twenty-first century."

The stack lit up and the noise from the engines was terrific as the shuttle left launchpad 39A; even at a distance of three miles I could feel the heat of the exhaust and the vibration of the engines!

"Houston now controlling,"
"Houston - *Atlantis* roll program."
"Roger rolling *Atlantis*."

"The roll manoeuvre is now complete aboard Atlantis…Vehicle is now in a heads down position on course for a 51.6 degree 201 statute mile orbit…Approaching thirty seconds end of the flight preparing to begin to throttle down of the main engines as the vehicle prepares to pass through the air at maximum dynamic pressure on the orbiter…Fifty seconds into the flight *Atlantis* is already down range from the launch site at two and a half miles and an altitude now of five miles."

"*Atlantis,* go and throttle up,"
"Go and throttle up!"

"*Atlantis,* three liquid fuel engines are back at full throttle and approaching one minute ten seconds end of the flight…All systems in good shape and the hydraulic systems auxiliary power units in excellent shape as are the electricity producing fuel cells aboard the vehicle."

A full moon rose to the east and Venus appeared high up as the first evening star in the west. The noise of the shuttle engine was a constant crackling sound.

"*Atlantis* already travelling 15,000 miles per hour down range from the launch pad ten miles and an altitude of thirteen miles one minute thirty seconds into the flight…At this point, *Atlantis* has already burnt more than two million pounds of fuel and weighs half of what it did at launch…All going very quiet, all going very smoothly, aboard the orbiter approaching one minute fifty seconds…The next event is burn out, and separation of the twin solid rocket boosters which consume about ten tonnes of propellant every second."

The smokestack broke out into the colours of the rainbow, proving sunset launches are the most spectacular. The beauty alone was enough to break your heart, as suddenly, for some strange reason, the azure blue of the background sky reminded me of 'my own Pacific', that field of bluebells from all those years ago.

"SRB separations confirm two minutes ten seconds end of the flight…*Atlantis* already travelling at 3,000 miles per hour at an altitude of 31 miles down range from the launch site 40 miles."

The shuttle was now just a pinpoint of light that suddenly flares. The noise of the engines was rapidly fading.

"Beautiful view of *Atlantis* on its external tank now, and main engine each producing 400 pounds of thrust…The twin orbital manoeuvring system is now firing for a duration of one minute -forty-two seconds to assist with *Atlantis'* climb to orbit."

Instead of the expected, "Hey kid, you ain't seen nothing yet... This is the *Millennium Falcon*, it can do the Kessel Run in less than twelve parsecs", a cool, calm and collected voice replied, "*Atlantis* to Houston two engine Tau."

"Two engine Tau."

"Two minutes forty-five seconds into the flight,*Atlantis* can reach zero go in stay in a single engine failure at this point however all three are continuing to perform in excellent shape."

The shuttle transferred into orbit as if it were the *USS Enterprise* jumping into warp drive – swish! The pinpoint of light disappeared, and then silence.

It was a balmy, warm Florida evening, the air was still, and all I could hear was the gentle lapping of waves on the shore as a lone heron returned to wade for fish. Just like a savage from the rainforest who had never seen civilisation before and is introduced to it by a view of the Eiffel Tower, I stared up in awe, thinking, *bloody hell, they've got people in that thing!*

With the exception of the savage, possibly everyone has seen a rocket launch, at least on YouTube, but to see it for real and so close-up is completely unreal. Suddenly I was aware of a different sound; pick-up trucks revving their engines as NASA personnel prepared to leave. Above this noise someone called out, "Come on Limey, the bird has flown. It's time to go home," and with that, I slowly trudged along the beach after them.